Sara

Once in a lifetime you meet Someone who changes *Everything.*
His Name Is Jesus

I missed you at my Book signing
Hope to see you before I leave
Thank you so much for your support.
Bless You
Frances

Seashell Prisoners

Kidnapped in Texas
Kidnapped on an Island
Kidnapped by the F.B.I.

Man's Laws vs. God's Laws

Story told by: Frances Collins

Seashell Prisoners

Story told by: Frances Collins

To order reprints of this book, please contact the author:
Frances Collins
seashellprisoner@yahoo.com
www.seashellprisoners.com/Seashell Prisoner Facebook/blog

Discounted rates available for clubs and organizations.

All proceeds from this book will be used to support ministries involved in teaching and encouraging Christian principles in youth and families.

All rights reserved. Except where permitted by law, no part of this book may be reproduced or transmitted in any form or by any means, electronic or otherwise, to include photocopying, scanning, recording, or use of any storage and/or retrieval system, without written permission of the author, Frances Collins or whoever she has designated to take her place.

Copyright © 2012 by Frances Collins

Acknowledgments

My special thanks goes out to everyone that reads and enjoys *Seashell Prisoners*. I had so much fun writing this book despite all the emotions' and ups and downs that go with writing.

It's an unusual story that never in a hundred years would I have thought it would happen to me and my family. God truly used a big box of crayolas as He walked along beside us through this life changing event. The story is SO COLORFUL, FULL OF DRAMA, AND SUSPENSE. Through the years God not only brought us out of it, but opened my eyes to His Mighty Power and His Abilities. The story is so full of drama it continues to this day to be mind-boggling to the many that hear about it, and especially the ones that lived it.

Some of the names have been changed. They are irrelevant and would possibly distract from the message that *Seashell Prisoners* is striving to bring about. There is a lot of information that has been withheld. Things that I would only have brought out in a trial. One day more books will come out of this story. I would not attempt to try and capture in words the thoughts and feelings of others intimately involved with the real life story called *Seashell Prisoners*. I leave that to the individual.

Many were involved with the editing and recollecting of events with *Seashell Prisoners*.

My gratitude goes out to my many friends and family for not only helping with this, but encouraging me along the way. For all my readers (friends) who patiently read and critiqued as I worked on this book. Thanks for arguing with me and not giving in.....You were awesome and patient in so many ways.

Paul, I especially thank you for your God given gift for professional editing. Everyone needs a Paul in their lives.

Anna, my beautiful daughter, thanks for being critical in a way that kept pushing me to do better. Thanks for calling me and telling me chapter eight ruined your evening and you cried your heart out after reading it. I also appreciate your letting me know the book has something in it for everyone and your trying to decide who will play your part in the movie. Arlene, thanks for saying you wanted your pastor to read it. Mandy, thanks for stating it sounded like something you would hear in Joel Osteen's church. That's the comments that encouraged me to go forward reconfirming what my spirit told me in 1994. This story would be our testimony and a book.

I especially appreciate Nocona for your patience in helping me improve my computer skills. Most of all thank you for laughing at me when I get so frustrated. You always have been and always will be sunshine on a rainy day for me!

I appreciate all of my friends for being a huge part of my life. God divinely placed each of you in our lives for a reason. We would never have survived without your constant support.

A special thanks to Gumbalimba Park on Roatan for the assistance in the photo shoot of the monkeys for the cover of *Seashell Prisoners*.

Author's Notes

SEASHELL PRISONERS WAS A LIFE CHANGING EVENT FOR ME AND MY FAMILY. TO SAY IT IS ALL TRUTH, I WILL LEAVE TO THE HEARTS AND MINDS OF EACH READER. I HAVE GROWN TO REALIZE TRUTH TAKES ON DIFFERENT MEANINGS WITH EACH INDIVIDUAL.

I AM ONLY SPEAKING TRUTH AS I SAW IT, FROM ONE PERSON'S HEART AND SOUL WHICH IS MINE....

Frances Collins
STORY TELLER OF: *Seashell Prisoners*
MY FAMILY AND I GREATLY APPRECIATE ALL COMMENTS FROM READERS.
seashellprisoner@yahoo.com
www.seashellprisoners.com/Seashell Prisoner Facebook/blog

DEDICATION

I dedicate my testimony, in the form of a book called *Seashell Prisoners*, to Thadd and Blanche Collins, (my parents) that recently passed away. To our prayer warriors: The late Ma Gibbons, Sister Laura and Frederick Tatum, Don Aschraft, and Joey Martin. They all aligned with us from the beginning of our struggle. To my precious young friend and soul mate on the Island, Lara Muller that recently went to see Jesus.

My appreciation goes out to the many that continue to stand in the gap for us: Miss Ruth Baker, Kayte Ashcraft, Sister Eleanor Cooper, Pastor David and Harriett Kelly, Pastor Frances Arch, and hundreds more. A special thanks to the many close friends and acquaintances having faith in me. Each stepping out from the beginning in various ways in the pursuit of Nocona's safety.

I dedicate this book to the country of Honduras God so divinely placed us in for Nocona's safety. To the late Governor Stavely Elwin. To the late Douglas Collins that worked side by side with us throughout the construction of Casa Calico. The many Islanders and foreigners on the island of Roatan. All of you stood up for Nocona, River JoNey, and myself even though you only knew us for a short time. To West End Community, Jerry Hynds, and many other business people that went beyond friendship...calling, sending letters to the judge and offering their time. It's people as yourself that kept us moving forward.

I dedicate this book to the thousands in the U.S. that supported us once we were brought back to the States. To the many that knew us and the thousands that never met us, yet believed and supported our endeavor.

I dedicate this book to the late Monte, Susan and Jake Price with the Cowboy Ministry. Both Don, and the Prices will always be remembered by the many lives they ministered to in Honduras. To Big Mike (our Santa) who left a ray of light in all he came in contact with on the Island.

To The Brave Hondurans that fought diligently for their country's Democracy... Despite the lack of support from surrounding countries, you fought hard and you won. Hondurans' you are truly our Heroes! You Banned together, you prayed, you fought, And You Overcame The Enemy. You Retained Your Democracy!

This book goes out to AMERICA!!!! I LOVE AMERICA AND THE PEOPLE THAT FIGHT DAILY TO PROTECT TRUE DEMOCRACY AND AMERICA'S GOD ....JESUS CHRIST....

I especially thank God for the brave people that make up the Tea Party movement. Thanks to them we now have hope that our country will return to the original constitution, its original goal, prayer returned to the schools and a safe haven to raise our children in.

Last but not least, my deepest gratitude goes to God for truly being my Lord and Savior and meeting my every need. I pray that every person not rest until they find Jesus...not just the knowledge of Him, but the love of Him.

Through my journey with *Seashell Prisoners* I found ...GOD REALLY IS THE ALPHA AND THE OMEGA....HE IS THE BEGINNING AND THE END!

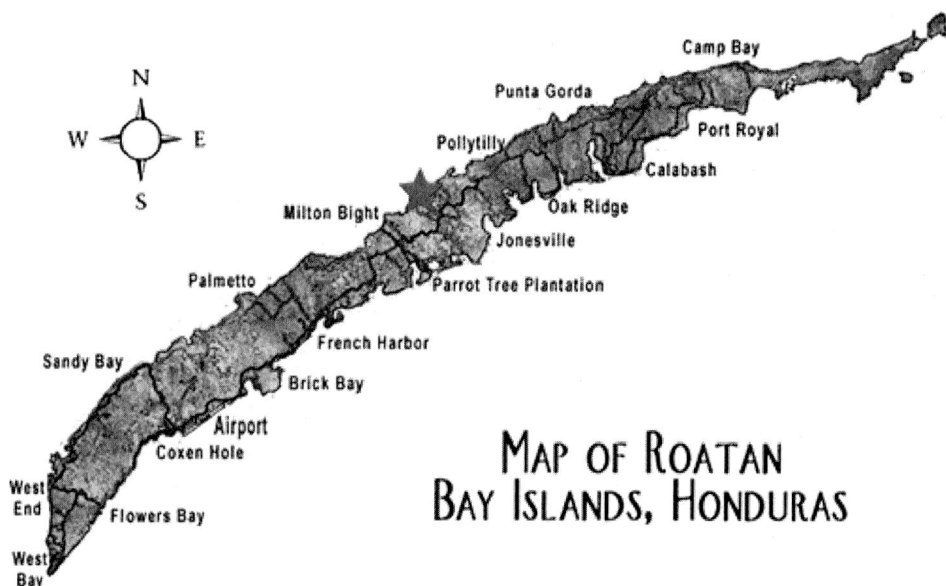

INTRODUCTION

Seashell Prisoners is not a book for people that are looking for perfection in story-telling. Nor is it a book for proper English. It's a book that has been written totally and completely from the heart. I literally poured my soul into this book using Southeast Texas slang words that I grew up with. Only until I used the editing, as each page was written, did I realize a lot of the words are not even words at all in the dictionary. I chose to leave some in because it tells the story in truth. Not a highly educated person, but a person with deep convictions and a great love for God, family, friends, and her country. This book I would say serves a fourfold purpose. One for God, one for our family legacy, one for healing, and one for helping others.

My desire for *Seashell Prisoners* was not to use it to tear down nor place anyone on a pedestal. *Seashell Prisoners* is a story full of color and adventure. The book is a powerful life changing story that altered the life of a small child, her mother, grandmother, family, and friends that were close to us. It's a story about overcoming against all odds. The book is full of truths. Truth as I saw and experienced....through the eyes of a grandmother.

My one desire is in some small way this book might help someone better understand an area of their life they are struggling with… whether it be a legal problem, human nature, child abuse, or a question about God.

Is This Book True ?

Each person or character listed in this book saw truth in a different component and in a different manner. Every professional involved in this story saw truth from their own prospective and from their own angle. For this reason I am not claiming everything that I have written is true or false. I am only saying the effect from the decisions of many professionals dramatically altered the lives of my three year old grandchild, my two daughters, my son, myself, and everyone close to us. Because of the power and variations of truth our world came to a standstill and was literally ripped apart!

Truth only lies in the heart of the individual....So I Offer To You, The Reader, To Seek Out For Yourself The Word... TRUTH !

Go To Seashell Prisoner website and Facebook and post your comments.

Table of Contents

Chapter 1	1
Chapter 2	13
Chapter 3	17
Chapter 4	23
Chapter 5	31
Chapter 6	42
Chapter 7	51
Chapter 8	69
Chapter 9	84
Chapter 10	91
Chapter 11	103
Chapter 12	122
Chapter 13	135
Chapter 14	159
Chapter 15	168
Chapter 16	185
Chapter 17	193
Chapter 18	202
Chapter 19	234
Chapter 20	245
Chapter 21	259
Chapter 22	270
Chapter 23	274
Conclusion	303

Seashell Prisoners
CHAPTER 1

FRIDAY, APRIL 1996, ROATAN, HONDURAS

Nocona and I were shopping in a small Tienda in West End, when suddenly we were interrupted by two Island policemen who were motioning for us to get into their truck. My knowledge of the Spanish language wasn't good, but the body language was simple. *We had no choice...but to go!* They pointed at the four-door truck and quickly ushered us to Coxen Hole, better known as the Centro of the Island. Not wanting to arouse panic in Nocona, I went along quietly as though it were a normal day, a role I frequently found myself playing on the small Island called Roatan.

Not knowing what to expect, I sat quietly as we rode. Nocona snuggled up to me. The winding road appeared endless today. The truck finally stopped and we were quickly escorted to Judge Ozcona's office in Coxen Hole.

The room was hot from the Caribbean sun and humidity in Honduras. I sat patiently waiting, and then a door opened. A lady motioned for us to enter the Judge's office. Nocona, normally being her inquisitive self would move about. Today, she clung to me, quietly asking why we were there. Trying to offset the intensity of the moment, I looked down and asked why it was bothering her. She tucked her head under my arm and replied, "This is where the bad people were when you were crying." Intense anger rose up in me. My thoughts immediately took me back to Texas and... *all of the whys!* Why didn't one of us just kill him. Each of us had the opportunity. Hundreds of people were shocked he got away with so much, yet no one took him out. I guess we just didn't have the guts to do it! Maybe, I should have taken Jason's offer. He was ready to do the job for us. How do you make that decision when so many were involved?

It all appeared so strange as to how we had the public support, but the entire judicial system including Interpol continued to work against us. What power did this abusive family have that would change up the whole judicial system in Orange, Texas?

Nocona's memory and recollection of events were vivid and unshakable.... Nocona is my granddaughter and was five years old at that time.

JULY 1981

My daughters, JoNey and Anna, my two nieces, Deborah and Cynthia, and myself were in Galveston, Texas, enjoying our favorite summer getaway. The sounds of the beach, the wonderful breeze, the seagulls swooping down on us, along with our ride on the ferry, all were definitely my idea of a wonderful escape from our hectic life in Mauriceville, Texas. Each year we laughed at the many humorous incidents from the previous years at the beach. My son Todd and his teenage friends' adventure, falling over the seawall, ranked at the top.

Anna & JoNey with family

The girls skated on the wide sidewalks along the seawall as I strolled, soaking up every breath of the salty breeze. I marveled at how the kids managed to make it in and out of the various crowded t-shirt and souvenir shops without some sort of fiasco. Browsing around the many shops was always fun even though the souvenirs failed to change from year to year. Despite the crude selection, the kids and I rummaged through them as though we were panning for gold. For whatever reason, it seemed important that we keep this tradition up each year.

Traditions were a monumental part of my life and my family's. Back home in Mauriceville, Texas, sat Grandpa Collins' old trunk in the large family room. My family heirloom overflowed with pictures and newspaper clippings of all the events that each of my children had experienced, reconfirming my devotion to family.

I never tired of the sound of the waves, people watching, and inhaling the wonderful salt air from the beach. I embraced each moment as though it might never return. The kids, being raised in the country surrounded by horses, cattle, and goats, were totally uninhibited and oblivious to everyone around them. They enjoyed every moment of the fresh breeze and salty environment.

JoNey's birthday party

The employees in the small souvenir shops never seemed to take their eyes off of them from the time we made our entrance. I often felt as though they would have preferred I tied them at the entrance along with the dogs. Actually, at times I did contemplate the very thought! On this particular day, as we were looking through all the many trinkets, I picked up an unusual souvenir that for some reason I felt the immediate need to purchase.

Yes, for five dollars I was now the proud owner of eight popsicle sticks with little seashells in the center of each. Each shell had button eyeballs peering through the sticks. It gave the distinct appearance of seashells imprisoned. From then on, my new highly treasured seashell prisoners were proudly displayed in my kitchen window. They were lined up in the window along with all the many baby pictures and valued mementos I had collected over the years.

*

My life, in many ways, was what you would refer to as typical. I was born in 1945 and grew up in southeast Texas in the city of Orange, Texas, population twenty thousand. My father, Thadd Collins, was an electrical contractor. I was the fifth child of a family of six children and was rather ignored, but grew to enjoy it that way. It didn't take long to see the advantages this would provide. Dad quickly wore down from stringent rules and regulations with all of my older sisters and brothers, leaving them with all the work. Mom and dad had worked hard for many years. They had graduated on to bigger things, frequently traveling. I was soon left in the care of my oldest sisters after many days of carsickness and complaining of being totally bored.

Dad was quite the disciplinarian, which called for a very structured home life. Dad and Mother were successful business people, but fell short in areas of communication. My father was highly respected amongst his peers for his honesty and ability to take care of his customers in ways that created a relationship of trust and loyalty with everyone that came to know him. There was no doubt Dad loved us, but his job and overriding desire to be perfect in everything he did overcame any thoughts of caring for the emotional needs of the family. The structured atmosphere was stressful and clashed with my tendencies of disorganization. My mother's name was Blanche. Her full-time job was caring for us and keeping Dad happy.

Being the provider was a huge focus to Dad, yet it didn't stop him from taking time to do special things for us during the year, especially during Christmas, Halloween, and Thanksgiving. These events created some of our fondest memories together. Dad loved giving and sharing with all our cousins in Louisiana. Almost everyone could expect gifts, fruit, and lots of fireworks at Christmas. Christmas was a great time for all of us.

Dad built our home right next to the Salvation Army Church. Each day I observed as the many transits walked into the church, all being greeted with food and clothing. I remember Dad's sister saying, "Thadd Collins, don't build that big house in Brownwood! You'll never get your money back when you sell it!" Her statement, I am sure, proved to be true. The example of the leaders of that church made a huge impact on my life as it taught me the importance of giving back what you have been blessed with.

Maybe Dad didn't get his money back on the sale of our home, but the life experiences I learned as a small child were deeply etched in my mind, life changing, and of great value to me.

※

Suddenly, everything began to change as my sisters and brothers began to go off to college and finishing schools. I had roomed with one sister for many years and now I was feeling totally abandoned. I was left to care for my younger brother, Ted, while Mom and Dad ran the family business. This left me taking care of many of the chores by all of which I quickly became bored.

I was never a highly motivated person in school, studying only enough to make passing grades. Neither did I work at being fashionably dressed or competing for friendships. I can remember from the second grade on, each year I was being elected to something. It started out being a princess, then later being elected most beautiful in my class. My freshman year I represented my class at the crowning of the Homecoming King and Queen. I was never into fashion or competing and didn't quite understand why I was continually being chosen for these activities. Most all of the clothes I owned were what my older sisters had outgrown.

I began to acquire more and more friends with each year in school. I loved basketball and played several years at my high school, better known as Little Cypress. It was through my favorite sport I met Owen Burton from Mauriceville, Texas. We later married. Owen was from a completely different background, raised in a small community, population 600.

Mauriceville was a place where going to the grocery store or the post office was never just about picking up things, but more often an event, stopping and visiting with everyone along the way. Many times getting in the car with friends or family and going to dinner was a common occurrence.

※

Owen had many goals all of which were quickly accomplished, but the marriage ended after twenty-two years. Later in life I realized the priorities set out from the beginning had definitely led us in the wrong direction for which I blamed him at first. Later, I realized submitting totally to his every decision was wrong on my part, making me equally responsible. We had succeeded as business partners, but failed in building our lives around each other and family. We had three children. JoNey was nine and Anna was five at the time of the divorce. Todd had graduated from high school and was on his own, traveling on the P.R.C.A. rodeo circuit.

The divorce was not easy. After twenty-two years of marriage, I ended up with a four-thousand-square-foot grocery store, our home, and the joy of raising our two daughters. Owen was awarded the large tract of land, farm equipment, and our hardware store. The legendary name, Burton's Grocery, soon came down and was quickly replaced with the initial of each of the children's names, T. J. & A's Grocery.

There was never an argument over the girls and where they would stay. Owen was always busy going forward. My time was pretty much consumed with raising JoNey and Anna and keeping up with the grocery business. Owen kept them once a week. After observing other divorces I soon thought of it as a blessing not having to go through the argument of who got the kids on the weekends, etc. I was totally unaware of what was in store as a result of the lack of a father's daily presence in the home.

Todd steer wrestling.

I had exhausted all areas of renewing the marriage and began once again putting my best foot forward. Moving forward with total peace came easy since I had done my very best in the marriage. The single life at times got tough. Daily I was trying to fill the new voids that continued to creep up on all of us. Dating and looking for marriage was put on hold until I could once again find stability for the girls. The thought of marriage and a sexual relationship with someone was rather eerie since Owen had been my only intimate relationship.

Anna & JoNey

JoNey's ability with horses, along with that of her brother, Todd, was evident from an early age. When JoNey turned nine, she was competing at the local rodeos and horse shows, coming home with money or an armload of trophies. JoNey was extremely competitive, yet equally naive. She had previously spent a lot of time trailing behind her dad on the farm. Anna was only five, and headstrong; she immediately set her priority at finding Mom a husband and someone to replace the absence of Dad around the farm. Anna was so intense, she became upset when one of the rodeo clowns flirted with me, and I didn't respond. I remember JoNey giving her a good scolding on the way home from the rodeo. At the tender age of five, the little independent redhead had made up her mind to do something and continued to pursue her goal!

Even though I had managed the supermarket from day one, I began to feel insecure and extremely apprehensive with the new breadwinner responsibility. As time went on, God continued to bless us, and money was never a problem. T. J. & A's flourished and we continued in the lifestyle to which we were accustomed. God was with us to the point that unusual things would happen. One day I felt a strong urge to cash in with Affiliated Foods, our distributor, and take out money they were holding in the sum of over eighty thousand dollars. Within months Affiliated went bankrupt, leaving all the major stores with losses of millions of dollars. Someone was definitely watching over us, obviously, setting us up for something much larger than our small minds could conceive.

Even though money never took precedence in my mind, I continued to be the object of my friends and family joking about money lying around the house and my car. LaDonna, a good friend of JoNey's, frequently stated it was nothing to see a thousand dollars in my glove compartment! Becoming wealthy was never one of my goals, so money never meant much to me, but family did! I worked day and night to keep my family together and keep us surrounded with wonderful friends.

God seemed to be blessing us. The girls and I never wanted for anything. They always had good horses, horse trailers, and trucks to pull the trailers. I never had to worry about bills—the money was just there! We were blessed!

Anna had a deep love for all the farm animals, giving every cow and goat a name. She quickly let anyone that arrived know which ones were hers. For some reason no one seemed to claim the goat that walked through the patio door or the one that made its way to the top of the Lincoln town car!

Now Anna was maturing into a beautiful young teenager, enjoying the malls and majoring in communication [telephone]; JoNey was just the opposite, begging to go to the feed stores and check over the latest horse equipment. As time went on, Anna began to share my love for the water, but only at spring break. I could always depend on Anna to continue the trips to the beach, whereas rodeos and horse shows took precedence with JoNey. As Anna aged, my beach trips grew into being dorm mother for many of her friends. The package included coverage of huge deposits on the cabin since something always got broken!

My recollection of my little redhead "Anna", from birth was that she was always ten years JoNey's senior. Headstrong, independent, and strong willed would be a good description. JoNey was just the opposite, extremely sensitive from birth, to the point that singing a sad song brought tears to her eyes. All three children were very smart. They never once asked for help with school and always made good grades. Anna was valedictorian at Mauriceville Middle School. JoNey, not only concerned herself with A's, but had the unremitting need to make high A's.

❧

As Anna grew older, she joined JoNey and Todd, competing in the rodeos, and she did well. Anna was a little different as she made sure both she and her horse, Hollywood, stood out in appearance as well as abilities. Anna's closet was packed with colorful matching boots and jeans. JoNey spent long hours with her horse JoLynn, working only on horsemanship. Todd at that time was riding professionally and ranked second in the world in bulldogging.

JoNey was a very multitalented child. After the divorce I did my best to help her explore her abilities in an attempt to see where she might progress. My deepest desire was to keep JoNey going forward in a positive manner. I enrolled her in gymnastics and later in karate where she once again excelled and continued winning in competitions. As JoNey grew older, she also had an unusual interest in the Spanish language. She went forward with her love for competing and entered high school contests and continued to win. Being a high achiever and loving education, she was always the teacher's pet, relishing in all their attention. Actually, JoNey had a way of grabbing everyone's attention. She had a beautiful personality, full of love and a great sense of humor. Everyone seemed to gravitate towards her.

❧

I continued my busy life traveling to all the rodeo events and keeping up with the supermarket, but soon took up the sport of scuba diving. I later married Richard Harris. We immediately had our daughters certified as divers and were going on family trips to the Caribbean. Richard wasn't exactly the rodeo clown or the cowboy Anna dreamed of. He had a prestigious job, was a really neat dresser, and was full of antics. The girls and I were ready for a few laughs!

JoNey, Christy, & Anna

Richard's only daughter, Christy, was a beautiful young girl, rather frail and whiny on arrival to our home. After my girls pulled a few pranks on her... the city life soon left! Richard was a diver, so we quickly found ourselves traveling to different Islands, the first being a small Island in the Caribbean called... Roatan! Our stay was on a key off of Roatan, but we stepped on the Island for a few minutes to purchase candy bars on one occasion. Our five-minute encounter wasn't good, and I vowed I Would Never Live In Honduras! An older gentleman had taken us across in a dory. When I requested why a home in the distance seemed to be at a standstill, I froze at his comment. He stated an argument arose and the owners head was cut off.

The new marriage was good, but short-lived. I had once again repeated myself with marrying a man extremely goal-oriented like my father and ex-husband. The pressure of his new job promotion soon became overwhelming for both of us, ending the marriage.

Richard & Frances

Once again single, I continued the dive trips for R&R, and the Caymans soon became a second home. Occasionally, I went on dive trips with a group from Davy Jones Locker, a dive shop out of Beaumont, Texas. We always had a great time, but I began to find solace traveling by myself, sitting on the beaches, and reflecting on past memories.

My experience traveling with a date usually ended up in a fiasco. One especially stood out when my sister fixed me up with a friend of hers. The man joined me on a "buy one, get one free" dive trip to Cayman Brac. Disaster would be putting it mildly. The man returned home by himself the following day after our arrival. My new underwater camera had taken precedence. I soon found that being single was not what I was definitely best at!

A.J. Judice, Frances Collins & Wade Granger

Each year the kids and I hosted a New Year's Eve party. Every year the parties flourished; we never knew where they would go with the wide variety of friends we had acquired over the years. It wasn't unusual for people like our good friend A.J. Judice to be on the radio prior to the occasion, poking fun at us, stating, "Don't miss Frances Harris's big New Year's Eve Party! Expect to see crawfish boiling in her hot tub!" Our new thirty-by-thirty-foot room was perfect for accommodating all the family and friend get-togethers.

The divorce was my first big letdown in life. I began to cover the pain with things. I guess the big thirty-by-thirty room was the first, and we had many fun events entertaining friends over the years.

We were all amused at the many scuba divers that appeared to dominate the parties, always entertaining themselves. JoNey, Anna and I laughed for days as the cowboys surprisingly sat back in their chairs just looking on. Their wives appeared to have more fun with the divers, enjoying the divers' humor and antics. Everyone knew if they wanted beer they had best bring it. I didn't drink, and everyone was aware that I had no desire to be around a drunk!

Whether it was a Christmas family gathering or a big New Year's Eve party, JoNey could always be found at the end of the evening sitting in my bedroom on the computer. She wrote stories of all the funny happenings that always occurred. JoNey had a God-given talent for writing, with an incessant and innate ability to find humor in everything. One of her favorite things to write about was Mom. It was as though something was always happening to me that was not always funny at the time, but the girls found humor in it in the end.

New Years Eve Party
Frances & Friends

New Years Party
Divers & Cowboys

JoNey &JoLynn

One morning I was bathing, getting ready for work, when JoNey asked if I would go ride the horses with her. It was early in the morning, and I was needing to be at work. I finally conceded, realizing how important it seemed to be to her. I was definitely not a horseback rider and never tried to act or dress the part. That morning I put a smile on my face and followed her to the barn. I commenced to saddle up my horse. JoNey was ready within minutes and had to help me. As we rode out in the field, I began to really enjoy the ride. My horse was walking very slowly. It was a beautiful morning.

JoNey was riding bareback. She took off on JoLynn, her horse, and was flying across the field. My horse got excited and began to run after JoLynn. I saw a ditch ahead and watched as JoNey's horse jumped it running very fast. As my horse drew closer to the ditch, I became so fearful I jumped off the side of my horse and fell very hard. I heard a loud cracking sound and knew instantly I had broken my ankle in two. JoNey ran to the house and Todd brought the Lincoln town car out into the field and picked me up. We raced to the hospital.

In my haste to go out and ride with JoNey, I decided not to put on underclothes, knowing I would have to shower again before going to work. All I could think of was how embarrassed I would be when the physician realized that! As soon as I got to the hospital, they sawed my leather boot off and cut my jeans down the side. Needless to say I did not make any dive trips that summer. I was in a cast all summer! As bad as it was, we laughed about it in the end and, as everything else, it became another one of JoNey's funny stories to write about.

As time went on, I grew weary of the grueling task of adding on to the grocery store and keeping up with twenty-two employees. I had added on to T. J. & A.'s twice. I had a unique relationship with each employee, enjoying many great times together. Tricks were often a part of the employees' day, and I never knew what to expect. As I made my entrance into the store on one occasion, I heard over the intercom, "Code three! Code three!" being called out. The employees burst out laughing as I entered. It was their alert... The boss was in the store!

They were not only my employees, but my best friends. We shared a lot and grew together with each trial in our individual lives.

I was in my early forties now having to make a life-changing decision. I made the decision to lease out the supermarket. I got the girls together one evening and made the big announcement. I reassured JoNey and Anna that we would be fine, but would possibly be on a budget. Anna immediately burst into tears as though her world was being ripped out from under her. JoNey was enjoying Anna's meltdown and ran down the hall laughing. I quickly reassured Anna we were fine and could keep up our normal lifestyle. We would just have to make a few cutbacks.

ૐ

 I was now retired, immediately purchasing a beautiful fifth-wheel travel trailer as a gift for having to endure all the trials of the grocery store, divorce, etc. I had driven Lincoln town cars for years, but soon traded it in for a new red Cherokee Limited Jeep. It all just seemed to fit in better with what now seemed to be...Retirement! Life was good!
 Not having the least idea of what I would do with all my free time, there was one thing I did know, and made the statement ring loud and clear to everyone, "I Would Never Raise My Grandkids!" Many a day friends were in and out of the store with their grandchildren. My visions were of making plans for my new life of retirement. Raising more children was not on my list! I was ready for relaxing, reading, scuba diving, and finding new interests that I never had the time for before.
 Despite problems that arose from time to time, I always felt blessed and compelled to help young people. I took on the job of organizational leader of the Dusty Trail 4-H Club in Mauriceville when Todd was young. With the help of friends, Reuben Stringer and Judy Baggett, we soon brought the Dusty Trail Club from a few members to a hundred youth within a year. We quickly felt the pressure of expenses for the larger group. With the help of Judy, Reuben, and other friends we started Mauriceville's first Flea Market. The Flea Market brought in five thousand dollars the first year. This not only covered expenses for the Club, but allowed us to pour the first slab on the grounds of the new Community Center in Mauriceville.
 The Flea Market soon grew into what is now a yearly event, The Mauriceville Crawfish Festival. A new group in Mauriceville organized the event and went forward year after year with parades, dances, and a large carnival. My new job was getting up a float entry in the parade each year. T. J. & A's had an energetic group of employees that were very competitive, taking great pride in winning. As a team we did whatever it took to win using drama, music, and costumes on a big eighteen-wheeler float. Together we were a tough team to beat with all the trophies to prove it.
 I went on to help the Orange Chamber of Commerce as Parade Chairman, and still later formed a drug awareness program in Orange County called S.T.A.N.D. Each program I worked on, either by myself or with my children, made front-page headlines. The new drug awareness program blazed forward with much enthusiasm from the Orange County Sheriff's Department, Dare

Program, school principals, and many businessmen involved. We held the yearly event at the local Mauriceville Crawfish Festival, always drawing huge crowds. Crystal Lyons, a young evangelist with the Cowboy Ministry, was one of the first speakers for the yearly event.

As my children grew older, I enrolled in a CASA program in Beaumont. I continued to have that growing desire to help others. Out of all the women participating, for some reason my face was on the front page of the newspapers representing everyone being sworn in. Within months, with the help of Judge Travis in Beaumont, I began to initiate a CASA program in Orange. I had come to know Judge Travis through the program and grew to respect him greatly. Within a short time I was forming luncheons in Orange, Texas, with the local judges and different civic groups. Judge Travis was lined up as the speaker. Newspapers once again gave full coverage on the new program with pictures on each event.

Life continued to bless me and my children with a unique fullness that was extremely rewarding. Each week I made it a point to have the children in church, but for some strange reason, as for myself, I just didn't seem to fit in as everyone else appeared to. I went to church, but definitely did not have a good understanding of the Word or the urge to dig further into it. I never cared to read any kind of book, and the Bible was just too complex.

S.T.A.N.D. Drug Program K.O.G.T.

T J & A's Employee Parade Float Entry

Seashell Prisoners
CHAPTER 2

Even though I had now experienced my second divorce, I continued to go forward. I had this unusual peace as though everything was working itself out. I always felt I had done my best in both my marriages. Now I just had to pick up the pieces once again and start over. I had many close friends that were like gold. At any given time they were there for me, never needing explanations. They were truly friends.

At this time in my life, men were of no interest to me. I had my children and loved doing things with them. I just wanted to enjoy my family, friends, and financial blessings.

Prior to the divorce, Richard and I frequented Galveston, enjoying our dirt bikes on occasion. On one particular outing we noticed a couple camping out and riding horses. Richard was more of a people person than I. He quickly approached the two and introduced himself. The lady quickly spoke up, introducing herself as Joni. Her husband was more subdued. Right off I sensed Joni and I would be good friends. I was excited! Joni was a lot younger, but we shared a common interest in areas that other friends couldn't relate to. She was the first female retail supermarket manager I had met! This was a huge change for me. In the mid 1980s, the retail grocery industry was primarily composed of men including all meetings, seminars, and conventions. Now having a friend that could relate with all the problems arising in business was truly neat.

Joni was managing on a much larger scale than T. J. & A's. She was employed with a huge supermarket chain. Joni had all the brains to go with the position. In my case, I was pretty much thrown into the business, but had good survivor skills of organization and management, and a deep respect for individuals. I was totally clueless when it came to bookkeeping. I quickly devised my own plan and...it worked! Somehow the right people appeared at the right time to fulfill any and all inadequacies I seemed to have.

When Joni's marriage failed, I suggested that she take up my new-found interest...Scuba Diving! It had worked for me, so I felt somehow it might add more friends in her life and expand on ours. Soon agreeing on our new sport, we signed up for a week-long diving trip to the Sea of Cortez on a live-aboard boat.

In preparation for the trip, we attended an orientation to meet other divers that had signed up. Many new faces were present including a very intriguing man unlike anyone I had met before. He was rather rough looking in appearance, yet worth checking into. I definitely was not looking for marriage. I was beginning to learn to appreciate and enjoy all the freedoms single life brought. However, this man certainly fit my criteria for having a good time. Phil was extremely humorous and had a beautiful red Mercedes which didn't hurt first impressions. Phil insisted we go for a ride after the meeting. I quickly saw he had an equally large ego to match his little red Mercedes. I later found out he was a very successful and respected entrepreneur in Orange. Phil had other business interests in other states, also.

We were all anticipating our new live-aboard diving adventure. Fate or possibly Phil's planning had a way of seating us next to each other on the flight to the Sea of Cortez. I immediately noticed he had to be in control of things, but it appeared to be in a fun way. The week was awesome! We all had a great time meeting many new friends, with half the divers being from Germany. Everyone had their underwater cameras anxiously ready to capture the hammerhead sharks well known to the area. That is, everyone but myself and Joni. We were just there for the adventure and to get away from the stress of the supermarket business.

By the end of the week all the divers were wearing down. I had to abort a morning dive, so I decided to make my last dive in the evening with a dive master on the boat. He tried to get all the hard-core divers to go with us and bring their cameras. The dive was awesome, and yes, hammerhead sharks were all around us. They were so huge they looked like whales.

The week ended with a surprise mock wedding for Phil and myself, due to our hitting it off so well. Everyone laughed and had a good time. It was a memorable trip!

⁂

My trips were good for more reasons than one. It gave me the opportunity to regroup and think my life over as a single mom and reminisce over the different happenings in our lives. I realized how blessed we were despite occasional setbacks. Like the evening I was at a rodeo watching Anna ride when I received a call from my store manager. T. J. & A's had been held up by a man with a sawed-off shotgun. It was late in the evening and JoNey was at the store sitting in the courtesy booth. The booth was closed for the evening and she was quietly doing her homework behind the glassed in counter. The man approached the window, pointed the gun at her and demanded money. Because of her innocent and childlike appearance, he turned and walked off. JoNey knew exactly what was happening. She also knew a lot of money was in a drawer right in front of her. She watched through the glass window as the man jumped up on one of the checkout stands and demanded all the money from the registers. We had drop boxes that all large bills were placed in, so the thief made off with a small amount of money. We were blessed to know the evening could have ended so differently.

My children and family remained my first priority, but in my free time I grew to enjoy Phil's humor and wit more and more. We both shared the ego thing in a fun way. We enjoyed competing against each other in many areas, including entering business floats in the local parades, always making the newspapers. With each year I continued to grow more confident in myself.

⁂

I wasn't one to go shopping for clothes often. Shopping wasn't one of my choice things to do. It had in time become a necessity, since I was attending so many meetings and conventions with the business, and working with different organizations. When I entered J. Harris, wine and cheese were quickly brought out. They knew at least a thousand dollars would be left behind!

At one point in our relationship, Phil bluntly stated, "You truly overestimate yourself." Momentarily, I was a little taken by the comment. As I thought about it, I guess I had possibly grown a little overconfident and maybe even a little arrogant over the years. After all, both my ex-husbands found answers to our problems through other relationships. My feelings and emotions had to divert to something!

Being overconfident obviously didn't affect Phil. He continued to call each time he was in town. I looked forward to an occasional get-together: The usual going out to dinner, boating, or just laughing and enjoying each other's humor. We had become great friends, but that is as far as either wished to take it. I was still very busy with the girls, taking them to rodeos and horse shows. The supermarket and the girls continued to be my priorities.

Phil had part interest in a yacht, but rarely used it. I loved the water and was wanting to purchase a pleasure boat. Phil discouraged me, saying there was too much upkeep involved. Being my own person, I went out and purchased a seventeen-foot Wellcraft pleasure boat. I quickly named it the Wild Wild West after a song we all enjoyed on one of the group dive trips to Florida. The girls and I had a great time in the boat, inviting friends occasionally. Needless to say, when Phil was in town he was always in the boat. With each trip he took control, knowing my inexperience. With each outing he broke a propeller. After two, he purchased a stainless steel propeller.

⁂

When boredom set in, I continued to slip off to the Caribbean or sometimes attend dive shows. One particular show I attended was in Las Vegas and extremely memorable. Being the typical female, I shopped the booths for the latest colors in wet suits and dive attire. As I strolled down the aisle looking over the merchandise, a total stranger working a booth reached out, taking my hand. I thought it unusual since he didn't have the appearance of a fortune teller, nor was there a sign up advertising his psychic abilities, but I went along. The young man scanned across my palm as though in search of something mystical. In a few choice words, the stranger boldly stated, "You have two daughters, one of which is pregnant with a child by a man twice her age."

I quickly withdrew my hand, being totally offended by the statement. I found it to be absurd, yet the words kept running through my mind and out of my mouth. The girls were maturing, but neither were old enough to date or even thinking about it. Each time I ran into one of my dive friends at the show, I repeated the bizarre remarks, and we would all laugh. We decided the man was obviously a jerk!

JoNey & JoLynn

Seashell Prisoners
CHAPTER 3

The girls continued working daily with their horses. Good farriers were hard to find. The last one had crippled JoNey's horse, causing her to miss several horse shows. Someone recommended a farrier, Trevor Reese. Anyone that came to the house with any knowledge of horses could be sure of one thing—*The girls would be under foot until they left!* They loved their horses and loved showing them off.

Trevor was very impressive to the girls. He knew all the right things to say. He spoke of all the Pro Rodeos he rode in throughout the U.S., and bragged about the many events he had won. The kids knew the names of all the famous rodeo contestants since Todd was on the pro circuit. To hear Trevor talk, not only was he on a first-name basis with all of them, *He guided them to the top!*

❧

The girls became more consumed with what they called their horseshoer and one day stated, *"Mom, he wants to meet you!"* With each return, Trevor became more and more persistent with his request to speak with me. I remember JoNey in particular begging me. She was rather pitifully asking me, *"Please just come out and say hello to him."* JoNey was in her teens; however, her maturity level was more akin to a twelve-year-old. Most people considered Anna, who was four years younger, to be the older of the two! Anna was much more mature and had a stronger personality. JoNey continued to be very naive.

My life was preoccupied with many responsibilities, but this time I couldn't ignore JoNey. I weakened, finding myself trailing off behind her to meet the famous horse farrier that knew all the famous people. I certainly did not want to hurt his feelings, considering the last farrier crippled her horse. I remember the excitement in JoNey's face as I approached Trevor. I greeted him and shook his hand as I normally did a stranger. I thanked him for doing a good job with the horses and within minutes turned and made my way back to the house. JoNey tagged along behind me with a huge smile on her face as though a mission was accomplished. Whatever made my kids happy made me happy. Later in the evening, Anna questioned me once again in an attempt to get Mom a relationship. I quickly reassured the little redhead telling her, "If he were the last man on earth, I wouldn't go out with him." I had absolutely nothing in common with him and he was younger than me.

Trevor continued to come by once a month to work on the horses. He began to play mind games with the kids. At the time it seemed trivial, so I didn't give it much thought. More and more, Anna would come in crying, saying Trevor was going to sell her horse, Hollywood. I would calm her down and reassure her that Hollywood wasn't going anywhere, so off she went.

ea

Fall was approaching with Christmas close behind—my favorite time of the year. I was determined this year was going to be the best! With each year, I felt more and more blessed. I was feeling confident and everything was going wonderful in our lives. I had made all the arrangements to take the girls to the National Rodeo Finals at Las Vegas for their Christmas present. My sisters were going with us.

Suddenly and without warning, JoNey's entire personality began to change. She became withdrawn, not the effervescent person we all knew and loved. She began to arrive home late from activities. JoNey, who normally never spent time on the telephone, was now suddenly making her way to the bedroom and locking the door.

More and more, the bedroom took precedence to everything in JoNey's life. I always thought all three children were perfect. JoNey, at that stage, had the world by the tail academically and in every sport she chose to be a part of! Now something strange and different was happening that I could not understand, nor explain.

For the first time I found myself pacing the floor waiting for JoNey to come in one evening, but it never happened. A close friend called. They began to state they saw JoNey sitting beside a man in a black dually truck. They were parked on the side of my supermarket. I immediately jumped in my car with no idea of what I would encounter. As I raced down the road, all I could think of was, Trevor drove a big black dually. I remember pulling up beside the truck and getting out. It was Trevor's truck. For the first time in my life I was confused and fearful of confrontation. Too quickly everything was beginning to fall into place, yet I was still in a state of shock. I was not sure what approach to take. JoNey had just turned seventeen.

I took a deep breath and got out of the car. I told JoNey it was time to go home, but she sat there as though she did not hear me. I immediately demanded Trevor to…*Get Out Of His Truck!* He looked me in the eye, then slowly rolled up the window. Fear raced through every part of my body as I realized what was truly happening. The truck didn't move. Anger rose up as I hollered once again for him to get out. He continued to look straight ahead as though he was basking in his power over me. I began to beg for JoNey to please come home with me, but she sat there as though under a spell. I screamed at Trevor once again to get out of his truck. He slowly rolled down the window and sat there as though he was enjoying my pain. I asked him what he was doing with my daughter, but he refused to answer. I then screamed at him, *"You're A Child Molester!"* At this point, I demanded JoNey to get out of the truck. The child I loved so much was so frail and naive, yet it was as though she was a thousand miles away. I could see her, but I couldn't touch her. The engine started and the large black truck backed up and slowly drove off into the night.

Excruciating pain raced through me as I stood totally numb and immobile. I felt a deep sense of helplessness, frantically searching my mind. He's twice her age! He is a child molester! Death would have been easier to face than the emotions that were racing through me.

This was the multitalented little girl that dressed like a tomboy, still slept with me, and was adored by everyone. JoNey was too naive for this! Guilt swept through my mind as I mentally beat up on myself for not preparing her for boys, much less men twice her age. She never talked about boys, nor dated, nor did she wear makeup or earrings, nor sit in front of the mirror. Her dress was strictly western jeans and boots; she never noticed if they were ironed or not.

Where did I miss the boat! My mind raced back to her transition from grammar school to high school. I knew it was extremely tough on her. She never really adjusted to the larger school, her not being the center of attention with the teachers. Where did I go wrong? After relentless hours of purging my mind, I went home and called her father. Owen was unavailable. I tried to call Todd, but he was in between rodeos in another state.

The next morning, I arose early, researching Trevor Reese, and what I was up against. I knew if he was in rodeos I could easily get information about him. We had many friends in the rodeo business. The information came too quick for what I was ready to grasp. It appeared that many knew Trevor, except me. Everything I did not want to hear was given to me quickly, sharp, and to the point. Trevor was thirty-four, and had been married twice. He was mentally and physically abusive to both wives. Trevor was a habitual liar and age made no difference with whom he decided to go to bed with. I thought that they were only a few opinions and searched for someone that would say something positive. Everyone that knew Trevor continued to repeat the same statements, yet each made an attempt to console me. No one seemed to have any comforting words or answers. Certain ones remembered Trevor prior to his marriages. The stories all had one common thread, abuse!

I was now faced with every mother's nightmare. My child was now living with a sick man. I sought desperately to contact JoNey and relay all of the stories I had been told about Trevor. But each time I attempted to call her, Trevor intervened stating, *"She's not here!"* or, *"She's busy!"* Nothing made sense. JoNey was neither mature nor developed; she looked like a child. I could not fathom why a grown man would be interested in an innocent tomboyish young girl.

Friends continued to call and console us. If they ran into JoNey at different places they would call and give me updates; all of which were bad. Bruises were seen on JoNey. She continued to spiral downward, losing weight and totally changing in personality. She didn't come home for a long time. One day, she showed up at the house looking pale and thin. Trying not to react was extremely hard. She wore a long-sleeved shirt with a high collar. I could see bruises on her neck, wrists, and arms. She refused to talk about it. I knew I couldn't force the conversation for fear of her leaving. Her visits were brief, but at least I felt a sense of progress.

Anna was taking more interest in horses and participating in high school rodeos. Sometimes we would see JoNey from a distance. She always had on the same jeans and loose shirts with high collars. JoNey never acknowledged us. She no longer participated in the rodeos nor showed her horse. My heart felt like it stopped beating. My world came to a standstill as I watched her from a distance. Anna continued to pursue her interest in the rodeos, but I grew to hate them relating them with JoNey's horrible fate. It was hard for me to discourage Anna since we had worn out trucks and trailers hauling JoNey to various events.

Friends continued to console me, letting me know each was praying, nevertheless, the pain got worse. It felt like all of the suffering of death, yet no closure. We continued to live with the pain of seeing JoNey from a distance. All I wanted to do was just be able to touch or hold her. We no longer enjoyed JoNey's humor over Mom and the way she drove her Lincoln, or the day the cinch strap broke when Mom was sitting on her horse holding her parrot. There were no more talks of college and becoming a veterinarian or competition in horse shows or rodeos.

JoNey continued losing weight and her body showed all the signs of physical and mental abuse. I made many attempts to call Trevor's house, with him refusing to allow me to speak to her. One particularly close friend called me one day letting me know all the abuse he knew about Trevor. The man held a public service job and was very much respected by our family. He went on to say I needed to get JoNey out of Trevor's life. I reassured him I was doing all I could and thanked him.

That night I got a telephone call. It was JoNey! Jumping on the opportunity, I quickly told her all the things people were saying to me about Trevor. I reemphasized our close friend and his deep concern for her. I knew it would make a big impact on her. I was hoping she would see Trevor for who he was since she had so much respect for this man's word. Instead, JoNey confronted Trevor, which resulted in his approaching our friend at his office the next day, threatening him. Co-workers were forced to pull Trevor off of the man. Trevor was quickly escorted out of the office. Other people who shared with me about Trevor were now being either stalked or receiving intimidating telephone calls.

From then on I never repeated anything to JoNey. I knew for the first time in my life I was confronting something that was bigger than me! I needed desperately to submit this to someone, maybe God, Whoever He was! If He really was out there, I would do my best to find Him.

A friend invited me to go to the Houston Livestock Show and Rodeo. Thinking it would take my mind off of the situation, I accepted his invitation. We walked around the exhibits for a while then ventured over to the arena. I looked across one of the arenas, and saw Trevor and JoNey. The same scenario, Trevor in his starched attire and JoNey very frail in appearance.

Later in the month, JoNey came by the house once again. By this time I had learned to be more subtle, to just listen in hopes she wouldn't leave. This time was different! She appeared ready to talk. I asked her why she was dressing the way she was. She replied, "Trevor would get angry if I dressed up." When I questioned her about her weight loss, she said, "Trevor thinks I am too fat." I then asked her why she was living with Trevor, with her reply being, "He loves me and promises to take me to a lot of rodeos in other states."

I came home from work one day and JoNey was once again at the house. She and Trevor had gotten into a huge argument. This time she decided to stay! We immediately began receiving phone calls with heavy breathing or sometimes a whisper. I knew the phone calls were from Trevor. I repeatedly told him I wasn't scared of him. The calls would come late at night with JoNey sometimes answering. He began telling her how much he loved her, and eventually she returned to his house. Once again, I was helpless! All I could do was pray and seek others to pray.

*

I searched deeper for this God that was supposed to be there for our every need. If He was there, then exactly *Where Was He?* I went from church to church seeking prayers. I needed something deeper than what I had seen and experienced in the past. I had been in church all my life, yet I was totally clueless and definitely *powerless!*

I began to reflect back on the Cowboy Church at the Tin Top Arena I attended with the girls when they were younger. I remembered I always avoided eye contact when I greeted the couple that was in charge, especially a young evangelist, Crystal Lyons, whenever she was present. The kids and I talked about each of them as we left the services. It was as though the leaders of the church could see right through us! At that point I was not ready for them, but I desperately desired to know and obtain what they had! I knew one and only one thing. I wanted their knowledge and strength, and especially their confidence in this person called God. Nothing about it made sense, but *I just wanted it!* They were sure of themselves. *I was no longer sure of anything!* Their sermons were simple, but powerful. These ministers were not afraid to talk about demons, and I had sense enough to know that what we were presently encountering was going to require more than a couple of prayers.

The Cowboy Churches in Texas and Louisiana rallied around us and our situation. Within weeks we had churches and Christian leaders in the community and all over Texas praying for us.

JoNey once again returned home.

Seashell Prisoners
CHAPTER 4

I'm not sure how it all came about, but I soon developed another relationship. Gary was a horse trainer with the girls taking to him like a duck on water. Gary trained race horses for different owners and ran them at Delta and Louisiana Downs. As Gary came to realize the situation with JoNey and Trevor, he did his best to console me. He always left me to make my own decisions on everything. Gary was definitely different from the others, and his quiet demeanor was soothing to my rigid lifestyle.

We soon purchased three horses together. Training the young colts at the house was great therapy for all of us. It had its way of taking the pressure off Anna and myself. Watching the three colts start off as babies and then advance with all the training was neat. Joining Gary at the races was totally new for me and a huge escape. The anticipation of the young colts getting old enough to compete became something once again to look forward to. At each race I envisioned myself one day stepping into the winner's circle, having my picture taken.

Of the three horses we had purchased, Gary had a favorite, Painted Imp. After many long hours of training, the colt was ready to race. Gary's choice of tracks for the young horse was Bossier City, so off we went. Being it was Painted Imp's first race, we had to get past the trials. To our disappointment, Painted Imp came in not only last, but limping. Gary, an extraordinarily confident trainer, boldly stated the following day, *"Painted Imp is ready for the race!"* I was totally shocked by the statement, but hesitant to say anything. Gary had proven himself as a trainer; I hadn't.

Within minutes, Gary had one of the best jockeys lined up to ride the young horse. We were ready! I was dressed for the occasion, anticipating being in the big picture. I had placed my bet! I knew Gary and I were probably the only ones betting on Painted Imp since he came in last in the trials. Despite that, Gary was walking tall and confident. As each horse made its way out of the paddock and began to line up for the race, there was something noticeably absent—Painted Imp! I scanned the paddock area only to see Gary now pacing and sweating profusely. I knew something was seriously wrong. At the last minute, the noted jockey had refused to ride the young horse that had come in last place in the trials. The jockey's reputation was at stake. After much confusion and frustration, the officials located a new rider for Painted Imp. The jockey now selected had not ridden in a year and had never won a race.

Painted Imp was now making his way to the starting gate. Everyone looked on, confused at the whole scenario. As the gate opened Painted Imp laid back, but within minutes the young horse with a big heart slowly began making his way to the front. To everyone's surprise, Painted Imp won the race!

The whole track was in shock as we stepped into the winner's circle. I am not sure who was the proudest—Gary, the jockey, or myself. It was a memorable day for the whole track! We collected our winnings and I counted my money as we exited the track. I was excited!

Gary, Frances & Painted Imp
1991

Gary and his two children, Lisa and Jason, stayed at the farm a lot. I was enjoying his presence and Anna enjoyed Gary's knowledge of horses. JoNey was once again back home. We all definitely felt more secure with Gary and his children with us. Our evenings consisted of sitting outside as Gary worked with the horses. This particular day Gary and I sat on the fence. Anna was working her new horse. She had outgrown Hollywood, and was now competing in high school rodeos with a fine new horse.

We were all focused on Anna, when we were abruptly interrupted with the roaring sound of a truck approaching. We all turned to see a black dually flying down the dirt road toward our house. It was Trevor! I heard the door of the house slam and glanced over to see JoNey running out of the house towards Trevor. As the truck came to a screeching stop, Trevor jumped out and grabbed JoNey. He immediately began hollering and screaming like a madman! The words were piercing, *"JoNey Is Going To Have A Baby!"* We all just looked at each other in shock!

JoNey angrily tried to push him back in his truck as he struggled with her. JoNey was small, but her tomboy side would kick in from time to time. Trevor continued to wrestle with her. Gary jumped off the fence and started in Trevor's direction. As usual, Trevor quickly made his way back to the truck and raced down the road. I heard the door slam as JoNey made her way back in the house.

I couldn't say anything. I just stood there, my eyes engulfed in tears. It wasn't exactly the way a mother expects to hear the announcement of her grandchild. It was obviously the Trevor Reese way! Once again Trevor made a flamboyant appearance. Then with pleasure, he made a spectacular departure. This form of pain became a frequent reoccurrence in our lives. *Flamboyant* fit Trevor in many ways.

We had heard story after story about Trevor's dad. He was an alcoholic and abusive to him and his mother when Trevor was young. Even though I genuinely felt sorry for Trevor, I repeatedly asked myself, why would Trevor select our family to persecute for his dysfunctional childhood? Never understanding why, I continued to be confused; especially not knowing to what degree this path of destruction would lead.

Desperate for help, I called Trevor's mother, Sarah, in an attempt to get her advice on the situation. Her noncommittal reply was, *"Trevor never hit on anyone and never hurt JoNey!"*

As a last resort, I then reached out to his sister Laura, only to receive the same rehearsed response, *"Trevor never did anything!"* Trevor had been married twice before he met JoNey. Surely if I had heard about Trevor's abuse to them, his own mother and sister would be aware of it. I knew immediately both of them were covering for him. It began to look as though the whole family was dysfunctional.

※

One day as I arrived home from work, I could feel something wasn't right as I came up the drive. JoNey's dad wasn't normally at the house. Today, he had Trevor backed up against the wall and was glaring into his face. The scene was threatening with once again seeing Trevor race down the road at high speed. Owen walked off extremely angry and never said a word.

Anna was upset, quickly filling me in. Trevor had arrived and an argument started between him and JoNey. Trevor began physically assaulting JoNey. Anna ran out to see Trevor throw JoNey up against the horse trailer and begin to choke her. JoNey was small and frail, but didn't back down to this madman. Anna was screaming at Trevor and trying to help JoNey. Anna quickly called her father. The huge question mark continued to grow as to why Trevor would be doing this to my child. Not only my child, but now my pregnant child!

Trevor began calling and once again convinced JoNey into moving back in with him. Months went by with all the same ups and downs. Finally, everyone fervently prayed as JoNey was to deliver within another month.

JANUARY 13, 1991

I received a call from Trevor early one morning. The weather was cold and wet and for some reason he was bringing JoNey over, but this time his voice was different with no emotion whatsoever. He never said anything other than that he was bringing JoNey to the house, nor did he come in to make sure she was going to be okay. It was all too strange and eerie. Trevor always had a plan or motive behind anything he did, and this was not making sense. As JoNey walked in, I wanted to cry because her body was so frail and void of life.

She stated she had been throwing up. JoNey was eight months pregnant, pale, and thin. I was trying hard not to take control or raise concerns. I slowly asked JoNey if she had seen a physician. Her reply was yes, but she didn't go into detail. I tried to discount the problem with the idea that it was dead winter and a lot of viruses were going around. I thought, maybe that was the problem.

Within an hour I noticed JoNey slip into my bathroom. I heard the door close and lock. Seconds later, I heard her screaming, groaning, and crying. Rushing to the door, I quietly told her to open the door. She screamed, "I Can't Find The Door!"

I frantically ran to the bathroom. I spoke softly and slowly until she made her way to the door. Within minutes, JoNey opened it. I immediately called her physician, relaying what had happened.

In a few words he very calmly, but distinctly, instructed me: "Get Her To The Hospital, Now!"

Gary was at the track, so I screamed at Anna and Lisa to help. We got JoNey into the car, turned on the emergency lights, and raced to St. Elizabeth's Hospital in Beaumont. As I drove I held my breath, noticing the color change in JoNey's complexion. She sat in the front seat agonizing with pain. Minutes before we arrived I saw her frail body becoming noticeably rigid. I was panicking on the inside. As we arrived in Beaumont, her body was twisting and her eyes were fixed. Seconds before we made our way to the entrance of the Hospital, JoNey went into a full seizure. Totally unfamiliar with the situation, I panicked, running into the hospital screaming for help. Within seconds, the medical staff had JoNey on a stretcher and in the emergency room. In thirty minutes they came out and announced the seizures were under control. Soon afterwards, we were informed JoNey would stay in the hospital for the remainder of her pregnancy. JoNey was diagnosed with later-stage toxemia. Her symptoms were elevated blood pressure, protein in the urine, and hyper flexia. The seizure was causing the baby's oxygen supply to get cut off.

Within minutes of receiving the news, a nurse once again approached us with the announcement that an emergency C-section was in progress. The seizures had started up again!

On January 13, 1991, Nocona Lynn was delivered. Nocona weighed 3 lbs., 14 oz. The physician came out stating, "It is a miracle that the two of them are alive, yet they are not out of danger!" He went on to say that JoNey's healing from this would take months and she badly needed to stay calm. She was having serious blood pressure problems. Nocona would also have to remain in the hospital for another week. She was to have supervised care, with controlled temperatures, and no visitors.

a

Par for the course, our stay at the hospital was like an Alfred Hitchcock movie! I stayed day and night by JoNey's side. It wasn't exactly the normal joyous occasion of a grandmother waiting for their first grandchild. Neither was it for JoNey anticipating her first child. Trevor was now back in the picture, continually present, pacing the floor with his ever-famous grimacing face.

Trevor's demeanor and appearance strongly suggested he was trying to intimidate all of us. This continued throughout the entire hospital stay.

One day the nurse entered the room with the birth certificate. She turned to walk out once she saw JoNey's condition. Trevor quickly grabbed the birth certificate and etched his name along the dotted line. It was as though it were a life and death situation. That moment will be forever engrained in my mind. He picked up JoNey's hand, forcing her to sign the birth certificate, because she was unable to raise her head much less her hand. JoNey was incoherent from all the drugs and problems of delivery. For some strange reason, Trevor demanded this birth be made official immediately!

Trevor continued his intimidation routine day after day in an attempt to force all of us to leave. JoNey was in critical condition, and I was not leaving even if he'd had a gun in his hand! We never had to explain Trevor's actions to friends and family. Everyone just knew this was par. The moment he would leave at night, everyone relaxed. Day in and day out Trevor repeated the same scenario. It appeared as though he were stalking us rather than paying a visit to his newborn child. Each day JoNey became more and more upset with his presence. At one point the nurse came in and boldly asked Trevor to leave. Obviously, this upset him. As he exited the room, he glared a death-piercing stare towards me. With each passing day, I felt more and more like my life as well as JoNey's was totally threatened by this man.

One day, as a last resort, I made my way to the phone, calling Owen, letting him know what was happening. Trevor then received the one call he most feared—a meeting with Owen! Owen was always extremely busy and didn't like interruptions. Trevor was aware of Owen's impatience and was obviously scared. Owen had made the decision on the location of the meeting. Accordingly, Trevor showed up for the meeting...with a bodyguard! Owen never revealed what was said, but choice words were obviously exchanged, letting Trevor know what would take place if he didn't back off.

It was a wonderful feeling as though I could breathe again, not having to worry about Trevor. JoNey and I had another long day, and we were both extremely tired. The nurses had moved JoNey to a private room since her condition was critical. I was grateful, knowing we could both rest better. Trevor knew nothing about the change in rooms.

I was tired of sleeping in my clothes. All I had was a slip so that was my gown for the night. JoNey and I talked late into the evening. As she relaxed, she broke down crying and began revealing more of Trevor's abuse to her. The two of us cried and finally went to sleep. I lay in a bed next to her with just a sheet over me.

At two o'clock in the morning I heard the door open to the room. I glanced over towards the door. The room was dimly lit, but I could see it was a male figure. Suddenly, I realized it was Trevor! My immediate thoughts were: The meeting with Owen didn't go well and Trevor was here to kill us!

JoNey and I lay motionless! Neither of us said a word. Trevor walked directly to my bed. He sat right beside me on the small bed. I could feel his body leaning towards me. I lay frozen as he looked into my face and made bizarre statements about JoNey's problem. He stated it had something to do with rabbits and a disease. JoNey and I never uttered a word, not knowing what his intentions were.

All of a sudden, he got up and exited the room. One thing was perfectly clear. Planting fear in people, especially women, was Trevor's favorite thing to do. It was obvious he was once again letting us know he could be present at any given time despite even hospital security rules.

❧

It was now time to take Nocona home. Trevor's house was short on conveniences with a lack of running water in the kitchen and other rooms. The long flight of stairs leading to his garage apartment had no handrails. It would make it impossible for JoNey to climb.

Trevor once again began to make attempts to get JoNey and the baby into his home. This time it didn't work. JoNey's weak, sickly body resisted his every attempt to manipulate her. JoNey readily accepted my offer to help out. She knew she couldn't take care of herself much less an infant. We also knew we couldn't deny Trevor coming to visit Nocona. JoNey was physically and emotionally crippled. She was totally overwhelmed with all the problems. Motherly instincts fell short as pain, suffering, and deep depression overrode the moment.

We had arrived home with Nocona from the hospital with a list of stringent rules to follow. The rules were not only for Nocona, but her mother also. Nocona was so frail, yet beautiful. She would have fit into a shoe box easily. Her first bed was on a small dressing table. No one was allowed to enter Nocona's room or hold her. A few exceptions were her mother, father, and maternal grandparents until she gained more weight. Everyone had to wear a mask at all times.

Gary was still living with us when he was in town. Todd was in and out from time to time. Trevor came for short visits, storming out the door each time as though he were upset. Soon afterwards, he began talking to JoNey for long periods on the phone. He continued to encourage her to live with him.

One night Todd was over visiting. It was freezing cold and raining. I heard a knock on the door. It was Trevor. He went to the back bedroom to see Nocona. I was busy in the kitchen. I heard JoNey screaming and crying, "He's Taking Nocona!" Both Todd and Gary reacted at the same time, bolting toward the door. They immediately apprehended Trevor in the hall. There was no resistance once he saw the two huge bodies glaring down on him. Todd and Gary both were large in stature and Gary had a reputation equal to Todd's. Trevor quickly handed Nocona over and once again cowardly stormed out of the house!

❧

A statement from Mr. Rayburn, one of JoNey's teachers, continued to jab at my inner soul. "Your daughter is very gifted. Whatever she focuses on she will accomplish, because she will pour herself into it 100%." I remember distinctly his emphasis on the word...*Whatever!* My only fear now was, would she do the same with this dysfunctional man? Would she continue to try to perfect this sick situation?

Trevor continued to call JoNey, begging forgiveness, and in return making big promises. With each event I began to realize JoNey would rather be dead than concede to failure. As horrible as their relationship was, JoNey was a high achiever, and failure was not a part of her character. Against my wishes, JoNey soon moved back in with Trevor. Trevor's ability to manipulate again took precedence over reality.

The problems persisted, and again JoNey and Nocona returned home.

Trevor continued to woo her back into his life with his soothing words, "I am so sorry, I love you so much, and I will never hurt you again. This time everything will be different." JoNey once again fell for it, moving back in with Trevor. Nocona was brought to me during the week, then Owen's or Sarah's on the weekends. JoNey got a job with her dream of one day going to college still tucked away.

I knew JoNey like the back of my hand, and this person I saw each time was only there in body. She was struggling to keep her sanity. She did not have the mental, emotional, or physical capacity to nurture and care for herself, much less an infant. She was a little girl with broken dreams, robbed of her youth, continually trying to piece her life back together.

Nocona grew and became a beautiful two-year-old, full of energy and always emanating love. Seeing her laughter and love was a constant reminder of her mother prior to Trevor's entrance into her life. Nocona continued to stay with me during the week when JoNey worked, so I had a set routine scheduled for her. Nocona needed release for her much stored-up energy. She loved music, so we played lots of music in the morning. Then we retired to the outdoors, spending many hours on the trampoline and playing with the animals outside. Nocona loved animals, especially her favorite dog, Hobbit.

Nocona was a beautiful baby full of personality. Everyone doted over her. In a way it was great, but in other ways I wondered how healthy it was for her. As Nocona was passed from grandparent to grandparent on different weekends, each dressed her according to their own individual tastes. Nocona had full wardrobes at each home along with all the baby equipment, toys, etc. Some dressed her in fancy dresses with all the bows, and some in jeans. Everyone was uniquely expressing their love for Nocona. Nocona was a very happy baby.

I loved keeping Nocona, but I had real problems to deal with. How would I get JoNey out of this sick situation and restored back to life?

Frances, Nocona & JoNey

Seashell Prisoners
CHAPTER 5

From the time I first met Trevor's mother she was always distant towards me. JoNey had mentioned earlier that Sarah had worked many years at the Orange County Courthouse in the county clerk's office. She once stated, Sarah literally had the keys to the courthouse.

One day I received a call from Sarah; she told me that she was coming by for a visit, which was totally out of character. Today it was as though we were good friends. As Sarah went forward in conversation, I sat back and watched her demeanor, not sure of what her intentions were. The visit was short and to the point with her subtly letting me know Laura, her only daughter, could not have children and wanted Nocona. I was totally and completely taken off guard! Trying not to react and keeping my composure, I simply said "No!" Sarah never entered my home again!

Vast changes began to occur in Trevor's personality. JoNey called me from his house with some unexpected news. She was saying Trevor was now encouraging her to go back to college. There was excitement in her voice. For the first time, Trevor was now agreeing to help JoNey by bringing Nocona to see her on the weekends. Her new plan was to register and attend Bryan College and later Texas A&M.

Trevor's whole demeanor changed to being extremely nice. I knew deep down there had to be an underlying motive. I quickly encouraged JoNey to go forward with her new plan. Right now the priority was JoNey getting out of Trevor's house and, eventually, his life! Without hesitation, I quickly located a trailer, setting it up at College Station for JoNey's residence.

Trevor made his first move of many that would soon become bizarre and life-changing for all of us. The new plan included putting Nocona in a day care close to his mother's house. Trevor would take Nocona to school and his mother would pick her up after work every day, conveniently taking me out of the picture completely. Not wanting to rock this new boat, I waited anxiously hoping Nocona would adapt to this sudden change.

I didn't see Nocona for two weeks. I called JoNey, who was totally confused, stating Trevor never made it to Bryan. The second weekend came around and JoNey returned to Mauriceville. She brought Nocona over, but never mentioned problems. It was evident JoNey loved school, and a small flicker of life had once again returned in her life.

Nocona was with JoNey, but not herself this time. She acted strange and disconnected. Her whole personality was different. It was evident she was not adjusting to all the changes. Instead of the playful child, she was crying over nothing and sucking her thumb a lot. I noticed small bite marks on her arms.

I began to visit the day care. On the second visit, one of the workers pulled me to the side and admitted Nocona wasn't adjusting well, and needed a change. Two of the workers informed me Trevor was extremely upset at my being there to the extent that he lashed out at the workers in the day care. The lady in charge recommended I get an attorney named Sonny Cribbs. She dropped the subject as quickly as she brought it up, leaving me with the distinct impression there was something very dark happening.

JoNey & Nocona

࿊

I began to get calls on the phone with no one talking, only heavy breathing. I started picking Nocona up a couple days a week from the day care. This infuriated Trevor. JoNey consistently came in on the weekends. Trevor made excuses each week as to why he never made it to Bryan.

My whole world that was rich with family, friends, and trips to the lake or the Caribbean had now come to a halt. All had been replaced with a new schedule, learning about stress and how to deal with psychopathic personalities! I had never known anyone personally that was abusive or defiant in any way and was totally clueless on how to deal with this situation.

Every day became more intense, unusual thoughts began to well up in my inner being, totally confusing me as to where they came from. I had previously had a dream about one of my aunts dying and the whole funeral.

Within a month my aunt actually died! Now even more odd thoughts began to surface.

I prayed daily and searched for who was, hopefully, God—Someone that could take this whole mess and turn it around. I wanted desperately for God to be real and be there for me and my family. My search for God grew more intense as our problems continued to grow with each passing day. I now realized there were many gods, and I didn't just need God; I needed The Most High God! The Bible mentioned there were many gods. Who were they and where were they?

My friends were many, each having their own form of religion. Everyone was doing their best to comfort me. One suggested yoga; others comforted me with what appeared to me as weird religious statements. At this point, I didn't want to hear about the god of peace and serenity or a god that could offer me comfort! I wanted to talk to The Most High God, a God With Power! My problem was huge! I wanted a God that could do huge miracles, as of...Right Now! I wasn't sure if He was out there, but if He was, I wanted to talk to Him.

I would take out my Bible and search endlessly for meaning. Comfort came, but the stories continued to confuse me and I would set my Bible down. One night for some unknown reason, I got down on my knees. I began to ask God if there was anything else He wanted to do with my life. I knew I was supposed to be saved, but just simply felt it was a question that needed to be answered. There was no big verbal yes or no, but from that day forward there was an unusual force that strengthened, driving me forward into what felt like a category-five hurricane. As an exchange for my submission to Him, I expected the Most High God to remove my pain and return the bliss back into my life. Instead, this force strengthened in intensity, plunging me deeper into what appeared to be a bottomless pit of pain and suffering. *What Kind Of God Was This?*

ەا

One Sunday I approached Dennis Vaughn, my Sunday School teacher. Dennis had an unusual walk with God and was different from most Baptists I had come to know. I often wondered if the pastor at the time was aware of things Dennis was teaching in his Sunday School class. Dennis reminded me more of a Pentecostal preacher—the kind back in Mamma's church. Dennis's walk with God was so intense that I deeply hoped he would have an answer for my unusual problem. Dennis began to pray for me, but there were no answers surfacing.

Within days after making my request to God, I woke up one night once again with this huge thought rising up in me. Unable to explain it, I awakened Gary and told him that something deep inside me was stating, we could no longer live together! It was so weird, but so plainly spoken to me in my spirit. I couldn't deny that there was definitely something in me that was totally different and now very much alive. I couldn't define it. I just knew whatever it was, it wasn't me!

Our lifestyle was the American way of living. Most everyone I knew found live-ins acceptable, and I never once questioned it as long as my children were in agreement. I thought one day I would possibly marry the person.

※

Weeks went by and once again I had another unusual dream—short in terms of time, but so profound I couldn't get it off my mind. I dreamed enormous rain drops were falling. The first one was coming to my sister, Arlene. As I watched, one was coming towards me. I reached my arms out to receive it. A huge ray of light was shining all around the large liquid drops extending up to heaven. There was such a calming aura to it. I remember basking in the moment, not wanting to turn loose. It was short in timeframe, but so surreal.

With each week as I came across my Christian mentors, I would ask if they had ever heard of such a thing. No one seemed to be able to interpret it. I remember the disappointment when I approached Ma Gibbons and another strong Christian friend. They always seem to know everything about God, but they had no answers for me.

※

Nocona, 3 years old

Each day had its own beginning. More and more problems appeared. Nocona began to complain of bugs being on her. She would scream as though she were being bitten, yet there was nothing on her. Nocona referred to a wolf getting her crying and doing bizarre things to her. Large bruises began to appear on her body. I was now having to take Nocona to a physician so he could witness all the changes and possibly help Nocona. Dr. Renaldi continued to be alarmed and eventually demanded I call C.P.S. After several visits, I came back at him with "You call C.P.S. They are not listening to me! I have made numerous calls to them."

I was becoming angry and confused at the lack of help. Nothing changed and Nocona's problems grew worse. She became more and more withdrawn.

JoNey never spoke of any problems when she came around. Every ounce of her was being poured into her school work where she was always achieving high grades in everything. I felt as though I should be doing something for JoNey, but I wasn't sure of what. At the present, I wasn't handling Nocona's problem much less knowing how to deal with JoNey's. I felt at this time college was the best place for her. I knew she was going forward with something of value and would deal with the other later.

I was normally a strong individual. With this bizarre situation, I was totally mindless as to how to handle this. The whole thing was like a cancer. The worst part was the cancer was attached to all of us. Every family member felt the impact from it.

ès

I received a call from JoNey. She was at College Station. This day was different! JoNey was confused and bewildered as she told me a constable came by and served her papers. Totally naive to the situation, she called Sarah hoping to get information from her, since Sarah worked in the office where the papers had been served from. JoNey stated Sarah was unusually nice, encouraging her to continue on with her schooling. Sarah explained to JoNey they were just trying to make sure Nocona's birth certificate was complete. She went on to say there was no need for JoNey to be concerned or leave college. I was confused because JoNey wasn't able to comprehend the papers served her. Something wasn't right! One thing was once again evident—Trevor was up to something!

I put in a call to Karl Perry, an attorney recommended to me. I was hoping my feelings were wrong. Within minutes, I received a call from Melissa, Karl's assistant, stating she had called the Orange County Courthouse. Melissa quickly explained it was a full-custody suit to take Nocona away from JoNey! She then stated "Tell JoNey to come home right now and bring the papers by our office!"

Within a couple of hours, JoNey had arrived and I received another call from the attorney's office. Melissa, stated "The reason your daughter could not understand the papers she was presented (was that) the main sheet was left out stating it was a full-custody suit!" She also noted that the office the papers were issued from was the County Clerk's office where Sarah worked!

It took a lot, but JoNey finally had her answer and never returned to Trevor's home. She picked up the phone and called LaDonna, her best friend. JoNey told her, "I have been praying a long time for a sign about me and Trevor, and God finally answered. I am never going back to him. Trevor is trying to take Nocona from me!"

There was no more wondering about what Trevor's new game plan was. The cards were now clearly out on the table with apparently his whole family in on the game. Trevor and his family's scheme was good, but apparently they had slipped up on one small detail. Nocona was in my possession when it was all said and done! We held on to Nocona, awaiting Trevor's next move. Within a short time Nocona had to released once again to her father.

&

We were now receiving the usual silent calls, along with Trevor's black dually undeniably stalking us. At any given time he could be seen driving up and down or just sitting at the end of our road. He was obviously attempting to plant fear in us. This was one game he would learn in time...*He Wouldn't Win!*

JoNey continued going to college, but in a sense in denial, refusing to talk about anything that had to do with Trevor. She had now come to know a wonderful Christian group called Cowboys for Christ in a small town close to Bryan College, called Trinity. The church knew her situation, stood by her in prayer and continued to support her throughout her stay in Bryan. God was good! They were definitely her encouragers! The pastors, Ron and Joe Conatser, along with an older member, Miss Ruth, were pillars in their faith. Both JoNey and I soon desperately clung to their every word for support. These people definitely knew something we didn't, an inner strength, something I was still determined to obtain.

Within a few weeks after being served the papers, JoNey got another big surprise. Trevor was getting married! I was shocked, but it all seemed to fit into his new plan. We were informed Jenile was very young, independent and pretty. Jenile had two children of her own, a boy and a girl.

Trevor smoked cigarettes and Nocona was very allergic to smoke. On each return to his home, Nocona reeked with smoke. Another problem we would try and deal with.

&

January came around, and it was my birthday. JoNey had picked up Nocona and taken her out of town for the weekend. I went out to dinner with my family, came in late, and was exhausted when I got home. I immediately went to bed.

Around midnight, the phone rang and it was Trevor. Momentarily, I froze at the mention of his name, much less his voice. I was determined not to be afraid of him, but pain and more problems always followed his presence. From his tone I gathered he was extremely upset, asking where Nocona was. Trevor angrily stated JoNey was at a hospital in Ft. Worth with a broken leg. He went on to say she had been riding bulls and bareback horses in a Women's Pro Rodeo that weekend. Completely blown away by the whole conversation, I just let him know Nocona was fine. I made him think I was aware of the whole situation and in total control. I thanked him for calling and told him I was on my way out to pick Nocona up when he'd called.

We were now facing a huge custody suit! Why would JoNey do anything to jeopardize this huge undertaking? Extremely upset, I woke up Anna and immediately left for Ft. Worth. There was always this deep sense of compassion for JoNey. Tonight all feelings left as my mind raced back and forth as to the effect this would have on the upcoming custody case. It was evident JoNey was doing everything she could to escape, but this was the limit!

When JoNey was younger I had caught her riding bulls at a rodeo, but quickly put a stop to it. I knew the Cowboy Church had brought a new spark into her life and was a huge support to her. JoNey failed to mention one thing. Their main activity after church was... *BULLRIDING!*

Early that morning we arrived at the hospital in Ft. Worth to find JoNey with her leg in a cast and hanging in a sling. As I approached JoNey, the conversation was short, consisting of three words: "Where Is Nocona?" As soon as she gave me directions to her whereabouts, I turned and left the room without one word of sympathy.

Relief came quick! Nocona was safe in a home of one of JoNey's friends and was well taken care of. The lady there was very cordial and it was obvious she and her husband were a part of the professional rodeo circuit. Each had much to say on how proud they were of JoNey's accomplishments. JoNey had just won $600.00 and was in the lead for Rookie of The Year in the Women's Pro Rodeo. She went on to tell me how great JoNey's rides were, until the pickup man ran over her leg as she was finishing her event. I guess I had a blank look on my face since she went on to explain what a pickup man was. "Frances, he is the man on the horse riding next to her horse or bull, whichever she is riding. He is responsible for making sure once JoNey finishes her ride she is safely picked up and out of harm's way."

I just stood there with a huge void on my face as the kind lady spoke. I tried hard to focus on her conversation, but it had a way of quickly fading. I knew exactly what a pickup man was, but at this point I just wanted to get the #@# back to Orange County!

It was a long quiet ride home and we arrived early in the morning. I was exhausted. Mauriceville never looked so good as we made the last turn off F.M. 1130, making our way down the narrow winding road that led up to our house. It was quiet as usual being out in the country away from everyone. The closer we got, the more evident it was that something was different about a new truck I had recently purchased for Anna. The truck was parked in front of the house. As we pulled around the drive I could see the whole side of the truck was caved in. Once again I was in total shock. Being out in the country we never had any problems with intruders. Only one person was aware we were gone, Trevor!

With each day, it became more and more apparent that we were dealing with a very sick man. The question was always there, Why us? What had we done to this man? We had never had any problems with anyone before Trevor arrived in our life. Now our whole world was spiraling downhill.

My only outlet was the organization I had formed. I continued working with the Drug Awareness program, making a desperate attempt to hold on to my sanity. Everything else in my life went on hold. I had no life! My total focus now was JoNey and Nocona. The relationship Gary and I had established had now diminished with all the problems surrounding me. He was so good with Nocona, but most of all we were best friends enjoying just sitting and talking for hours at the end of each day. Now that was gone.

My life quickly took on a whole new profile filled with seeking out attorneys. I spent every minute desperately searching out ways to protect ourselves against a very sick man. I was totally illiterate when it came to legal jargon. Nothing about it made sense. Lawyers, courts, and abusive people had never been a part of our lives nor of anyone we knew.

Our many friends continued to surround us. Phil was coming by and calling to check on us. New friends began to surface as we needed them, but the pain never wavered. Not one person had experienced anything like this, but it was comforting having their moral support.

My strong point was definitely not working with or choosing attorneys. I quickly reflected back on the divorce with Owen. I probably would have slit my throat if I had known this was only a small glimpse of what was going to confront me repeatedly down the road. My choice of attorneys for the divorce was a suggestion from an acquaintance, which quickly ended in total disaster. My lawyer stated as we left from the first courtroom hearing, *"Why are you expecting anything? You never did anything in the marriage!"* I soon learned Mr. Ramsey had worked with Owen on a project prior to our divorce. Quickly firing him, I recovered my losses with a new attorney. This one had a different perspective about a woman that had spent twenty-two years with a man raising the children, caring for the home, and managing the family business.

The biggest problem was the only good attorney I knew was now an elected judge and not able to help with my huge problem. The more I sought out professional help for JoNey, the less support I seemed to have. Karl was highly recommended to me and had a good reputation as an attorney. On the first visit with him, he had come on strong. He boldly stated he would have Trevor in prison by the time it was over, since JoNey was seventeen when the relationship started. Trevor was twice JoNey's age, and was abusive to both wives he had been married to prior to his and JoNey's relationship. Karl stated that in Texas, when a female is seventeen or under, in a relationship with an older man, that is statutory rape. She is considered a minor. That day, I poured my soul out to Karl with him looking me directly in the eye, reassuring me he could handle the job and that it would be a piece of cake.

I remember as I left his office, I truly thought this would be the shortest jury trial ever with Trevor's abusive reputation. Karl met with us once again. He very casually informed us Sarah had picked the judge, but reassured us he saw no problem with it. He also stated he was best friends with Trevor's attorney, Jay Runnels. He reassured us again that that also would not be a problem. I was rather bewildered by it all and totally ignorant of the whole new legal crisis I was now faced with. I momentarily sat in a mute state as I began to realize how totally dependent we were on this man. It felt excruciating! Not a position I savored. I would just have to trust Karl since he came highly recommended.

There were hundreds of people that knew Trevor and his violent background, and saw our dilemma from day one. Each knew a different horror story. They readily called or came by to warn us, but finding enough to come forward and testify was like finding needles in a haystack. Everyone feared this man, and the thought of getting involved with this psychopath and the legal system was mind-boggling. Trevor had a reputation of harassing anyone that came up against him. With much prayer, enough people came forward and we were now ready for the custody suit!

We had what we felt was a strong defense, but we were badly needing Trevor's ex-wives to testify. They knew the abuse first hand, and continued to live daily in fear of him. But they wanted no part of our bizarre problem. They had experienced enough in their own lives. One was now happily married and lived close by, but stood her ground, wanting nothing more to do with Trevor!

I was forced once again to release Nocona to Trevor for visitation. Letting go of Nocona every other weekend was extremely hard, knowing what kind of person we were dealing with. Each time Nocona came back we could see continued changes. She not only talked about a wolf, but now refused to go outside. Most of my time was spent with Nocona in my lap since she no longer felt safe. The visual bruises on her body became more apparent. I continued to call C.P.S., but their response was strange as though their hands were tied. After several calls they said they would go out for a visit, but I never heard from them.

The following weekend Nocona returned from Trevor with a black eye and scrapes all over her arms and legs. With each return, I continued to take Nocona to the physician and pour my heart out to him, not only for Nocona's problems, but to continue getting everything documented in hopes someone would believe me and help us. I begged Dr. Renaldi to please put pressure on C.P.S. He reassured me he would, and he would be there for us with whatever we needed. He always appeared to be deeply concerned for Nocona.

On one occasion Trevor returned Nocona and she was crying. Her thumbs were blood red. Nocona said Trevor was putting hot sauce on them all weekend. Again I took Nocona back to Dr Renaldi. He was extremely upset, and reemphasized the importance of C.P.S. getting involved. I told him the last time I spoke with C.P.S. I ended up screaming at them, but nothing was being done. C.P.S. finally made one announced visit to Trevor and reported they couldn't find any problem.

Nocona continued to go downhill with more and more visual signs and emotional problems. I picked up the phone and called Karl. I knew he was supposed to be working on the custody case, but the problem with Nocona was getting worse. I was very upset. I boldly let him know if I didn't get help I was going to leave the country with Nocona!

Karl was outraged at the statement! He came back at me saying if I left that would kill JoNey's case and she would not have a chance with the upcoming custody suit! Karl must have mentioned the problem of abuse to Trevor's attorney. The visual bruises on Nocona immediately stopped. But the emotional problems were still present.

The custody suit was fast approaching. I thought Nocona's abuse would be brought out in the trial. In the back of my mind I was thinking that the trial would solve all our problems.

૨૪

One weekend, JoNey decided she wanted to have her picture made. This was very unusual for JoNey. She was always rather tomboyish and dressed simply. Today she wanted to dress up and have her picture made with Nocona and JoLynn, her favorite horse. I was truly surprised at how feminine JoNey looked after she had done her hair. She was very pretty and dressed up, anticipating the photo shoot. Nocona was also ready with her best dress on. This was a nice break from the daily stress of Trevor. Good memories flooded me as JoNey posed with her horse. We all embraced this small moment of normalcy. *It Felt Wonderful!*

I took picture after picture of JoNey and her horse while Nocona played nearby. She and Hobbit were running in the grass. At one moment I looked up and Nocona was a few feet from me. She had stooped down in the monkey grass next to the sidewalk. As I picked her up I noticed a few ants on one foot. I took off her shoes as I started toward the house. I set Nocona in the kitchen sink to run cool water over her foot. As I picked up the ointment to put on her foot, I noticed small welts on the back of her neck. Within seconds the welts doubled in size. I had never seen anything like that! Immediately the welts grew larger. I hollered at JoNey to get in the car! We were taking Nocona to the doctor. Dr. Renaldi's office was just a few miles down the road beside Owen's hardware store on Highway 62. I knew we didn't have time to go to a hospital in Orange or Beaumont.

I raced down FM 1130. Within a mile down the road I looked over to see that Nocona's small body was now twice the normal size! Within minutes we were at Dr. Renaldi's office in Mauriceville. We burst into his office carrying Nocona's lifeless body. As Dr. Renaldi worked over her, we watched in shock. All I knew to do was pray. We were totally helpless. At one point Dr. Renaldi became pale, stepped back and calmly stated Nocona wasn't breathing! The look on his face was easy to read. It was apparent he didn't know anything else to do. I quickly intervened hollering, *"Call 911!"* He immediately made the call and under their instructions administered another shot of epinephrine to Nocona. The ambulance arrived shortly afterward and took us to St. Elizabeth Hospital. Nocona was doing much better by the time we arrived.

As much as we didn't want to, I knew I had to call Trevor. The hospital experience was the same with Trevor's arrival. His eyes were piercing. His sister and his mother kept their distance. The physician came out and explained that Nocona was extremely allergic to fire ants. He went on to state it would be necessary for all of us to carry an epinephrine shot with us at all times. Trevor refused, saying he would give Nocona Benadryl if anything happened.

કર

Nocona continued to go to Trevor's every other weekend, only to return with problems. From the moment Trevor dropped her off, my time was consumed. I made every attempt to get Nocona back up mentally, emotionally, and physically so she could once again return to Trevor.

I was very sure the custody suit would bring about help for Nocona. I would regroup and call C.P.S. hoping they would intervene, only to be told there was nothing they could do. I continued taking Nocona to Dr. Renaldi so everything could be documented for us to use in court.

A few weeks went by and I receive another call from JoNey. Something was wrong, but I couldn't make out what she was saying. I struggled to comprehend her, asking her to repeat herself. I could tell she had been crying. I soon realized her trailer at College Station had mysteriously burned to the ground while she was away for the weekend! JoNey was supposed to have been there, but at the last minute decided to go out of town. It's like we never recovered from one thing before something else happened. Terrorists had nothing on Trevor! He was a natural, who needed no time in training camps to know how to break people down.

I went forward in an attempt to nurture JoNey and keep her mental state up. I knew the trial was coming up, and it was going to be tough. Trevor's name was never brought up in conversation. If it was, you could be sure of one thing, JoNey would exit the room! Mentally and emotionally, she was weakening on me. I didn't know if she would hold up to the week long suit.

Seashell Prisoners
CHAPTER 6

The miniature horse, the playground, the animals that were always a haven for Nocona had now become a threat. With each attempt to take Nocona outside to play, it always ended in panic and tears. Nothing made her happy spending most of her time in my lap. I began to notice Nocona was more relaxed at Owen's. I realized the connection: Trevor never went to Owen's!

Nocona always referred to Trevor as Dedi. From time to time when she spoke of the wolf, I would ask her who the wolf was. Nocona appeared to be fearful, not replying.

Later I asked Nocona where the wolf lived—"Was it at Granna's house or her grandfather's?" But I got no response.

Finally I asked, "Does the wolf live at Dedi's?" She quickly replied, "Yes!"

I now had her confirmation: it was Trevor! I better understood why Nocona was refusing to go outside, because she was afraid the wolf would return and get her at my house!

A few days prior to the custody suit hearing, I was shopping in a store in Orange when I met up with an acquaintance that was a long time friend of our family. Adam frequented the rodeos and knew all the contestants. Adam knew both Todd and Trevor. Today, for some reason, his demeanor was different. Looking me in the eye very seriously, Adam asked very pointedly "Do you know why Trevor hates you so much?" The question startled me. Completely taken off guard, I quickly made an attempt to regain my composure and look equally as confident. I boldly looked Adam in the eye and stated, "Yes, it's because Trevor knows how much I love JoNey. He knows I do not want my daughter in his life."

Adam quickly replied, "No. It has nothing to do with your daughter. Trevor was interested in you and obviously your money. He was furious at you, stating you stepped on his ego! He said he got back at you with your daughter!"

A huge wave of nausea came over me—the thought of someone being so sick! As I turned and walked off, I thought, *surely there is more to this. No one could be that sick!* I quickly began to dissect the statement. I was older than this man; it's common knowledge I don't even ride a horse, so I have absolutely nothing in common with him. His goal had to be money!

That entire day, my mind was racing, unable to clear. I couldn't seem to dismiss Adam's remarks. At the end of the day I called Todd, hoping to discount this sick statement. I knew Todd, being around the rodeo scene, would know and tell me the truth. Sure enough, Todd, along with another rodeo friend, reconfirmed the statement. Trevor was bad news and definitely up to no good, and their suspicion was the same. He was an obvious psychopath and yes, mother, he was after your money! This sick man and his despicable scheme continued to immerse our lives every day.

JUNE 1993

The Cowboy churches along with other native churches in Orange County were picking up momentum with their prayers. Trevor became outraged at the Baptist Church in Mauriceville for supporting us in prayer. He stated to the press that he was going to sue them! No one seemed to be surprised by his statement. Trevor's support group remained small with only his sister Laura, his mother, and a couple of his friends and relatives.

Prayers were going up from many, with a team of prayer warriors meeting with me daily. Each person's goal was to prepare me for the custody suit and my testimony. Ma Gibbons, one of Mauriceville's biggest prayer warriors, headed up this prayer circle.

Today was the first day of the custody suit. We fervently prayed for God's divine intervention.

Many friends and family members filed into the Orange county courtroom. As I entered the large room, I immediately noticed a strong presence of heaviness in the air. With my new search for God, I was now being educated on what obviously appeared to be demonic spirits! I later brought it up to our attorney and LaDonna, a close friend of JoNey's. Karl commented that this was common in family court, reconfirming that other attorneys also noticed it.

I looked up to see Laura in the courtroom, walking towards Jay Runnels, Trevor's attorney. Not knowing otherwise, a person would have thought Laura was the attorney from her attire and demeanor as she made her way to the chair.

Trevor was in his usual white shirt and jeans. His presence was equally as strong as his demeanor. Trevor had no influence, but his mother's and Laura's influences were definitely turning this into a David-and-Goliath situation. We searched daily for the right stones to pick up!

Karl had schooled JoNey on what to wear and how to best protect herself in the courtroom. Upset by her lack of response, he demanded we tutor her on the importance of reflecting self confidence in the courtroom. Little did he know LaDonna and I were just praying JoNey would show up for court, much less be told what to wear or what to look like! JoNey was just a child, whose foremost thought was to run from this whole dysfunctional mess. Actually, that was everyone's desire, except for Trevor and his family. They appeared to be enjoying the moment.

The whole scenario was excruciating, just knowing JoNey would be in the presence of this evil man all week. She knew her entire life with Trevor would be publicly broadcast. JoNey was supposed to represent a strong, healthy, loving mother in court. The truth was she was void of life, feeling absolutely nothing for anybody or anything.

The courtroom filled with our friends and family. Judge Davis immediately instructed all witnesses to wait in the hall until called. Not knowing what to expect on the first day, I sat anxiously waiting in the foyer for Karl to call in our witnesses. No one was called in! Several of us waited patiently in the foyer all day.

I was told JoNey was on the stand. I knew my kids like the back of my hand and JoNey would only go one route—total honesty! That trait burned deep in all of us, making this situation ten times worse. I knew everything that came out of Trevor's mouth would be lies and deceit. JoNey was too young to have an understanding of the power of words and the importance of protecting herself in court. So much was hanging on her motherhood! It was all very stressful knowing the very things JoNey would say might cause her to lose custody of Nocona, in the end, placing her in the hands of this sick man. From that day forward, we saw how appropriately Nocona had labeled her father...*The Wolf!*

On the second day, JoNey was called to the stand. Once again it was another long and grueling day. It was difficult leaving JoNey alone as I took my place once again in the hall. She was now expected to be a grown-up woman ready to defend herself against a pack of wolves! Each day JoNey exited the courtroom, she was always pale and distraught. She had obviously been in the lion's den under fire. She never spoke a word all the way home.

We picked up Nocona at a friend's house. Nocona was two and a half, and appeared to have picked up on the emotions of her mother. JoNey was in such deep thought it was as though she were in a trance. I dropped JoNey off and took Nocona to the Dairy Queen to entertain her in hopes she would not notice the stress surrounding our day.

On the third day we regrouped and went back to court. Once again, JoNey was on the stand. Once again Karl never called any of our witnesses. We continued to sit anxiously waiting our turn. All day, JoNey was under the grueling attack of a professional and it was now obvious she was getting no help from Karl, our attorney. With each day, friends reconfirmed the heaviness in the courtroom. They informed me that at one point Jay Runnels pulled out a cassette tape and nervously fidgeted with it as though he were going to use it. LaDonna stated, "My eyes stayed glued to it. Then, all of a sudden, a bolt of lightning thundered across the room, quickly grabbing everyone's attention! The electricity went out, unsettling everyone. It was all very strange! The tape was then set down."

Another day ended and once again JoNey came out lifeless from a full-day attack by Trevor's attorney. We returned home and JoNey refused to eat. It was apparent she just wanted to be left alone. I joined Nocona on the deck, entertaining her while JoNey sat in a stupor, totally stripped of emotions. I went in and sat quietly by JoNey in hopes of finding something to say that might help relieve the pain she was suffering. We both sat and watched Nocona as she played in her small swimming pool on the adjoining deck. Suddenly, there was a loud scream! Both of us jumped up, running towards Nocona. Her body was stiff and her hands were clenched in a fist! We frantically examined her thinking something must have bitten her. There were no signs of anything. We continued to console Nocona, but she wouldn't stop screaming. Her body was stiff and rigid. She finally settled down and went back to playing. I sat back down by JoNey, hoping in some way to comfort her.

Within minutes we heard Nocona scream once again, and this time it was more intense. Her small fist was clinched shut as though she had something in it. She continued to scream. We jumped in the car and raced to the hospital with her. JoNey drove as I held Nocona, softly singing and praying as tears ran down my face. We were all exhausted from the grueling day in court, but now it was going to be a long night. I continued to sing, then all of a sudden Nocona began to lean into me. I felt her body going limp and she stopped crying. I held her clinched fist. I felt it opening as she dropped off to sleep. I looked thinking there might be an insect, but there was nothing. We turned into the parking lot of the hospital and sat there a while to see what was going to happen. Rather than sit in the hospital three hours and try to describe something that wasn't visible, we just returned home.

On the fourth day as we entered the courthouse, I overheard whispers as we walked down the long hall. I was looking over my notes as we made our entrance to the courtroom. Laura and Jay Runnels were walking up ahead of us.

Someone whispered, "Look at her!" I turned and looked up. Laura never looked to the right or the left as though she were of great prominence or maybe an honor graduate of Harvard. Then I overheard someone say, "No one would ever guess her past background was living with a man on drugs that ended up in prison for cutting a man's head off!" Shocked at the remark, I asked Karl if he was aware of that; he reassured me it was the truth, and went on to say Laura's mother rushed her off to Houston to get her out of Orange when it happened. Laura later married an attorney in Houston!

The fourth day of court repeated day one and two. The courtroom was packed with friends and family. Once again Jay Runnels grilled JoNey on the stand. You could cut the tension with a knife it was so heavy. Today, Owen showed up! Trevor and Laura immediately alerted security! Owen was stopped, and a full body search was performed including the removal of Owen's boots. You could hear a pin drop as everyone watched in awe at the event!

It was extremely colorful as Trevor, his Mother, and Laura plotted each turn of the day. It was abundantly clear who was in control in Orange County, and it wasn't us! They had all the legal experience and obvious strong connections. We had neither, but we had prayer warriors! All eyes continued to focus on Owen's reaction, but he appeared totally unaffected by the whole charade. From that point on, there were guards at the door as each person filed into the courtroom. Everyone was searched for weapons. The only weapon that was needed was a knife, to cut the tension in the air! It was as though no one was even breathing during the whole day.

It was the fourth day before they called our witnesses. Our first witness called to the stand was Crystal Lyons. Crystal was brought in as a character witness for JoNey. Crystal was a beautiful young lady in full-time ministry with the Cowboy Church. She also rode in the pro rodeos. Crystal's lack of intimidation and straightforwardness was piercing. I knew she would be long remembered in the Orange County courts. Crystal's indebtedness was to one Person, and that was God. Her integrity rang loud and clear to the courts and the jury. It was evident from day one all our friends were loyal, honest, and to the point.

Crystal and JoNey, from a distance, were frequently mistaken for each other in the world of rodeo. Both had long blonde hair and slim figures. Both were frail but fearless when it came to horses and bulls, neither intimidating them. Today it was different: Crystal was standing tall, facing the courts head on. JoNey was emotionally ripped to shreds, wishing she were a million miles away.

During a break in the proceedings, Karl called LaDonna and I to meet with him and JoNey. Karl was nervous and mentioned his concern for the case. LaDonna and I quickly intervened, stating we were looking to God for the victory. Karl brushed off our statement as though it were offensive. Karl then stated, "Stop all the foolishness. It's up to us!"

LaDonna and I just looked at each other! What happened to the statement that Trevor would end up in prison? What happened to the statutory rape charge? And the fact that Trevor was an abusive man to two previous wives and twice JoNey's age? No charges were obviously filed against Trevor. Our lack of knowledge and experience in this field continued to be paralyzing. What we had anticipated to be courtroom justice was more an appearance of a courtroom holocaust!—JoNey being the Jew, rather than an innocent child who needed protection. Karl had come highly recommended, but when and at what time would he start the defense and help JoNey?

Later that night, Owen received a call at his house. The person stated they were on the jury and were sympathetic. Owen was immediately suspicious. Owen thanked them for calling, but refused to give out the information they were seeking. I relayed the message to Karl, with him reporting it immediately to the judge. The next day the judge shut everything down until each juror was polled and questioned individually. There was an answer, but it was evident it would not be from the jury: Just another deceitful attempt by our enemy! With each day, Trevor and his family's deceptive scheme became more and more mind-boggling. It was not looking good for us.

I was to take the stand on Friday. It was the last day of the trial. I was the last witness. For the first time, I knew what it was to be "prayed up." My team of prayer warriors had met with me every morning. I felt they had prayed a double portion over me knowing my anxiety over the week. Everyone had done their part, and now it was up to me. I was feeling confident all of which was evident as I took the stand. You could have heard a pin drop as I walked towards the witness stand. I sat down then immediately turned and looked at Karl. He appeared to be extremely nervous and distracted. Normally, I would have come in like a lion protecting her cub lashing out at anyone that was attacking my child. Instead, I was calm, collected, and conscious of everyone there.

Looking Trevor in the eye came easy as he once again tried to intimidate me as I turned and glanced over to the right at him. Karl began his questioning. When asked if I thought JoNey was a loving, caring mother, I answered emphatically, "Yes!"

I did not consider it a lie with my comparison being Trevor! JoNey did not whip and beat on Nocona, nor did she soak her thumbs in red sauce. Her youth and being away at college maybe didn't rate her as the world's best mother. Nor was JoNey mentally, emotionally, and physically after Trevor's appearance in her life. As I looked the attorney in the eye, I thought, JoNey was one heck of a mother! *She brought Nocona to each of us to care for and nurture when she wasn't able to. JoNey fought daily to keep Nocona out of the dysfunction.* I truly admired JoNey.

Earlier, Karl had instructed me on things not to say prior to my taking the stand. I disregarded everything he said and went totally with whatever God brought up in my mind. Karl asked me very few questions. Karl sat down and Jay began to question me, but that didn't last long either once he saw how bold I was. I continued to glance over at Karl and then over at Trevor. I wanted all of them to know despite my lack of knowledge of the law and legal connections not one person there was going to intimidate me.

During the break Karl once again pulled us off to a private room. He was extremely nervous. This time he suggested we pray. Earlier it seemed to be of no value, but now it appeared to be a priority. He made a remark that it wasn't looking good for JoNey. I couldn't concentrate on his prayer for looking at him, thinking, *What a charade.* Does he really think I am that stupid? It was obvious we had been compromised. He and his good friend Jay Runnels had a plan, but it definitely had nothing to do with protecting JoNey and Nocona.

By the end of the day, I was totally disgusted with everything I saw from watching the weeklong lawsuit from the hallway. Each day I was observing my innocent daughter's defeated demeanor. Trevor, Laura, Sarah and their attorney daily walked out confidently with heads held high. Something definitely wasn't right!

The jury would give their decision Monday.

As we all left the courtroom, I avoided Karl. I was so upset I was afraid of what I might say. I wanted to think it over and talk to him when I was calmed down. No one had to tell me anything. I knew Karl was not doing his job.

Later, after I regrouped, I called Karl and made an appointment for Saturday morning. The next day I made my way to his office. With each mile I grew more and more livid thinking about everything we had gone though totally unprotected through the week. I wasn't an attorney, but neither was I stupid. When I opened the door I looked straight at him and immediately noticed fear in his eyes as he watched me walk across the room. I never sat down and I never took my eyes off of him. With few yet choice words, I let him know he was not there for my daughter and I knew it. I very calmly looked him in the eye and told him I did not know why he was not there for JoNey, but he wasn't. I went on to tell him regardless of how badly he handled the custody suit, JoNey would win! It was strange, but deeply embedded in my inner soul was a voice stating so strongly, *Just go forward. Don't look to the right or the left; JoNey Will Win!* Karl never said a word. I turned and walked out of his office. I was furious with him and he was now aware of the extent! I accomplished my goal and went back home.

I was learning the hard way, attorneys are not your best friends; they are businessmen like any other businessman. You are only one of hundreds that will cross their paths. Their main priority in life is not your case or the outcome, but how they can profit from your demise. You may be looking at your moment of justice, but they are doing the human thing and looking at their best interests. Money was definitely taking precedence over whatever code of ethics attorneys should have! As a result, we were suffering tremendously in every way! Not only had we endured a week of excruciating pain and suffering, now our enemy had gained a foothold that would soon become devastating for all of us.

ે⁂

The following Monday, friends and family surrounded us as each filed through security once again. The tension was heavy as we all made our way down the long hall to the entrance of the courtroom. This time there was silence and reverence, with a wide look of expectation from everyone present. The courtroom was once again packed. Today, as I entered the courtroom, I was calm and began to look around. There was a noticeable difference—a lightness in the air. It was as if a refreshing breeze was blowing through the room. The heaviness was no longer present! I knew then that something was in our favor. For some strange reason, I was sure this presence had to be God and everything was going to be okay. What else could cause that? No windows were open, yet there was a definite lightness in the air and a soft breeze flowed through the room.

Prior to our entering the courtroom, Karl had warned us. If JoNey should get custody, he wanted us to clear the courtroom as quickly as possible. From the tone of his voice, the day was serious and carefully plotted. He quickly briefed us that we were to follow him to a room down below this floor. We were to stay in the room until Trevor and his family cleared the courthouse.

Everyone had entered the Orange County courtroom. We sat motionless awaiting the jury's decision. We all knew it was truly a flip of the coin from all that was evident during the grueling week. Judge Davis moved slowly across the room as everyone sat intensely watching his every move, waiting for him to be seated. No one looked around; everyone was keeping their eyes focused on the one man that would decide Nocona and her mother's fate. Each party there was hoping to be able to foretell the result by the judge's expression or his gait. There was a long silence as he sat down. Very quickly and unexpectedly, Judge Davis mumbled something. Everyone was looking at each other in a stupor, totally confused! No one obviously understood him or...*Most Everyone!* I looked over to see Karl grabbing JoNey and making their way to the door. I immediately thought of Karl's statements. I took Anna by the arm, quickly exiting the room and down the long stairway. Karl and JoNey were below us, but Karl looked back and motioned for us to hurry. We were soon in the small room where Karl reconfirmed, "JoNey Won!" We were all cautioned to keep quiet.

Karl reemphasized we were to wait until Trevor and his family cleared the courthouse. It was obvious the judicial system was concerned about Trevor and his family's reaction if they lost. Later I found out nothing was brought out about Nocona during the trial. The judge was giving Trevor full visitation rights with Nocona.

⁂

Within days, Trevor appealed the jury's decision. I was told Laura called the jurors requesting information on the case. Once again ignorant of the legal system, I was totally shocked thinking a juror's personal information would be confidential and not available to the public. Knowing how badly the trial went and what we might be up against, once again I decided I would call two of the jurors. I just wanted to know why they even gave JoNey custody since Karl did not appear to be defending her. I built up my courage and made the call. Their reply was, "We have served on other juries when Karl Perry was defending someone. Karl is a very good attorney, but for some reason Karl was not defending your daughter."

It wasn't the statement I wanted to hear, but it certainly reconfirmed my thoughts. I paid this man to put us through a week of hell and help destroy our lives mentally and emotionally! A week went by, and then we received the news that Judge Davis had denied the appeal! This was a relief, but we later realized Karl's lack of support had given Trevor's family another foothold. Trevor, Laura, and Sarah knew they had Orange County's support even though they didn't have the jurors. An important tool they would soon use against us.

He who justifies the wicked, and he who condemns the just,
Both of them alike are an abomination to the Lord. Proverbs 17: 15

Seashell Prisoners
CHAPTER 7

River JoNey Burton
W.P.R.A. Rookie of the Year

JoNey and I were in a state of trauma by the end of the trial. JoNey's search for escape quickly ended as she was reminded of her standings for W.P.R.A. Rookie of the Year in bareback and bulls. With her competitive nature and ability to regroup, she quickly started packing for the road. As for myself, I was barely able to peel myself off the couch. My mind was totally bogged down with the past week's bizarre event. My body was equally showing the wear and tear of the trial.

An old friend called encouraging me to visit them in California. The idea of touring vineyards and dining out in beautiful restaurants danced though my mind. Reality soon had its way of kicking back in. Maybe this would be in my best interest, but definitely not for the party that invited me. JoNey wanted Nocona to go with her on her trip, so I thought, what the heck! I threw a few things in a bag and joined them.

Just getting the heck out of Dodge seemed the perfect thing for all of us. With very few clothes and my nervous system a total wreck, I dropped my lifeless body into the car and down the road we went.

We traveled to Colorado, New Mexico, wherever the circuit led us. This definitely wasn't my idea of a vacation, but getting away from everything that had anything to do with Trevor and this nightmare was.

Most of JoNey's rodeo friends called her "River." I liked that name. She truly flowed like a River. As time passed, the name definitely fit her personality. She was always unique and full of adventure, and you never knew where she would end up. Just like a river! When people asked me where she got the name, I just said, "It was the name God chose for her."

I quickly came to know every fast food business along the route as we looked for outlets for Nocona's stored-up energy. McDonald's seemed to be the favorite. For lack of better things to do, I found myself comparing playgrounds and service. The whole trip was like a shot in the arm for all of us, with Nocona relishing every minute. It appeared as though the further down the road we went the more relaxed we all became.

River JoNey once again was finding humor in Mom's unusual situations. The roads were long and empty of restrooms, leaving me little to no choice but to use the wooded areas. I continued to leave every decision to JoNey, not realizing to what extreme our personalities were. Whether it was sleeping in a tent or eating fast food, I just quietly went along, just to be with JoNey.

As we drove from rodeo to rodeo, I began to meet more of River's friends. I realized they were just people with a vision totally different from what I considered the norm, but still a vision. I found the trip was for more reasons than just my escape. I began dropping preconceived ideas of my daughter, all the dreams I'd mapped out for her in my mind. I was finally seeing River JoNey for who she was and who her friends were. With each day as JoNey got her gear together, I sat in the stands in awe at her ability to get back up and go forward. As for myself, I still couldn't see past the moment.

We soon returned home with more winnings and a new accomplishment. River JoNey had now earned the title of Rookie of the Year in the W.P.R.A. Women's Bullriding event. Adding to her many accomplishments were a big silver buckle and pictures in the newspapers to add to our family trunk collection.

❧

Despite the chaos, Anna was also going forward with her life. She was getting ready for her senior year; anticipating her most memorable year.

Todd's first marriage to Sonya had failed, but they had had a beautiful daughter named Whitley. Todd was now married to Kim. Kim had two daughters from a previous marriage, named Kayla and Lacy. Within a year a new arrival came, and they named him Sam. Everyone doted over Sam. Kim soon enrolled in college with a goal of becoming an attorney. Life was good for all of them.

River then landed a job in Baytown, so I continued helping each week with Nocona. The court's decision was for Trevor to pick up Nocona at my house for his visitation. With each return from Trevor's, Nocona continued to struggle. Daily I searched for things that would be entertaining and relaxing for Nocona. My routine was pretty much the same, but now more intense—taking Nocona to the physician, calling C.P.S. and pleading for help! No one was interested in a small child's problem! As much as I tried to reach out, it was the same. No one was listening to me.

❧

I continued to read to Nocona and play music to entertain her. Nocona gravitated to anything that had to do with music and drama. Amongst her many books, her favorite was a small condensed children's Bible from which she quickly memorized the stories. The more stressful her life became, the more essential it was that the little Bible be there, to the point that she cried if it wasn't visible. On one return from Trevor's, she began to search for her Bible. We couldn't find it. Once again, seeing how stressed she became, I immediately went to the store, purchasing one for each room.

I always found it strange the way Nocona reacted each time Trevor came for her. She became despondent and sobbed as he grabbed her up to leave. She had the appearance of being under a spell. It was more like she had to go rather than a child anxious to see her father.

On one occasion when Trevor returned Nocona, she wouldn't even look at me, but crawled under the table and curled up into a little ball and sucked her thumb. Her eyes were empty. Once again I called C.P.S., only ending up screaming at them. I continued to pray and consult professionals for advice, but everyone wanted to shy away from the word abuse—even the paid professionals. Out of frustration, I made a call to one of the judges that I was acquainted with. He was sympathetic, but all I received was more legal jargon of no value to Nocona.

It was too late! Nocona was now returning with more bruises and a black eye. I knew I had to do something! This time I panicked, asking Trevor, once again, what had happened to her. Trevor just turned and walked off, never answering.

My relationship with Owen was far from the best. I knew anything that had to do with the grandkids was considered neutral ground, so I gave him a call. Owen came over immediately to check on Nocona. He had also noticed all the changes in Nocona. Outraged by it all, he carefully planned his approach to Trevor.

It was now time for Trevor's arrival once again. Trevor's truck was approaching the house, making the last turn. Owen waited until Trevor drove up into the driveway, and then Owen quietly pulled up behind Trevor's truck. Trevor's face was white with fear as Owen stepped up behind him. I stood from a distance with my telephone in my hand in case I had to call the law. I was relishing every second as I saw fear engulf Trevor. Owen backed him up against the wall, threatening him. As usual, as soon as Trevor found space to sliver through, he cowardly grabbed Nocona and quickly jumped in his truck. He raced down the road in his black dually.

Owen and I talked once again about all the changes in Nocona and what to do. C.P.S. was not intervening, and no one else seemed to have the answers. Owen was concerned not only about all the physical and emotional changes in Nocona, but her conversations. Nocona had changed from baby talk to fearfully talking about wolves and guns. She frequently stated, "My Dedi has big guns." Owen and I agreed to hire another attorney in an attempt to get help for Nocona.

I was now receiving more strange telephone calls with either silence or heavy breathing. Trevor continued to stalk JoNey. On several occasions he could be seen just sitting quietly in his truck at the end of our road. Once again we placed another call to the Sheriff's department, but they just took down the information. Trevor's actions daily revealed to me how sick he was. My priority was not only to help Nocona, but also to not allow Trevor to destroy our lives.

·❧·

Phil called, and we got together for the evening. Once again we had a great time visiting and laughing about the dive trip and other outings we had been on. As he left out, my housekeeper left out soon after. I immediately walked over to the table to pick up a rhinestone necklace and bracelet I had placed on the table early that morning. It was very strange…the jewelry was not there. I had placed it on the table just hours before Phil's arrival and he and the housekeeper were the only ones there.

I dismissed the problem from my mind, and the next day I searched the whole house for the jewelry, but I couldn't find it. It was a beautiful set of rhinestones that looked like diamonds. I had a special event to go to and Kelly, a friend, had loaned them to me. I never found the jewelry. I hated it so much, but I called the housekeeper and explained the situation and stated that, under the circumstances, I would have to let her go. I explained to her she had not given me any reason not to trust her over the past year; I just couldn't find the jewelry.

·❧·

Nocona was back again for another weekend with Trevor. I was sick all weekend, worrying about Nocona and what was happening to her. I thought surely Trevor would not do anything else to her after Owen threatened him.

Over the past years we became more aware that Trevor thrived on three things: Hate, glory, and winning. All three took precedence in his life. We all knew there was no limit to the extent he would go to inflict pain on all of us. I thought surely there was a limit as to just how far he would go.

Two weeks had gone by and Trevor's truck was making its way up my drive once again. I was at the door anxiously waiting for Nocona. This time Nocona was draped over his shoulder as though asleep. Trevor pulled her off his shoulder and handed her to me. I immediately noticed her body weight didn't feel right. She felt much lighter. Nocona's body was limp and lifeless. I looked into her eyes and they were open, but strangely fixed. I got in Trevor's face, demanding he tell me what was wrong with her. Trevor turned and once again arrogantly walked back to his truck.

Totally distraught, I walked into the house and began crying. I sat down in the rocking chair and just rocked and rocked Nocona as her limp body clung to me. Totally traumatized, I got up and called Dr. Renaldi, but he was not at the hospital nor at home. All I could think about was, Who do I call? Who can I turn to? I sat back down and noticed Nocona's ears were blood red. I asked Nocona why her ears were red, and she began to sob. Nocona cried and cried and later began talking about the wolf whipping her. Over and over she stated, "The Wolf Beat My Heinie!"

I thought of Owen, but as I turned to make the call, I saw his truck through the patio door going down the road. It was late in the evening. I was emotionally drained of the whole sick situation. I slumped back down and rocked Nocona until we went to bed. I placed Nocona in my bed, but she only slept for minutes at a time, waking up crying during the night.

The next morning I waited frantically for Dr. Renaldi to get to his office. I quickly relayed the message to his secretary, only to hear her cold arrogant reply, "Frances, Dr. Renaldi said there's really nothing he can do for Nocona at this time and there was no reason to bring her back in."

I was furious! I wanted to scream at her; instead I slammed the phone down!

Dr. Renaldi was definitely not a physician—he was a jerk! My lack of experience in this was playing a heavy toll on Nocona, and I was feeling the guilt.

My list began to grow of paid professionals that operate through greed and lack of integrity with no true feelings for their patients or clients. Maybe the physician, C.P.S, nor the attorneys would be there for Nocona, but I would! Trevor Would Never Touch Nocona Again! I was prepared to do whatever it took, not caring what the outcome would be. I was determined from that day forward Trevor would never touch Nocona again!

I didn't have a plan. I decided until I did, I would just not be at home when Trevor showed up, nor answer the phone. I began to pray more and more for that Big Creator to kick in and scream at me on what to do next. I needed advice quick; lots of advice. Everything was way over my head. If He was there, I needed to hear from Him not softly, but loud and clear! I was not trusting my judgment for one second. I knew something really bad could possibly happen. With each day I prayed and waited for answers.

The week went by too quickly. It was time for Trevor to pick Nocona up once again. I sat in the back room with Nocona and waited until he left.

Two weeks went by and he was back again. I could tell Trevor was enjoying what he considered a game, and he began bringing a witness with him on each arrival. I am not sure if they were there to be a witness or he was a coward expecting Owen to be around the corner. With each return, I would not answer the door.

I never told anyone what I was doing. I just quietly went forward hoping something positive would come about. The timing was not good with so many unfinished projects in full swing. I continued on with the upcoming drug awareness program and the CASA program as though nothing was going on. As crazy as my surroundings were, I couldn't just drop the projects I had spent so much time working on. I knew I had to go forward despite what was happening in my life. I prayed every minute as to what my next decision should be. I thought about past remarks from a friend and one of my relatives. They stated I needed to find someone to get rid of Trevor! One stated he could find the person for me. As bad off as we were, I couldn't see myself agreeing to a hit man! God would have to intervene.

Nocona was absorbing most of my time, but the annual Drug Awareness Program was coming about in just a few weeks. I was in charge. The event was to be held once again at the Mauriceville Crawfish Festival. This would be the seventh year, and I knew it would have to be God giving me the fortitude to keep it going forward. The CASA program in Orange, Texas, was just beginning to form. I decided to test the new leader in my life: God! I was sincerely hoping what worked for one would work for the other. Sure enough, I called all my prayer warriors. I let them know I didn't have time to work on these projects and needed their help. I didn't let on to anyone what was actually happening with Nocona.

It worked! The Drug Awareness event continued to go forward even stronger with little to no effort on my part. I was totally in awe at the money and help that was flowing in for 1994's event, totally and completely on its own.

Initiating the CASA program in Orange came easy. I had previously coordinated luncheons with area judges and various organizations. Now all I had to do was keep it going forward. Judge Travis from Beaumont was the main speaker and the main person instrumental in the CASA program going forward.

I was monitoring Trevor's actions daily as to what my next move would be. Trevor had been in our lives long enough that I now pretty much knew his thoughts. He was definitely embellishing the fact that I was breaking all the laws on visitation. I went forward with life as usual, despite the circumstances. The S.T.A.N.D. Drug Awareness meetings were held at the Crab Shack Restaurant in Orange and were going great. Representatives were there from the Sheriff's Department, principals from the area schools, local businessmen, and the Dare Program. Two of my favorites were A. J. Judice and Wade Granger. Both were highly respected and loved by Orange County and always added humor to whatever they were involved in. Wade was married to my sister Charlene.

Nocona was in hiding, but it still was not public knowledge. One meeting on the Drug Awareness program was memorable. Most of our meetings were at the Cajun Cookery in Orange. From year to year at each meeting, the officers of the Orange County Sheriff's Department would always sit directly across from me. For some reason on this particular day as they entered the restaurant, the officers sat on both sides of me and never said a word throughout the meeting. I thought, This is it! They are here to pick me up! Normally, they were extremely nice. Today, they were serious, with their whole demeanor making me totally uneasy. As I presided over the meeting, I visualized them at some point slapping handcuffs on me as they ushered me out. I would glance around the restaurant from time to time, looking to see exactly who all would witness this horrible scenario. Surprisingly, nothing happened. As the meeting finished, I slowly walked out to my car as they left out in front of me. I was thinking that any minute they would intercede, but nothing happened! They just left!

As each day passed, I struggled with Nocona's pain. Her whole personality had changed, making her extremely difficult to work with. My nerves were slowing me down to a turtle's pace. I was desperately trying to have patience, knowing the struggle Nocona was going through. It was very hard on both of us. I spent hours trying to do simple things like combing her hair without her sobbing or falling onto the floor crying. Nocona wanted to stay in my lap or right under me all the time. If I handed her a doll she threw it down and screamed at it. If I went out on the porch, she would be cruel to Hobbit, our dog. Hobbit was normally her favorite dog.

This went on for days, then weeks. I began taping her conversations and videoed her actions with the dolls.

Nocona talked frequently of her dad having big guns. One day she stated, "My Dedi killed Kahli's rabbit, and he hates you, Ganna!" Nocona cried as she told her story as though she was fearful for all of us.

Our lives had not only been interrupted by this dysfunctional man and his family, but now I was totally consumed to the point I knew everything I had lived and worked for was at risk. Nothing meant anything anymore! My home was no longer filled with laughter and family, but wreaked with the pain and anguish of Nocona and River JoNey's abuse. It was now a constant reminder of Trevor. Our whole lives were coming to a standstill, with this sick man and his family taking precedence over all our lives. Somehow, some way, everything was going to have to go on hold: Anna's graduation, my new grandson, everything!

I continued to call C.P.S, but still no results. Sarah's ties were too strong in Orange County. C.P.S. would talk to me, but continued to state their hands were tied; there was nothing they could do. Out of desperation, I called the D.A's office, letting them know I was not getting help from C.P.S. I let them know my plans were to leave with Nocona if I could not get help. All I got was more legal jargon.

I was continually told I would need a lot more evidence if we were going to go to court for Nocona. Someone suggested a counselor for Nocona. I checked the CASA program, with them saying Wanda Aldridge from Beaumont was the best. They stated she was highly respected by the courts with her twenty years' experience representing abused children. Relief came and, for the first time, I felt someone cared, someone was actually listening.

After a couple of weeks working with Nocona, Wanda was ready to go to court when we were ready. Wanda worked with Nocona using dolls. Out of three dolls, Nocona was horribly abusive to one to the point of pointing a gun at it and killing it. The other two she loved and comforted.

Wanda was amazed at Nocona's ability to verbalize for a two-and-a-half-year-old child. She was videoing every conversation and movement with Nocona.

Owen and I brain stormed, both being down on attorneys, but finally contacted Steve Carter. Steve's reputation was quite different from the others. Many were saying he would do whatever it took to win. This is what we wanted! Prior to this we had used attorneys with whom we thought had integrity, but that didn't work. Now we didn't care what it took! We just wanted someone that would take the reins and go forward, stopping this abusive man in his tracks and then in the end helping Nocona.

Steve immediately let us know I was to hire a certain psychiatrist named Dr. Groban from Beaumont. He reassured us he had influence with him and the man would say whatever he wanted. I was totally set back with the statement and reluctant to stop the appointments with Wanda. Once again, neither Owen nor I had the law degree. Steve Carter did. I had to trust this man, and he was saying to drop Wanda Aldridge.

On the next visit Steve accepted the two-thousand-dollar retainer fee, and then let us know his schedule was full. He quickly reassured us his associate could handle the job with his assistance. He stated the judge had already reassured him he would be there for Nocona.

FEBRUARY 1, 1994

A motion was filed in Orange County Courts by River JoNey Burton to modify Trevor's visitation with Nocona. Reasons for this were Nocona was showing physical and psychological damages after visitations with Trevor. The goal was for Trevor to have a professional with him at all times when visiting with Nocona. Judge Davis would preside at the hearing. The court date was scheduled for March 10, 1994. This hearing would immediately give Nocona relief until we could come up with something better for her.

After our visit with Steve, it was like all I had to do was take Nocona to Dr. Groban. He would show up, intercede for Nocona, and the problem with Trevor would be over! We were rather set back with the whole plan; yet we had no other alternatives.

I immediately got on the phone, making appointments with Dr. Groban. We were now down to just a couple weeks before we went to court. His testimony was of extreme importance. On the first appointment as Nocona and I sat in Dr. Groban's waiting room, I was reading a book to Nocona about Little Red Riding Hood. I realized that this is where Nocona had obtained the understanding of the word "wolf," from this children's book. I had read this book to her several times. This was obviously the parallel with Trevor.

After the second visit, I found it strange Dr. Groban never asked to speak to Nocona. Actually, he never asked to speak to me, either! On the third visit, I asked the receptionist if I might speak to Dr. Groban. I reemphasized we would be going to court in a couple weeks. Finally, I was called in to his office. I had a cassette tape of Nocona telling what the wolf had done to her. Dr. Groban listened to the tape and became nervous, immediately asking if my attorney had heard the tape. Once again Dr. Groban did not ask to see Nocona, but acted as though he would soon.

With each visit I paid Dr. Groban a hundred dollars. Everything was so different than the visits with Wanda. Wanda spent at least an hour interacting with Nocona, using dolls and other toys. She always commented on how verbal Nocona was for her age. Dr. Groban could not even tell you what Nocona looked like!

With each visit, Dr. Groban's attendant directed me to a young lady that appeared to be totally disinterested. She would ask me a couple of questions, then let me know the visit was over. I became irate at the lack of interest. I asked when Dr. Groban was going to talk to Nocona. She evaded the question. I kept thinking, The attorney had such confidence, maybe they already had their story prepared for the courts; yet the whole thing just didn't feel right!

After six visits and $600.00 in payments, I became even more irate at the lack of empathy towards us. It was only days before we were to go to court, and Dr. Groban still had not seen Nocona and continued to evade me. I became extremely upset and approached Dr. Groban in the hall. I asked him why he was not talking to Nocona. He looked me in the eye and stated, "Three-year-olds are not verbal." He went on to say that he had no intention of going to court for Nocona, and walked off as though I had never made the first appointment. I walked out in a state of shock! As I returned home, fear totally engulfed me, not knowing to what degree Sarah and Laura's influence was.

I regrouped and called Wanda, and she agreed to resume her work with Nocona and yes, she would go to court with us. The problem was she didn't have much time left. Games were being played, but I couldn't comprehend why or how to stop the games and obtain justice for Nocona. Just how far-reaching was the game? Was it just Dr. Groban, or was it what it was looking like, that Trevor, our attorney, and the whole judicial system were against us? I called Owen to let him know what was happening, but he stated we didn't have time to change attorneys. We would just have to have faith!

ે

Pressure was rising. I realized there was no way I could go forward with my projects. I wasn't sure what I might do next. I knew at any time my actions could all break out in the news. This could place a horrible stigma on the projects I had put so much energy and time working up. I began to worry about everything turning into a huge fiasco, embarrassing not only myself, but everyone involved. Prominent businessmen had invested time and money into the drug awareness project. Now it was all in jeopardy along with the CASA Program. Many articles and television promotions had already come out on both programs with my name as the promoter.

Once again, everything just seemed to fall into place, with a couple phone calls. The new headlines hit the press now stating The Orange County Sheriff's Dept. was heading up the upcoming S.T.A.N.D. Drug Awareness program to be held at the Mauriceville Festival Grounds. The same thing happened with the CASA program. It was like a divine intervention! There were many qualified ladies more than ready to take the program and go with it, totally freeing me of the whole project.

It was as if so many things in my life were rapidly changing. Everything was going into place like a giant puzzle Someone was putting together for me. There was a strong presence emerging, something I had never experienced before. With each day I was sensing it more and more. I was beginning to feel as though all I had to do was stand up each morning and take a few steps forward. Everything for the day was going to happen according to this huge plan that appeared to be divinely set up for me and my family.

❧

With each day this new presence in me began to speak louder in my spirit. I knew I had asked God to talk to me, but this was not a voice, just something coming from my inner spirit. Now something deep inside of me was stirring in me, telling me to get rid of my two-caret diamond ring and my mink coat. The presence was so strong it not only told me to give it away, but whom to give it to. I tried to bargain with the voice. I thought it would be much better to sell the things, but the voice told me distinctly whom to give it to. The ring was far from average. Some are known for their fine cars. My Lincoln town car was different for a rural community, but this ring was unusual in beauty and noticed by many. I felt this voice had to be God. I was needing desperately someone on our side, so I made up my mind I would follow through with whatever the voice said.

With each week stranger and more unusual things continued to happen. In a weird sort of way I somehow felt I was beginning to connect the dots; I was definitely beginning to experience God!

Many fun things filled my closets that I held onto strictly for parades and friends like Johnny Ruth Clark to plunder through year in and year out. I reflected on the past as my evening lit up with Johnny's arrival, full of stories anticipating her annual trail ride. One of her favorites in my closet was this neat, little, short, fur jacket with all the little coon tails on it. The coon tails dangling from the side guaranteed to make her the envy of the trail ride. Johnny Ruth may not have been the youngest rider on the trail, but she was always the best dressed and most talked about during the event.

My friend Cheryl was another one that would slide in on a Friday—just in time to get on board for a trip to Mardi Gras in Galveston. Cheryl could amazingly go into my closet and within minutes come out stepping tall, ready to take on the world.

But for some strange reason, my spirit was saying I was now supposed to get rid of most of my clothes? It was real plain my mink coat was to be given away also. Nothing about it made sense! Actually, nothing about anything was making sense anymore.

❧

Anna had always been such a perfect child, considering she was rather pampered. I remember a prediction from a friend stating I would one day have trouble with that little redhead, but that never happened. Anna had always made good grades and with every day grew in beauty and talent. I knew I focused too much on my kids, but they were just good kids and it was fun rewarding them. One of my fonder memories was coming in from a sale at Dillard's and handing Anna six pairs of shoes I had purchased on sale. Anna loved new things and I enjoyed giving them to her. When she was younger, her hair was long and beautiful, so I kept her in big colorful bows. Now she was into makeup and the latest fashions in clothes.

It was now Anna's senior year, the year of all years. One night she arrived home late, rebelliously stating, "All my friends come in late, and I will, too."

As with all my confrontations with my children, I went right to the point. I stated my rules, reinforcing them once again. She listened, then proceeded to say if I would not concede to her new time schedule, she would go live with her best friend, Amber. I never argued with the kids, I just stated the facts and, within seconds, she made the decision to go live with Amber. I knew Anna required a lot and Amber's mother would not want to take on another teenager. Within a couple of days, Anna ended up at her father's under much worse scrutiny. Within a few weeks, Anna and I were back on good terms, but she remained with her father.

☙

With each turn of events, I continued to feel even more this strange sense of a stage that someone larger than myself was setting up. I found it unusual that I was the only one sensing this.

By this time, I was pushing this new-found God to the max, leaning on Him for every move. I prayed a lot, and weird things continued to come out of my mouth, only to leave me questioning them as: Where Did That Come From?

I reflected on something that came up in my spirit so strong a year earlier that totally made no sense. It was so strong I never forgot it. Did it have anything to do with this? I remembered as I was walking in my yard this very profound thought was dropped deep into my spirit. It was telling me the very place I lived was only mine for a season. I thought it to be so bizarre, being I loved my home and living in the country so much. It was my home where I raised my children and I had no plans of ever selling or leaving it. Why would that pop up in my spirit?

One night, Phil came in from South Carolina. When he walked in the door, he said, "You would not believe all the problems I am having with my business here in Orange."

I looked at him and said, "Phil, your being here has nothing to do with your job. It has something to do with your helping Nocona." I remember stepping back in awe at why I even said that. I did not have the least idea of the next step that would come about with getting relief for Nocona. I refused to fixate on any plans of separating from my family, friends, home, boat, and brand new travel trailer.

❧

Our good friend, Miss Ruth, came over for the weekend. As usual, I was hanging on her every word that came out of this bold Christian friend's mouth. When the moment came, I expressed my feelings that I felt very strongly that I would be leaving. She boldly stated, "I cannot see God having you leave when you have so much going here." That was exactly the words I wanted to hear, but it wasn't what was burning in my spirit. Something so strong in me was saying, "I Was Leaving!" It was totally unexplainable, but I had hoped so much Miss Ruth would sit down and say, "Yes, Frances, God is telling me the same thing," but it never happened!

❧

As the court hearing for Nocona grew nearer, I grew more intense with my search for God. I attended a weekend Women's Conference with Miss Ruth at the Triumph Church in Nederland, Texas. We soon found ourselves sitting quietly in the back of the church. I was seeking any tidbit of Godly wisdom or knowledge they might pass on to me. Maybe a prayer, a few words, or even a hand sign, anything that might help make sense or bring relief to this obvious satanic attack on Nocona and my family. I think I hoped in some way they might have a straighter line to God than I or my friends. I just wanted God to know how badly we were all hurting and needing Him as in, Right Now!

At the end of the service I didn't have to think twice, I got up and boldly walked up front to be prayed over. There were several ladies up front, but for some reason the pastor's wife prayed over me. Within seconds she stated I was speaking in tongues. I didn't want to argue with the lady, but I never noticed any change. When I went back to my seat and started singing with everyone else; many were raising their hands. I followed suit. As I raised my hands, I felt this intense heat rising up out of my hands. It was like my hands were on fire. It only took minutes after I cleared the doors to realize these people had a much better grip on God than I did and I knew for sure I was going in the right direction. It may have been strange and really far out, but I knew this had to be God! At the end of the service, the pastor's wife announced a lady from Mauriceville was filled with the Holy Spirit! I was a little taken back by the announcement and momentarily embarrassed, but I knew she was referring to me.

As Miss Ruth and I made our way back home that night I thought maybe I should mention it to her just to see her reaction. Of course there was no reaction; she knew exactly what was going on. I remember sitting up very confidently explaining to her that they obviously had made a mistake. I really did not feel any different at all. Miss Ruth was her usual quiet, confident self and never argued, yet had this big smile on her face, so I dropped the subject.

Each session of the Conference I was one of the first going up for prayer each time the request was made. I had no shame. I knew my ignorance in this field and readily admitted it. I poured my heart and soul out to them, and they prayed diligently.

The next day Miss Ruth and I were late for the individual classes. We slivered past the ladies on the back row hoping we wouldn't interrupt the speaker. As the lady closed the session, she asked anyone wishing to be prayed over to stay. No one walked out of the room. She looked around the room, then began to walk and lay hands over each individual, with each falling out on the floor. I watched in awe thinking, I am just not ready for this! We were in the very back and couldn't get out until the others left. Miss Ruth was not budging, and I could not see an easy way past her. The lady walked slowly down the first row and made her way to the second. Every person went to the floor as though they were fainting. As she steadily grew closer to us, I thought, there is no way I would do that. I had seen this in Mam Maw's church as a child, but it wasn't going to happen to me! Even a hypnotist once said I would be extremely hard to hypnotize. I peered out the side of my eyes to see how Miss Ruth was reacting. As usual she was calm and relaxed as the woman made her way down our aisle. As the lady approached, I went flat out on the floor with her never touching me. Miss Ruth was the only one in the room left standing. As I lay on the floor I thought, I could do this forever! I didn't want to get up. Something was going through my body that was so cleansing and refreshing, I was now feeling wonderful! Now how can I make that last?

As the hearing for Nocona drew nearer, more strange things continued to happen. It was as though a path was being laid ahead for us. I continued to reach out for prayer from anyone. I really didn't care who it was. I just needed help and if I thought a person had a God-contact, I wanted their double portion.

Anna was going forward planning her senior year. I tried to put on a good face for Anna, making an attempt to be a Mother. It was evident to her and everyone else in my life that I was totally consumed with Trevor's dysfunction.

ze

One day I was working on the computer in the bedroom when I heard Trevor drive up in another attempt to pick up Nocona. I was caught completely off guard with Nocona sleeping in my bed. The sound of his truck was embedded deep in my memory. I knew it was him. I glanced around. As I heard his truck door slam I jumped up and locked the bedroom doors where Nocona lay sleeping. I shut the blinds going out to the patio. I knew I had left the kitchen door unlocked. The knocks got louder and louder as Trevor went from door to door. I searched frantically for my gun. I knew I had one, but never really had a need for it. My nerves settled down once I found it. I slowly made my way to the side of the hot tub and sat on the steps going up to it. I quietly loaded the gun as I anticipated Trevor's next move. I kept glancing over at Nocona, making sure she was still sleeping. There was no doubt in my mind if Trevor came in and gave us trouble, that that would be his last time. I was ready. I wanted him to come in. I was mentally prepared to put a bullet right between his eyes. I sat there praying to calm myself. I had only shot the gun once practicing one day, but for some reason I was calm and ready.

I knew if he came to my bedroom door he would wake up Nocona. I sat there thinking, Please, Please, God, keep her asleep. Trevor was hollering louder and louder. He kept saying he knew I was there. I thought, you coward, that was obvious being my red jeep was sitting out front and my T.V. was on. Within minutes I heard the truck start up and he left.

I went to the phone and called Wanda to see if she was ready to go to court. She was! I called Dr. Renaldi, demanding all the documentation of Nocona's visits to him. I went down and picked it up, but most of it I couldn't read since he scrawled the information on the paper. How stupid could I be? If I would have just insisted on getting a copy of his record each time I took Nocona, I would have had something to go on.

Finally a positive note. As a last resort, I called Trevor's ex-wife, Evelyn. Many had told us the abuse she had received from Trevor. Evelyn was not wanting anything to do with Trevor nor to be around him anymore. It was a Saturday and JoNey was at home. JoNey got on the phone and began to tell Evelyn all the problems Nocona was having. Evelyn once again expressed her fear of Trevor. She went on to say she was now happily married and didn't want any problems from Trevor. JoNey kept talking to her, and Evelyn began to soften up. She told JoNey how her children slept with a bat under their pillows when she and Trevor were married. After an hour of each exchanging horror stories, Evelyn finally agreed to testify. Within a few days, she let us know Trevor was stalking her again, but she was still going to testify. What an accomplishment! Things were looking up!

ે♣

Exhausted by all the ups and downs, I took an invitation to go out of town for the evening. Friends of mine were giving a Christian concert. Nocona and I stepped on the big bus totally exhausted, but ready for an escape from the week. I felt so disconnected from everything, but the wonderful Christian music proved to be the antidote for the week. On the long way home, Nocona snuggled up to one of the ladies in the group. Later the young lady told me Nocona had told her about her abuse.

MARCH 10, 1994

The long-awaited court day arrived. It was the week before spring break. As much as I wanted to dismiss the idea of having to leave with Nocona, it continued to be a constant reoccurring thought. The one and only thing I knew for sure was I had to stay focused on the moment.

My friends were many and I knew to what extent each one was willing to go over others. The stronger the Christian, the closer they were to God, the more value they were to me and Nocona. There were some whose walk was shallow, or not at all, but our friendship was so deep they took chances. Not one minute was spent in plotting or planning the "what ifs" with anyone, nor did I pack. I just knew I would have help if needed, so I took each hour at its face value.

Every minute felt as though God was directing my every step, despite the boulders in the road and the fear that daily attempted to paralyze me. This morning I arose early, carefully placing Nocona in good hands, safely out of town. We were now back in the hands of the Orange County Courts. Many friends and family members flooded the courthouse in support of Nocona. The intensity was heavy. Judge Davis made his usual entrance. This time Trevor had changed attorneys. They were now using Denison from Houston. Denison was large in size and very much like Trevor and Laura, doing his best to intimidate whomever he passed. They made a good team. Laura made her usual entrance. Her head was held high as she walked closely alongside Mr. Denison. As far as our attorney, Steve Carter, I was told he reeked with the smell of alcohol.

Immediately, each person present to testify was asked to leave the courtroom. A friend of mine was called to the stand first and then Wanda Aldridge. I had an unusual calmness as I sat in the hallway awaiting my turn. I sat by myself, then decided to go over and sit with Evelyn, Trevor's ex-wife. I tried to make conversation, but she was withdrawn. It was as though she was fearful and anxious to get through as quickly as possible and make her exit. Actually, that was everyone's desire—to break and run from this sick man and his family. Evelyn finally began to make conversation. She stated Trevor was once again stalking her.

The intensity grew as the minutes went by. The courtroom door suddenly flew open! I looked up totally shocked to see everyone pouring out the door! I knew something obviously went wrong! I thought, It can't be over. They Just Got Started! After seeing all the expressions on different familiar faces, the fear began to become reality. I stood totally numb, now desperately looking for Wanda Aldridge. For some reason, I just wanted to see her face. I knew I would have the answer if I could just see her face. I did not want to speak to anyone except Wanda!

The moment came as I saw Wanda clear the courtroom door. Wanda's face was pale. She looked distraught. Her eyes were fixed on me as she made her way through the crowd towards me. She stopped, looked me in the eye and boldly stated, "Never In My History Of Doing This Has A Judge Ever Stated What Judge Davis Just Did!" Judge Davis had ordered Nocona to be returned to her father and stated court would reconvene after spring break. Wanda then turned and walked off. I never saw Wanda again.

It was an obvious setup right before spring break, at the end of the day, so the Judge could get Nocona back into Trevor's hands. Once again we had been sold out! I knew Wanda had done her best and had no part in the corruption.

I couldn't tell you who was around me at that moment. I turned and calmly walked off going down the stairway and out of the courthouse. I knew what I had to do and no one could do it for me. I had driven a different vehicle just in case this happened and parked it down the road from the courthouse. I had someone else drive my red jeep in case they were watching it. I looked around and couldn't believe Trevor nor Laura were anywhere around! No one suspected anything!

܀

I picked up Nocona from my friend in Beaumont, and left totally without a plan other than to protect Nocona from what appeared to be, not one, but many wolves in this case! I went directly to the trailer park in West Orange where Phil had my travel trailer. I was needing to think and regroup. Phil joined me shortly afterwards, filling me in on Owen and friends who were back at the courthouse panicking over my whereabouts. I was truly traumatized by the morning, but my purpose was clear. I never wavered; I knew what I had to do. I didn't know from one minute to the next who may be in or out as far as helping me, but it didn't matter. The only thing I knew for sure was, I had to help Nocona! I would leave the country with Nocona!

I was exhausted so I laid down and finally went to sleep. The next morning Nocona, now three years old, for some reason looked over at Phil and asked, "You're going to help God take care of me?" Phil and I just looked at each other.

I dressed Nocona, packed a few things, and made my way to the car. Phil was insistent on going with us. I didn't give it much thought, I just knew what I had to do. After leaving Orange, we went from place to place hiding out. Fear of the law gripped family and friends, but I had acquired many friends over the years. God daily opened doors, preparing every step we took.

Friends and strangers were appearing from nowhere, offering help. We stayed in a home on Texla Road for a few days. The elderly gentleman entertained Nocona during the day by reading, and letting her paint his toenails. Each in his/her own way did whatever it took to minimize the stress for Nocona and to help me. As soon as we left the residence, the Sherriff's Department searched the person's home. From there we went from house to house and on two occasions stayed on the river.

෴

Once I realized the F.B.I. was involved, I then knew it was time to leave the country. I knew I had to return to Orange and pick up a few things before making this change. I would need money, and my passport. In one day I removed everything from the banks, sold my supermarket, and liquidated everything I had. I later got word Trevor was spreading the word he would be suing several of us for over ten million dollars. Friends arranged it so I could get into my home one night and get my passport, important papers, and a few clothes. Everyone worked together doing their part, many knowing nothing about me personally. They just knew a small child needed help!

A friend called and told me when everyone was leaving the courtroom the day of the hearing, they overheard Trevor tell Denison, his attorney, they had better watch me that I would probably leave with Nocona. Denison told him that was what they were hoping for.

Everything of material value that I had spent a lifetime building up was quickly diminishing before my eyes. Financially, I had lost over half a million dollars in one day!

The news media continued to have a field day with what they were referring to as "The Underground Grandmother!"

Seashell Prisoners
CHAPTER 8

While the press continued to have a field day with my pain, I stayed focused on one thing…*Getting Out Of Texas!* Decisions had to be made and made fast. In one sense leaving my home and family was extremely hard. In another way it all seemed as though I was just going through the motions. Something much stronger than myself appeared to be leading us. It was apparent we were headed towards a whole new destination.

Phil re-emphasized what had previously been told to me by a professional. Once you make the decision to leave you cannot stay in the U.S., the F.B.I. would get involved immediately. Phil knew I would do whatever it took to keep Nocona safe. He also knew I would listen to one person and only one and that was God, even if it meant leaving the U.S.!

I was now beginning to see that more than family and friends would be leaving my life. Privacy and being in control quickly perished along with everything else of meaning.

Word got back to me that Dr. Renaldi wanted to purchase my home! The man took my money, but wouldn't help Nocona. Now he wants to profit from my having to leave? I was livid when I heard this!

Phil suggested we travel in his 1986 cream-colored Cadillac, and I agreed.

I knew I would have to take as much money as I could. Where I would put it was the big question, now that I had made up my mind to leave. I had checks and large sums of cash. Since I frequented the Caymans on dive trips, I had an account there. I quickly found myself being forced to put trust in many people, something totally new to me. I found acquaintances on their way to the Caymans. I asked if they would deposit a check for a large amount of money in my account. That problem was taken care of, but with the sale of the supermarket and c.d.'s I had cashed in, I still had large sums of money I needed to secure. Phil and I talked it over along the road, with him making a suggestion. Phil had an outstanding loan he would cancel and replace with my money. Phil would invest the $237,000.00, in turn getting a 12% return on my investment. He was a great friend and accomplished businessman so I agreed. I would only take $20,000.00, with Phil agreeing to invest the rest, making monthly payments to me. I knew the invested money with Phil would help finance the remainder of my trip and build towards my future retirement. As soon as I got settled, Phil would meet me and bring more money to finance my endeavor. Everything seemed to be falling right into place. All corners were covered!

We soon found ourselves traveling from state to state, staying with different families. Nocona was too young to realize the magnitude of what was coming about, but was content and relaxed with all the new changes. We stayed in Texas for a short time. At one home, a pastor and friend prayed with us and then handed us a license plate to use if needed. At another home, I was given a driver's license and credit card to use. God just seemed to open door after door, and Nocona and I stepped in. Friends and strangers were taking huge chances. The ones that knew me were well aware it had to be bad for me to make a decision of this magnitude. This was just not me! We would stay a couple days at one home, then move on to another. Nocona was enjoying the children in different homes. Just being away from Orange County, Trevor, and his family was now making us all happy!

One particular home in Louisiana I will never forget. Each night the small children formed a circle and prayed over us. Trish, the oldest daughter, got us all in a circle each evening and led us in prayer. I didn't know any of these people, but they fully understood Nocona's life was in danger and never thought twice about helping us. It was hard leaving this haven, but we knew for everyone's best interest we couldn't stay long.

Previously someone had mentioned Costa Rica. The person had vacationed there, and said it was a beautiful bilingual country. From the recommendation, I felt this was obviously it. I just knew, *This Is Where God Was Sending Us!* Costa Rica sounded perfect. The person was convincing, and went on to state Nocona and I both loved the water, so living by the sea would be perfect for us.

Anna Graduation

We seemed to stay one step ahead of our enemy. I just wanted to get on a plane, go half way, and finish by bus to my destination. No way! Phil, our knight in shining armor, had his own agenda totally focused on driving us to Costa Rica!

One day as we traveled I spoke with Phil about his walk with God, and asked if he even knew God. I felt it was important that I make sure he knew and understood the plan of salvation, since I was becoming more acquainted with God. Phil was quite pleased that I cared, and said he was ready to go forward with his walk with God. A few days later, we stayed in a motel. I noticed when I got back in the car there was a Bible laying on the seat. Phil admitted he took the Bible from the hotel. I thought it was odd, but rather amusing. I had never known anyone to do that.

From time to time Phil would get us settled in a home, go back to Orange, check out the situation and return. His reports back to us were the newspapers and T.V. feature story continued to focus on the new Underground Grandmother. Phil stated wanted posters were all over the county, including Anna's High School with my and Nocona's pictures. He said Anna's graduation went forward, but men were seen vigorously searching the crowd for Frances Harris.

At one point when Phil returned, he surprised me with a letter from the Orange County D.A., Raymond Jones. Raymond was requesting that I return, stating they would do all they could to help me this time. I immediately replied, letting him know they had had their opportunity to help. I had been lied to and deceived enough. Why would I trust them now?

Later, in a more adamant demand, a clipping from the newspaper read that if I didn't return, the Orange County Sheriff's Department would have me in custody in a week! I wrote the news media and let them know my opinion on the matter. My reply was that we would only return when God so decided. I really didn't care what they thought of my statement. I didn't completely understand it myself. All I knew for sure was a force much larger than me was now leading us and I was in total agreement. The force was stating that I was not to return. I just knew I was to keep going forward.

Underground grandmother is talk of town

By ANN GRAY
Staff writer

MAURICEVILLE — In the beauty shops, small-town stores and cafes of a close-knit community, Frances Harris and her flight to protect her granddaughter from alleged abuse is a topic of conversation.

Before her name hit the press as an underground grandmother, Harris was better known for a number of civic activities in both Orange and Mauriceville. She helped start a 13-year-old anti-drug bonfire program for Orange County teens, supported the Mauriceville Crawfish Festival and, during this past year, spearheaded organization of a Court-Appointed Child Advocate program in Orange County state district courts.

For the family members that Harris left behind, the ordeal keeps them busy day and night working, waiting and praying for the safe return of the little girl and her maternal grandmother.

"It's a matter of just getting through the day," family member Nelda Harrison said. "But it's like you're not swimming and getting ahead, you're just treading water. Every now and then your head gets dunked under and you come up for air and go right back to treading."

Three-year-old Nocona has been at the center of a child custody battle since her birth in January 1991 to a couple who never married, River JoNey Burton, then 17, and then 34.

Her custody case turned into a criminal matter after Harris — who is JoNey Burton's mother — disappeared with the child March 10 after a judge ordered

Nocona to spend an 11-day spring break with her father in unsupervised visitation.

Orange County grand jurors on June 29 indicted Harris on a felony charge of interfering with child custody.

Harris and other family members contend abused Nocona and JoNey Burton earlier this year asked the judge to limit the father's visitation rights.

denies the allegations. He countered the action, asking the judge to grant him custody of Nocona. He later filed an additional civil suit seeking more than $1 million in expenses and

See HARRIS, page 8B

HARRIS

Phil became extremely nervous as we approached the Mexican border. He pulled over to the side to stop and regroup, thinking the F.B.I. would be expecting me to leave the country. There was a huge sigh of relief once we cleared the border.

Traveling in Central America was totally new and a huge change for me in more ways than one. We drove for hours ignoring all the threats. Everything that felt like home quickly changed. I watched Nocona as she peered out the window for hours watching all the people and surroundings. As unusual and crude as the areas were, it still looked refreshing in comparison to the stress we had left behind. With each mile, Nocona relaxed as though she knew life was taking on a whole new meaning.

After many hours of traveling I began to grow numb, as reality kicked in. Everything in my life was taking on rapid changes. The roads were long and rough with no conveniences in sight. I focused on the vastness of the countryside, being in complete awe at the scenery and people. I had heard tales from many others about Mexico, but this was a first for me and totally different. The further down the road we got, the more the countryside changed. At one point, I felt as though I were in the National Geographic, going back into time. Nocona continued to stay mesmerized at the changes in scenery, the ox-pulled carts, and different homes than what she was familiar with.

We woke up early and once again began to travel. This day would prove to be educational and surreal as I stared across the new frontier, now feeling totally out of place and disconnected. The absence of my family, my home, and conveniences became more and more evident with each mile. Thoughts began to flood my head, like ...*Where could God be taking us? I sure hope He knows what He is doing. Did God possibly have a bigger plan for one of us?* It had to be Nocona; I certainly was not God material. Was Nocona going to be raised in a third-world country to be used by God later in life? I could only embrace the moment and pray it truly was a part of His plan and not just a figment of my imagination!

We knew we needed more documentation on Nocona, being she wasn't our child and we had more borders to cross. We talked our way through the first border crossing, but we might not be as lucky on the next. We came to a small town, and I found a place where I could make a document for Nocona in case I was questioned at the borders. After typing out a letter, I copied a seal off of a U.S. document I had in my briefcase to make it look official. It worked!

ès

We finally arrived at the Guatemala border. Everything had gone extremely well up to this point. We were told with each border crossing we approached, we could expect the unexpected. By this time we had a better understanding of the term, *Third World.*

We quickly learned approaching the borders was always pretty much the same with skinny, poverty-stricken men, women, and children overwhelming us as they begged for money. I felt threatened and totally overwhelmed at times. We always held our breath until we cleared. Most of the time it took hours.

As we made our attempt to clear the Guatemala border, the unexpected happened. After waiting several hours and going through a car search, the border patrol noticed my passport had expired. We tried every way possible, but they were steadfast, not letting us through. I never even thought to look at the date on my passport when we first left the U.S.

Not prepared for this setback, we made our way to the closest city, Tapachula, Mexico. No one was saying a word now. I was completely taken by surprise, not knowing what could happen from here. We immediately found a room in the city and began to regroup. It would take a huge miracle to get a new passport! I was sure by now I had to be on the wanted list by the F.B.I. There was no way I would be able to get a new passport!

వ

The hotel we chose in Tapachula was called the Hotel Fenix. It was quaint in its own way with small rooms and a large veranda where many businessmen met from day to day. The hotel had their own restaurant and many businesses surrounded the area. We were right in the heart of the Centro.

What had appeared to be a clear picture, that I was supposed to go to Costa Rica, was now dulling with the border problem. Troubled by the crisis, I became restless. Phil drove us around the city the next day, but nothing about it felt right. No one spoke my language and the food and surroundings were definitely not home. Nocona instantly took to the people and the city, but I felt totally alien to everything. We would walk around the Centro in the evenings, listening to the music and watching the many vendors selling their tortillas, roasted corn, and jewelry.

I soon regrouped and made a mad attempt to get a new passport. It would take contacting friends and getting help from them. I knew it would be a total miracle if I applied and the F.B.I. did not intercede, but I had to give it a try. I made several calls to see who might be able to make this happen. Once again friends came through. They would be willing to take a chance.

Phil realized this could take a month, so he decided to take a flight back to the States. He would leave Nocona and I until the passport problem straightened out. Phil asked a new acquaintance to check on us, then off to the airport we went.

As we walked around the airport waiting on Phil to make arrangements for his flight, I became agitated over something. For some strange reason, Phil and I got into a hellacious argument right in the middle of the airport! As a whole I was always extremely easy going, but today I was tired and feeling bad. Phil knew when I did get upset, to expect the unexpected! That was when I caught my first glimpse of the culture I was now about to become a part of, all of which had an obvious lack of respect for aggressive women. The people definitely weren't used to seeing an outraged female speaking loudly to a man! I immediately felt their reaction. They were glaring at Phil as though he should gun me down or at least knock me to the floor. I quickly turned and exited the front door, then reality kicked back in.... *I Had No Place To Go!* I quickly rescinded and made my way back to the car. Phil was soon on his way back to the States, but not without laughing over the airport altercation.

Miguel & Nocona

Tapachula, our new-found residence, was a large city in the Chiapas. The streets were badly littered with trash, yet the sporadic torrential rains preceded by large bolts of lightning had a way of daily cleansing them. Within a few hours the city would once again return to its unique quaintness. All the residents were extremely nice. As we made our way around the city, I found it unusual how even the business people went out of their way to greet us with warm, friendly smiles. We began to relax in the small comfortable hotel in the center of the city. Miguel, the owner's son, and Nocona, now three years old, quickly became best friends. Both were the same age, yet neither understood the other. Laughter quickly became their common language.

Telephones were hard to come by and averaged $50.00 to $100.00 per call to the U.S. Few calls were made. I was deeply concerned about Anna. She had graduated and I was not there. With each call to Texas, something new had come up on the news. I was told I was placed on America's Most Wanted List!

Much of our time was spent walking the streets checking out the different shops, or resting at the hotel. Phil heard there was a beach close by, so prior to his leaving, we made an attempt to locate it. He knew my love for the water so he thought maybe that would be a nice getaway for Nocona and I. Several miles before we approached the beach, we saw a huge pipe going out over the water. Phil and I both broke into laughter at the same time. We realized all the sewage from the city was being emptied into the beautiful ocean! After we arrived at the beach, I noticed no homes were on the beach and the sand was black. Small thatched-roof restaurants were there and many locals were on the beach, but few were swimming. We sat and watched the huge waves as they broke over the rocks on the shore.

Phil had left me with his car, which was in great condition, yet an older model, cream-colored Cadillac. He was now back in the States and I was told he was driving my Cherokee jeep. I was surprised since it was a bright red, and everyone knew it was mine.

As days went by, I searched the small stores for books that were in English, but they were unattainable. I continued to make attempts to find things to do to entertain myself and stay focused.

I found out, too soon, that Tapachula had its own problems. It was a beautiful city, but Guerilla Warfare was going on in the outskirts of the city, getting worse with each day. News in Guatemala was an American lady had been captured for stealing children and selling body parts. It was not a good time to be in Central America!

❧

    I went forward as though everything was normal. I entertained Nocona with daily walks around the busy Centro. My heart melted as the small children surrounded us selling their Chiclets. I bought them despite the fact that I quickly grew sick of them, usually giving them away. As I watched the children each day, I knew they would be forever etched in my mind.
    The people, the buildings, the food, the culture, everything was different. Armed guards were everywhere with machine guns. With each day, I felt even more detached, being so out of touch with everyone and everything that surrounded me. Not one person spoke English. Nothing felt like home and nothing felt familiar. Nocona, on the other hand, was like the golden girl, totally fearless, with each passerby reaching out to touch her hair. She obviously felt very much at home; I didn't. Within days, everyone knew her by name. As Nocona skipped down the long crude sidewalks, tasting the vendors' beans and tortillas, you could hear people calling out Nocona from a distance! She was obviously different with the red hair, white skin, and high energy. Her smile and laughter had obviously won the hearts of everyone.
    Day in and day out I would go up to the little ice cream stand, relentlessly making an attempt to order ice cream. I had learned ten words of Spanish, but no one ever seemed to understand me when I spoke them. One of the words was helado (ice cream). I always ended up pointing to the object I desired. Despite my lack of knowledge or adaptation of this new environment, I continued each day to visit the shops with a desire to educate myself. I was hoping one day I would wake up and the new surroundings would bring a familiar feeling and a sense of home.
    Out of total boredom, we returned to the beach so Nocona could play with the children. The difference in cultures daily amazed me. On one occasion, a young girl was left to babysit her baby brother, and obviously grew weary of watching him. Being creative, she very quickly buried him in the sand, then made her way off to play. He never cried even though his little head was the only thing visible. Nocona found it to be totally mesmerizing and lay beside him, entertaining him.
    With each day I pondered on the next step of the journey and the possibility of normalcy returning possibly in the next country. *Just how long would I have to live with people that I could not even talk to or relate with?*
    After a couple of weeks I started checking daily with the hotel to see if my passport had arrived. Each day was disappointing with no arrival. After a few weeks, I decided to register Nocona in a small private school.

*Nocona
School in Mexico*

Nocona was so excited with each new day and entered the classroom as though she had been there all her life. It never seemed to cross her mind that all these children did not understand a word she said! I would watch from the street as Nocona interacted with the children. I was always in awe at how disciplined the Mexican children were. Each child was sitting erect in their chairs as the teachers appeared to be teaching them. I often wondered how they could keep three-year-olds seated for such long periods.

That is, all except Nocona! For some strange reason, Nocona was treated totally different. By the second day it was obvious an extra teacher had been assigned to the classroom, her one assignment being to *Keep Up With Nocona!* Nocona, being very vibrant and hyper, never walked, but skipped. This teacher never missed a beat, skipping right along behind her. I never really cared if Nocona learned anything. I just wanted her to be with children and hopefully adapt to this new environment.

Each day after I picked Nocona up, we would go for lunch at a little restaurant. On one particular day we were ordering our food. A young man approached us and began to talk to us. I noticed from time to time the youth that were in the private schools had a desire to learn the English language. If they heard us speaking, you could see them stop to listen to us. Nocona very quickly motioned to the young man and said, "Sentarse."

I laughed, realizing she had actually learned something at the school. The words meant, *Sit down!*—which, I am sure, was drilled into her daily. The young man quickly sat down. Somehow, Nocona was able to communicate with him with the Spanish she had learned.

ɞ⚘

Nocona and I sat out on the veranda of the hotel daily as she played with Miguel and watched the loud bolts of lightning and torrential rains. I entertained myself just observing the people, always finding it amusing as to what might be going on in their lives. Some were obviously businessmen. Others would be all dressed up as though there might be a big gala event in the city. At any rate, it had a way of keeping my mind off my problems.

I soon met a young European writer who spoke English. He had recently backpacked in the mountains of the Chiapas. His stories were exciting, yet his stories ended with sadness since he was unable to obtain pictures to show for his trips. He stated that the Indians in that remote area were uneasy about his presence. My curiosity grew as to what it would be like to enter the lives of a tribe that was in such a remote area on the mountains. One day I approached the young writer to take us with him when he returned. He agreed and, yes, we would go in the cream-colored Cadillac!

The day was beautiful. I was highly anticipating the trip and knew it would be unforgettable. I finally had found someone that spoke English even though he was just there for a short time. Nocona and I were both so excited about the day.

We traveled around and up the mountain in Phil's big cream-colored Cadillac. With each second, the scenery changed, becoming more and more remote. The path continued to narrow, but we pursued going forward. From the looks on the people's faces, no vehicle had ever been there.

We observed as small, short people carried firewood and flowers down the mountain as we traveled up. Each looked at us very strangely.

As the path ran out, we began to make our own road. Everyone continued to stop and watch the cream-colored Cadillac as it made its way up the mountain. They had obviously never seen an American here, much less an automobile! We continued to pass little herds of sheep and goats as we peered at the tiny shanties dotting the hills.

Finally, it came to a point we needed four-wheel drive. We stopped, parked the car, and finished up by walking. I am sure there were dangers, but there was such a feeling of tranquility. I really didn't care what lay ahead. I just wanted to experience it.

When we got to the top we just stood for a few minutes. The young writer and I watched in awe at the beauty and the simplicity. There really were not words to express the aura and beauty in the people and their modest adobe houses dotted along the sloping mountain. We sat back in the distance at the top of a hill, monitoring the Indians for a few minutes, then we made our way closer. The Indians went about their chores. I was so caught up in the moment I failed to notice Nocona. When I looked up, she was sprinting down the mountain and up to their modest homes as though she were invited. My first thoughts were to race down and grab her, then I noticed the people continued to go about their business as though she were one of them. They never changed their pace, but continued on with their chores, occasionally looking back at her. I stood in awe at their response.

The homes were built on the side of the mountain, with pigs and chickens running freely around them. It was like something from a storybook, and Nocona was embracing every moment of it. The people would occasionally stop and smile, keeping their focus on the little, redheaded gringo. She was running and dancing across their lawns, picking their flowers out of the window boxes and chasing their pigs. Nocona felt totally at home, and they appeared to love the way she embraced their home and life.

My friend saw the camaraderie between the Indians and Nocona and quickly pulled out his camera, taking many pictures. I could have stayed there forever, but it began to get late, and it was soon time to go.

As we slowly made our way down the mountain, there was a stream of children gathering and chasing after the big Cadillac. Nocona was hanging out the back window waving at all the people along the way. As we wound down the narrow path, one small lady came out to the road. The elderly lady began handing Nocona bouquets of flowers.

For the moment I felt as though I was in a movie setting. I knew no one at home would believe this! There was no way to express going even further into another culture's world for the day, then driving out as though you were reentering another time zone!

Days continued to go by and boredom set in once again. I continued my search for books in English. I went through my small bag of things I had brought. All I had was Nocona's toys and a book of Dr. Lester Sumrall's cassette tapes on *Dreams and Visions.* I picked them up at a church service I had attended in Huntsville, Texas. I was with my good friend Miss Ruth Baker prior to my leaving. Why I had chosen them over everything else in my house to bring was not apparent, but what the heck. I went into town and shopped until I found a cheap radio with a cassette player in it. I made my way back to the hotel.

After the third tape, I began to cry as the speaker told of a missionary that had brought thousands of people to the Lord in Argentina. Before the missionary died, he had had a profound dream of huge drops of liquid light. The light was falling on different people around the world. The people that they fell on would be in one country one day and in another the next. These people would go out in Jesus' name and heal the sick, feed the poor, and cast out demons.

All I could think about was the dream I had prior to my leaving, about the huge raindrops falling on me like liquid light. Something in my spirit was now pointing to me. Me! How could that be? Could this be another part of this huge puzzle? *Could God actually have a plan for me, too? No, I Don't Think So! I Don't Even Know How To Pray!*

With each day I would make an attempt to rationalize this whole scenario. I wondered what the purpose of all this might be. By this time, it was evident God was in this, but the question was still there. What was up? I was only getting bits and pieces. Maybe Nocona was like Joseph and had to be taken out of her country. God might have a plan for her in Costa Rica. But He couldn't possibly have a plan for Frances Harris! That would be too weird!

I began to teach Nocona more about God and how special she was. She found that to be exciting. Even though she was extremely comfortable in this new environment, I wanted to continue keeping her focused and positive. Every day, I made an attempt to make her think everything was going as planned. Each day we drew pictures of the new home we would have on the beach in Costa Rica. We drew lots of neighbors and friends with flowers and a school. I always drew pictures of the church on the beach with Nocona walking to church on the sandy road with the native children. Each day we repeated the same story about our new life. Nocona was excited. I was trying to be!

For some reason, I felt the need to write her grandfather's telephone number in the back of her small Bible we had brought with us. I felt if anything ever happened and we got separated she might have the Bible and have the number. Every day I would have her repeat the telephone number, hoping she would memorize it.

My private time was when Nocona slept. Occasionally, I had my cry. It wasn't just the loss of my home, family, and friends, but not knowing from one day to the next what lay ahead. I knew something bigger than me was in charge, yet I continued to feel I was walking daily in total darkness. I was really needing more information. I was in control for years. Now I had no control! I did not have the least idea where we were going or what we were going to do after arriving.

Day in and day out I continued to check the front desk for mail, hoping to get my passport. Each day the Hotel Fenix employees were extremely warm and friendly, with the exception of one. On our day of arrival, this employee asked to teach me Spanish and seemed to be outdone that I wasn't interested. My mind was too fractured to concentrate. How could I learn Spanish? I really did not even want to be in Mexico!

The churches were all Spanish, and I tried going to one in hopes of gaining something. I had a Bible, but it still wasn't making a whole lot of sense. The family and material things were missed greatly. Now I was totally grasping for things of the spirit and totally aware of their importance to our survival. More and more I deeply longed for God to show Himself to me in some way. I was needing friends badly. I was missing my wonderful friends and encouragers from back home. I never thought that much about the importance of encouragers until I arrived in Tapachula. Now, it was just me and someone I knew so little about—Jesus!

こ

With each call to Texas, more trauma was added to my life. The latest news was that the girls were told to sell everything out of my home because of the lawsuit Trevor was now filing against me! Everything I owned had to go or possibly end up going to Trevor. My mind and body continued to be racked with emotional pain. I was devastated! Every inch of my house, in and out, to every brick, had great sentimental value. I had lived there for at least twenty-five years! I now found myself crying over simple things—

the loss of my little seashell prisoners, the pictures of all my babies in the window, or the cake plate filled with all my favorite little seashells. I had so many things that meant something to just me, even the pots and pans I used to cook in while raising the kids.

JUNE 1994

Once again I was sitting out on the patio in a lounge chair watching Nocona play with Miguel. I was patiently waiting for the mail delivery in hopes today would be the day my passport might arrive. I leaned back to say a little prayer, only to be interrupted by the loud roar of two large black trucks. They were driving up within six feet of where I was sitting. The trucks were loaded down with what appeared to be junk. Loud-talking, dark-skinned men could be seen in the front seat. Rough-looking Spanish guys jumped out, making their way towards us. Fearful of what might happen next, I sat quietly plotting as to what I should do. *Should I grab Nocona and run or should I look more confident and unafraid of the situation?* I quickly glanced over at the second truck as the door opened up. Out stepped a beautiful young lady with long blonde hair and beautiful legs. They were all laughing and speaking Spanish as though they knew each other. The girl suddenly looked up and broke out in a huge smile as she saw me. It was River JoNey! I couldn't believe my eyes! She had changed so much! It wasn't the frail little girl I had left back home. *How did she find us?*

Never once had I spoken to her. The last I knew she was living with her father. After telling her story, I was even more shocked. I thought, *There Obviously Is A God!*

River had become upset with the way everything was going in the States and decided to join us. I was hoping she would make all the court sessions, but it was great seeing her. She stated when she drove through Houston on her way here she saw license plates on a truck that had Guatemala on them. She followed the party until they stopped. She then asked if they knew where Tapachula was. Their reply was, *"We are going right through Tapachula."*

River quickly joined up with them. I grimaced at the thought of her crude companions and what they might have done to her, but was thrilled she was with us.

It was good having River along, but it was evident she may have been maturing on the outside, but inside something was still missing. There was an unexplainable void that she kept only to herself. With each day she continued to be in total denial, refusing to talk about anything to do with Trevor or the past. I was needing someone to brainstorm our situation with, but it would not be River. She just wanted to go forward with her life.

River JoNey, like Nocona, adapted quickly to Tapachula and the Spanish people. She had won awards in high school in Spanish, so she embraced each person and place she visited. River loved everyone and they quickly fell in love with her.

Despite my warnings about all the ruthless taxi drivers, JoNey had brought her bike and was determined to ride it. The first day, she came in, telling me she fell in the middle of the street in the city. Many businessmen helped her out of her precarious situation. It seemed to be the opportunity she needed to make friends.

By the end of the week, she was going out to all the plantations and knew all the owners on a first-name basis. She continued to amaze me! After that it was like every business we passed, the owners wanted to stop and talk to us. They not only loved Nocona, but embraced River as though she were their own.

We were close to the Centro, so each night we frequented the little sidewalk cafes. It was special being together, tasting the different foods. JoNey and Nocona loved everything, but I continued to be selective in everything I ate, hoping it would stay down!

The evenings were always interesting. We never knew what might happen. We didn't need entertainers; the local people took care of that. As we walked the streets, the owners of the small businesses were now requesting we come to their homes to visit them.

One night it was a little much as we sat out dining at a small sidewalk cafe. I heard a loud thud! A reckless taxi driver hit someone walking down the street next to us. I would always look around at the people around us and marvel at their response. There was no response! It was as though it was a normal day!

One evening a purse snatcher raced down the sidewalk, taking advantage of an innocent old lady. There were always guards in front of all major businesses with loaded machine guns. They never as much as flinched or moved a muscle in an attempt to help this person. The heavily armed guards in the city never moved from their position no matter how loud the woman screamed. This extreme drama was not a daily thing, but often enough that I never seemed to get over one incident before something else would happen. But the business people were always extremely nice. With each day it was as though they were trying to make an attempt to make up for the problems there.

We soon learned Tapachula was a haven and stopover for everyone trying to escape the U.S.! The people here were quite used to people like us and never questioned us. It was obvious they sensed our dilemma and had made their choice. They were obviously on our side. They continued to encourage and uplift us.

Days went into months and finally we got word from the U.S., the passport was on its way. More problems were arising in Tapachula, and the locals continued to warn us daily that guerilla warfare was getting closer. They were now more intense stating, *"You really have to leave! It is not a safe place for Americans!"*

I continued to check the mail often, anxiously anticipating my passport. When Phil heard the passport was in the mail, he began driving my Cherokee jeep to meet me. One day out of frustration, I finally called the post office, only to hear the passport had been hand-delivered to the hotel employee that worked the front desk. The employee informed the postal service that we had checked out. The postal service therefore had sent the passport back to the U.S.!

I wanted to cry so badly, but my anger overrode the moment, stopping the tears. I knew exactly which man it was. He had not spoken a word to me since I refused his Spanish lessons on our arrival. The hotel was small and he saw us on a daily basis. In seconds, everyone in the hotel, including the owners, knew my dilemma and how outraged I was. I called the person in the States handling this for me. They stated there was no way the passport could go back to them. They did not put the correct return address on the envelope and did it on purpose. Phil called and made the decision to return to the States.

I began to pray for a miracle. I then got word the passport had returned to the person's home! It was clear to all of us we had witnessed a miracle and the passport was now back on its way to Mexico! Once it arrived into Tapachula, the man from the post office walked the passport to the hotel and handed it to me personally, knowing my frustration. Phil flew to Mexico and once again joined us.

༄

During our stay at Hotel Fenix, River had become acquainted with a young businessman. He was very persuasive, telling us all the great things about Honduras. He was quite convincing in River's eyes. I guess you would say a little too convincing? Neither Phil nor myself was intrigued, but River JoNey was falling for his sales pitch. River insisting Honduras was possibly where we were supposed to live. She decided she would follow him and check out his thoughts.

Phil and I stayed on course and continued on our way to Costa Rica. I was totally convinced this is where God was obviously leading us. I didn't go around telling people God was sending me to Costa Rica, but I just knew... *He Was!*

VANISHED

OUR CHILDREN, OUR FUTURE

IF YOU HAVE SEEN OR HAVE ANY INFORMATION, CALL: 1-800-VANISHED OR (408)296-1113

NOCONA LYNN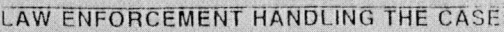
Date of Birth: 1-13-91
Date Missing: 3-10-94
Missing From: Orange Texas
Green Eyes & Reddish Blond Hair
Ht: 2' 6"   Wt: 30 lbs.
Missing Type: Family Abduction by Grandmother
Race: White
Other: Fine scar above left eyebrow, ant bite allergy

ARREST WARRANTS ISSUED FOR INTERFERENCE WITH CUSTODY & UNLAWFUL FLIGHT TO AVOID PROSECUTION:
FRANCIS ANN COLLINS HARRIS
A.K.A. Francis Burton
Born: 1-2-45
Blue Eyes & Brown hair with gray
Ht: 5'6"   Wt: 145 Lbs
Other: Wears Glasses and has unusually rapid eye blink

LAW ENFORCEMENT HANDLING THE CASE:
Orange County Sheriff's Office, Orange Texas (409)883-2612 Or your local FBI

Seashell Prisoners
CHAPTER 9

Phil, Nocona, and I made our way through Guatemala and on through Honduras and Nicaragua. Everything was going smoothly. I was feeling accomplished with the new passport and now once again making our way towards our goal. The changing scenery kept us all entertained and the time went by fast. As we arrived at the border of Costa Rica, it was the first sign of civilization. What a relief!—A very professional, organized border crossing, with the car being sprayed down with insecticide by men in white suits. We all sat back in awe thinking, wow, civilization at last! I was now once again anticipating our new homeland. I just knew this was it! We had finally arrived! Now God would take over from here and I could just sit back and relax! I had followed His direction to the T and now had a total feeling of achievement.

We immediately began to try to get a feel for the new country and its layout. We found a quaint little Italian resort on the ocean with monkeys jumping from tree to tree. This would be our first place to stay. Late in the evening, Phil and I took Nocona to the beach for a walk, but Nocona was surprisingly afraid of the waves. We each took a hand and let her jump over the waves as we walked through the water until she got used to the waves.

The next day after breakfast we were back on the beach for a day of relaxing. It was the first time I had ever seen topless women walking around on a beach. I realized at that moment we were definitely not in the little town of Mauriceville, Texas. The sign on the resort did say *Italian*, so I guess I would just have to get used to a few culture changes.

After resting a couple of days, the decision was made that it was now time for Phil to return to Texas. Phil reassured me he would be checking on us frequently. He would soon return with more of my money to finance my endeavor.

We made our way to the airport and bid him farewell once again. It was now up to Nocona, myself, and this new God I was totally dependent on. I felt great and totally at peace, assured that I was now at the divine location God had led us to.

It didn't take long to see Costa Rica was definitely beyond anything I had ever experienced in beauty! As I traveled the roads, I was in awe at the mountainous jungles and beaches. Each day I ventured out more, and soon we made our way to the capital for a few days. Little did I know San Jose would soon become the worst place I had ever been in my life! The hotel and the people that worked there were very nice and friendly, but the city itself was extremely stressful. The taxi drivers gave you the feeling they were fresh out of prison with no respect for anyone. The traffic was so hectic that it made it easier to take a taxi than to drive! It didn't take but a few rides to realize our lives were truly in danger with each experience!

The restaurants, including Kentucky Fried Chicken and Burger King, employed no one that spoke English. I found the workers in one place to be rude. On one occasion, I overheard a businessman in the booth next to me speaking English. I turned and asked if he would please let the manager know how rudely I was treated by one of the employees. On the next arrival, the manager came out to my car and opened the door for me!

❧

We soon had our fill and made our way out of the city and back to the beach. I thought, *Where is this bilingual country that my friend recommended?* I traveled for days, beach after beach, nothing of which was what I envisioned. The water was pretty, but mostly for surfing. I saw one dive shop, but there wasn't much business. With every stop I continued to find only Spanish-speaking people. Where had I gone wrong? I thought this was God's choice for us, but now nothing seem right about Costa Rica. I decided to check on land and homes to purchase. Prices were extremely high and everything with any potential appeared to be bought up. It was obvious Costa Rica had reached its peak in development years ago. Nothing felt like God or home! At that time I began to think, *Where exactly did I go wrong?*

Each morning I would regroup, and once again look for that special place that God had picked just for us. I was determined to make this God's plan. One evening I was touring the coastline, looking for a different beach. I noticed on the side of the road two young women hitchhiking with babies. I decided to give them a ride. I tried to make conversation, but that didn't go anywhere. They got very quiet. I glanced into my rearview mirror to see how they were doing and realized they were stealing Nocona's toys and clothes. As I drove down the road I was trying to decide what was the best and safest course of action. Did they have guns? Were they criminals? Regardless, I had to make a decision. I quickly pulled over to a business with people around it and demanded they get out. It worked, and off we went again! Nocona had a few less bows for her hair and no videos, but we still had our lives.

❧

Every day I became more confused. I was so sure this was where God had wanted us to be. The God-puzzle was now missing an important link. Where did I go wrong? Or was there ever a God to begin with? Fear and disappointment began to take over my thoughts. My prayers became more fervent.

There were very few children on the beaches, since most of the places catered to tourists. Nocona soon took up with a skinny little calico kitten that hung around the restaurants. We nurtured it back to health and quickly claimed it. We kept it in the little room we had on the beach. We soon had our fill of Costa Rica, but not of our new friend, Rican Kitty.

I decided to quit trying so hard and enjoy the beauty of Costa Rica a few days before leaving. It definitely was the most beautiful country I had ever been to. I certainly got crossed up with the language and people, but the beauty was awesome. Maybe a new plan would come to me once we got away from the beach. We began to drive around the country and explore the tourist attractions. I purchased a collar and leash for Rican Kitty, and Nocona walked her daily at each stop. People laughed at the little redhead with the kitten on a leash. Maybe it was a first; I just couldn't come up with a better idea, and it seemed to work.

Nocona and I spent one day horseback riding up to one of the volcanoes and walked down to the waterfalls. It was a long adventuresome climb down the cliff and very exciting. I was in awe at the beautiful waterfalls, but felt a little uneasy at the long climb back up. Thank God the young tour guide was strong and able to carry Nocona. I was exhausted, but loved the adventure. The next day we bathed in the natural pools of hot water from the volcano, and I treated myself to a massage. It truly was a beautiful country, but not my choice of places to live. I soon had my fill of the scenery, and reality was kicking back in.

I contacted River JoNey, realizing we had to come up with a better plan. River sounded excited that I wasn't interested in staying and encouraged me to join her in Honduras. It was good talking to her, but I noticed she wasn't too happy with the outcome of her new Honduran business friend.

When I hung up the phone, I hesitated, trying to decide if I wanted to make any more calls, being pay phones were almost non-existent. As I was stalling, I noticed two young Peace Corp workers discussing their plans for the next day. Yes, they were going to Honduras! I quickly invited them to join us, and the next morning we were on our way back to Honduras. They were obviously Christians and enjoyed listening to the music I had of the Martin Family, our friends in Mauriceville.

❧

Once again the countryside was beautiful as we made our way down the winding roads in the big cream-colored Cadillac. We made only one quick stop. The Peace Corp workers quickly bargained for a monkey some small children were selling alongside the road. We continued on with our one goal and that was to make it to the Honduran border before it closed.

We flew down the road, but as we approached the border, patrol men with large machine guns were walking off. Despite our begging, they insisted we come back at nine the next morning. Normally, I would win with my compromising arguments. With these guys, it was obvious they had the guns. *We Didn't!* They were not going to budge from their statement.

They did reassure us there were good places to stay right down the road. I obviously had overlooked them. We were all starving, and there were no restaurants or what I considered a decent place to eat for miles. It was late in the evening and we did not have time to get back to civilization. We drove up to the place they highly suggested, which was a little, run-down shanty. As I peered over at it, I was concerned for the car's safety, much less ours. The owners showed us our room. Dirt floors with grungy little knotted-up mattresses. No pillows. The shack had mud walls and an outdoor outhouse. There was a wooden door with a loose latch that Nocona could have pushed through. We were each given a bucket of water, so we took turns bathing. It was truly an unforgettable experience!

Food would be ready soon, we were told. I was starving so I didn't ask questions. The meat was tough, but the beans were hot. It was kind of hard eating with all the border guards staring at you, holding AK47 machine guns. It was obviously their hangout.

I decided to go to bed, but the lady motioned that it wasn't safe to leave the car outside. I looked at her thinking, *Where was I supposed to put it?* There was no place! She quickly took me out and pointed for me to pull it up in between the rooms. I couldn't believe it! There was a hairline crack between the car and the shack! I thought it's probably best that Phil was not here! My new Peace Corp friends decided they would sleep in the car. By morning, I knew they were truly the wiser.

Surprisingly, we woke up to no tarantula bite marks or men in our room. I guess that's the most grateful I've ever been in my life to God! I was extremely thankful to be alive!

We soon were on our way, finding it much easier to get a child through the border without her rightful parents than Rican Kitty. It took a few bucks and a couple hours of hard fast talk, but Rican sat proudly beside me as we made our way through the border crossing.

We were now arriving at the capital of Honduras, and this was where we would part ways with the Peace Corp workers, but not with the memories. I wanted to give the young couple a gift, so I gave them one of the Martin tapes they enjoyed so much. We hugged and parted ways.

❧

Now it was up to Nocona and I to find our way to San Pedro and hopefully find her mother. Problems momentarily dissipated as I traveled down the winding roads overlooking beautiful mountains and valleys. It soon got dark, but I could tell I wasn't far from the city. I began to speed up as I saw lights in the distance. I was going 65 miles an hour when I came upon a huge pile of rocks and dirt right in the middle of the road! I came to a screeching stop, took a deep breath and slowly made my way into the city. Reality definitely kicked back in! I was still in a third-world country. No caution signs, No nothing! I began to see what appeared to be civilization. Wow, Burger King and American food restaurants, up and down the street!

I drove around town wondering how I was supposed to call River JoNey with no phones in sight. I soon made the connection with the help of an employee of Pizza Hut. Telephone booths were nowhere to be found, but the employees were very gracious and appeared to understand my predicament.

It was wonderful seeing River JoNey again. The next day we gathered up our little bags. Off we went, not having the least idea where we were going or what we were going to do. I was thoroughly confused by this time. I continued to question divine guidance other than the help of the Peace Corp workers, and the fact that we had found JoNey. I guess that should count for two miracles! I continued to look back at how sure I was that God had been taking us to Costa Rica...But look at us now!

We stopped at small towns and made an attempt to find something to take our minds off our problems. The surroundings didn't help matters. The country was struggling in more ways than one. Poverty was prevalent, and there was an obvious shortage of electricity. Everywhere we went, the roar of generators and the smell of the exhaust were excruciating. The whole scenario was overwhelming.

I grew more and more despondent, not knowing what direction to take at this time.

One day as we were relaxing and eating at an outdoor roadside restaurant, we overheard one of the locals mention the Island of Roatan. I was momentarily taken back in time as I remembered a dive trip I made on a small key off the Island thirteen years back. My spirits picked up as I thought how neat it would be to see the actual island of Roatan. I had forgotten Roatan was a part of Honduras. For some reason, it was never advertised as Honduras on any of the brochures or web sites!

The next day, for eight dollars each, we found ourselves leaving the mainland of Honduras on a large yacht. We observed the hundreds of Islanders loading up their supplies to take back to Roatan as they boarded the large boat. It was obvious the yacht was their main transportation going to the mainland of Honduras.

We were now on our way to the island of Roatan, leaving the big cream-colored Cadillac behind! By that time, we were down to a very small bag and a keyboard (piano) River had brought from home. I'm not sure why she singled it out to bring on her trip since no one played, but we brought it along. As we all got on the boat, we immediately made our way to the top deck. The large boat slowly drifted out to sea. It was a wonderful feeling as the boat left the dock and the mainland began to disappear. Immediately, I was mesmerized at the vastness of the ocean. No more fumes, and no more loud generators. I was told the problem on the mainland was temporary, but it was nice getting away from it. From here on we did not have the least idea what to expect, but anything would have to be better than our past experiences.

One couple aboard, obvious alcoholics, immediately approached us desiring to make conversation. Personally, I just wanted to locate a place to relax and gaze out over the water. I really didn't want to talk since I couldn't understand them very well, and I was anticipating a quiet boat ride. The couple were obviously foreigners, looking nothing like an Islander or a Honduran. I harnessed my inner thoughts and made conversation despite that they reeked with a strong smell of alcohol. For some reason they were persistent that we stay in a small village they referred to as West End. At this point I thought, *Who cares, West End, East End— It Really Didn't Matter To Me!* We were just going to visit the Island and leave in a couple days so I really didn't care where we stayed. I reassured the couple we would give West End a try.

There was a nice-looking young man on the boat that lived on the Island. The drunk couple thought he and River would make a perfect couple. Immediately, they began to fix them up. I slowly worked my way over to the front end of the boat, leaving them with River to do their matchmaking. Nocona and I sat down to enjoy the view. I looked back to see River JoNey within minutes walking over to the other end of the boat.

I became totally lost in time as I sat watching the ocean and how beautiful it was against the sky. You could see a little island here and there, yet endless, beautiful, blue water. The peace and tranquility was so wonderful! I reflected on the thought of just remaining on the boat forever. The yacht was huge with several floors, air conditioning, and T.V.'s. Enjoying the quietness of no one around, my eyes continued to go from the blueness of the sky to the blueness of the water.

Suddenly, I noticed in the distance a beautiful rainbow. The colors were brilliant and unusually large. I pointed it out to Nocona and quietly reminded her of the story of Noah and his ark. And then another rainbow formed on top of the one we'd been watching, and it too was unusually large. Nocona and I just sat in awe at how it filled the sky. I immediately thought of God's promise to his people, and reminded Nocona. The moment I said the word, *Promise*, I felt something come over me that warmed my whole body. I Knew It Was God! Immediately I became very emotional. I felt tears rolling down my face. I knew the Island of Roatan may be strange and new to me, but Someone higher than me was making it our destiny in more ways than one. I glanced up to see JoNey coming across from the other end of the yacht. I watched as she made her way over to us. When she looked up, she appeared to be fighting back tears. Very emotionally, she looked me in the eye and stated, "Mother, something just came over me. I just need to tell you I know this is…" For some reason, there was a pause, then she went on to state, "This is where you are going to live!"

I'll never forget that moment as long as I live. It was my first huge revelation of God! I knew without any doubt: This was God and it was intended for no one else on this earth but us! Once again, a supernatural leading and another piece of the huge puzzle had finally connected together!

Seashell Prisoners
CHAPTER 10

NOVEMBER 1994: Nocona, Age Three; Roatan, Honduras

We arrived on the Island completely unaware of what lay in store for us. I'm not sure what I expected, but one thing quickly became evident—it wasn't exactly the Caymans! It was pretty obvious the Island was relatively unknown to most, but in a quaint way, extremely laid back and interesting.

For the moment we felt more like strangers on another planet; making it difficult to make simple decisions, like choice of taxis—a choice of run down, worn out, or totally dilapidated! We soon cringed, said a prayer, and stepped into the first one we came up to. The door failed to shut, so we hung on as best we could, trying not to interrupt the Islander next to us feasting on fried chicken. The driver was obviously insistent on impressing us by turning up the Spanish music. It definitely had a way of adding to the misery of the hot, humid, stifling heat. As the taxi wound along the narrow roads, the first impression we received wasn't good—run-down buildings, trash-littered streets, and a man urinating along the side of the road.

Everything quickly changed as we left out of Coxen Hole and approached the long winding road now on our way to West End. I was now totally and completely mesmerized at the unusual beauty—the lush jungles, the wide assortment of mango, cashew, banana, and almond trees. Small simple homes were spotted along the road with Islanders going about their day in total simplicity. It was obvious few had cars or any form of transportation other than walking. The narrow, paved roads had more people on foot getting to their destinations than in vehicles.

As we made our way down the long winding road, it was evident most of the Island was heavily laden with a wide assortment of tropical plants. As we approached West End, the driver suddenly exited to the left, taking us to what he referred to as West Bay. I didn't question it since it all added to the adventure of seeing a whole new Island. As we made our way to the top of each hill, the view of the beautiful blue Caribbean down below was breathtaking!

Scattered across the sea were various dive and sailboats. I sat quietly reflecting on all my travels to various dive destinations; this was truly beyond anything I had ever seen anywhere. The Caymans were nice along with Bonaire and Cozumel, but nothing in comparison to Roatan! Now bubbling up inside of me was a renewed feeling of life. This had to be handpicked by God! I felt like Christopher Columbus, as though I had come upon a little secret kept from the world. With my background of traveling to dive destinations, I wondered how long it would take for others to come to know and love the nostalgia, beauty, and tranquility of this little virgin Island called *Roatan!*

After we dropped off an elderly lady, we continued the drive down the winding road and back toward West End. With each mile, we traveled to the sound of rusted-out propane bottles rolling around in the trunk as the taxi made its way to the hotel. We were headed straight for West End for no other reason than that's where the merry, intoxicated couple told us to go! I continued to just flow with whatever seemed right for the moment. It just became easier rather than stressing myself out as to the reasons for it. It was as though at this point God didn't need me, and it felt good. Since I had no other options, I just hung on from point to point.

I felt a strong sense of calmness in my spirit as we arrived in what we would soon come to know and love as the unique and notorious West End.

As the main road ended and we were approaching West End, we came upon a beautiful large bay. The taxi slowed down, made a sharp right turn, then made its way down a sandy, bumpy road. The path wound around the bay and came to a dead end at a small place called Half Moon Bay Resort. There were rustic cabins overlooking the beautiful bay.

We immediately made our way to the front of the resort where a restaurant consisted of a large deck overlooking the bay. The handsome waiters were quite personable. We soon knew them all by name. Mark always knew exactly the right words to say to pick you up with the Island jargon. All the male tourists were called Captain and the ladies Princess. Mark never seemed to notice the irritated husbands' dislike for his flirtatious remarks.

It was obvious George Jones was the waiters' favorite musician. Like him or not, you would dine to his music! It was quite different from what the norm was for previous Islands I had visited, but Roatan really wasn't your average Island!

I found the music unsuitable at first and often suggested Reggae to the waiters. After several requests, I realized this is what the Islanders liked! This is what made West End special and unique. They were just who they were with no pretense whatsoever.

Dotted along the sandy beaches in West End were Islanders' homes, a few rental places, rustic, outdoor, thatched-roof restaurants, and small dive operations. It was obviously a haven for backpackers and adventure seekers. I often looked for the couple on the yacht that directed us to West End. I continued to wonder why they insisted we come here to begin with, other than possibly...*Was this just another God thing?* It was nearly a year before I saw them again.

My soul felt totally secure each day as I slipped off my shoes and walked barefoot down the sandy beach in West End. As the heat from the sun became more intense, I knew my biggest problem would be adjusting to something totally new to me...Sweat! As I listened to the English-speaking Islanders, I knew for certain this Island and West End were exactly where

God wanted us to be! This was my first time in four months to hear people speaking English! How wonderful it sounded! Everything about it felt right. I immediately began looking for something more permanent for ourselves and our new Rican calico kitten.

※

The quaint little section of the Island called West End was extremely laid back. West End was beautiful in its own way and full of character, not only with the modest homes dotting the sandy beach, but also the people that lived there as well. Calico cats lay on many doorsteps. Yes, Rican Kitty would love it here! The more I strolled the beach road, the more I became enlightened to the new life we were quickly becoming a part of.

Each day as I walked the beach road the voice of Charles Stanley echoed out the windows of the Islanders' homes and across the bay. I listened to Charles Stanley every day prior to leaving the U.S., so I took this as another confirmation. Yes, this had to be God directing us here.

One day as I strolled down the sandy beach, a young child from a distance smiled and waved at us. I quickly asked her name. She replied with a beautiful English accent, "I am Lara Muller from South Africa."

I was totally mesmerized as she skipped out to the water in her little blue dress, diving into the sea so innocently. We quickly grew attached to this beautiful child, making friends immediately with Lara, her mother Averyl, and father Guy Muller.

The following week I rented a small one-room cabin and began my search for property to build on. With each day I felt secure I was doing something right. I continued to take it one day at a time, striving not to look too far ahead.

My wardrobe was down to a few pairs of shorts and a couple of long skirts. Everything I put on was hot! I was constantly searching for ways to get cool. After several months I found a very nice lady (a seamstress) named Melda. Within a few weeks she had me back up and going in a totally new wardrobe consisting of colorful, sleeveless, Island dresses. They were so much cooler than shorts, and I was now for the first time taking on the Island look.

With each day River and Nocona were making friends. I was so intense and focused on survival that friendships never entered my mind. At the end of each day, River and I would relax at dinner and laugh about the daily humor. There were so many changes in our lifestyle and unusual ways of the Islanders and tourists from all over the world. We found ourselves laughing at simple everyday happenings. What appeared to be normal in the lives of the Islanders and foreigners on an Island was humorous to us. We often thought how boring and uneventful our lives had become in the U.S. compared to theirs.

Almost every structure in West End was modest. Air conditioning was obviously not a known invention. I loved the beautiful Half Moon Bay, so we rented a one-room duplex not far from the water. It was a small room with a curtain across the bathroom door, with no running water coming out of the shower or kitchen sink most of the day. We quickly adapted to the shower problem, learning to save up water in gallon jugs. For some reason the water went off frequently.

Holes were in the wall large enough for snakes to come through. Islanders reassured me they never saw snakes, so the cracks didn't bother me.

The only fan in the room went out the first week, so we peeled off as much clothing as possible to sleep at night. The heat became more and more excruciating with each day. I tried to be patient for the owner to bring us a fan. But after several nights of intense heat, I gave up and quickly purchased my own fan.

There was a young lady in the unit next to us, and every day we could hear every word she said. The walls were thin so River and I would whisper for hours into the night, usually ending with a burst of laughter. Our first lesson learned as Island residents was, no longer would there be privacy in our lives! Even walking down the road there were always Islanders or tourists sitting under the nearby banana or mango trees. I often longed for a boat just to go out into the ocean to have a private conversation or release my frustrations. We had quickly learned the importance of guarding our mouths at all times.

Hiding was next to impossible for me since that was never a part of my life before Trevor. I found it hard to not allow Nocona to run freely like the other children. I knew I was a fugitive of justice and my first priority was Nocona's safety, but after the first few weeks, I released Nocona to live a normal lifestyle like the other children. Nocona's happiness had to come first, so she was now right in the middle of all the activity on the water and land with all the Island children. Nocona was having a wonderful time! Daily, I would sit on the beach as Nocona played in the sea.

Our favorite place on the Bay was beside a large, two-story, yellow-framed house to the right of the entrance of Half Moon Bay. The house overlooked the Bay and had a beautiful sandy beach in front of it. The owner had a variety of macaws and parrots. There was a large dock going out into the water in front of the house. Daily the Island children could be found playing and jumping off the dock. Everyone referred to the house as Ms. Mandy's house. We frequently watched Ms. Mandy as she fed and interacted with the birds each day. You could tell her Macaws and exotic parrots were a huge part of her life, and they were cared for as though they were her children.

I finally took a day off to get a glimpse of the rest of Roatan. It didn't take long to see that the whole Island was beautiful in appearance. A friend rode with us to help us come to know the different parts of the Island. After we passed West End we came to Sandy Bay, where the oldest and very upscale resort called Anthony's Key was located on the sea. Many Island homes were scattered along the winding seashore. Then further down the road and to the right was Coxen Hole.

French Harbour lay pretty much in the center of the Island. I found it strange that many of the upper class residents chose to live there, but did not reside on the beautiful sea. On the right was Eldon's Supermarket, a seafood-processing plant, a hardware store, and a few other businesses.

As we made our way East down the winding road, it became more mountainous and, once again, breathtaking. We soon arrived at Jonesville and then Oakridge. We had already driven for about an hour and we still had not come to the end of the Island. Everyone was tired, so we made our way back to West End. Our friend stated the Island was approximately twenty-eight miles long and three miles wide.

※

Within the first year, it became evident we were not alone. The talk was that almost all foreign residents that originally landed here were running from problems in their countries. Now more and more tourists were beginning to discover the Island of Roatan. International Living was bringing in entrepreneurs from various countries with most of them purchasing property. Many had talents in restaurant and resort operations. The Island began to take on change.

※

Months went by and we were beginning to settle in. I was sitting on the tiny porch of our duplex trimming River's long hair. A very pretty business woman on the Island casually strolled up to our porch. She was visiting with the young lady in the duplex next to us. I had seen this lady many times at the Eagle Ray Dive Shop thinking she and her husband were part owners.

The area was so small we overheard every word of their conversation. We especially took notice when the lady stated she was from Orange, Texas. It took all we could do to keep a straight face as she stood inches from us. Not knowing what to do, we chose to sit quietly. As the lady went on with her conversation it was obvious she was either from Orange or had family there. I couldn't help but wonder if they were keeping her updated on our situation. The thought entered my mind that she probably knew exactly who we were.

River and Nocona adapted quickly to everyone and everything around us. They were continually making more and more friends. As for myself, I was a little more subdued. I only knew one thing. I was where God wanted me to be and that was it! As far as what lay ahead the next day, I would just have to take that when it arrived. Little did I know how quickly that would be!

Regardless of all the "what if's," the incident on the boat was etched in stone and had made a huge impact on me. It was the boost I needed to go forward each day. I now knew for certain God definitely had His hand in all of this. That one experience alone would be my cornerstone that I would return to on all future problems.

Now it was up to me to find a way to make an income and go forward with my goal of helping Nocona.

I continued to search daily for property. I found the perfect acreage on the water only to find another party was in the process of purchasing it. I continued my search and found a few small lots down the road east of Half Moon Bay in West End. I purchased it from an elderly Island couple named Laura and Frederick Tatum. The property overlooked the Mangrove Bight. We were close to the end on the North side of West End. On one side of the new property was a vacant lot. On the other was a large, two-story home. A young couple, Garnel and Tonya, lived in the home with their beautiful little girl named Tallany. Directly past the home was the Eagle Ray Dive Shop overlooking Mangrove Bight. Mr. Admiral's Seagrape Resort lay at the very end, overlooking the ocean.

The Tatum's' home was located on the water directly in front of our property. On the side of the road was a large open field. Every day the West End boys of all ages could be seen playing baseball or soccer. Within weeks of living in West End, we came to realize baseball was a huge sport on the Island. The West End team had made a name of being one of the toughest and best teams on the Island, frequently winning championships. As far as the West End teams' favorites went, they never missed watching the Atlanta Braves or the New York Yankees.

The more I looked around, tourism seemed to be the only possibility for me. It was obvious there were two choices. The Islanders were either commercial fishermen or they catered to scuba divers. I was only familiar with one, so that is what I went forward with. I had people skills and knew all about diving, since I was a diver. I would build and operate a small hotel for tourists. I knew even with the money I had entrusted to Phil, I couldn't put all my faith in that. I would have to do something to make a living.

The rooms for rent in most of West End were very small and modest; the majority being unfinished on the inside with wiring exposed. The more upscale had ceiling fans. The electric company called RECO was not known for its efficiency. The electricity was well known to go off during peak periods. Pretty much the same was true with the water. The tourists either came with survival skills or quickly adapted, otherwise you would not make it in West End. I noticed water cisterns at a couple hotels in West End. No one seemed to have generators except a few large dive resorts further down the Island.

Many Island homes lined the road opposite the beach. West End was a beautiful and quaint little village. There were a couple small dive shops spotted along the beach in West End. Being a diver, I noticed right off at how professional they were though their operations were small. They were all foreign-owned.

I now had a piece of property and began researching home builders. I started collecting information from different foreigners that had already built homes. All I seemed to get were horror stories! After lengthy research I soon decided on one home builder and contacted him. The man was extremely nice, came highly recommended, and I was told he was an excellent builder.

I was now low on the money that I had brought. I wasn't concerned, knowing Phil would be bringing what I needed soon. If there was one person I could depend on it was Phil. I used an Islander's phone to check on him. Yes, he was coming, but it would be Thanksgiving.

His last words were, "Check on some property for me. I would like to do some investing." I laughed, knowing the statement I had previously made to him was, *"I would never live in Honduras!"*

A couple weeks went by. It was before Thanksgiving and we were sitting around the room. We heard someone knocking at our door one night. I knew of no one that would come here at all, much less late at night. I heard the man's voice and it sounded okay, so I opened the door.

The stranger stated he and his wife wanted to meet with us later, after dark, and talk. He said we had met in Coxen Hole. He looked at me very seriously and said something important had come up about us. From the tone of his voice, we knew it had to do with Nocona. We met with them the following night. They immediately let us know he had overheard an F.B.I. agent at a small business. He stated the F.B.I., Embassy workers, and local police were all showing wanted posters of Nocona and I to a select few on the Island. Later, the man with the help of others quickly arranged for us to get off the Island, and seek help through a Human Rights organization. We were told to contact an attorney in Tegucigalpa, the capital of Honduras. We were extremely grateful and thanked them, realizing they had to be a part of God's brigade of angels.

The first thing that came to my mind was that we were expecting Phil, not the F.B.I.! Surely not! My best friend wouldn't do that! Thanksgiving came and went, yet no Phil. I realized then that Phil had told the F.B.I. where we were. I was devastated, but I had no time for anger; I had to let go and go forward.

I called Phil, letting him know I was aware of what he had done. He quickly made excuses, yet agreed, yes, he had turned us in. I asked him to please wire my money to me, but there was no reply. Totally confused, the thought went through my mind: *Was Phil a thief on top of being a traitor?*

From the very beginning throughout our journey as I shared our plight over and over, the statements were all the same. This is going to be a book and a movie! These statements were repeated from the first week I left with Nocona. With each turn of events, I was beginning to think, *Yes, it would definitely be a book.* We now had enough to fill a book just on human nature.

Despite each obstacle, a strong force continued to push me forward. Reports from home were that Phil was thoroughly enjoying being the center of attention. The Orange County Courts, the D.A., and Sheriff's Department were all keeping in touch with Phil. Everyone at the local bars were now his best friends, desiring the latest on the infamous Frances Collins Harris. Reports were he was driving my Cherokee jeep, flaunting his involvement with me. Out of the hundreds of people that protected us along the way, I could now better understand why he was included in the ten million dollar lawsuit Trevor filed against myself, my ex-husband, and his fiancée. Phil's main objective was obviously the same as Trevor's: attention and money.

I tried not to focus on my anger at Phil and continued on with my goal despite his. I would have to go forward and try to get the money from the Caymans and hope it would pull me through until I could get something up and going.

❧

We stayed in Tegucigalpa a month, making appointments with attorneys, Human Rights, and Immigration. I was prepared with documents, plus River and Nocona, to back up my story. I was amazed at the response and support we were getting from many organizations. Human Rights was very strong in Honduras. The head person, Dr. Leo Valederes was constantly putting his life in danger to protect the innocent in the country. His name was front page news frequently as he went against big names to protect the innocent.

We finally got a meeting with Dr. Valederes, and he stated he would do all he could to help us. We had found favor and he quickly made us an appointment with the U.S. Embassy. Dr. Valederes let us know Honduras had not entered in with the U.S. Hague Convention Treaty. We had protection to a degree. The U.S. could not come in on its own and pick us up without Honduras agreeing. Thank God, so far, Honduras was definitely not agreeing! This, too, had to be God, since I was totally ignorant when choosing countries! However, I had a mission, and we obviously had God on our side!

On the day we arrived on the mainland of Honduras, it was evident many of the residents on the mainland of Honduras lived in poverty, yet the U.S. Embassy was majestic and beautiful in appearance.

The U.S. Embassy was supposed to be our protector, but we felt uneasy as we entered the large building with a representative from Human Rights by our side. We were seated in a large lobby. While waiting, I glanced around at the many people working there. I began to notice individuals coming out of their offices. They would look at us, then return as though trying to decide what steps they should take. There was definite tension in the air. It was obvious they all knew who we were and why we were there.

We were soon called into an office. An Embassy worker came over and asked if it was okay for Nocona to go with her for some cookies and a drink. It sounded innocent enough, so I said okay. When I saw Nocona go with her, I felt deep down I had made a mistake.

Our Human Rights' representative introduced all of us then went over our situation. I observed each person present as he spoke, trying to analyze the Embassy's intent. The meeting was rather strange. At times I felt there was concern for us, but I could tell the Embassy official was picking his words. It began to look as though it was a no-win situation, regardless of what we said or how much proof we presented. He went on to say many calls were being made by Trevor's sister insisting on our return. He said they were also getting calls from congressmen and senators in the U.S., but did not say at the time who they were. I knew Laura's husband had political strength and she would use every weapon she could find to go against us.

There was a very large, dark-skinned man standing behind the desk of the main spokesperson. He stood to the right of the U.S. Embassy speaker. I found it odd that the man was standing there and watched to see just what part he played in this whole scenario. I spoke of our appreciation of the Human Rights organization and others that had helped us.

At that moment, the large man burst out as though he was outraged at my statement! He made a sharp derogatory remark about the Human Rights, adding we shouldn't be looking to them for help. I was shocked at his statement and looked over to see the response of our representative. He was totally composed as though nothing was said!

At that point I found it necessary to once again introduce the representative accompanying us. It was obvious someone did not understand his title. He was the Human Rights! The large-framed man was totally embarrassed, but continued talking in an attempt to correct his blunder. It obviously made the situation awkward for the Embassy. Our representative continued to plead our case.

As we left the office, I knew deep down something wasn't right about this meeting, but I couldn't put my finger on it. The official appeared to be speaking out of both sides of his mouth, not letting me know what the result would be or where he stood. At times I felt he was deeply concerned about our problem and other times it appeared he was going where the political strength was, and it wasn't looking like it was in our favor.

After we left the building, Nocona excitedly told us they had taken pictures of her. I knew then they were not our friends nor would we be getting any help out of them. It was now obvious we would have to dig deeper for help.

We made more meetings with attorneys and Human Rights. We continued to stay in a small hotel in Tegucigalpa. We were in the Centro section of the city with a lot of restaurants and businesses surrounding us. The nights were long with all the fireworks and loud Spanish music, making it hard to sleep. Thank goodness there were no more loud, roaring generators. They obviously had overcome the problems they were having on our first arrival to Honduras.

During the day I enjoyed the sidewalk markets with lots of fresh vegetables and fruits. We seldom found this on the Island, so I was enjoying this part of the stay. We would go for lunch sometimes at a quaint little outdoor restaurant close by. There were tropical plants and trellises in the garden area with a couple rabbits hopping around. It was a very relaxing atmosphere that I frequented whenever possible.

There were many small retail businesses and restaurants, some actually being American. Our advisors had cautioned us with safety tips. To be obscure was out of the question since we were the only white people amongst a sea of dark-skinned bodies. We didn't go out that much, but I used every precaution. I was fearful of River coming and going on her own.

One day we were walking in search of a place for lunch. Suddenly, I felt a sense of danger. There was a small group of kids approaching us from behind. It was a street gang. They rushed us from the back. For some reason, I grabbed Nocona and crouched under River JoNey. River pushed me and Nocona into a small bakery. The teens became outraged, grabbing River's cap. What they didn't know was the now beautiful blonde still had enough tomboy in her. Laced with a past of karate, she quickly chased the young gang and retrieved her cap. Locals stood along the sidewalks in awe at the Gringa. Each enjoyed the whole scenario, yet no one offered help. They all applauded as River recovered her cap!

୧୭

We had more meetings set up with Immigration the following Monday. To get through another weekend, River insisted we go to see Honduras play against Costa Rica in a big soccer game in Tegucigalpa. I thought that sounded innocent enough so I took her up on the idea. We were both getting totally bored of the small apartment with nothing on the television that was entertaining or that I understood.

As we arrived at the large stadium, I noticed right off no one had children with them. Nocona was the only one present. I was very dressed up with a colorful long skirt and blouse. River was in her usual shorts and

Honduras Soccer Game
Tequcigalpa

sandals. As we made our way to the stadium seats, hundreds of people were pouring in. Little carts pulled by vendors immediately made their way to the front and began selling their tamales, baleatas, and beer. As we sat down, the people crowded all around us. We were sitting like sardines amongst a sea of people. As the game started, everyone was loud and screaming as they drank their beer and cheered Honduras on.

Suddenly, I began to feel this hand going up and down my leg. At first I thought it was accidental. I looked over to see this little old man with few teeth staring at me, with his hand rubbing my leg. I pushed his hand off and he did it again. This time I became a little more assertive. The game grew more intense, with the crowd's roaring becoming more upset as Costa Rica continued to score.

I began to feel beer on my head and going down the back of my dress. As the crowd became more aggressive, it was obvious it was not looking good for Honduras or us! People were throwing their beer, then they began to throw fireworks from the top of the stands. The vendors frantically began to run with their little carts. We got up and tried to make our way out, but the crowd was now starting fires in the stands! We finally made it out. Needless to say, that was the last Honduran soccer game I attended!

ࢥ

It was now time for our visit with the head of Immigration. We sat in the lobby awaiting our turn. I said a short prayer, not knowing what to expect. We were soon called to enter the office. The air-conditioned room felt awesome! Cold air was a first in a long time, and it felt good. River and I sat in the two chairs in front of the desk. Nocona took the small sofa behind us. To my surprise, at the large desk sat a very distinguished lady named Angelina Ulloa. For some reason, I was expecting an older man. Angelina had a uniqueness and professionalism about her that definitely set her apart. I immediately began to present our case. As River JoNey and I desperately made our plea, pouring our heart and soul out to this prominent lady, I began to realize her attention was not on us, but totally focused on Nocona! I looked back, and Nocona was enjoying the coolness of the air conditioning on the large leather couch, occasionally standing on her head. Nocona's red hair was flowing down her face. Air conditioning had obviously made her energy level pick up.

Unsure of how this was being taken, I knew I only had minutes and went forward with our plea. By the time the meeting was over, we had found favor! Angelina's statement was, *"I will personally make sure no one takes you out of Honduras!"* She warned us on the way out that we needed to get a residency as quickly as possible. We continued to gain favor with people in prominent positions, but obviously not with our own U.S. Embassy.

After a month of working with officials on the mainland, I was now needing to return back to the Island. I had run completely out of money. Phil was refusing my calls. This was truly embarrassing! Desperate, I took out a loan with new friends, reassuring them I had an account in the Caymans. They helped us until I was able to wire money from my Cayman account and repay them. I placed more calls to Phil, hoping he would send my money, yet it never happened.

On our return to the Island, we began to have frequent visits from the U.S. Embassy. We knew we had no choice so we tolerated each visit. The more they came, the more it became evident we could not trust them. With each visit it was never what they could do for us. They continued to speak of many calls from Laura and the same U.S. Congressman and Senators from Texas.

River had previously told me Laura's husband had big parties at his ranch and was very politically connected. I later found out through U.S. Embassy files the names of the U.S. Congressman and Senators.

Throughout the whole scenario, Trevor appeared to be a silent partner. Laura was the main person in pursuit of getting Nocona back. Trevor was mentioned only occasionally.

Seashell Prisoners
CHAPTER 11

Every day seemed to grow more intense, yet I went forward with my plan, daily asking, *Who can I trust?* We knew from day one we could be picked up at any given time, but there continued to be something in the air that was unexplainable. Not knowing that much about God, I still felt that strong presence inside. It continued to state, "Frances just keep going forward, don't even look back." I really had no other choice than to follow the voice. I had absolutely no plan or original ideas of my own or really any feelings toward anything. All I knew for sure was one of my best friends had obviously betrayed me, and now the U.S. Embassy was monitoring us.

River and I daily made attempts to look at the lighter side of living on an island. I would sit back at times and think, I can now relate to Gilligan's Island with all the cultural changes we have gone through. Regardless, the Island was now becoming more and more difficult for me. With each summer month, the heat became more intense. Every now and then a glimmer of family and friends would enter my mind, but the daily stress and pressures had a way of pushing that thought to the side. It was like there was nothing I could do to help myself, much less my family, so it made it easier just to block everyone out of my mind.

The water was beautiful, but up to this point I had not taken the time to dive or become a part of any social activities other than attend church. My first priority was to protect Nocona and then, hopefully, one day bring normalcy back into our lives.

I finally purchased some snorkeling equipment, took off a day, and went snorkeling. I was amazed at how beautiful the corals were and how shallow they were. I had never seen with all my travels coral reefs so shallow and so easy to access from the shore.

As I studied the Island and its potential, I knew I had to do something different. I would go forward and build a small hotel, yet not copy the existing hotels run by the Islanders. That way my endeavor would not affect the existing residents and their means of making a living. Life appeared to be going well for them with many backpackers providing their income. I had a vision of drawing a different crowd. I felt like every tourist would love this Island, not just the backpackers that were predominant in West End. Roatan was so beautiful and had so much to offer not only divers, but snorkelers, fishermen, and adventure seekers as well. The coral reefs were the best I had ever seen and were listed on the Internet as the second in the world in beauty.

I had traveled many times with divers to various locations in the Caribbean. I knew deep down this Island had so much potential that some of the Islanders possibly were not even aware of it. Maybe in some small way I could be a part of helping bring this feature out. Yes, I would take a big chance with my construction and hope to bring in a completely different group to West End.

Nothing about it made sense, being our lives were in total limbo. We could be picked up by the F.B.I. within the next hour, but something just kept saying, *Frances just go forward*, so I did.

I was sitting down one night in the small cabin. I began to draw out on a paper sack exactly what I wanted the hotel to look like. No, I had no talents in architectural work, but it just flowed. The drawings were rough and crude, but I knew what I wanted. Instead of small unfinished rooms I would go with large rooms, tiled kitchens and baths, large decks with hammocks, etc., totally finished on the inside. With all the research and other home-building horror stories, I worked diligently to avoid the same situations.

Douglas Collins, Frances & River JoNey

No one could prepare me for the soon-upcoming nightmare I would encounter with this project. I think back now and know I truly witnessed the Pits of Hell, and that would be putting it mildly. By the middle of the project, I knew I had made a grave mistake with choice of contractors. He had the skills, but obviously no integrity, abusing the money for the project and definitely taking advantage of a female entrepreneur. By the middle of the project, the contractor disappeared, leaving his helper, Douglas Collins; other workers; and myself to figure the rest out! I was totally overwhelmed! The man never said anything to any of us, but just didn't show up after the end of the week.

On the lighter side, I stepped back one day, and began taking pictures. I found it amusing and immediately claimed Mr. Collins as a relative, even though he was very dark skinned and I was rather white. Thank God, Mr. Collins was a righteous man and easy to work with. After a few days, between Douglas, myself, and my brother we took over the project until it was finished. I realized almost all the workers on most construction projects had no knowledge of finishing work, since the majority of homes and rooms rented out were not finished.

My brother, Thadd, had flown in and took charge of the electrical work with the help of Tony, a very skilled electrician from West End. With no previous experience on finishing work, between River JoNey and I, we practiced on the walls with texturing until we got it down, then we taught the workers. Douglas and his helpers went forward with all the carpenter work. Like somewhat of a miracle, the project went forward.

Curiosity was obviously abounding. Every week locals and Island businessmen checked on us to see how the Texas ladies were coming along on their project. Now that I think back, there were probably many bets made on the side as to whether we would make it or not, knowing the many building problems on the Island.

We decided to move into the building, being we were on the project all the time. We were always there late at night. There were no doors on the building, but we had running water and electricity. Obviously, by some much Higher Power and a lot of perseverance, this horrendous experience within a year took on the countenance of a beautiful small hotel. Douglas Collins, myself, my brother Thadd, and River all stood back in awe at the accomplishment!

To my amazement, by the end of the project, the hotel wasn't only very beautiful, it was obviously a showplace for West End and the Island. People continued to drive to West End to view the new "Gringa Project."

Casa Calico Hotel

To finish off the little hotel, River JoNey used her artistic creativeness. She sketched out a logo of a cat with a dive flag, which was soon a beautiful sign with the name, "Casa Calico," named after our little Rican Kitty. We were the perfect fit for West End!

Thadd originally had come to oversee the wiring of the hotel. With all the problems, his stay was extended to helping throughout the project, but it was now time for him to leave. This day was difficult, leaving me feeling as if everything were once again back totally and completely on my shoulders.

Now I was working equally as hard as I began to take in tourists. I often thought of the remark I made on a dive trip I took to Little Cayman ten years back. The whole week of my stay, I had watched a female resort owner labor from morning to night. The lady was exhausted at the end of each day. As I sat on the beach one day observing her, I made the statement, "I would never have a resort!" Now, I was beginning to think, *Maybe I need to stop saying the word, "Never!"*

Casa Calico Rooms

Casa Calico

Casa Calico

Throughout the year of building Casa Calico, young Spanish boys would bring birds by the building project. Each day I tried to explain to them that after I finished the project I would purchase a yellow-naped parrot since they were easy to teach words to. "Do not bring me the green-headed parrots referred to as conures! I don't want the green heads," I kept telling them.

Regardless, they continued to arrive with the little green parrots perched on their arms each day. After many interruptions, I began to shut the door when I saw them coming. As soon as Casa Calico was finished, the Spanish boys were at my door once again with their little green parrots. This time I was rude, refusing their birds. I explained one more time: "I want to purchase a yellow-headed parrot. Don't bring the green heads!"

The following day, the Spanish boys once again appeared at my door—this time with the yellow-headed parrots. I smiled and they smiled as we agreed on a price. I was so happy I purchased two instead of one.

One of the birds came up missing within a week, so we named the remaining bird Petie. Petie was mean, not allowing anyone to touch him. We continued to warn the tourists, but many ignored us and always got bit.

Casa Calico

One day as I worked on my computer a young man strolled in. Our back and front door were always open. As I turned and looked at him, he said, "Frances!"

It took a moment, then I realized it was a young man from Mauriceville, Texas, that River had gone to school with. I was rather startled at his being here and was not sure what to say. River was resting in the next room, but heard his voice and came running out to see him.

Steve Yerby was working at one of the dive shops at West End and quickly became a frequent visitor of Casa Calico. Steve would lay in the hammocks on the porch and play with Petie with each visit. We all watched in awe, since Petie didn't allow any of us to hold him. On one particular day while I was working in the kitchen, Steve was sitting in the hammock once again....playing with Petie watching him do all his tricks. All of a sudden, Steve hollered, "Frances, you need to come see something. The yellow paint is coming off of Petie's head!"

I was momentarily in shock. Everyone laughed, realizing the young Spanish guys had definitely taken advantage of me on the purchase. I paid the price for the yellow-naped parrot, but obviously didn't get the right bird.

It wasn't long before Petie was trailing me daily, wanting me to hold him. He rode on my shoulder and frequently ate with us. He hung out during the heat of the day in the banana and coconut trees, and in the evening he visited with the guests upstairs. Within a few months, Petie fell in love with me, wanting to ride on my shoulder daily. Actually, he had stolen everyone's hearts, with tourists taking pictures with him and looking forward to seeing Petie on each return visit to the Island. Petie's value was beyond a dollar figure now. Petie didn't need to talk, his personality definitely filled that gap. Petie worked daily on new tricks to do to get attention and his favorite snacks out of everyone.

Steve Yerby & River JoNey

The name Casa Calico quickly grew in fame along with our reputation. Casa Calico was now the hot spot on the Island with large, beautiful rooms overlooking the Bay. All of our guests loved the cool, spacious rooms with large, front and back porches, hammocks, and tropical breezes blowing across the decks and through the rooms. A winding, wooden stairway went from the ground up on both ends of the front of the building, taking guests to the top floor. The kitchen and baths were fully tiled with hardwood floors. The rooms could accommodate as many as six people.

Nocona along with our new pets—Petie (parrot), Puffer (dog), and King Kally (cat)—also grew in fame as they daily entertained the guests.

Word of mouth spread through Costa Rica, Guatemala, and Mexico, and the rooms filled—with no advertisement, no telephone, no faxes, no emails—with what was better known as "walk-ins." Everyone loved Casa Calico! With my background in the supermarket and various organizations, my guests were treated special, as I worked hard to meet their every whim.

The bottom floor of the hotel was one big open room with hardwood floors. There were large posts dividing the kitchen from the living area with a wide assortment of pots and pans hanging to the side of the kitchen. The kitchen counters had beautiful, dark, green tiles with a large, wooden, handmade, preparation table with matching tile. This table divided the kitchen from the living area. There was a large picnic table with benches in the middle of the room with swirling ceiling fans hanging above them. The table had an Indian handmade cloth on it, with a large piece of glass covering to protect it. The Indian cloth was another item River had chosen to bring with her from the U.S., so I put it to work.

The beautiful, handmade, double doors going out front were always open and so were the windows, allowing the breeze to flow across the room. All the wood in the two-story structure was from Honduras. I found it unusual that my guests were constantly bragging on the beauty of the wood in the building. All the windows, doors, and cabinets were also handmade. The shiny, mahogany-wood floors gave the room a warm feeling that seemed to make everyone feel welcome.

Most of our friends and new guests would enter Casa Calico from the back door, being it was the closest to the road. The front entrance faced the Bay and the double doors were always open. As the guests made their way into the large open room, they frequently checked out the latest seashells I had collected, viewing them from a glass cake cover in the entranceway. Over to the side of the room, I had a couch that could be used for a bed when needed.

My office was a simple, handmade, wooden counter with a five-foot area next to a window. That is where I did all my computer work and business transactions with the tourists. King Kally always sat on the counter as I checked each guest in and out. She was like a little statue. Sometimes my guests would do a double-take to make sure the cat was alive! For some unknown reason, Nocona called our calico cat King Kally, even though it was a female. King Kally pretty much ruled the place, coming and going throughout the hotel at will.

All the windows had shutters and screens that were kept open. They were only closed at night, since the airflow was so much better with them open. If King Kally got shut out at night, she would be scratching at my bedroom window, and I always let her in. She would crawl into my bed and immediately go to the foot of the bed to sleep.

All was going well with the business. Nocona was enjoying Sister Laura's grandchildren next door and right off claimed Naomi as her best friend. I continued to hear from individuals back home and things seemed to be going well.

Then I receive a message that Anna was getting married to Brandon, her high school sweetheart. Knowing Brandon was from a wonderful family and was good to her was extremely comforting, yet the fact that I would not be able to take my rightful place in this special event haunted me.

&

My good friend, Ashley, sent word she and her daughter, Kalin, were coming for a visit. Nocona and I were so excited to see anyone from home, especially close friends. Kalin had grown to be a beautiful child. For a short time after their arrival, everything felt normal once again. I took some time off and we were having an awesome week together swimming and snorkeling. It was nice laughing again with old friends.

Late one afternoon as Ashley and I were visiting, two young men stepped into the hotel. They were not typical tourists even though they were making every attempt to act out the part as they made inquiries about purchasing property and places to eat. Ashley and I immediately went forward, making conversation. Our immediate goal was to eventually see what their true intentions were. Ashley and I had been on many trips together. We were both skilled with a gift of perception and found these two to be a small challenge.

The two men inquired of restaurant choices, then asked where we would be eating. Once we told them, they remarked they would be dining at the same location which was on the other side of the Island.

On arrival to the outdoor restaurant, the two men asked to sit with us under the palapa. We knew their intentions were not on the up and up, but we were not concerned since so many people surrounded us. Ashley and I went about the evening laughing and talking as though it was a normal get-together. It was one of few outings that I had the opportunity to simply have fun. I was not going to let anyone spoil it, not even these guys. As the evening progressed, Ashley and I exited to the restroom. We went over our thoughts about the two plotting the next turn, and laughed about it. The men were well dressed with a look of businessmen. We continued to find the situation amusing and somewhat of a test. By the end of the evening, the guys knew we were on to them, admitting they were investigators from the States. Their mission was to check up on Frances Collins Harris and get as much information as they could. We all laughed even though it probably should not have been a funny moment, but what else could we do? They obviously had a good evening, picked up the meal ticket, and we all called it a night.

Ashley wanted to see the mainland. There were some things I was needing for the hotel, so I took a day off and we left for the mainland of Honduras. We rode on the very boat we originally arrived on. I wasn't aware that there was a huge festival going on in LeCeiba, but we finally found a small run-down place to stay for the night. We definitely wanted to take it all in, so we watched the parades, did the tour of LeCeiba, had a bite to eat, and then made our way through the large crowds to the hotel.

The room was small, with Ashley's bed being closer to the door. There was a lot of hoopla going on in the halls with all the people celebrating the biggest festival of the year. Finally, we went to sleep, only to be awakened by the door rattling. As we looked up, we saw a man's hand trying to take the chain lock off the door. Ashley immediately screamed and slammed the man's hand in the door. Somehow he got it out and we made another attempt to reinforce the lock on the door. I had been in Honduras long enough that for some reason this didn't bother me. I just turned over and remarked, "Welcome to Honduras," and went back to sleep. Needless to say, Ashley got her money's worth in the country during its biggest festival, and was ready to get back to the Island!

Fame, as always, has its problems. The comforts and conveniences of Casa Calico soon filtered through every dive shop, hotel, and restaurant. The news spread like wildfire across the Island that Casa Calico's business was booming! Competition began to surface using similar ideas. Many foreign investors were now making their presence on the Island. Several came and toured Casa Calico. They were obviously impressed with the concept, boldly stating as they left, "We are going to build on the same order!" I took a deep breath, knowing the effect it would have on my business.

The need for communication was not only a top priority, but now, of grave importance! There were quite a few Islanders in West End with telephones, most not working half the time. I had applied over and over at Hondutel, our local telephone company, for a phone, offering whatever was the going price, but for some reason, year after year, I continued to be overlooked. After seven years, the man let me know I reminded him of a real estate lady in West End. I was told the lady had become so outraged with him, she jumped over his desk and attacked him. Needless to say, I knew exactly who he was referring to and ... I never got the phone!

Kris Holt was quite an aggressive real estate agent in West End. She was the only volunteer I could get for a Christmas program I started in the community. The first Christmas program was a total disaster, but Kris and I had lots of laughs and, as everything else in my life, it was quite memorable.

Kris was known for her many friends on the Island and always had a funny story to tell. I always thought the best one was about herself. I'm not sure if she ever told the story about her last investor she took around the Island. From the tale I heard, while she was showing a man named Al a piece of prime property, Kris backed off a small hill and rolled the SUV she was driving. Surprisingly, she landed the deal and Al purchased the property.

Despite the daily problems it was like a day never went by that something funny didn't happen to someone on the Island. It quickly became the main element in each day that kept you going through the worst of days.

Times got harder for us with the influx of foreign entrepreneurs saturating West End. The little Island of Roatan was becoming more and more known to the world. My hotel was located approximately half a mile from the entrance of West End on the Mangrove Bight. All the property on the Island was growing in value. Islanders on the beach in West End began selling off their homes to foreign entrepreneurs. Within a few months the new owners quickly converted the properties into small resorts. Casa Calico was losing all new walk-ins. With no phone, I was now totally dependent on word of mouth. The same large rooms with tile kitchens were now spotted up and down the West End beach. Casa Calico was only getting return customers or the overflow from peak weekends. Everyone loved the rooms and the fresh cool breeze off the Bay flowing through the rooms, but now, I just had to get better situated with communication to be able to compete. I was desperately needing the Internet for booking my rooms.

The phrase, *Third World*, was now becoming more defined and stressful in various ways. There were many problems living on an Island trying to communicate with authorities and fellow Islanders. The only sure thing you could totally depend on from year to year was no electricity during peak tourist weeks and sometimes no water! The quickest lesson I learned in Honduras was that what may have been normal or logical to me wasn't logical at all to most! Any problem that came up pretty much had to be resolved within yourself. Everything worked so opposite to the U.S. that many days I would do a mental check, making sure I was okay.

Town meetings were held in West End, but usually ended up in more confusion, yet they were always quite memorable and entertaining, totally Island-style. They were held at Mr. Orties and Ms. Gretas by the Tienda. They were full of color and drama with few problems solved. The extremely hot summers grew more and more intense as so many problems seemed to go unresolved.

I continued to go forward daily with my one and only reason being that I was so sure that Roatan was God's plan, not mine. I knew I was where God wanted me to be. I was now taking it one hour at a time, practicing my new faith walk with each new day. I blocked out everything that appeared hopeless and futile around me, even the thought of being on the F.B.I.'s Most Wanted list.

I began to go snorkeling and visiting around the Island on occasion. As I began to relax, I often wondered, would family back home just forget me or would I ever get to see them again? Questions continuously flowed through my mind.

The heat became more intense during the middle of the day. In July and August we would take a break around lunch time and make lemon grass tea. We sat in hammocks until the day cooled off. That was my time to relax and sometimes people watch. I observed the Islanders going about their daily activities despite the heat. It really didn't seem to affect them as it did me.

I was learning each day about Island herbs, and lemon grass was my personal lifesaver. It was a very refreshing drink with a sedative effect, helping me get through each day. I noticed my European guests digging up the roots and using them in various recipes. They were obviously familiar with it. The herb grew like grass so there was always plenty.

Beautiful mangos were everywhere on the Island with the taste being different from tree to tree. The people were the same, with each village being different. People on one end would be very serious while on the other end, all smiles and warmth. The languages varied—some being English, Spanish, or Garifuna, and some just very broken.

I didn't really see that much extreme poverty. Most had plenty to eat and a roof over their heads. Each were quite content, enjoying their simple lifestyle surrounded by family. They seemed to have an ingredient that many in the U.S. had lost over the years. Actually, most all of my guests, no matter what country they were from, lived a fast life and enjoyed the simple laid back Island life.

I remember one guest when he slowly got out of the hammock to make his way back to the airport, he sadly stated he had to get back to reality. I stated "No, this is reality." The Islanders never got in a hurry and lived each day with a much slower pace than most countries.

The foreigners were just the opposite of most of the Islanders, all partying, diving, snorkeling, and enjoying the night life. I found it amusing that the residents tolerated them so well, seeing the difference in lifestyles. I enjoyed sitting back and observing everyone's personalities. There was never a dull moment in West End.

Some of the foreigners had little bars on the water with grass roofs. As Nocona and I walked the beach road in the evenings, we would stop and visit with them occasionally. Nocona adapted quickly and continued to grow and learn with each new day.

On our arrival, it was hard to tell exactly where I stood with everyone, but I knew I just had to be me. Each denomination had a strong understanding of the Bible, but worshiped in different ways. I never questioned anyone. I just loved visiting with the different churches and learning what God meant to them. With many, the smiles and warmth would overwhelm you.

In West End, the huge smile of Pastor Eddly Bush not only was a welcome treat for us, but soon became a tourist attraction! Everyone not only enjoyed watching him, but found his whole family intriguing as they walked the sandy beach road. Day in and day out one would see them with either their fishing lures or Bibles on their way to church.

Harriet & Pastor Eddly Bush

As time went on, I came to understand and appreciate more and more the strong bond the Islanders had towards each other. Watching them interact day to day with their families was beautiful, but it was a constant reminder of the loss of our family and friends. The ladies daily walked up and down the beach road, exchanging tasty Island dishes. They had craft classes, or just enjoyed visiting with each other. One could hear them passing the day away talking about the latest events of the Island. It always brought a smile to me as I compared them to the people in the U.S. We were definitely out of touch, not taking time for each other. With most Islanders, talking softly was not in their vocabulary. To get the attention of their neighbor or children, they hollered, always getting an immediate response. They were all extremely nice and protective towards us, making us feel like family. Most knew our situation in the U.S.

છા

I soon grew tired of having Petie ride on my shoulder. Petie was becoming as aggressive as a Rottweiler, as people would approach me. I was getting concerned for my guests the more protective he became. To resolve my problem, I found a friend for Petie.

I had purchased Ronnie from a local bar off of Mangrove Bight. Petie right off hated Ronnie, so Ronnie daily perched at the end of the porch, spending his day mimicking me or people at the bar he had previously come from. He had a cough that sounded just like a smoker's cough.

At the end of the day, Ronnie hollered for Nocona. If Nocona didn't respond, he got louder and louder and began screaming, "Nocona Lynn!" The tourists all thought of it as being funny, but it did have a way of making me stop and think how I might sound to those around me.

I would always know when someone was approaching the back entrance of the hotel. Ronnie would say, "Helloooo," or sing Happy Birthday to them. Until they got to know him, the tourists stayed confused as they looked for someone to help them.

Petie & Ronnie

As Nocona grew, it didn't take her long to see who the good cooks were on our end of the village. Nocona could frequently be seen either on the Islanders' porches or at Welba's Restaurant, enjoying their delicious Island food. Lily, our neighbor in front of us, always had a big pot of rice con pollo or iguana cooking. Nocona knew exactly what time it was ready. Each day the breeze from the Bay kept the aroma flowing through our hotel. Blackie, Marty, and their family lived right across the road from Welba's. Nocona played with their daughter Tashana and seemed to know exactly which day the fried chicken was on the menu.

With each week that passed, Nocona was taking on more and more of the Islanders' ways. Everyone treated her as if she were their own, even to the point of disciplining her. By the second week on the Island, she had picked up the Island talk, sounding just like the other children. There was only one word in the children's conversation that I daily tried to delete from Nocona's vocabulary. Everyone used the word *molest* as in an innocent way as though someone is harassing you. Nocona being full of drama, picked up on the word the first day and used it frequently. I tried to explain to her the importance of dropping that from her vocabulary. With the frequent visits from the Embassy and one day return to the States, it could definitely present a problem!

Nocona swam almost every day. If she wasn't in the water, or climbing trees, she was at her friend Naomi's house. For the first few years we watched hundreds of tourists, but seldom saw the Islanders in the water. I often wondered if they really understood what a prize their beautiful Island was! Some had been to the U.S., but most had never left Honduras.

When business was slow, I would take a few hours off and lay out on a raft in the bay. It was one of the few times I could lean back, look up at the beautiful sky, and let my mind relax and reflect. I remember thinking back on the days right after I left the U.S. with Nocona. I recalled the young fearless family in Louisiana with the small girls, that encircled us and prayed every night as they hid us out. How neat it would be if the girls could see what a beautiful place God had brought us to for Nocona's safety. I wanted very much for them to see the results of their prayers.

After relaxing in the water, I would always float over to the Half Moon Bay Resort, and Mark or one of the friendly waiters would bring my order right up to the water at the end of the dock. These days were priceless!

One day as I lay out in the water, I noticed Nocona skipping down the sandy beach. I hollered at her to see if she needed money for lunch. Her reply was, *"No, I have money; Ganna, the resort owner, paid me and Tashana to leave his resort!"*

Shocked at her reply, I asked what she was doing. Her reply was, "We were sweeping in Don Renee's office and the dust was going everywhere."

I couldn't help but laugh, knowing the owner.

That evening I took Nocona back to the resort for dinner so I could apologize. The owner came over to the table with Nocona's favorite virgin Piña Colada. We all laughed about the day! That was definitely one of the better moments!

❧

When I first purchased the property, we had a surveyor survey the property. His name was Carlos Ortica and he was from LeCeiba on the mainland of Honduras. Ortica was unusually nice, with a warm friendly personality. River and I right off gravitated to him and quickly became good friends. Each time Ortica came to the Island, he kept insisting we go with him and see his property in Trujillo, which was on the mainland by the Sea.

River and I, after many requests, decided to join him, being he was so insistent, wanting us to meet his family. Arrangements were made and River, Nocona, and I left for the mainland of Honduras. Ortica was very happy we were with him and drove us across the country, stopping at various family members, finally reaching Trujillo.

Everyone was hungry after several visits, so we stopped to have lunch. I noticed right off the restaurant was very clean and neat. I wasn't that hungry, so I decided to have something light. Later we went on to Ortica's property. We walked his property, then that evening went to a nice resort in Trujillo for dinner. We were to stay at his family's home after dinner. We all went upstairs to the dining area. We were exhausted from the long hot day, and placed our order for dinner.

Suddenly, I began to feel very bad. I excused myself and went back downstairs to the restroom. I became ill so fast I could hardly stand up. I walked out of the restroom and made it up to the front desk and asked for a room. The walls in that room were thin, and I could hear the television on in the next room. The noise was making my problem worse. I leaned over and called the front desk and asked for another room. After two room changes, I finally got a room that was quiet. I was so ill. I knew I had food poisoning.

When I didn't return, River and Ortica started searching for me. Out of frustration, they described me to the desk clerk. He told them I had gotten a room.

I was up all night in great pain. The next day I was very weak, but able to leave. Everyone had a good laugh, but it was far from funny that night. That is the closest encounter I had experienced with death.

Ortica introduced us to a lot of his family and as Ortica was, so they were all very friendly. Throughout the weekend I heard him say over and over and over, *"My house is your house!"* I had never heard that before and could not comprehend why anyone would say that. Were they really that nice? We then made our way back to the Island of Roatan.

Working daily with tourism we were quickly meeting people from all over the world. We had now come to know a young German entrepreneur name Wolfgang. He had a beautiful dive boat that he kept docked on Half Moon Bay. Through an Alternative Ministry group, Wolfgang had come to know the Lord. On a couple occasions I would join Wolfgang on slow days when there were not that many tourists. Wolfgang knew if I dove I would make sure I was the last to go in the water. After so many years of previous diving, I considered diving with beginners to be very stressful. I pretty much went in the opposite direction of the other divers on each entrance into the water. It was nice, relaxing and seeking out the beautiful fish and turtles. Most of the time I was diving thirty-foot dives or less, since the coral reefs were shallow.

Several years later, Wolfgang asked me to go on a dive trip around the Island with his group. At this time Harriett Bush, a beautiful young Islander, was helping me a lot with the hotel. Her father, Bro. Eddly, was the pastor of the Baptist Church in West End. Nocona loved Harriett and her very feminine ways, so Nocona stayed with Harriett, and I took the day off and joined Wolfgang and his group on the dive.

Halfway around the Island, I began to get very seasick. I finally decided to call it a day and swam back to land. I dried off and took a taxi back to West End. The Island was so unique in that way. No matter where you were, you were really not that far from home and would definitely know someone around every curve.

Everyone in West End was distinctive in their own way, but I continued to look around and wonder just where I fit in. It was like my choices were limited to going to church every night or hanging around in the bars. Somehow neither seemed to be me. The bar owners were a little too high energy, and the Christians were unusually quiet, reserved, and intimidating with their Bible knowledge. Even the Baptists dressed extremely modest. Actually, all denominations dressed pretty much the same, which I found to be quite different than the States.

I continued with my usual sleeveless dresses, being the heat was so intense. Yes, I definitely used lipstick on special occasions, trying to maintain a little feminine side of myself. As far as the makeup went, I didn't have a problem living without that. The heat did away with that quickly, so I never bothered with it.

I had to be me and somehow everyone would just have to accept me as I was. Actually, with all the changes, at that point I was not sure who I was anymore or who I might be tomorrow, and often wondered if God even knew! River JoNey and Nocona were quite different. They not only related, but seemed to find common ground with everyone they met. It all continued to be a perfect fit for them.

Daily I racked my brain as to why God would place me here. River was more like the tourists, enjoying the nightlife occasionally, and now playing on the ladies' softball team. She certainly wasn't showing any missionary material, neither was Nocona or myself. Did God make a mistake? All the Christian Islanders were in church every time the doors opened and knew the Bible backward and forward. Where could we possibly fit in if this was God's plan? I still made attempts to study the Bible, but it just was not all coming together for me.

One day a missionary, totally unannounced, came to stay with us from Guatemala. As soon as I opened the door, this stranger took one look at Nocona playing on the floor and profoundly stated, *"This child will be singing prophetically one day!"*

With each month, I never knew what to expect. Strange things continued to happen. I began to log events and thoughts in a computer that Thadd had sent me. Maybe this would help me make sense of all of this.

❧

Daily, I observed the Island culture, finding more unusual and humorous incidents. The big event of the Island was baseball. The huge West End field lay directly behind Casa Calico. Ball teams from around the Island would gather on Saturdays and Sunday afternoons to compete with the West End team. We could watch the games from our back decks. The game was never normal, always guaranteeing a full-fledged fight within minutes. Sometimes players brandished knives and on occasion even guns! At one ball game, the fight was over a juguito (a popsicle in a bag).

Since my hotel was close, I found myself constantly having to scold the men. They were either urinating on my water cisterns or throwing their trash on my property. Everything outside had to be anchored down or it would probably come up missing at some point during the game. The tourists on the top floor found it amusing, yet I thought of it as ghastly. In time I became more desensitized, with almost everything becoming normal, humorous, and less annoying. With the influx of tourism, new rules were introduced, not allowing any more misbehavior between the players. The baseball games became more civilized, but less amusing!

❧

I began to meet more people in different ministries around the Island. In a weird chain of events, I was talked into going on a mission trip with a powerful women's ministry into the Mosquito Coast. Phyliss, a new

Phyliss, Sister Harriett, Frances & Women's Conference missionaries to Mosquito Coast

property owner and acquaintance, had asked me to introduce her to people that did mission work on the mainland. I took her to Oakridge and introduced her to Sister Harriett Kelly. Sister Harriett was well known for organizing many Women's Conferences on the mainland of Honduras. I sat and listened as they discussed the next trip and then set a date. When asked if I would assist them, I quickly replied, "No!"

The next thing I knew, I was boarding the plane. This was totally not me! I always hated the heat and roughing it! Everything about this trip was not good and definitely was not me. We were now headed into the deepest, roughest part of the country, the *Mosquito Coast*, and I could not believe they talked me into going!

Sister Eleanor Cooper and Sister Harriett Kelly were over the ministry team. They had picked up chickens and an assortment of food for the Women's Conference to be held in an area called Palacios. For what reason I was there, I did not know. I sat back and observed as everyone went forward very seriously with everything they did. They were all big ministry people. I only knew a few Bible stories, but I had experienced that one big God encounter and felt maybe that should count for something!

We all entered the crude tiny aircraft early in the morning. I sat towards the back of the plane. The small plane alone, built for race horses, was an experience of its own. My number one prayer was that we would just make it there! I looked over to see one of the Honduran ladies sitting near a gallon of honey, right by the aisle in the middle of the plane. Within seconds, it was on its side and the honey was flowing down the aisle. My eyes searched each lady for a reaction, but no one moved a muscle even though everyone was aware of the dilemma. We made one stop prior to our destination. The pilot made his way down the aisle, never reacting as he carefully stepped around and through the honey as though it were a normal day. As he opened the door, the honey flowed down the steps! Still, no response!

Upon arrival, the heat was so intense I could not believe it. We were told to bring umbrellas, but it wasn't for the rain. It was definitely for the heat! We were truly in the jungles and stayed in a cinder block building that Canadian missionaries had built. The only problem was we were not in Canada. The windows were small and very high on the wall. There was no air flow and no fans! The heat was horrible, and there was very little clean water.

The next morning I watched as women and children began to gather as they made their way through the dense jungle of banana and tropical trees. Most arrived barefoot, with their small children walking along beside them. Some came up river in dories, taking them all day to get there. Many women slept on the ground during the event. They just wanted to hear about Jesus.

I will never forget the hard looks on their faces on arrival. It was the most humbling sight I had ever seen. They lived their whole lives with no running water nor electricity. Small thatched roofs were their homes. I stood and wiped back tears, momentarily forgetting the sweat pouring off of me.

The weekend was powerful, spiritually. Things happened that no one would believe back in the States. At night in the jungle you could hear these very eerie sounds in the distance. A demon entered our room the first night, speaking for hours over my friend sleeping below me. Demons showed themselves physically in the nightly meetings, immediately being cast out. One morning I relayed what I heard and saw during the night to the ministry team. A young Spanish lady sleeping in the kitchen area repeated the same chain of events as I was telling the American missionary (Phyliss) outside. The confirmation was comforting. I was so happy, momentarily thinking I could possibly be delirious from the heat and drastic change in environments.

The team leaders knew everything about me on arrival, yet during the meetings introduced me as a missionary. I would shrink back at the statement, but they knew my heart and didn't seem to care about anything else. The people living here obviously had worse problems, and my being a fugitive of justice with the F.B.I., Interpol, and a long list of people after me was totally irrelevant to them. I feel certain not one person was even familiar with the word fugitive that far back in the jungle.

I would sit in the back during the church services only to be called up front at the end of each service. Sister Eleanor and the team needed help praying over the women at the end of the meetings. There were a lot of women and they were all having problems with witchcraft and demons of every kind.

I was totally clueless to everything I was observing in the meetings. Sister Eleanor started off each service by breaking off curses on the women. At the end of each meeting I would go up front feeling totally inadequate. I thought, *The only thing I knew was what I had recently seen on TBN.* As the women came forward, I would just have to go on pure faith that God would show up. The ladies were small-framed and innocent-looking. I felt like I towered over them. As the ladies stood in front of me, I would raise their frail arms just as I had seen them do on TBN. I began to pray. God would just have to do the interpreting. Neither knew what the other was saying, but obviously God did.

The unexpected happened. I was totally shocked as demons presented themselves. The first one darted out to the right side of my face. It scared me so bad, I jumped back and looked around. I nervously looked down on the small-framed lady. She was so intense and helpless-looking. I glanced over at Sister Eleanor and Sister Harriett, and they were going forward with great intensity. I regrouped and once again went forward praying over the small lady. Finally the demons left. I could see each demon's face as they left the women.

There was such a strong presence of God surrounding us. I knew it was nothing I was doing. It was all about God and His power.

At the end of the Conference, there were soft smiles on the ladies' faces as they made their way back to their homes. On their arrival, the ladies looked so hard, but they were obviously set free and now totally at peace.

On my return to Roatan, I often wondered why God was visibly showing me demons and not all the women on the ministry team. I never once asked to see them physically. I had prayed and prayed desperately for God to show me His power before I went to the Conference. *I Guess He Did!*

On the Island, unusual and humorous things continued to arise with each week, including Sunday church services. Nocona and I not only enjoyed the Baptist Church in West End, but more and more I was acquiring acquaintances from all over the Island. We tried to move around the Island as frequently as possible on Sundays to visit. We enjoyed Sister Frances Arch's Church at French Key and made many friends there. We always looked forward to taking a boat and visiting Pastor David and Sister Harriet Kelly's Church on the Oakridge Key. Eventually, we made our way over to St. Helene and visited the people there.

It would not have been a normal day if something funny didn't happen from time to time. Sometimes it was a skinny dog with matted hair laying at our feet as the people sang their hearts out in an outdoor service. As a child played one day, the bench fell in, yet the choir never missed a beat. Whether the dogs were fighting or an Islander was switching her children for being disobedient, pastors compensated by getting louder. To them it was a normal day; to me it was seeing God in all His different personalities! I never left a church that I didn't come back with something special. It gave me a whole new meaning to life and a deeper understanding of this new Person in my life called Jesus!

During the summer months, the churches were extremely hot, the pastors were loud, and so were the people's singing. On our arrival to the Island, Nocona started out by covering her ears, but rapidly joined in with them. Many paid the price as Nocona sang daily in the hotel at the top of her lungs!

The Island was beautiful, but lacking in every area as far as constructive activities or organizations. I saw no 4-H Clubs, Crawfish Festivals, CASA

Programs, or parades, much less a Chamber of Commerce. But I continued to build on the Christmas program in West End each year.

With no entertainment, we continued to walk the beach daily for exercise and relieve the stress from various problems. Nocona would ride her bicycle, with Petie on the handlebars amusing all the tourists. Island and foreign businesses lined the sandy road, with various businessmen hailing Nocona as she skipped and ran down the beach—first John, then Paul with the Cocoanut Tree Restaurant, who quickly nicknamed Nocona, Flossy! The two never missed hailing her as she skipped along the white sands. Nocona was full of drama, continually drawing attention. Nocona was petite, but far from dainty as she skipped and ran along the beach with her red hair flowing in the Island breeze. Naomi and her sisters Mel, Britnie, Shanie, and Susan, always walked properly on their way to West End's Baptist Church, making sure their beautiful dresses didn't get dirty. Nocona always skipped, usually arriving with spots from falling or just kicking up the dust.

The elderly couple next door to us, Sister Laura and Frederick, lived in a small concrete house on the water in front of our hotel. Their granddaughter, Lilly, and her five beautiful children, lived with them. Laura was struggling with her health from the time we arrived, but with every day she counted her blessings with very few complaints. Lilly daily cooked for all of them and cared for her grandparents and her children. On arrival this family opened their home to us, and in a few weeks I became Sister Frances to Sister Laura and Frederick. I shrunk back at her labeling me, knowing I was far from perfect, yet somehow she came up with the title. I felt there must be two categories, and I definitely wasn't a party animal. I soon learned every Christian woman on the Island in most of the denominations were referred to as Sister.

Nocona, Naomi & Mel

*Ms. Ruth, Frederick Tatum,
Nocona, Mel & Naomi*

Seashell Prisoners
CHAPTER 12

Living on an island was similar to living in small towns. On arrival, I was a little overweight so...some thought of me as possibly being pregnant! After I went into the construction of Casa Calico, I lost thirty pounds; the word came back, I had AIDS!

The construction of Casa Calico along with the new lifestyle of being a fugitive of justice was taking a toll on me. I continued to get up each morning, regroup and start over. River JoNey was struggling with her own problems. She kept busy filling all voids with people and trying to find a job that made more than two dollars an hour. There were definitely no colleges to finish her education and no horses to work with. Anything that had to do with the past and reality continued to stay conveniently tucked away.

My life was burdened with survival, and I was not able to help JoNey. Problems back home continued to be placed on the backburner. I found a place to do emails in Coxen Hole, so I would drive several times a week to a small business called Paradise Computers. I was once again able to communicate with the world. Occasionally, we would get feedback from Texas. JoNey's father was daily working with attorneys, fighting the ten-million-dollar lawsuit. He was now married and he and his wife were fighting the lawsuit together. He was spending thousands of dollars in legal fees on something they had no part in. Proof obviously was not needed by the law for Trevor to go forward inflicting pain on all of us.

River JoNey struggled with each bad report from the U.S. She continued to keep a lot to herself, but there was one thing she and I did discuss and we were in total agreement on: If the F.B.I. picked us up and returned us to the States, we would both go straight to prison rather than suffer more at the hands of the Orange County Judicial System, or another lying, deceiving attorney. I reassured River, I would never hire another attorney! The courts would just have to appoint one if they brought me in. My thoughts were, "Let the courts pay for these creatures of prey!" I knew if there was one attorney on this earth with integrity and honesty, I would never be fortunate enough to find him!

※

Nocona was doing great and continued to go through different stages with each growth spurt. She woke up singing and went to bed singing. Nocona felt secure and safe and was loving the Island. With each year I grew more suspicious of the U.S. Embassy and their casual visits. In one sense I felt safe on the Island, but more and more questions continued to arise with each fax or visit from the U.S. Embassy. They were getting more persistent with their request for us to return to the States.

It was comforting knowing the Islanders were very protective of our situation. Total strangers had better identify themselves quickly when making inquiries, or they would be led on a wild goose chase by the locals. Reports came back on several occasions of strangers being a little too nosy about our situation. By the end of the conversation, they knew they were not welcome in the village of West End.

Nocona's 4th Birthday Party

Daily, I was being educated on the culture. When Nocona had turned four, we gave her a birthday party on the beach and invited a few children. I made a big cake and planned a few games. An Island friend brought another large cake. I was a little confused, but she explained Islanders are a little different from Americans. Sure enough, each child not only took food for themselves, but helped themselves to extra cake to take home to their families. We soon came to learn this about anything we organized—that is the protocol, whether it involves adults or children. Everyone thinks of their families that are not there. It took a while to adjust to this, but it finally sank in that my ways would not work on the Island of Roatan.

After Nocona's fourth birthday, I enrolled her in the Roatan Bilingual School. She loved the burgundy and white uniforms and, as everything else, she went at it with total enthusiasm. By this time, Nocona had mastered the Island lingo and was highly anticipating her first day of school. The teachers along with all the kids embraced the new redheaded Niña.

Within weeks, Nocona was elected to represent the school in the Island's biggest parade. She would be one of the leadoffs in the parade with other classmates. It was the biggest event of the year for Hondurans! Nocona never noticed her skin was a different color, as she pranced along the long dusty road with cameras flashing all around. It was a grand moment for all of us! Her mother and I looked on in awe at how much she was enjoying her life on Roatan.

Nocona
Roatan
Bilinguil School

Nocona in Roatan Parade

Daily I listened to the radio and television, hearing many sermons on purpose and being predestined. As I watched Nocona interact from day to day, maybe I didn't have the least idea of how this would all end, but I knew one thing for sure—this is exactly where we were supposed to be living! Even if it was just for Nocona and myself to learn more about this new person in our life called God!

Our neighbors, Sister Laura and Frederick, lived directly in front of us. Daily they could be seen in the heat of the day, laying in hammocks that were tied to mango trees out to the side of Casa Calico. Inside their small, cinder block home the heat became more intense as the sun rose directly over us. Daily I watched them from my window as I worked on my computer. Frederick was usually sitting in a lawn chair sipping cold fruit drinks that his granddaughter Lilly made them. Laura would be in the hammock. The cashew and mango trees seemed to be the favorite spot for all their activities, including their grandchildren's birthday parties and frequent visits from family and friends. In my free time I would join them. We never had a conversation that we didn't talk about Jesus. They were so looking forward to seeing Him.

With each day that went by, I was even more determined we would not live in hiding nor in fear. My greatest worry was what Frederick our neighbor might do if someone did attempt to take Nocona. Mr. Frederick and Sister Laura were deeply concerned about Nocona's safety and very protective of all children. Nocona never thought of herself as being any different from the other children that played at their house. Frederick, Laura, and Miss Lilly did, and lived each day watching out for Nocona's safety and well being.

Sister Laura was definitely a leader of the community. If you were not aware of it when you met her, you would definitely know it by the time you left. The whole Island had much respect for both her and her husband. There were many quotes about them around the Island.

Once in conversation while visiting at Coxen Hole, Mr. Frederick's name came up as being the only honest man on the Island. I was always amused by certain statements made by individuals, but nonetheless I knew Mr. Frederick was definitely my choice of a fine example of a Godly family man. I always sat next to them in church when possible. Most of the time they were surrounded by grandchildren, always dressed to perfection, so I would find Ms. Greta and Mr. Orti and sit with them.

Sister Laura was a lady of few words, at one point inadvertently getting me elected as a Sunday School teacher for the youth. On that particular Sunday, Pastor Edly Bush passed by, greeting us. He asked Sister Laura if she would teach the youth Sunday School class. Sister Laura looked him straight in the eye, then glanced over at me and boldly stated, *"Sister Frances would love to do it."* I shrunk back at the response, knowing I had never held the title of Sunday School teacher and still did not have a full understanding of the Bible. I reluctantly agreed, knowing Sister Laura would never have accepted my refusal. I was still the only person in the church wearing lipstick and sleeveless blouses! Who would listen to anything I had to say?

Nocona and I made our exit from the service and took our usual walk on the beach road past the beautiful Half Moon Bay and around the corner to Casa Calico. As I watched the dive boats leaving out of the bay, I smiled and reflected on the last West End Church Conference I attended. The pastor had announced everyone was to dress casual since they would have a picnic and singing on the beach. I took them literally. The churches were always hot, but when I thought of an outdoor service, picnic, etc., I showed up wearing a sleeveless blouse and long baggy shorts that had the appearance of a skirt. People were there from around the Island. Missionaries from the States were singing for the event.

As we all sat around listening to the music outside, all of a sudden Bro. Solomon, pastor from Coxen Hole, stood up and made a profound announcement: "Everyone should be there enjoying the music and not get upset over the dress of certain individuals present." For a moment I froze, realizing... *It Was Me He Was Referring To!* Then I looked around, and the missionaries were dressed similar to myself. I was normally very perceptive, but totally missed this one! I decided, what the heck, and I just stayed until it was over, hoping everyone would be okay with his statement. I thought, who knows, maybe that was the reason God had me there! Maybe my dress was not what they desired it to be, but my heart was in the right place.

The youth knew from the first Sunday that I appeared in their class, that they were in for something totally different. I put up the small teaching guide given to me and went straight to the Bible. I handed them all a pen and paper and told them not to put their names on the paper. I had a list of questions for them. I was quite curious as to how many were saved and what exactly their idea of salvation was. I just needed to know where they were in their walk so I would know where to start. Just how hard would it be to stay ahead of these teenagers?

I asked them several questions and, surprisingly, they went forward jotting down their answers on paper. After gathering up the answers, it was apparent they knew the Bible much better than I did. I found it disturbing when I asked how many of them were saved. Their reply was… "No one!" I asked how many of the youth in the other classes were saved? They stated… "No one!" I left, totally confused, and determined it was time for change. How could they be so knowledgeable of the Bible and not be saved?

※

Today it was back to town for shopping and picking up emails. Trips to Coxen Hole were far from enjoyable! I considered the little Centro to be hot, dirty, and grungy with trash-littered streets. I cringed when Vonnie, one of my friends, stated it was the highlight of their vacation and jokingly requested to stay at the only hotel present. Along with all the run-down government offices were many novelty shops with local art and souvenirs. The only enjoyable part of the day was running into our friends and business acquaintances either on the street or in Warren's Supermarket. There was always someone we knew, lined up at the counter on the right. Each person rested on bar stools as they enjoyed the fried chicken and potato salad loaded down with hot sauce Warren's was famous for.

Miss Ivy always had time to stop and chat as she went up and down the aisles working in the supermarket. She had a famous saying when the people asked how much were the prices going up. Her reply was, "Ever how much I think we can get." Her brother Tim was a little more serious, but we occasionally got a smile, letting us know he was happy we were shopping with them. Curby Warren could always be seen helping customers at the desk by the front door or visiting with his friend, Larry McLaughlin. His job seemed to lean toward the intellectual; he was rarely seen doing physical work.

With each return to Coxen Hole, I was always amazed. There were many business transactions that could be taken care of simply by walking the streets through Coxen Hole or shopping in Warren's Supermarket. Not having a telephone made me totally dependent on God to make many things happen…and He always did.

Each week we were bonding with more and more people around the Island. We now truly felt a part of Roatan. This particular day in Coxen Hole, a local judge stopped and told me men were in his office asking about us. He felt they were U.S. officials. I thanked him for his concern for us. As all other incoming news, I tried to dismiss it. I knew it had to be someone up to no good. I was just grateful the judge didn't tell them where we lived.

The following week on my return to Coxen Hole, I was shopping once again in Warrens, and a female resort owner from West Bay quietly passed me a Reader's Digest. She whispered in my ear that there was an article in it about my leaving the U.S. with Nocona. I thanked her and quietly dropped it into my purse and kept walking. I never knew with each return trip to Coxen Hole what may come up.

ಷ

The U.S. Embassy workers began to frequent Casa Calico more. They obviously had an agenda and so did I. I used each visit to monitor our situation in the States. As they played on me, I played on them! They continued to say Trevor's sister was calling daily, putting more pressure on them. With each visit they would ask if I was going back and would encourage it. My answer was always emphatically, "No! Not until Nocona is older!"

Owen and his wife Nelda came to the Island for a week to visit Nocona and River. Nocona enjoyed their company and excitedly showed them around the Island. I visited with them on a couple occasions. They discussed the problems going on in the States with the judgment and trying to keep River's custody of Nocona. When River JoNey left the U.S., Trevor had Judge Davis illegally transfer Nocona's custody to Trevor. Owen hired an attorney and had the custody placed back with River. This scenario happened several times. Trevor continued every form of harassment he could!

ಷ

One day as I went about working with guests, I was sent word from an Embassy worker. A party wanted to meet me at a large resort on the other end of the Island. It was an Embassy employee I had not met before. The person was attending conference meetings, but wanted to take this opportunity to speak with me in person. I thought, *how much more damage could it bring about*, and made my way over to the middle of the Island and met with the party. The person was quite different from the other representatives of the Embassy. I wasn't sure why the party asked me there, being the person never made a real point of the meeting. I just knew I felt unusually comfortable with this person as though I could trust the party, but left totally without knowing the purpose of the meeting.

JANUARY 1996

I continued to hear from Anna and her wedding plans. I had been deprived of Anna's graduation. Now I would be deprived of her wedding! I would get letters and videos of her wedding shower, which only made me feel more disconnected. I sent word requesting Anna and Brandon to come to the Island and reenact the wedding for Nocona and me. Anna finally agreed.

More news from back home! Anna's wedding in the States had a change of plans with all the mass confusion. She was going to simplify it and go to Las Vegas, but the plans were still on to come to the Island afterwards!

Once again, I got word from a neighbor that the Embassy wanted to speak to me. Now it was referred to as an Emergency! When I returned the call, the party stated he was an F.B.I. Agent, and his name was Fred Lucas. He boldly announced my charges had been dropped in the U.S. and I could come and go as I pleased to the States. Somehow it just didn't add up! Why now, right before Anna's wedding? I thanked Mr. Lucas, but never let on my feelings about his statement.

The caller was enticing, but a huge red flag was definitely going up. I went back the next day and called the Embassy, requesting to speak to one of the Embassy workers I trusted. The party quickly informed me they had recused themselves from the case and could no longer speak to me.

I later receive another call from an Embassy employee. This person's last words were piercing: "Frances, what they are doing to you is immoral! People are using your case to make points. *Do Not Trust Anyone!* Do you understand, Frances? *Do Not Trust Anyone!* Do not go to the States and do not trust anyone! They are setting you up!"

Their words were hard, ringing loud and clear. For days I couldn't get it off my mind. I was totally blown away! The thought kept going through my mind, *This is my country speaking, my U.S. Embassy, my protection from all enemies. They are into something that is totally immoral to us? What could it be?*

Once again I heard from Anna. They had a wonderful time in Vegas with family and friends and now it was time for her and Brandon to make their way to Honduras. They were ready to redo their wedding vows due to my demands. Nocona and I had planned and anticipated for months for this grand day. River and I now had many friends that would attend and everyone here loved weddings and birthday parties. I also knew some would come totally uninvited. That's just the way they were and yes, I had hired the best chefs in West End for the occasion to make sure I had plenty food. Nocona began practicing a special song for the grand event. New dresses were in the making for Nocona and Naomi. They were to be the flower girls.

I then receive another call from the Embassy! This time it was not what I was expecting. F.B.I. Agent Fred Lucas was threatening me, if I did not return, they would come and get us! I knew he had been lying to me about my charges being dropped. He actually thought I would go back to the states for Anna's wedding. Now he confirmed it, but failed at his attempt of setting me up and it was all evident in the tone of his voice. By this time, I was outraged, leaving nothing for guess-work. I loudly stated, *"I lost everything in an attempt to help Nocona, my home, my family, and my money. I will continue to do whatever it takes to protect Nocona from this sick man!"*

He then stated that if I didn't turn myself in I would have new charges, including International Parental Kidnapping. The new charge would bring Life Imprisonment! Outraged, I screamed, *"That's fine...Put me in prison! That would give me plenty of time to write about all the injustices that have come about by the Judicial System, including yourself."*

There was a pause.... He very boldly retaliated stating: *"We Will Get You!"*

That was the wrong thing to say. My last words rang loud and clear: *"I will find a gun and use it, if necessary."*

There was another long pause, ending with, *"It won't be me!"*

I questioned the whole scenario.

I was later told Mr. Lucas had put in a request for Angelina Ulloa (Director of Immigration in Honduras) to deport us. Angelina Ulloa's reply to him was, *"Forget It!"*

ع

A month went by. I receive word from the Cayman Bank I was doing business with that the F.B.I. was intercepting all faxes, emails, etc., in an attempt to seize my account. The official from the bank reconfirmed my account was safe due to the way I had originally set it up.

I had no choice but to go forward. I embraced each day in hopes that the next would bring about an end to all of this. I had taken on the new job as a hotel owner leaving no rock unturned. I continued to make sure all guests were comfortable and knowledgeable about the Island and all it had to offer. My background in business and working with organizations had definitely prepared me for this time. My instincts quickly picked up on each guest's wish for his dream vacation. Most were there for diving. Some desired to have a cookout and some desired to purchase property. Others became engaged, desiring a wedding. Whatever they requested, I made it happen! It was important that each guest return home with a wonderful story to tell about the little island of Roatan and Casa Calico.

No one sensed my personal struggle deep within. I had obviously become an excellent actor with no one realizing our presence on the Island was far from normal. I had my story well prepared for the tourists and used it frequently. They were all full of questions with their favorite being: "What brought you to Roatan?" I repeated the same story starting off with the fact that I was a diver for twenty years and enjoyed traveling to Islands. I used a lot of detail and always told the truth; I just didn't tell the whole story.

ع

On our arrival to Roatan, one thing was obvious. Christmas was like another day to most. It was usually hot, humid, and rainy. The closer it got the first year, I began to inquire around to see who was preparing turkeys and just how many friends were gathering at each home, but there was no response! This was stifling to me, being that Dad had made it such a huge event in our lives. I sent word back home for anyone and everyone to please send me any old Christmas decorations they did not want. There was definitely nothing in the stores to purchase. I began to get decorations in the mail. I was determined we would celebrate despite the stifling heat and humidity. Each day I played my one Christmas CD over and over to the point that friends made fun of me. It was Christmas and I didn't care if I was the only one excited, I was going to make it a special day.

My guests soon came to know Christmas dinner would be on the table on their arrival to the Island. Our favorite Island friends would join us.

River JoNey and I spent two days cooking and preparing all our favorite foods. We put out the tablecloths in the outdoor garden area and decorated them with all kinds of beautiful flowers. The Europeans were a little confused with the Deep South Christmas dinner with cornbread dressing, but greatly appreciated the vegetables, and the fact that we had gone to all the trouble. I was soon to be the only one listed in tour books as "The hotel with the nice friendly owner!"

❧

With each letter from home, I was told my life was still headlining newspapers. Now the word was that I was listed in the Top Ten Most Wanted Women in the State of Texas!

Once again I made my way to Coxen Hole to do my shopping and business. I always held my head up and went about my shopping as though everything was normal in my life. I visited with old friends and businessmen, going over daily happenings as I went from the bank to various shops. I was proud since I could now carry on a decent conversation about tourism, Island recipes, and Jesus. I was always curious about the latest revivals, etc. I was enjoying being able to relate to people about God and now I could actually add to the conversation.

Upon each entrance to Coxen Hole, I never knew who or what may take place on each arrival. On this particular day it would be a strange turn of events. As I was making my way from the supermarket to the post office, I was approached by a total stranger on the sidewalk. It was normal for people in various positions on the Island to approach me. Today was different and more intense. The public official strongly suggested I go with him into a nearby government office. I followed the man as he made his way behind the post office beside Warren's Supermarket. I was struggling to understand the man's language; his tone and urgency were clear and demanding. It was a short walk across the street and down a row of buildings. I reluctantly entered the office, sensing it meant more problems. I thought of Nocona, then had a sense of relief that she stayed at the hotel with my brother.

As I entered the dimly lit room, there was silence and a serious look on the man sitting at the desk. He never said a word and immediately handed me the telephone. The party on the other end spoke broken English, explaining his authority in Honduras. He went on to say I was to meet him in San Pedro Sula at a certain time and place. He emphatically stated that I was to go by myself. No one could be with me!

I thought about it as I returned to West End. I knew this was all way over my head; what exactly were my options? I felt at this moment they were expecting me to go to San Pedro and possibly ask me to slit my own throat! To what degree was I to trust these people, and just exactly who were they? The Embassy employee statement kept reoccurring, "...Don't trust anyone, Frances!"

It was all getting to be too bizarre. I went by and visited with a couple I felt I could trust. Deeply concerned, one of them insisted on joining me on the trip.

We made our way to San Pedro, totally unaware of what to expect next. We checked into the designated room, and at exactly the right time, there was a knock at the door. My mind reflected on all the armed men with machine guns that were frequently seen on the streets of Honduras. Were they going to burst in and just gun me down, or was he coming as a friend?

For some reason, once he entered the room, I couldn't look him in the eye. He sat down in the chair closest to the door. The room didn't have much light and now he was in one of the darkest areas. That made me nervous.

I walked across the room and sat on the bed closest to the window. For what reason, I was not sure, except I wanted to be as far from him as I could get. The party that came with me sat quietly on the bed closer to him. The stranger was well dressed and spoke with authority. I could tell he was not an average Honduran. He never really said whom he represented. He just made it evident my name was on a list to be picked up and returned to the States. After a short conversation he began to relax and started to come across as sympathetic. He then asked if I would let them put us into hiding.

At that point my nerves gave way and I began to cry. I let him know I was not up to hiding anymore even though I had never truly hidden to begin with. Regardless, this whole scenario had become way too stressful. Once he made his statement and understood I would not leave the Island, he left the room. It was all very strange, leaving me to wonder as to what was next. He never said, but I had the strong sense he was with the military. We then made our return to the Island.

Tourists came and tourists went. One day a rather large Italian gentleman came to stay at Casa Calico for a couple of weeks. Eric Wilmeth looked to be in his fifties, immediately boasting of his many languages. He quickly informed us he was here to vacation and to look into purchasing property.

Everyone was now wanting a piece of this little utopia. What began as a sleepy little virgin island was now growing in popularity every day. It was obvious it would soon become one of the hottest spots in the Caribbean. Once again I did the task I had performed hundreds of other times—I would fill Eric in on different real estate properties and realtors to contact—just one of the many frequent requirements of my job.

Eric was typical Italian and obviously here to have a good time also. He asked about the other Italians here, etc., as though he may want to link up with them. Being a huge people-watcher, I had come to realize Italians always requested Italian places, Germans want to link up with Germans, but Americans, they could care less. They just wanted to have a good time! The more diversion and adventure, the happier they seemed to be!

Eric talked a lot about his love for cooking. In conversation I chimed in, boasting about the great cooks I had lined up for Anna's wedding. He quickly asked if he could join us, with my reply being, "No Problem." That was another advantage to being a guest at Casa Calico. Whatever was going on in our lives, the guests were always invited. Between Nocona's friends and our friends we had come to know, we were frequently making homemade pizza or doing something in our outdoor kitchen.

It was getting closer to the day for Anna and Brandon to arrive for the wedding. We were all excited, finalizing last minute arrangements.

Everything was coming along great, and then Nocona became ill. Suddenly Eric, our new Italian guest, shortened his vacation, stating he had to leave, but would return at a later date. Prior to his leaving, Eric asked if I would check out more property for him. He would fax from time to time, letting me know his arrival date. That would be easy since I knew all the right people that would make that happen, so I agreed.

Suddenly, big red bumps were appearing all over Nocona. I couldn't believe it! How could God do that to me? Here I had waited so long, and Nocona now had the chicken pox! I consulted with my friend Ms. Marie who always knew the latest Island herbal remedies. Within a week I had Nocona up and going once again.

❧

Candice, a very colorful American lady from the States, dropped by the hotel one day, promoting a big event she was organizing at Fantasy Island. I knew Candice well, and she was not at Casa Calico for a casual visit. I also knew she was definitely needing something! I nonchalantly asked Candice what was up, knowing it probably had something to do with her job at the resort she worked for.

Candice made casual conversation, then asked if Nocona would be in the swimsuit contest at the upcoming event she was coordinating for the resort. She stated she needed more entries in the four- and five-year-old category. I was totally against that type of thing, but knowing Candice's expertise in organizing, agreed on one account. Nocona would participate only if Candice would help with the upcoming wedding for Anna and Brandon. I desperately needed Candice's help! The agreement was made.

Swimsuits made up 90% of Nocona's wardrobe, so getting her ready for the event would be an easy task for me. Everyone that came to visit us brought swimsuits! On the day of the event, JoNey and I never told Nocona she was in a contest. We were just taking her to Fantasy Island to the beach for the day.

Fantasy Island's guests were upper class, so there were entries from Costa Rica, the mainland of Honduras, Guatemala, and Roatan. When we arrived, the children's parents were sitting around visiting. Each was sipping Pina Coladas and margaritas relaxing under the umbrellas close to the beach. They were anxiously waiting for their daughters to step forward in the contest.

The girls began to line up. We told Nocona everyone was getting ready to go to the beach, so she ran up to the children and lined up. I instructed Nocona to just do whatever the other girls did. Nocona walked out with the others smiling and waving, thinking she was headed for the beach. She was quite noticeable with her long red hair and white skin alongside the Central American children.

At the end, the judge walked up and down the line, then surprisingly placed the crown on Nocona! Nocona still did not know she was in a contest and had actually won. She turned and walked off, waving as though she were in the Miss America pageant! We let her play on their beautiful beach, then headed back to West End, quite proud of the day's accomplishment. Candice got her contestant, I got my wedding planner, and Nocona got a crown at the beach party!

APRIL 13, 1996

The big day was finally here, with my daughter Anna and husband Brandon arriving with what we counted to be a miracle—fourteen pieces of luggage full of gowns, presents, and one suitcase full of cokes! It was obvious Anna thought of Roatan as being a deserted island. T.A.C.A. at that time was notorious for losing luggage, but by some small miracle all fourteen pieces were here. Bro. Solomon, the pastor of the First Baptist Church in Coxen Hole, would officiate the big event.

The wedding went over with great camaraderie. The outdoor kitchen tables were set with green-over-white tablecloths. Beautiful tropical flowers from all the neighbors' yards graced the tables. The twinkling white lights in the banana, cocoanut, and palm trees made it a beautiful setting. All the salads were iced down in an extremely old dory I had found on the side of the Bay. The dory lay under the cocoanut and banana trees and was decorated with all the Island flowers.

Brandon and Anna each came down the long winding stairway on opposite sides, just as I'd planned. Anna was beautiful and so was the moment. Nocona and her favorite little friends were all a part of the big event. Bro. Solomon with his deep baritone voice and in his usual diplomatic manner performed the ceremony beautifully. Friends from around the Island came. Many stated it was one of the most beautiful weddings they had seen on the Island.

Everyone was having a great time enjoying the delicious lobster, shish kebabs, and seafood gumbo. All were prepared by some of the best chefs on the island. Yes, there were some present totally uninvited, but we all had a grand evening. Nocona sang her song she had practiced, but few heard it since the musicians pretty much drowned her out. Everyone clapped, and she stepped down beaming. The whole event was totally Island-style and was all caught on video.

Anna & Brandon's Wedding Day

Anna

Seashell Prisoners
CHAPTER 13

The following week we saw Anna and Brandon off, then Eric Wilmeth returned. When he walked in, I found it unusual that he only had a small handbag, yet he was staying a week. Despite my exhaustion from the wedding, I once again put on my smile and made an attempt to welcome him back.

Later that evening, Eric brought spaghetti downstairs for me and Nocona. He wanted to know all about the wedding since he arrived too late to attend. As we sat at the table, I filled him in on all the details. I was a little uneasy when I noticed a bottle of vodka in his hand. He offered me a drink and set the bottle in front of me. I thanked him, but returned the bottle to him. This was just not the norm for our guests. Almost all guests were very friendly and frequently came down to visit, but never offered liquor of any kind.

As Eric left the room, I had to ask him to please take his bottle with him. He insisted I keep it so I walked to the door and handed it to him on his way out. Two days later as I straightened the living room, I noticed the video of Anna's wedding was missing. The large living area was like a common room for everyone to use, but I couldn't imagine anyone being interested in taking it. I was tired so I just dismissed the problem, putting it on the back burner, thinking I had misplaced it. The next day I continued my search for the video, but it was not there.

All tourists have a routine, and they are pretty much like clockwork. All follow the same pattern. Eric's pattern was different. He got up very early, and returned late at night. I never saw him carrying snorkeling or dive equipment. He never came in to rest in the afternoon. It was all quite unusual, but I continued to rationalize his odd behavior. Anna's wedding had taken a lot out of me, and I was not feeling well. I was desperately trying to get my health and energy level back up and going.

One morning, JoNey came into my bedroom looking confused. She had come in late that night and looked up, feeling as though someone was watching her. She went on to say she saw Eric coming down the stairway outside in his underwear. She made sure the front door was locked and went to bed. I knew deep down this man was not on the up and up. I felt I needed to search his room once he left for the day, but again I put it off. I was now having flu-like symptoms, feeling worse instead of getting better.

APRIL 23, 1996

The day was normal in routine. I got up and once again began to dress Nocona for school. It was her first day back after she recovered from the chicken pox. As usual she was excited. After packing Nocona's lunch we were once again ready for school. We got in the black Chevrolet truck, but this time the truck wouldn't start! As I struggled with the hood of the truck to check on the battery, I felt as though someone was watching me. I looked up to see Eric looking down at me from the upper deck adjoining his room. He quickly stated he would come down and fix the problem. I had this eerie feeling about the offer, yet it was obvious I had no help this early in the morning. Within minutes he had the black Chevy up and running.

I went forward with my day, dropping Nocona off, watching her run up to the school, then returning to Casa Calico to start my day. On my arrival to the hotel I went about with my usual list of chores. This day would soon prove to be different.

Within minutes, I heard a truck door slam. Two friends were at the door stating their daughter called them from the Bilingual School. *Nocona Had Been Kidnapped!* Everything that was within me was not there anymore. I felt no life whatsoever. I got in with the couple and we quickly drove to the airport. No words could come out of my mouth. As we made our way down the road, they began to fill me in on details. Trevor, Eric (thought to be an ex-C.I.A. agent), Laura (Trevor's sister), and another thug entered Roatan Bilingual School. They entered Nocona's classroom with guns and grabbed Nocona, throwing her into a truck. Nocona's teacher made two attempts to save Nocona, but was knocked to the ground by one of the men. The kidnappers raced to the airport, narrowly missed hitting a couple of Islanders and airport guards. Waiting at the airport was a private plane from El Salvador where Trevor quickly placed Nocona.

The whole school was in shock and traumatized by the event. Teachers, students, everyone that had cars, mopeds, and bicycles, did their best to catch up with the assailants. Maria Del Carmon Enrique, the school director, immediately contacted the airport. Teachers and all persons in authority arrived at the airport in time to see airport security taking Nocona off the plane. Cheryl Galindo, the owner of the school, met us at the door extremely upset. It was obvious a lot of planning and many were involved with this tragic event.

Someone brought it to our attention that a lawyer was standing in the airport and mentioned we might need his help. I thought it strange that he just so happened to be there.

Trevor's character stayed true at all times. He never did anything on the up and up. It always had to be underhanded, with a bang, and certain to get everyone's attention. River and I knew he wouldn't be the gentleman and write or make arrangements with the U.S. Embassy to see Nocona. That just wasn't Trevor!

Attorneys universally have bad reputations, with no exception on the Island. The echo continued... *"Frances, do not trust anyone!"* It just got louder and louder.

It didn't take long to see a select group on the Island, including a few in the legal system, were involved with this devastating ploy on our lives. Evidence was strongly pointing to employees of the U.S. Embassy, political leaders in the U.S., Interpol, and the F.B.I. as the main players supporting Trevor and his sister. They were supporting what would end up being devastating mentally and emotionally to not only us, but the whole Island.

Rumors were flying, stating who was involved, and large amounts of money were being dispersed to judges and anyone in authority on the Island, helping to set this up. An attorney I had previously used was obviously one of the recipients.

Honduran Newspaper Kidnapping Article

The minutes were more like days in our attempt to get Nocona back. We raced home and quickly found the documents proving River had legal custody when we left the U.S. Finally the courts released Nocona to us. Within a few hours, we had Nocona back home again.

The kidnapping news spread like wildfire around the Island. There was front page coverage in Honduras, with the airplane from El Salvador in the background! All six assailants were now under arrest and had to stay in the custody of the police for six days. They broke many laws, yet money influenced the right people, and they were free to return to the States after six days. Immediately after their arrest, Laura had the U.S. Embassy make a call to her husband, stating he was to call a certain U.S. Congressman, a Senator, and Laura's attorney.

The whole Island was in an uproar and appalled at the legal system's lack of punishment to the assailants. Due to the residents' attack on the judicial system, on April 10, 1997, Trevor, Laura, Eric, and Bradley were sentenced to two years and nine months. If they entered the country of Honduras, they would immediately be arrested!

River JoNey, Guy Muller & Frances

Once again wonderful friends rallied to the hour. River and I both were numb to everything, with our nervous systems hanging by a thread. Courageous friends and businessmen stepped up to the platform, staying with us day and night—Guy Muller, Carlos Ortica, and Mauricio Constaneda, each not knowing what could happen at any moment, knowing Eric Wilmeth and possibly others remained behind on the island. The question was how much more money did they disperse to individuals on the Island still leaving us prey? Up till now the whole country had protected us, but money was overriding morals and integrity with some.

The U.S. Embassy-influence was obviously strong. One of the first things we learned upon arrival to the Island was the importance of Hondurans being on the right side of the U.S. Embassy. No Visa—no trips to the United States. This was definitely working against us with a few.

Casa Calico overnight turned into a fort instead of a hotel for tourists! It was decided everyone would stay in the same area at night. I quickly relinquished my bed to the men, knowing the danger we faced. I would look over from time to time during the night to see one of our friends with a gun in his hand.

Man arrested, jailed in Honduras

BEAUMONT (AP) — A Texas man and his sister have been arrested in Honduras after the man's attempt to leave the country with his previously missing 5-year-old daughter, family members said.

Police took   his daughter Nocona and his sister,   , the Orange County man's wife, told the Beaumont Enterprise that family members were making contacts in an attempt to gain the group's release.

             has been involved in a legal battle for custody of his daughter since her birth in 1991. The child disappeared with her maternal grandmother, Frances Harris, after a March 1994 Orange County court hearing.

Harris and the child were later joined in Honduras by the girl's mother, River JoNey Burton, according to Houston private detective Clay Titus, who worked to locate the trio last year.

Harris has said she is trying to protect Nocona, alleging that the child had been abused by her father.

             , who denies the abuse allegation, gained emergency temporary custody of Nocona last June with hope that he would eventually find her.

Titus said the girl, her mother and grandmother have become Honduran citizens whose efforts were embraced by residents in the Central American nation.   accompanied by two soldiers, apparently took his daughter from her school on Tuesday, Titus said.

             said she knew about her husband's plans to bring Nocona back to Texas.

Beaumont Enterprise article on Trevor's arrival in States.

SENTENCING OF ~~BOY JOHN~~
SISTER ~~MARY SUNHOONG~~ & OTHER
INVOLVED IN KIDNAPPING OF
NOCONA ON THE ISLAND OF ROATA

EVIDENCE:

The undersigned Secretary of this Court of Appeals CERTIFIES: That under date of the tenth of April of nineteen hundred ninety-seven, the Departmental Court of Letters of Rontén, Bahía Islands, pronounced final sentence in the cause brought against BRADLEY JAMES ROBINSON, ERIC WILMETH, JORGE ANTONIO COLORADO BURGOS and JAIME ANTONIO APARICIO BORJAS, for the crime of ABDUCTION OF MINORS to the detriment of the minor NOCONA by means of which sentence the Court resolved: 1) SENTENCING the defendants BRADLEY JAMES ROBINSON, - ERIC WILMETH and as responsible for the crime of ABDUCTION OF MINORS to the detriment of the minor NOCONA, to serve in the Penal Farm of the Municipality of El Porvenir, Department of Atlántida, the penalty of TWO YEARS AND NINE MONTHS; and 2) ABSOLVING THE DEFENDANTS JAIME ANTONIO APARICIO and JORGE ANDINO COLORADO BURGOS, who were assumed responsible for having committed the crime of CONCEALMENT. The mentioned proceeding is found in this Tribunal, by virtue of the recourse of appeal interposed against the sentence of which mention has been made.

And for the purposes which suit the interested party, the herein Evidence is issued, in the city of La Ceiba, Department of Atlántida, on the 14th day of the month of May of nineteen hundred ninety-seven.

(SEAL)   (Signature)
          M. AUXILIADORA DE CARDINALE
          Secretary

(SEAL)   (Signature)
          JOSE EFRAIN MONTOYA RODRIGUEZ
          President

Honduras Sentence of Trevor, Laura & Accomplices

Father denies death threats

By LAURIE D. HAYNES
Staff Reporter

The family of Frances Harris, who fled the country with her granddaughter, say that the girl's father, has threatened to kill Frances and the child's mother, River JoNey Burton.

calls that accusation false as well as Harris' allegation that he abused his daughter, Nocona.

Nelda Harrison, fiancee of Owen Burton, Nocona's grandfather, said, "What are they supposed to do when he has threatened to kill Frances and JoNey? He stalked them when they were in Mauriceville."

Anna Burton Breaux, River JoNey's younger sister, accused of just trying to get Harris' money.

"He first tried to date my mother, but she wouldn't have anything to do with him," said Breaux. "So he went after River JoNey. He was 34, she was 17. He took advantage of her. I once saw him beating her out in the yard. He wanted her to marry him, but she wouldn't do it."

Harrison said used to yank Nocona up by her arm and would hold a gun on her.

"That baby told me he beat her against the wall and stuck a gun in her stomach," said Harrison. "She would come home and say, 'My daddy's got a big gun.' Frances and River JoNey are terrified of him."

Harrison noted that has named Owen Burton, as well as Harris, in his suit against Harris for interference with child custody.

alleges Burton knew where Harris had gone.

"Owen spent $20,000 of his own money trying to find them, but he couldn't," said Harrison. "He's threatened to sue just about everybody. He's just out to get money."

Although River JoNey is now with Harris and Nocona, in a deposition taken in April 1994, after Harris and the child fled the country, River JoNey said the child should not be deprived of its father's presence, that Harris was wrong to have taken off with the child.

The FBI located Harris, River JoNey and Nocona in Roatan, Honduras, and informed the Department of State as well as . The State Department, said , did nothing, so he took matters into his own hands and hired some "consultants."

He said his consultants found where Harris was living on the island of Roatan and one of them struck up a friendship with her to gain more information about how to get to the child.

and his sister, flew down to Roatan and with the consultants, went to Nocona's school to get her.

Harris' family said and his people terrorized the children, assaulted a teacher and made off

Please see FAMILY, Page 2A

with Nocona, screaming and crying. Honduran police arrested _____ and his group and gave the child back to Harris.

"All their allegations are false," said _____ "I have never threatened them and I have never abused my daughter. The allegations were investigated and no charges were filed. I hadn't seen Nocona in 27 months, but she knew me. She was glad to see me and was hugging and kissing me."

_____ said during the two hours Nocona was with him, they visited in her schoolmates' homes.

He said the reason he showed up at the school to take the girl was he feared if he had gone to the authorities, Harris would have fled again.

"I showed the police and the judge all my papers," said _____ "The judge ordered them not to leave the island, but within an hour, she (Frances) was trying to get plane tickets."

_____ said he will do whatever it takes to get his daughter back.

"I want the child back because I love her," said _____ "Frances doesn't know when the next consultant will be knocking on her door. I could leave at any time to go get Nocona."

Father denies death threats (continued)

```
VS OFFICE Electronic Mail        Friday       07/11/97  04:23 pm   Page:

heard
from _____ either, except that, as I believe I told you, the criminal case
against _____ , .    and the two commmandos is proceeding, and all would
seem
to be subject to arrest if they were to set foot in Honduras again. By the
way, you speak of asking for a "fresh" Hague application by_____ . I can't
recall ever having seen or received a previous one, and to my knowledge,
nothing was ever submitted to the CA.   Am I right?
```

U.S. Embassy Note on Trevor

Each day became more intense as news continued to surface. We were now picking up more information as friends brought new updates from Coxen Hole each day. We learned Trevor and his thugs were in jail the first day, then later placed in a small hotel with guards watching them. The jail was overcrowded. Two locals overheard Eric and Trevor in the dining area of the hotel plotting to murder me. The plan was to have someone along when I went diving. There was only one problem with that plan, I seldom ever went diving, and if I did it was with someone I knew very well.

Different ones recognized Trevor and Laura from the hotel they were staying in prior to the kidnapping. They said Trevor was a real party animal enjoying the company of one of the female workers at the resort. Other feedback was that people in authority on the Island continued to be paid large sums of money to aid the criminals.

Within a few weeks Owen had brought down a legal team to Roatan to take depositions of every detail of the whole kidnapping. Many Islanders were quick to testify everything from the bizarre kidnapping of Nocona at the school, the thugs and Trevor plotting to kill me, even to the partying going on by Trevor, his sister, and other members of his party.

※

Mandy, a beautiful, middle-aged entrepreneur from the States, quickly took charge in West End. With her background and influential friends, changes would soon come about. Mandy had been on the Island many years with her colorful personality, brains, and beauty placing her in all the right places. Mandy's jobs were many, one being to assist the U.S. Embassy and Island businessmen on various projects. Mandy was well-known across the Island. Her residence was the large beach house in West End on Half Moon Bay where Nocona and other children frequently played.

Up until this point, Mandy was an acquaintance, but quick to speak and hold casual conversation as we crossed paths from day to day. Today, Mandy became our best friend and biggest angel, insisting on helping us in whatever way we needed. God never let us down, once again placing people in our paths at the right time.

Previously, I had sent out letters to Senators and state representatives requesting help for our situation. I had tons of paperwork explaining our problem. Most of the people on the Island knew only bits and pieces. Only the people closest to us were well informed. Everyone now was deeply concerned and wanting to help in whatever way they could.

I quickly passed detailed information to everyone who was getting involved, so each would understand exactly what they were quickly becoming a part of.

Mandy's whole focus turned to our dilemma, working on it daily. She never realized some of the very people she thought would be there for us were a part of the whole deception. I made attempts to inform her of my beliefs of the U.S. Embassy's involvement. She couldn't comprehend deception by people she had trusted and worked so closely with on many projects. She continued to go forward in her usual manner.

Mandy and I met on a daily basis to brainstorm. The thought came up of getting support from our friends that were government officials on the Island. We contacted Governor Elwyn Stavely, Mayor Merren, and other leaders. Each was very supportive, sending letters to the U.S. Embassy, Congressmen, Governors, and other U.S. officials, all pleading support of Nocona.

U.S. Embassy article on Angelina Ulloa refusing to help them.

```
VS OFFICE                TUESDAY   02/27/96  05:14 PM              1
PACKAGE SUBJECT:  NACONA SMITH
ITEM TITLE:  NACONA SMITH          UNCLASSIFIED
```

MICHAEL,

YOUR MATERIAL IS EXCELLENT AND CORRECT. I WOULD ADD THE FOLLOWING BY WAY OF AMPLIFICATION AND CLARIFICATION:
1) RE REMOVAL OF NOCONA TO THE US UNDER THE HAGUE CONVENTION, EXTRADITION, OR DEPORTATION, WE HAVE AND WILL CONTINUE TO PURSUE ALL AVENUES:

--HAGUE CONVENTION CANNOT BE EFFECTIVELY INVOKED UNTIL GOH DESIGNATES A "CENTRAL AUTHORITY," WHICH WE ARE ACTIVELY PUSHING THEM TO DO. WE'VE SENT TWO DIP NOTES SO FAR, AND "DEMARCHED" THE VICE FOREIGN MINISTER IN SEPT. WE'RE RENEWING THESE EFFORTS THIS VERY WEEK. LACK OF RESULTS SO FAR REFLECT (SADLY) GOH INDIFFERENCE AND/OR INCOMPETENCE RATHER THAN SHORTAGE OF ZEAL ON OUR PART.

--WE HAVE YET TO RECEIVE ANY EXTRADITION REQUEST FROM WASHINGTON. IF WE WERE TO GET ONE, WE WOULD PURSUE IT ACTIVELY, ALTHOUGH GOH TRACK RECORD ON ENFORCEMENT OF THE OLD TREATY WE HAVE IS EXTREMELY POOR TO SAY THE LEAST, AND WE ARE NOT AT ALL SANGUINE THAT OUR REQUEST WOULD GET ANYWHERE. (NEVERTHELESS, OCI MAY WISH TO CONSIDER THIS OPTION.)

--DEPORTATION: FBI REP RIVERO TOLD ME HE LONG AGO ASKED ANGELINA ULLOA, DIRECTOR OF HONDURAN IMMIGRATION AND A CLOSE FRIEND/CONTACT OF THE EMBASSY, ABOUT DEPORTING THE FAMILY, AND SHE FLATLY REFUSED AND TOLD HIM TO FORGET IT.

3) "COLLUDING WITH THE HONDURANS:" THERE IS ABSOLUTELY NOTHING TO THIS CHARGE. I BELIEVE THAT IT WAS VALLADARES (WHO IS NOT ACTUALLY A MINISTER BUT RESPECTED DIRECTOR OF A PARA-GOVERNMENT, QUASI-INDEPENDENT HR ORG) WHO ACTUALLY (AND PHYSICALLY, I BELIEVE), FIRST BROUGHT _____ RIVER, AND NOCONA TO OUR ATTENTION. ALTHOUGH IT'S TRUE THAT VALLADARES SEEMS TO BE THE CHIEF "PROTECTOR" OF ___ AND RIVER WITHIN THE GOH, TO MY KNOWLEDGE WE'VE DONE ABSOLUTELY NOTHING TO SOLICIT OR ENCOURAGE THIS. I'M NOT AWARE OF ANY SUCH DISCUSSION WITH THE ANYONE IN THE GOH, AS ALLEGED BY ___)

STEVE DOESN'T NEED TO INCORPORATE ALL OF THE ABOVE IN THE LETTER, BUT SHOULD FEEL FREE TO DRAW ON ANY/ALL OF IT, AS HE DEEMS APPROPRIATE. G

---------------------------------- REPLY ----------------------------------
TO: GREG T FROST   FROM: MICHAEL A BARKIN
SUBJECT: NACONA SMITH   DATE SENT: 02/07/96

DEAR STEVE,
WE THINK THAT THE RESPONSE TO THE LETTER SHOULD BE BRIEF, AND WE (GREG AND I) DON'T THINK IT NECESSARY TO RESPOND TO EVERY CHARGE. WHATEVER OUR PRIVATE OPINIONS OF THIS CASE MIGHT BE, I DON'T THINK ANYONE HERE HAS DONE ANYTHING TO OBSTRUCT THE CRIMINAL CASE AGAINST RIVER AND ___ / WE CONTINUE TO ADVISE THEM TO RETURN TO THE STATES TO DEAL WITH THE CHARGES, EVEN THOUGH WE REALIZE THAT THEY ARE UNLIKELY TO DO SO.
HERE IS OUR INPUT ON THE INDIVIDUAL CHARGES IN THE LETTER:

Dept. of State, RPS/IPS, Margaret P. Grafeld, Dir.
( ) Release (X) Excise ( ) Deny ( ) Declassify
Date 04/01/03 Exemption _____

UNCLASSIFIED

```
VS OFFICE                TUESDAY   02/25/97  10:46 AM  PAGE:      1
TO:       SENA, STEPHEN             IN STATE
FROM:     GREG T FROST              CURITY:     LIMITED
SUBJECT:  NOCONA SMITH CASE         TE RECEIVED: 02/24/97
```

STEVE,

INTERESTING. GUESS ROATAN IS PRETTY UNANIMOUS ON THIS ONE! MAYOR MERREN AND GOV. ELWIN ARE FROM DIFFERENT PARTIES, SO THERE IS A LITTLE RIVALRY BETWEEN THEM. THERE IS A GUY WE'RE TRYING TO EXTRADITE FROM THE ISLAND. ELWIN IS PUSHING TO GET RID OF HIM, BUT MERREN FALLS STRANGELY SILENT WHENEVER THE GUY'S NAME IS MENTIONED--PERHAPS IT'S BECAUSE THE GUY'S WIFE IS A MEMBER OF HIS CITY COUNCIL?

AS FOR NOCONA, I WOULDN'T SWEAR TO IT, BUT I DON'T THINK THEY EVER WERE IN COSTA RICA. I THINK THEY FIRST CAME INTO THE EMBASSY HERE IN FEB. 95, AND I RECALL ___ TELLING ME THEY HAD FIRST FLED TO MEXICO. G

---------------------------------- REPLY ----------------------------------

U.S. Embassy on kidnapping, (Mayor & Governor).

Secretaría de Estado en el Despacho de
Gobernación y Justicia

REPUBLICA DE HONDURAS, CENTRO AMERICA

Roatan, 24 of January, 1997

President Bill Clinton
White House
1600 Pennsylvania Ave.
Washington, DC 20010
Attention Marcia Hale

President Bill Clinton

Tuesday April 23, 1996 on the Islands of Roatan, Honduras, Three U.S. Citizen forced their way into a private school with guns and kidnaped a five year old child by the name of Nocona Lynn _____ (father of Nocona), _____ and Erick Wilmith, forced the child onto the floor of a truck as the child cried and screamed for help, Nocona's teacher in an attempt to help Nocona was knocked down twice by the assailants. The result of horrendous action not only left the children and the teacher devastated but has also left scars that will never leave the minds of the many children and adults present that day.

The teacher's children and parents of the children live in fear of _____ return. _____ not only endangered the life of Nocona Lynn with his reckless high speed race to the airport but the lives of the many residents that walk and travel these roads daily. The narrow roads with sharp curves are traveled normally at a rate of 20 to 25 miles an hour with caution.
high speed in excess of 55 mile an hour showed no respect for anyone. At the time of the kidnaping, I was off the Island due to illness. I feel at this time it's in my best interest that _____ and his accomplices need to be informed I will in no way tolerate such actions by people of his nature.
This case is still pending and will get my upmost attention if they choose to return. It is my duty as the Governor of Roatan to look after the safety and well being of the residents of this Island and in no way will I tolerate such disrespect.

Sinceraly Yours

Stavely Elwin
Governor, Bay Island, Honduras.

CC. JAMES F. CREAGAN
AMBASSADOR OF THE UNITED STATE OF AMERICA.

January 28, 1997

Islas de la Bahía, Honduras, C. A.

David Dunn
163rd District Judge
801 Division
Orange, Texas 77630

David Dunn

Greetings from Roatan Island, Honduras and thank you for taking the time to read my letter.

As Mayor of the City of Roatan I have had the privilege of meeting many warm and friendly Texans who visit our shores for the purpose of diving our beautiful reefs. I have even had the honor of performing the rite of marriage for a couple of your constituents.

On April 23rd of 1996 my opinion of Texans was tainted by _____ of Orange, Texas and _____ of Houston, Texas. They brought to this island two professional thugs, Mr. Eric Wilmeth and Bradley Robinson for the purpose of committing international child abduction. They chose to violate the most sacred ground on Roatan, a grammar school. Disguised as well meaning tourist they entered a classroom of innocent pre-kinder children and assaulted their teacher when she attempted to rescue her pupil.

This was not the act of a bereaved father, but an act of terrorism. The money and influence these people yielded was even terrifying to me.

These four US citizens had no respect for the laws of Honduras, our judicial system, our schools, our teachers and our national treasury, the children of our nation. Unfortunately epitomized the "Ugly American" and left a difficult legacy for the many fine Texans who come here with good intention.

As Mayor of the City of Roatan I will continue to welcome the many great people who come from the state of Texas with the exception of these four individuals. I hope that one day you might visit our shores and we can discuss this matter in person.

Respectfully yours,

Ricardo Merren
Mayor

Each day was now surrounded with stress not only for us, but the whole Island felt the pressure. Nocona and I were picking up a few things at the Tienda in West End. My nervous system had pretty much collapsed, so I was there mainly just to get out of the house. As I began to pay for the items, I noticed two local policemen walk into the small store. They turned, abruptly spoke, and motioned for me to go with them. Nocona normally interpreted for me, but today it wasn't needed. The body language was simple. I knew they were giving me no choice. I had to go.

I soon found myself in Coxen Hole, face to face with the presiding Judge over the whole kidnapping case. As we entered the building, Nocona became extremely nervous. She told me that this was the place that the mean man was at, and the place where I'd cried on the day she was kidnapped.

Nocona and I sat quietly until called into the Judge's office. Once we were seated, the Judge asked several pointed questions. He then let me know a U.S. Senator and Congressman were calling daily, putting a lot of pressure on him. He ended by telling me not to go out of the country. I sat, patiently waiting for the purpose for the meeting, but that seemed to be it, and I was told I could leave. I left, totally bewildered by the whole incident. Why would he say, *Don't go out of the country?* There was no clear reason for meeting with him at all! I was not the one that committed a crime in Honduras.

Within a few days, I was approached by my attorney and a resident of West End. I was told to go to Tegucigalpa immediately to meet with Human Rights. I found it to be rather strange, since River and I had just finished that route only to be told they could do no more. The person became persistent as though they knew something I didn't. My desperate needs overriding my personal thoughts once again placed me in the hands of an attorney. Feeling as though I had no choice, I went forward, taking their advice. Within minutes, a lady showed up, encouraging me to do as he stated. I thought of the whole scenario as being strange at the time, but I went forward anyway and the lady joined me.

I spoke with River JoNey, requesting she take care of some things at the hotel and later join Nocona and I. We immediately made our way to the airport with one of the attorneys and a friend going with us. With each mile, I felt something was totally wrong about this. It all became even more confusing when the attorney stopped in Coxen Hole and suddenly left us, stating he would join us later at the airport. Something wasn't right! I now had this profound feeling that I was being set up! It kept going over in my mind, do I go back to West End or do I go forward in what the professionals are telling me to do?

As I made my entrance into the airport, my instincts continued to kick in, leaving me feeling totally helpless with this huge problem. I went forward and purchased tickets to Tegucigalpa, the capital of Honduras. I paused again, thinking I should go back to West End. With each step I prayed I was wrong, but deep down I knew I was being set up. Everything within me screamed this was totally and completely incorrect! I felt so much drama, feeling as though I was in a movie setting and hoping, once again, someone would loudly announce... "Cut!"

At this point I felt I had no choice but to keep going. The party that stayed with me was now turning and walking off. As I lay my purse on the conveyer, I noticed uniformed men watching me. They were moving around nervously from each side. I knew for sure I had been set up, but I also knew despite, any change in decisions now would not help. My main thoughts were to get through whatever was going to happen with as little hoopla as possible, hopefully not upsetting Nocona.

Nocona was totally unaware of the whole event. I made it through security and continued to go forward. I noticed people from the side, all in uniforms, making hand motions to each other. I had frequented the airport many times and this was not the norm. As I made my way to the seating to await the plane, I could see uniformed policemen running back and forth outside. After a while I became annoyed at the drama, wondering ... *Does it really take thirty men with machine guns to pick up an unarmed grandmother and a small child?*

The policemen began to approach me from all sides as though it were a drug raid, letting me know I was to follow them. Nocona and I were ushered into a small room. I immediately handed them my tickets, showing where I was going, but no one was interested. They had a purpose and a plan and nothing would change it.

They went on to state I was trying to leave the country. I tried to explain I was told by my attorneys to meet with Human Rights. I calmly told them to call Human Rights or look at my tickets. The tickets plainly stated I was going to the state capital, Tegucigalpa. I was totally ignored and could tell that no matter what I said, they were focused on one thing and it wasn't on letting me go. It then registered with me there never was a meeting set up with Human Rights! I knew for sure now that I had been set up not by one, but many. I continued to sit quietly as though it were a normal day, hoping Nocona would not become alarmed. I waited for their next move.

An hour went by and then all the men got up and motioned for us to follow. An arrogant young lady grabbed Nocona's hand, but I pulled Nocona back. The lady was upset by my response, but the police motioned for her to stop when they saw my persistence. It was as though she was appointed to take Nocona from me and obviously turn her over to someone else.

A truck was waiting outside the airport and we were told to get in it. As we left the airport, others surrounded us and followed. We were definitely on our way to jail. We came to a stop and began to walk the rest of the way. I had heard all the rumors about this place, and I was now going to experience it firsthand. As we approached the muddy trail going to the jail, it had the horrible odor and appearance of sewer on the ground. I looked up to see only one cell with a dirt floor approximately the size of a small bathroom. It was hard to tell how many men were in it since the enclosure was dark from so many bodies being in it. From the sound of their voices there was standing room only. I was grateful they had us sit outside.

I made a request to call the Embassy, but the request was denied. I may be down, but I just wanted the Embassy to know I was totally aware of their position in this. They finally allowed me to make a call. I called a friend and local businessman that we had come to trust, but he was not in.

It was extremely hot. I knew Nocona would start crying if she got nervous, just making things worse. She wanted to get down and play, but there was only one clean area on the ground where the officer's bicycles were. I let her down to play for a few minutes.

I monitored the demeanor of the policeman as he sat at a desk outside as though he were waiting on someone. No one told us anything as to why we were there or what their plans were for us. An acquaintance quietly walked up and sat beside me.

Several hours went by. Three large men in suits abruptly strolled in. They approached the policemen, flashed a badge very arrogantly, stating they were with the U.S. Embassy. I quickly grabbed Nocona and held her close to me. The men were very loud and haughty. They stated they were here to take Nocona into their custody. The Islander sitting next to me interpreted. I lost it at that point, screaming, *"You're not taking Nocona anywhere!"*

The policeman in charge stated something to them and they wheeled around and spewed out crude words as they walked off. They were obviously not the party the policeman was waiting on. He was a small-framed man, but he was not intimidated, nor did he respond to their harsh remarks. My interpreter stated when the men walked off, "They were calling you dirty names and said they would return with handcuffs for you."

I finally got the policeman to call a friend of mine that was politically connected. The word was soon out, and River JoNey along with others began to come. Late in the evening, a judge came by. It wasn't long afterwards that I was free. No one stated why, and I didn't ask. We were now back home and that felt good!

My nervous system was totally traumatized. The next day all I could think about was getting away from the Island and this whole horrific mess! The hotel, West End, and everything that surrounded me was now a constant reminder. I hired a bodyguard, picked up Nocona, and headed for West Bay for the day. West Bay was a secluded area with one restaurant called Bite On The Beach at the end of a long sandy beach—the perfect spot for Nocona to run on the beach and play in the water. No hotels, no dive shops, no tourists, just a quiet, peaceful, beautiful beach.

As we pulled up to the sandbar, a few Island children quickly ran up to play with Nocona. I sat on the beach and watched them swim and play in the sand. As the sun began to go down, an Island fisherman paddled up in his dory. He had caught some very large fish and began cleaning them on the beach. One had live babies and the children began to play with them in the water before the fish swam off. I took pictures as I watched Nocona laugh and interact with the children.

I began to walk the sandy beach, looking at beautiful seashells that had washed up. My eyes became fixed on the small, lifeless shells as the water flowed over them. I reflected on the little sticks I had purchased in Galveston with the seashells peering through, as though they were imprisoned. Now that had become my own plight! *We were now Seashell Prisoners!* I now felt totally imprisoned by an island, surrounded by water, sand, and seashells.

MAY 4, 1996

Mandy had now organized to take us off the Island and get us settled on the mainland. She had friends all over Honduras including lawyers and physicians. Once we arrived in LeCeiba, we drove for hours arriving at a beautiful hotel in San Pedro called the Grand Sula. Friends from the Island and the States immediately began contacting us, stating that Nocona's father, sister, and thugs had returned to the U.S., but Eric remained on the Island. From all evidence, Trevor continued his plot against us, and Eric was obviously the thug left behind determined to finish the job. The bounty for Nocona apparently was high.

We were told upon Trevor and his sister's arrival to the U.S., they were approached by the press. Trevor made the statement that he was suing Stephen Sena, State Counselor/Officer for Children's Issues.

```
VS OFFICE                 THURSDAY    05/09/96   05:26 PM   PAGE:
YES, I DID LOOK AT THE TWO NEWS STORIES ON(     ]  HE WAS FILMED AT THE
AIRPORT UPON HIS RETURN.  HE TALKED ABOUT GOING TO "RESCUE" HIS DAUGHTER AND
HOW HE IS GOING TO SUE THE STATE DEPARTMENT AND STEVE SENA ALL THE WAY BACK IN
WASHINGTON, D.C.  UNTIL LATER, REGARDS, STEVE.
```

U.S. Embassy Report Trevor's Arrival to States

The next day, Mandy was introducing us to a team of famous attorneys and physicians on the mainland. We once again began adding new friends to our list. Mandy's close friend, Dr. Redolpho Bendena, not only cared for us as patients, but quickly became an integral part of our support team.

Redolpho accepted us into his home and his life, making us feel accepted and safe in Honduras. Once again I heard the warm greeting, *My home is your home*, as he introduced us to his family and friends. Redolpho treated me for my nerves, but I soon realized my situation was needing a lot of time to heal. The medication was like taking an aspirin.

We were eternally grateful as with other friends that continued to go the extra mile each day. People daily stepped up to the plate with each catastrophe, helping us to continue going in a forward motion. No one stated, "God sent me"...I just knew….

We had many appointments with the attorneys in San Pedro, and they made progress as far as getting our residency, etc., settled, to keep us more secure in the Country.

On Mandy's return to the Island, she gave us a call. She let us know she was being stalked by Eric Wilmirth. He was frequently seen racing up and down the narrow road of West End harassing her as he searched for us. Children narrowly escaped being run over as he daily stalked the Island. She stated one of Nocona's good friends would not return to school after seeing Eric in West End. Nocona became upset when she heard us talking about it! She turned to River and myself, with everything from the past flooding her mind. She began telling us everything Trevor did to her as a two-year-old. Both River and I struggled as she talked about her nightmare and spoke of guns and different forms of abuse. I hugged Nocona, letting her know her friend would be okay and so would we.

The Grand Sula was very nice, with a huge swimming pool. I was emotionally drained with only the energy to go down the elevator and slump down in a chair, while Nocona spent her days in the pool. We quickly became a well-known fixture in the Hotel, watching people come and go. Nocona loved the pool, mesmerizing all the guests with the small figure swimming like a fish in the huge pool.

Two weeks passed. The thought came up of just selling everything and staying at the Grand Sula until I ran out of money! I felt safe there. I was so sure I could raise Nocona in the Hotel. All I needed was water and food to keep her happy, and we had both.

༄

PRESIDENT OF THE UNITED STATES
GEORGE BUSH
WHITE HOUSE
1600 PENNSYLVANIA AVE.
WASHINGTON D.C. 20010

TO WHOEVER IT MAY CONCERN:

WE UNDERSTAND THAT FRANCES ANN HARRIS CARRIES A CHARGE OF KIDNAPPING IN THE U.S. IF THIS IS TRUE ,AND IF BY ANY CHANCE FRANCES IS PUT ON PROBATION, WE WOULD LIKE TO REQUEST THAT SHE SERVE HER PROBATION TIME IN HONDURAS HERE ON THE ISLAND WHERE HER TALENTS ARE NEEDED.

THE PEOPLE HERE ON THE ISLAND OF ROATAN HAD FALLEN INTO A STATE OF COMPLACENCY AND BECAUSE OF THIS THE YOUTH ON THE ISLAND WERE SUFFERING FOR IT. THE SPIRITUAL DEATH OF THE YOUTH WAS RECOGNIZED BY FRANCES AND SHE BEGAN WORKING UP PROGRAMS INVOLVING YOUTH WITHIN A YEAR OF HER ARRIVAL..

MOST OF THE FOREIGNERS THAT COME HERE PUT THEIR PRIORITY ON MAKING MONEY THAT WAS NOT THE CASE WITH FRANCES. AFTER HER ARRIVAL ON THE ISLAND, FRANCES WAS WORKING UP PROGRAMS FOR YOUTH , WOMEN, AND HELPING WITH MANY CHURCH GROUPS AND MISSIONARIES, HERE FROM THE U.S..

LIVING ON AN ISLAND IN A THIRD WORLD COUNTRY HAS MANY HARDSHIPS, ALL OF WHICH I FEEL FRANCES AND HER FAMILY HAVE ENCOUNTERED....DESPITE THE MANY HARDSHIPS OF THE ISLAND AND HARDSHIPS FROM THE PROBLEMS WITH HELPING NOCONA, FRANCES CONTINUED TO GO FORWARD AND NOT ALLOW THE PROBLEMS TO DISCONTINUE HER WORK WITH THE YOUTH AND COMMUNITY.

JUST FROM WHAT WE HAVE LEARNED FROM SPEAKING WITH FRANCES ,
SHE CAME TO THE ISLAND AND STARTED WHERE SHE LEFT OFF IN THE STATES. FROM SPEAKING WITH HER FRIENDS AND FAMILY FROM THE STATES , FRANCES WAS CONTINUALLY ORGANIZING AND INVOLVED WITH NUMEROUS ACTIVITIES INVOLVING YOUTH IN ORANGE AND MAURICEVILLE, TEXAS.

WITH FRANCES'S BACKGROUND IN ORGANIZING YOUTH EVENTS AND WORKING WITH YOUTH PROGRAMS, SHE HAS IN TURN BEEN ABLE TO BRING SIMILAR ACTIVITIES TO THE ISLAND. BECAUSE OF THIS, MANY YOUTH AND THEIR FAMILIES HAVE BENEFITED BY THEM.

PROGRAMS FRANCES HAS STARTED HERE OVER A FIVE YEAR PERIOD :

1.TWO YOUTH REVIVALS FOR THE WHOLE ISLAND INVOLVING OVER 500 YOUTH
2.HELPED ORGANIZE MONTHLY CHRISTIAN WOMEN'S MEETINGS: INVOLVING WOMEN FROM ALL OVER THE ISLAND
3.CHISTMAS ON THE BEACH PROGRAM: YEARLY EVENT FOR THE PAST FOUR YEARS INVOLVING ALL THE YOUTH AND FAMILIES OF THE COMMUNITY OF WEST END WITH PARADES/ YOUTH DRAMA , DANCE, & DRAMA PROGRAMS , FIREWORKS DISPLAY. BOAT PARADE WITH SANTA AS THE HIGHLIGHT OF THE EVENT, ALL OF WHICH FRANCES ORGANIZED AND WORKS UP WITH THE BUSINESS PEOPLE AND COMMUNITY
4.PASTOR AND MISSIONARY CONFERENCE: HAD THE FIRST ONE AT HER BUSINESS AND LATER HELPED OTHER MINISTRIES WITH THERE PROGRAM

5. HAS MONTHLY DINNERS FOR WELCOMING NEW MISSIONARIES TO THE ISLAND AND BRINGING THE ISLAND MINISTRIES TOGETHER
6. USED HER HOME & BUSINESS FOR NEW MISSIONARIES COMING IN
7. WORKED WITH YOUTH SUNDAY SCHOOL CLASSES IN WEST END
8. SUPPORTS MINISTRIES IN HONDURAS WITH HER INCOME
9. STARTED A DANCE TEAM WITH CHILDREN OF WEST END
10. HAS YOUTH OVER DURING THE YEAR TO HEAR VARIOUS SPEAKERS COMING ON THE ISLAND/
11. WORKED UP A CHRISTIAN PROGRAM FOR THE YOUTH ON HALLOWEEN NIGHT
12. HELPS MINISTRIES ON THE ISLAND TO COME IN CONTACT WITH MISSION TEAMS FROM THE STATES, AND WORKS WITH THEM IN BUILDING WEBSITES FOR THEIR MINISTRIES.

FRANCES AND HER FAMILY ARE VERY RESPECTED HERE. ITS OUR DESIRE TO SEE PEOPLE LIKE FRANCES & NOCONA CONTINUE TO LIVE AND WORK WITH US HERE. ISLANDS HAVE A WAY OF ATTRACTING MANY, OF WHICH AT TIMES, TAKE AWAY FROM THE ISLAND.

FRANCES WORKS WITH MANY MINISTRIES HERE AND BECAUSE OF HER INTEGRITY WAS CHOSEN TO SERVE ON A BOARD OF A NEW MINISTRY HERE, (EUROPEAN OUTREACH), CSI. THIS MINISTRY IS IN THE PROCESS OF BUILDING A YOUTH CENTER, ORPHANAGE, AND BASEBALL FIELD, FOR THE YOUTH ON THE ISLAND.

FRANCES ALSO WORKS THROUGH HER BUSINESS WEBSITE TO BRING NEW MINISTRIES IN TO THE ISLAND TO SUPPORT THE CHURCHES HERE.

WE WOULD LIKE TO ASK ONCE AGAIN, IF THERE IS A CHANCE OF FRANCES ANN HARRIS / COLLINS BEING ALLOWED TO BE ON PROBATION WE WOULD LIKE TO SEE THAT PROBATION BE USED HERE WHERE IT IS BADLY NEEDED IN THE COUNTRY OF HONDURAS..

OUR DEEPEST APPRECIATION OF YOUR TIME

MAYOR OF ROATAN   GOVENOR OF ROATAN

CHIEF OF POLICE/ ROATAN   PASTORS: OAKRIDGE CHAPEL/ ROATAN

PASTOR/ OVERSEER :FIRST BAPTIST CHURCH ROATAN   FRIEND/SHIP INTERNATIONAL: HONDURAS

PASTOR/ OVERSEER CHURCH OF GOD ROATAN   PASTOR: SEVENTH DAY ADVENTIST ROATAN

PASTOR : CHURCH OF GOD COXEN HOLE ROATAN   PASTOR : CHURCH OF GOD FRENCH HARBOUR ROATAN

ALTERNATIVE MISSION: HONDURAS   EUROPEAN/ CARIBBEAN OUTREACH: ROATAN BRAD Warren
                                                   (504)445-1915

One night I decided to do something different and take Nocona to eat in the formal dining room on the top floor. River was in the hotel bar watching soccer games on T.V. It felt good being in an elegant environment with tablecloths and nice silverware on the table. Nocona and I dressed up for the occasion. As we sat in the dining room, I thought of West End and the many thatched-roof restaurants on the beach that we had frequented many times. The cool air-conditioning was quite a change from the sand and heat of the Caribbean.

As we sat in the luxurious dining area eating, the room began to fill with many distinguished American men in blacks suits. They just kept pouring in. I cautiously watched them as they each sat down at the tables around us. There was an intense urgency about them. From their dress and demeanor, I had this strong sense it was F.B.I. agents from the U.S.

The longer I sat, the more concerned I became. As soon as Nocona finished her meal I paid my bill, and quietly made our way out the side door and back to the room. Within minutes, River entered the room extremely nervous, stating she was at the bar watching a soccer game, and the room filled with F.B.I. agents! Most of them spoke good English and she thought one of them was Fred Lucas. It was all reconfirmed as we watched the news on television. River interpreted the Spanish station saying U.S. F.B.I. agents were in Honduras on a special mission, but it was not made clear what all it entailed.

We continued to meet with attorneys and make contact with Human Rights. Finally, after two months, Island friends convinced us to return to Roatan. I was growing weary of the whole problem. My life had come to a dead end. I felt totally dead mentally, physically, and emotionally. I reluctantly made the decision to return to the Island, but in body only. I really did not care what happened next. I just wanted life to be over with!

JUNE 1996

On our return to the Island, Nocona was clinging to my every move. She was now very insecure, not wanting to be out of my sight. River's friend, Ms. Ruth, was writing faithfully along with many others. This time she was coming to stay a month. On her arrival, I tried to act like I was okay, but I wasn't. I was in a deep depression and everything was making me extremely nervous. It was like I got up in the morning just to make sure I wasn't dead! River was communicating with her father. Owen and Anna came to the island and took River back to the States.

With each month my nerves got worse, with depression setting in. At one point, I begged God to please take my life; I did not want to live in this world one more hour! To my sorrow, I would wake up only to find the request was not fulfilled.

The first week back on the Island, Nocona was asked to return to the Bilingual School. I appreciated the invitation, but was totally unsure how that would affect Nocona. I decided I owed it to Nocona to give it a try. As we approached the school this time, ten-foot-high fences had been erected. After a few weeks of attendance, it was obvious Nocona was not able to focus. Her lack of attention caused her to become a disruption to the class. Nocona was outwardly making an attempt to be happy, but inwardly was feeling confused and insecure. I would now have to look into home schooling. Within a few weeks, River JoNey sent the ABeka home school program for Nocona.

As I poured myself into depression, Nocona poured herself into her home school program and playing with Naomi and her sisters. She would constantly check on me, making sure I was okay. Frederick, Laura and the grandchildren watched Nocona every second. I knew Nocona was safe with them.

Nocona & Grandfather, Owen Burton

The hotel was now much harder to run with my frayed nerves. Each day on the Island became more and more stressful for all of us. River's dad and Anna flew in, insisting River return with them. She emailed and let us know she was okay and attending Texas A&M College. It was a relief knowing she was now going forward with her life.

Mandy came by each day to encourage us, and continued speaking with U.S. Embassy officials and judges in an attempt to make sense of this whole bizarre thing. She felt sure these people would help us. They were all her good friends and people she had worked with for years. With each day, it was evident more and more mind games continued to be played, not only on Mandy, but on all of us. Mandy wouldn't let go and was determined to get to the bottom of all of this. Mandy had always been able to make things happen with whatever she attempted. As the weeks went by, her brother, Joe, demanded she return to the States.

I made every attempt to get the hotel back up and going. I dreaded rainy days when Nocona had to stay in. It was extremely hard keeping her quiet on the hardwood floors. The guests would always come in and rest in the hammocks after their morning dive, then go out for dinner. They wanted it quiet in the afternoon and evening before going out.

Living below the three rooms, I always knew when the guests left for dinner in the evening. We all had a sigh of relief. Nocona and Puffer dog were then allowed to run throughout the bottom floor and play. Up and down the winding stairway she ran with her usual game, chasing Puffer dog around the large room and upstairs. His long white hair flowed across the floor. Petie bird always got in on the evening entertainment, ending in a big fight with Puffer as each vied for our attention. It was all very amusing, in its own way, taking my mind off of my problems.

I continued to make an attempt to keep my guests happy and was meeting new people each week. I was introducing guests to real estate agents and missionaries to church leaders around the Island, and recommending restaurants to guests. I was now having to work harder at my acting, but it worked, and all my guests continued to be happy and to love their stays at Casa Calico. The hotel continued to grow in name in many countries.

❧

The tourists varied, some from Italy, Germany, Canada, Britain, and the States. One day, as I was on Ms. Mandy's beach watching Nocona and her friends, I noticed a young American couple playing on the beach. They were enjoying the sun and blue water. I loved their enthusiasm. I watched them from a distance, reflecting on myself and all the fun dive vacations I had been on prior to my arrival here. I found myself wanting to speak to them just to possibly find someone that might share just one moment of something that felt like home. Maybe they did not know my family, but could possibly say something that would reestablish myself with my country. I finally approached them, and they were quite friendly, letting me know they were missionaries doing work in St. Helene. Jeremy and Melissa were only in West End for the day. As I gathered up Nocona to leave, I invited them to use Casa Calico if they needed a shower or a place to get out of the sun. They later showed up and, as always, Nocona took over entertaining them with her usual antics.

I continued to study my Bible, daily learning more stories. It was as though I had an overall idea of how all the stories went, but I was still unsure in areas. Each day, I would sit down and teach the stories to Nocona, and together we would journal our thoughts and favorite Scriptures in a notebook. I added pictures of Nocona and her friends to each page.

❧

Casa Calico soon made a sharp turnaround. The new hotels may have taken a lot of my European business, but now missionaries began to flood Casa Calico. The young couple, Jeremy and Melissa, loved my hotel and spoke to their leaders about it. The young ministry of Alternative Missions was soon bringing in missionaries from the States doing work in various places. I never knew a missionary prior to my arrival on the Island, but I soon gravitated to all of them. Once I noticed them attaching to Nocona, it definitely made my job a lot easier. This was also a great opportunity for me to learn more about God. All the missionaries arrived with a purpose, lots of enthusiasm, and lots of love.

The missionaries' jobs were many—some being physicians, teachers, ministers, dentists, etc. I loved their excitement for life and enjoyed listening to all of their stories. They were definitely full of personality and certainly were not the image I had in my mind for missionaries!

A few of our favorites were Dan, Tim, Dr. Ron, John (a dentist), Laura, Miss Jen, Margie and Miss Peggy. Laura was a vibrant young lady that always wore glitter on her eyelids. Nocona was fascinated with the glitter, so Laura left Nocona with a good year's supply behind on her departure.

Nocona was a perfect fit with all the missionaries, quickly learning new ways to get presents. She entertained them with songs, dances, and playing the piano. They were quite different from the tourists. I could now breathe easily, not having to keep Nocona reigned in. These people had their own agenda. They focused totally on doing God's work on various islands and the mainland! I soon took advantage handing them the keys to the place, and taking a day and sometimes a weekend off.

From this, I met Tom Hackett, the Director of Alternative Missions. Dan Fortune, a phenomenal young man, headed up the team. With the help of Dan's good friend Tim and many others, they constructed a medical and dental clinic in a very remote area off the East end of the Island, called St. Helene. Nocona and I quickly attached to this group, looking forward to each return. We were always treated as though we were a part of their team, frequently going to dinner at the end of their stay. It wasn't long until other mission teams found Casa Calico also.

Nocona at the age of six was fluent in Spanish and quickly became a PR person for new missionaries, showing them all the favorite snorkeling places and best places to eat and shop in West End. Nocona was well known by the boat taxi drivers and all the residents of our area, making it easy for them to get around.

Within months, Dan's father and mother were now making plans to come to the Island and would be staying at Casa Calico. All we knew was that Katie was a Christian author and speaker, and she and her husband Don had traveled to different countries giving talks. Interesting and fun people were always showing up with more stories and much knowledge of God. I soon found with each group that arrived that our lives would be changed in some way once they left. Nocona and I both gravitated to all of them, and now we were anticipating getting to meet Dan's parents.

On the arrival of Don and Katie, it was apparent Dan was quite different from his mother and father. Dan was serious about his work, but full of humor and always poking fun. If I had Nocona settled down on his arrival, change came about quickly as Dan and his good friend Tim entered the room, always picking Nocona up and hurling her around, leaving her laughing and screaming! It was hard to get aggravated with them since they brought laughter and normalcy back into our lives with each visit.

Dr. Ron, Laura & Alternative Ministry Team

Miss Jenn, Nocona, Dolton at St. Helene

Dan, Wolfgang, Frances & Friend

Don and Katie were very gracious, but totally focused and totally business. I was a little surprised at the interest they took in Nocona and me. I was not sure if they had heard all the notorious stories. With each person that arrived, I always tried to make conversation without sounding like the fugitive of justice that I was or show concern over any recent happenings. (Interpol was now pushing harder seeking out our capture and return to the U.S.)

One evening as we sat around the table visiting, Katie let me know God had given them a word for me. As I sat at the table, they began to take charge, speaking strong words into me that sounded very strange at that moment. I intensely listened as Katie went forward, explaining God's plan for me on the Island of Roatan. They obviously knew a lot more than I did. I wasn't sure who I was or what my presence was doing here, but it was reassuring that they seemed to know. It was as though God were using them as some sort of messengers.

They went on to state God was using me as a catalyst and a connector on the Island. Katie went into more detail as to the many ways God planned to use me in Honduras. With each word she spoke, she was writing it on paper. They spent time praying with me, then I tucked the writings in my Bible and graciously thanked them. I was in complete awe at the evening and very grateful for their time and knowledge, but still a little perplexed by it all.

Over the years, our friendship grew with each time they stayed at Casa Calico.

Seashell Prisoners
CHAPTER 14

Time seemed to be the only thing going forward. Each day was long and difficult with nothing but huge voids at its end. I then received the news that Anna was pregnant! What should have been a cherished moment just brought more disappointment. I would try to keep in touch and let her know how happy I was, but the truth was—I wasn't happy! I wouldn't get to be there for the birth of Anna's first child! I would just have to be content with a long-distance call from the hospital along with a few snapshots in the mail.

During Anna's eighth month of pregnancy, I requested a photograph of her since it was her first time to be pregnant. Shortly after, I receive a picture of this huge, nude stomach. I thought, *Well, I guess I should have been more specific!* The day of her delivery, I got my call and I was excited for her. I was also told either Trevor or the F.B.I. had someone staked out at the hospital, thinking I might be there.

Once Rylan was born, Anna sent us hours and hours of videos of simple things like Rylan lying in the water or Rylan laying on a blanket. It was obvious Anna was crazy about her baby! Nocona and I desperately searched each video upon its arrival for a presence of Anna, Brandon, or just anyone back home. They were never in the picture, just hours and hours of Rylan; Thank You Jesus!...*Finally crawling!*

The Island had always proved to be tough on me, but now it was physically, mentally, and financially draining. Once again, despite each setback, God continued divinely placing people in our paths. This time it was a young islander named Dennis Castro. Words could never express Dennis's importance to me, Nocona, and Casa Calico.

I hired Dennis from a restaurant River JoNey had previously managed. Dennis was young with four beautiful children. He worked hard, taking care of the rooms and the guests' needs. He was an extremely detailed person with quiet movements. My nerves were shredded, so his mannerisms and personality were perfect for me at the time. Dennis knew little English, but we worked beautifully together despite the language barrier. Within a short period we both came to have the same goals—great pride in Casa Calico and seeing the guests happy! We quickly became family, forming a unique bond. Dennis nurtured and protected Casa Calico, and protected Nocona and myself, as he did his own family.

I frequently saw Dennis's mother and family as I occasionally walked the beach road in the evening. She only spoke Spanish so we exchanged few words, but I could always expect a big hug. On one occasion, Dennis told me his mother was very sick, daily going down in her health. He went

Dennis Castou & family

on to say she wasn't able to work anymore and she was in a lot of pain. He said there was a strange movement in her side. He went on to say the bush doctors told her she had an iguana living in her.

I spoke to my friend Wolfgang, and we decided we would try to help her. I had been around enough missionaries and felt confident in the attempt, and Wolfgang had been reading a lot of books on demons. It was a slow week with the tourist, so Wolfgang didn't have any divers to take out on his boat for a couple days. The timing was perfect!

Dennis brought his mother to the hotel. I thought if there was any chance of helping this lady, I would give it a try. Wolfgang and I were in total agreement. I felt the problem wasn't an iguana, but possibly a demon of some sort! We took her into one of the bedrooms on the bottom floor while Dennis kept the guests distracted. Wolfgang began to read from the Bible what Jesus said about demons. While he read the Bible, I laid hands on Dennis's mother. Within minutes she became very relaxed, and the demon left. Dennis's mother was healed! A week later I saw her back on her job at the gift shop, and once again she gave me a big hug.

My arrival back to the Island became strained in many ways. Prior to my introduction to Honduras, I knew absolutely nothing about mental illness. I never even knew one person that had a problem with their nerves. Now my whole being was ravaged with confusion. Deep depression continued to haunt me. I knew I had a serious problem, but how was I supposed to get through this on an island? I was able to help other people, but I wasn't able to help myself. At each dead end I was reminded of the inner voice, and once again I was totally dependent on it leading me out of this.

My brother Thadd had sent me a computer from the States. I began to sit at the computer more and more, finding comfort in journaling. It was as though somehow I could empty my mind of anything that was stressful by placing it into the computer. I journaled every day.

One day as I was writing, I saw this small booklet filled with Scripture, called the Gospill Capsules, lying at the side of my computer. Obviously, the missionaries had left the pamphlet behind. They were Scriptures for overcoming difficulties, and I definitely had more than my share of them. I quickly put the Scriptures into my computer and kept a copy by my bed. I had no other alternative, so I gave it a try. Day in and day out I repeated the long list of scriptures, sometimes four and five times a day. Within weeks my brain once again began to show life. I continued this with each day, feeling a huge difference.

On each of Miss Ruth's visits, she would pray and encourage me. We would sit on the porches in the hot evenings, drinking lemon grass tea and blended melon drinks, having long talks. She daily cautioned me against speaking negatively. *"Frances, Speak Life!"*

After hearing it over and over, I became angry. She obviously had a good understanding, but I didn't. I wanted to scream, *What Life*, as she repeated it over and over and over! I respected Miss Ruth so much, but had to work at restraining my inner thoughts with her repetition of the Word.

Miss Ruth convinced me to purchase cable so I could watch more Christian television, and therefore gain more spiritual strength. I finally did and it helped me so much. I grew to love watching Pastor John Osteen.

I remember the day his son Joel stepped into his Dad's shoes, giving his first sermon. I was in awe, questioning God as to how that could possibly work! Joel's dad had so much wisdom and power and years of experience. His congregation was huge! Joel was relatively unknown in the ministry since he was young, and he obviously worked behind the scenes. I had attended a funeral at Pastor Osteen's church prior to leaving the States, so I felt as though I related in a small way. Could God really pull that off? Once again God proved He is God, and Joel not only did it, but with a totally different style of sermon than his father's. Obviously, it was God's timing. As the years passed, you could hear Joel's name mentioned around the Island. He became a favorite of many with his encouraging sermons.

Each day I continued to watch Nocona running and playing, yet I was still not back to my old self. Nocona was so precious. I knew God had a big plan for her. I felt deep guilt because I could not meet all her needs. I continued to struggle with depression. I bathed and fed Nocona, but that was all I could do. I was empty and totally void of life.

Day in and day out I repeated the Scriptures, and read my Bible. Something inside me began to state I was too inward-thinking and I needed to do something for someone else. I began taking my mind off of my problems by reaching out to help others.

Each day I prayed fervently for God to show me His power. If He truly had power, I wanted to see it. As each day passed and I saw no change, I began to demand it! I felt as though He owed that to me. As I sought God daily for change, He appeared to keep me at bay. Then He began showing me things in the spiritual world and soon began setting me up in positions that would be totally different than that of the old Frances Collins Harris.

With each minister I came to know in Roatan, I continued to speak my concerns for the youth, requesting youth revivals. Months went by and each time I passed a pastor throughout the Island I would continue to bring up the subject. I grew frustrated since no one acted on my request. One day I felt something in my spirit so strong stating, *"I Was Speaking To You! Why Aren't You Doing It?"* It became more and more dominating in my thoughts. I would often wonder, why was I becoming so fixated on the young people and their salvation? I never had a problem with it in Texas. It was as though I felt this horrible spiritual death encompassing the Island. God was telling me, I, Frances Collins Harris, was to get up and do something about the youth! My time as a Sunday School teacher was short lived with all the cultural differences, and now I was supposed to promote Youth Revivals on the Island of Roatan? I finally stopped fighting it and decided to give it a try.

Crystal Lyons

My nervous system was far from totally being back into place, but I was soon organizing youth revivals for the Island, planning picnics on the beach at the end of the week. God was definitely in the middle of it. My friend Miss Ruth, with awesome contacts back in Texas, would bring in dynamic speakers from the only church she was associated with…The Cowboy Ministry! The first were Ray and Crystal Lyons from Texas. The Island was in for another culture shock they were totally unprepared for! They just thought I was different, until they met Crystal! I had met Crystal and her husband Ray at a Cowboy Church at the Tin Top Rodeo Arena, which was close to my home in Mauriceville, Texas. I had used Crystal at one of the S.T.A.N.D. programs we had at the Fairgrounds in Mauriceville, Texas. Crystal was a very attractive lady. She was not only an awesome minister of the Bible and a great singer, but also competed in the rodeos including the event of bull-riding. Despite badly damaged nerves, I continued to go forward, with an unusual force pushing me forward to bring about the Youth Revival.

I was once again back into organizing, passing out fliers and posting them all over the Island in my spare time. I was on a total faith walk. I knew if this was truly of God, He was going to make it happen, despite me. I quickly began my promotional campaign. I taped a song of Crystal's and gave it to the Island radio station to play. Everyone began to get excited about the upcoming event. I spoke with Bro. Marco Galindo, and he agreed to help. Bro. Galindo was a highly respected Pastor and businessman on the Island with a beautiful family. We could have it at his church and have the picnic on his property at West Bay.

The first revival was unforgettable in more ways than one. God failed to prepare me for many things, one being Crystal Lyons, our speaker, arriving with a suitcase full of jeans and boots! As I watched Crystal exit the plane in her jeans, I reflected back on our arrival when one of the Islanders told River JoNey she had to wear a dress to church or she couldn't go! Now here I am with a female minister in jeans with the boldness of a lion! I looked at Miss Ruth like—surely you did remember to explain the culture to Crystal? Miss Ruth never flinched at the whole scenario. I remember thoughts flying through my mind of the upcoming revival thinking, *Exactly what could be the worst case scenario? Could I be banished from the Island?* I certainly didn't have money to start over. What would I do if this all turned into a huge fiasco?

Prior to the first meeting of the revival, I explained the situation to Crystal, talking her into wearing one of my dresses with a white jacket. The first night was to be at a Church of God in French Harbour. I remembered as we entered the church everyone was very accepting. As Crystal was introduced, she made her entry to the podium. To my shock and everyone else's....her honesty and forthright personality quickly emerged despite my plea. I sat frozen as she very boldly let the congregation know she was in my dress tonight, but tomorrow night she would be in her natural attire, boots and jeans!

I did not have to look to the right or left—you could just feel the effect of the statement. There was total, dark, stormy-like heaviness in the air. I wanted to slither under the bench, but I thought, *Okay, God—either You're God or You're not! You will just have to take care of this.* After the service, women were approaching me from all sides as I walked to the truck, all offering to purchase dresses for Crystal to wear at the next two services! I walked forward as though I never heard a word. I knew there were no words for this situation and the decision would not be left up to me. They were as strong in their belief as Crystal was in hers. I refused to get in the middle and just prayed fervently.... *There really was a person called God!*

The following night, the meeting was held in Coxen Hole, in an open-air building by the water that belong to Pastor Marco Galindo. This night the winding road to Coxen Hole seemed to be extremely long. On arrival, I could tell the tension was high as Crystal stepped out of the truck. Some were definitely not accepting her attire.... I was just praying somehow God would show up! Tension grew as she strolled across the grounds in her boots and white jeans and through the open-air building, making her way to the stage. As Crystal passed the congregation, there were a couple of light handshakes expressing what we could possibly expect through the service.

The building was close to the sea and packed with hundreds of people.

I love the sea and the cool breeze that flowed from it. Normally, this was one of my favorite places for church services, but nothing about this night was normal.

I sat nervously on the front row not knowing what might happen at any given time. I noticed right off how unusually hot and stifling the night was. Normally, there was a cool breeze from the sea. Tonight there was only intense heat. I sit quietly looking around to see if there was any way I might exit without being noticed, if the need came up.

I intensely watched Crystal as she stepped up on the platform and made her way over to speak to an Islander I had never seen before. The man was sitting at the keyboard to the back of the stage. I continued to watch to see what his reaction would be to Crystal, but there was no reaction. The person seated beside me told me he was from Pastor David Kelly's Church in Oakridge. Crystal then turned and picked up the microphone and walked toward the front of the stage. Crystal was looking confident! I braced myself as the man began to place his hands on the keyboard. Crystal began to sing.

Instantly everything changed! There was a lightness in the air. A cool breeze began to blow with a sweet presence that quickly overrode the heaviness. I sat in awe, knowing I had just witnessed another huge miracle! *This Had To Be God!* I never looked back to see the people's expressions. I just knew this was God.

Bro. Galindo stepped up to interpret as Crystal began to minister. Crystal preached with her usual boldness. Once again the presence of the Holy Spirit quickly overrode all strongholds. The night was awesome! As Pastor Galindo interpreted, every person there was intensely listening to every word of the sermon. At the end of the service Bro. Galindo made a profound statement as to how wrong people were for judging people by appearances. Maybe I didn't have much faith or knowledge of what was about to take place, but God did and was obviously aware of the outcome. I knew at that moment I had seen another side of God, realizing that people spend so much time trying to fit Him into a box, but the truth is He just won't stay there!

2nd Annual Music Festival
YOUTH REVIVAL & BEACH PARTY
Cowboy Ministry
THE PRICES
From Texas.....Monte, Susan, Leann & Jake Price
APR. 13TH - 17TH   7 PM
Location: Outreach Ministry, Coxen Hole.
Everyone Welcome!

Crystal Lyons had made a lasting impact on the Orange County Courts and, once again, in the lives of the hundreds of people of Roatan. Before she left the Island, we had one more request of Crystal. Nocona was desperately wanting to be baptized. Nocona was six years old. Miss Ruth, River JoNey, myself, and Crystal's family all made our way to the sea at Half Moon Bay by Mandy's house. Under the beautiful blue skies of the Caribbean,

Crystal not only baptized Nocona, but myself also. It was a great end for the memorable Youth Revival on the Island of Roatan, Honduras.

Time went on. With the help of Miss Ruth, another young group with the Cowboy Ministry from Texas made an equally big impact on the Island, but in a different way. Monte Price, a calf roper, and his wife Susan, his son Jake, and daughter LeAnn ministered and sang at our Second Island Youth Revival. The islanders were mesmerized with the talent and anointing of Monte's beautiful wife Susan and daughter LeAnn as they sang. Their son Jake worked with the music. Monte ended the sermon doing various tricks with his rope, entertaining everyone with his great roping abilities. All this was once again so different for the people present, but amazingly accepted and loved by everyone. With each event I was also learning more about God and finding Him now to be...*Truly Cool!* I knew I had learned a new lesson: Just listen, go forward, and let God take the reins. Don't even try to figure it out!

Day in and day out while Dennis worked cleaning rooms, Miss Ruth took long walks on the beach visiting with everyone along the way. I never let her go snorkeling without me since she knew no boundaries. Many days I would have to swim out and redirect her since she continually snorkeled out to sea. She had a huge appreciation of the beautiful corals below.

Everyone loved Miss Ruth. On her return from her walks, we could always expect her to come back speaking words of wisdom straight from the Bible. She had words for every situation that came up, and there were always plenty. Now, I had a brand new neighbor giving me problems over property lines, like an inch off the road. Day in and day out, this man was either attacking me or the seller of the property, Sister Laura. I tried to ignore him, but he was persistent, bringing in judges and municipality personnel to check out property lines. One day Sister Laura and I were served papers to show up before the judge in Coxen Hole. It was a cold, rainy, miserable day. Absolutely nothing seemed to be accomplished from the day. I never hired an attorney even though the other party appeared to have a couple; neither did I understand a word anyone was saying since they all spoke Spanish. Everyone continued to be as bewildered as we were over the situation.

Nothing about it made sense, being it was a road that everyone had legal access to. The man was single and had shown interest in me when he first arrived. I was so focused on survival, it never went any further than "Hi and how are you doing?" I introduced him to a couple of other ladies and thought everything was going well with our friendship until the man began giving us problems.

One day he verbally attacked my brother as he was working outside at the end of the hotel. Thadd came into the hotel very upset, letting everyone know his dislike for my new neighbor. I stood there, not sure what action to take now. The quiet, effervescing Miss Ruth had obviously all she could stand also. She boldly began walking throughout the small hotel, loudly claiming our neighbor was in serious trouble. He was coming up against a Child of God! She was very loud and adamant as she paced around the room! I stood at a distance, totally in shock at this normally, mild-mannered woman's remarks. The more I thought about it, the more I became amused, hearing this from this very small, Godly, elderly lady.

This very same man within months had to go back to his home in the States, and never returned to the Island. We were told he'd passed away. Months later, two other men that attacked me in other ways also had unusual deaths. After that I became a much stronger believer, listening intently to whatever came out of Miss Ruth's mouth. I didn't have to go to the Bible to check this lady out. If she spoke it, I knew it was there. I could tell she had obviously leaned on God enough to prove all her points. We always looked forward to her return visits.

Each year as Christmas came and went, I longed to be back in the States with my family. As I watched the beautiful Island children play each day, I decided to make an attempt to show the people in West End what Christmas meant to us back home. Nocona and I collected the children, taught them songs, dances, and skits, and had a Christmas program on the beach. The following year several West End businessmen and missionaries joined in. The kids and I would walk the beach taking up donations and soon built a stage, all of which became a yearly event called, "Christmas On The Beach." Signs and banners would show up all over the Island advertising our Christmas celebration.

Vincent Bush, owner of Cocoanut Tree, always welcomed the event by letting us set up the stage in front of his store and restaurant. The Cocoanut Tree was the perfect location, at the entrance of West End on the Half Moon Bay. A friend from the States had sent me a Christmas CD named "Christmas on The Beach." It was exceptionally upbeat and perfect for the occasion. We played it extremely loud every year, getting everyone in the Christmas spirit.

I looked forward to seeing the tourists hanging over the rails on the second floor of Vincent's restaurant, watching the local children do songs and dance routines on the stage below. Each year I would go to my closet, and pull out colorful serapes, Christmas decorations, or whatever I could find to dress the children up to make them feel special.

As the years went by, more and more decorations were collected, making each year special. The evening started with a walking parade, then went into a colorful, flamboyant program, fireworks and, last but not least,...Santa

Claus! Even though we were in the rainy season, nothing stopped the magical night as Santa made his way in beautifully decorated boats across the Bay. Others with the same love and vision joined in with our Santa, like Big Mike, Kris, Ron, Judy, Rose, Harold, Marcos, Delsey, Averyl, Bill, Gloria, Kevin, Tom and many others—all making it a night to be remembered by tourists and hundreds around the Island, especially the children.

Each year we would surprise the children with something different. One year we had a skinny Santa that snorkeled up from the sea. As he came up out of the water in his dripping wet suit, the children looked on in total shock and disappointment. We then brought out the real Santa! Another year we had three Santa's, since hundreds of children had overwhelmed the one the prior year.

The most memorable event was the year Santa fell through the stage when all the children jumped on it! This was a year no one would forget! Everyone laughed as the tourists captured it all on video.

At the end of the evening we would be so exhausted that I would swear I would never do it again. The tenacity of this group and their love for children made it happen year after year. As years passed, homes began to decorate and twinkling lights were appearing up and down the roads in West End.

I continued to struggle with my nerves, but knew the Bible was the only thing working for me, so I stayed in it.

Frances, Kris Holtz, Krista & West End Children

Big Mike, Frances & Nocona

Seashell Prisoners
CHAPTER 15

JULY 29, 1997

A breath of fresh air and great news on the Island: The Friendship Ministry was coming and setting up full time! Since they were docked in Galveston, Texas, prior to my leaving, I was familiar with them from different newspaper articles. I remember at one point in my life reflecting on what it might be like living on a ship and going from harbor to harbor helping people. Now the Friendship Ministry would be on the Island of Roatan, and I just knew God would place them on the West End...*Just for me!* Now I would have friends around daily from the States that knew all about Texas and things I was familiar with.

The Friendship Ministry arrived with great excitement, but politics quickly took precedence, placing their entrance on the Island back for weeks. It was election year in Honduras, and that is just the way it works. It was evident certain parties were trying to profit from the work of the ministry. This was leaving the Friendship Ministry momentarily paralyzed and left out to sea until the elections were over. Despite the problems, many were going out by boat to visit and welcome the huge ship full of excited missionaries.

Nocona and I got the opportunity through Dan and the Alternative Ministry team to go aboard the ship and meet the new missionaries. I was so excited the day we stepped onto the ship and totally felt the presence of God with every person we met. I looked each missionary in the eye, knowing God was going to supernaturally place at least one of them into my life.

Friendship Ministry & Friends

December was approaching. Don and Sondra Tipton, the founder and director of the Friendship Ministry, had appointed Don and Kayte Ashcraft to be project managers on the Island. I had casually met Kayte on the ship and later visited with her at a friend's house. I knew the whole Friendship Ministry crew was still held up on their ship, so I invited them all over for Christmas dinner. To my surprise they were not only accepting, but also as excited as I was. It wasn't long before Kayte and Don had become awesome friends and wonderful soul mates to Nocona and myself. I finally had close friends from Texas! It felt good!

With the help of Dennis, Nocona, Naomi, and Mel, we immediately began decorating the hotel and getting everything in order for the big day. They went up and down the winding stairway putting out strings of artificial holly and poinsettias. Dennis and I prepared food for days, blending all the Island fruit surrounding Casa Calico. We made over twelve gallons of fruit punch, freezing it into a slush, along with preparing many dessert dishes.

One of Nocona's favorite pastimes was rummaging through all the unopened snacks the guests had left behind. I confiscated the rum left behind, making wonderful rum cakes for whomever arrived at Casa Calico on Christmas Day.

Christmas Day came with everyone arriving as excited as we were. We had most everything prepared in advance, with some of the missionaries jumping in to help us with last-minute details. As we set the table and finished the turkey and dressing, the rest of the crew joined Nocona at the beach for swimming and snorkeling. It was a special day with lots of laughter as all the punch, turkey, dressing, rum cakes, and pies were quickly consumed. I was a little concerned about the rum cakes, since they were missionaries, but as all the other food, it quickly left the table.

For some strange reason I found myself connecting more and more with Christians, one being a lady on the far end of the Island. My mother's relatives were Pentecostal, and I guess it just began to surface in my spirit. Pastor David and Sister Harriett's Church had a presence of God that I needed at this time. I never related before to strong Christians, but more and more it had a feel of normalcy to it. As I sat in their services, I often thought of the Easter Sundays at Mam Ma's Pentecostal Church in Ragley, Louisiana, when I was young, and how I stayed crouched under my mother. I was so afraid of all the unusual activities going on in their services, and now I was loving the strong presence and understanding exactly what it was all about. I very much wanted to learn more and more about God in every aspect.

Sister Harriett was bold and powerful with a personality that would have intimidated many back home. With each visit I grew to love and respect this strong woman of God, her husband Pastor David, and sons Michael and Mica. The small church on the Key surrounded by the beautiful Sea quickly became a haven for Nocona and me on many weekends. We were quickly adopted into their lives and spent memorable nights in their huge dorm built over the sea. Nocona never lacked for entertainment and ran freely with all the beautiful children on the small Key surrounded by the Sea.

On an average evening the wind off the water would rush through the windows at hurricane speeds at night to the point that we had to close the windows just to keep the sheets and pillows on the bed! The long trip to Oakridge plus the dory ride to get to Pastor David's church was always an adventure and well worth the trip. I often thought one day there would be a book and movie on the unusual history of this beautiful church and its people.

Nocona, Frances & River JoNey

With each trip to the Key, something strange would always happen, like a powerful Conference we attended. Many speakers were there from different countries. The main speaker was from Haiti. On this particular day, my friend Kayte had joined Nocona and me. We were all sitting in the back of the church gleaning over every word that flowed out of the mouths of each speaker. Nocona nervously fidgeted for lack of space and more entertaining things to do. The building was packed and extremely hot, with no air-conditioning and, more surprisingly, no children!

A prophetess with the End Time Hand Maidens made her way to the podium. Within minutes into her talk, she began to prophesy. Many pastors from the mainland and different parts of the Island were called up as she prophesied. I sat quietly listening since I knew a lot of pastors and was in awe at her accuracy in words she spoke over them. It wasn't long before I looked up to see Sister Harriett coming down the aisle towards me. She reached out for my hand through the people standing in the aisle. My friend Kayte joined me and we were pulled through the crowd towards the front. I thought about Nocona and reached back and brought her along with us. We waited patiently as the speaker prophesied over each minister standing beside us. The prophet then turned and walked over to me, immediately laying hands on me. I went out on the floor. I was told she approached Nocona and down on the floor she went. She started towards Kayte, then turned and went back to Nocona, boldly prophesying over Nocona. She very profoundly stated, "This child is of the generation of Caleb, and God has big plans for her. She will go in and break down strongholds and conquer areas no one else would." As usual we left the service totally in awe.

※

I always got a boost from the Conference meetings and soon found myself organizing a women's conference at Casa Calico. Everything I was learning about God, I was feeling the need to pass on. This type of conference was something new on the Island, but it was being spoken very strong in my spirit. I had met Pastor Connie Weisel with the Assemblies of God Church in Florida through Bro. Galindo, and she agreed to come and speak. With Sister Harriet's assistance, it was an awesome experience for all who came, and God showed up.

Once again, God sent a forerunner to help, my cousin Sue. When I heard she was coming, I discouraged the party helping Sue organize her trip. I had not seen Sue in a long time. I knew I would not have time to visit or take her anywhere since I would be working with the conference. As it turned out, Sue arrived and was extremely helpful; I could not have made it without her.

As a token of gratitude, I took Pastor Connie Weisel to St. Helene to see the clinic. From that day forward each year, Connie felt the call of God to return to St. Helene to have women's conferences, and from there began organizing men's conferences.

Ladies Conference Beach Outing

I was approached to write articles for the Bay Island Magazine and a newspaper on the mainland. I capitalized on the opportunity, realizing it had to be another door God was opening. Even though I was far from a college grad with great writing abilities, surprisingly, my articles were published, bringing in donations for a young Island minister in need. I named my articles, "Look What God Is Doing on Roatan." I had come to know a lot of the churches, their activities, and their needs. I wanted everyone to know the great things God was doing on the beautiful Island of Roatan.

Earlier God had connected me up with Sister Frances, Sister Betty, and Eunice Jackson from French Key. Sister Frances was from the States and pastored a church in French Key. Together we worked up monthly women's meetings. Ladies were attending from all over the Island. Seeing so many needs on the Island, I continually found myself encouraging others. The more I went forward doing what I felt God was directing me to do, the stronger my nervous system and mental health was getting.

Despite the new friends, I still missed my family in the States and desired to see them. My closest friends were not around me daily, but in and out, sometimes not seeing me for weeks. Even though I worked on different projects, it wasn't enough. I sought God daily for more.

I observed the countenance and demeanor of the hundreds of missionaries as they came and left Casa Calico. Year after year I watched them come and go. Deep down I wanted to do the same. I wanted to be able to come and go, also.

On each of the missionaries' arrivals, I observed them. I couldn't believe there were so many happy people totally at peace with themselves using their vacations to help others. I remember my friends and I questioning prior to my leaving if there were even one happy marriage on this earth! Not so with this bunch! The more I watched them and their excitement in serving others, the more I decided most Americans were too focused on money and themselves. The void I had been missing for so long was now clear. I was happy, but it was happiness from the outside in and not the inside out. Missionaries were all focused on helping others. I always focused on me, my family, and friends.

Each year brought friends and family to visit us for a week. Arlene, Charlene, Judy, Harris Willey, Vonnie, and my dive friends, Bill Childers, Keith, Jeff and Sandra Ayo, Toni and many others. It was great seeing all of them, but I was sad when they left.

Another good friend of mine returned to the Island with her daughter. From time to time during the week, she would try to talk me into going back to the States. She could tell I was struggling in every sense financially, physically, and emotionally. The only reply I knew to give her was what I felt deep within my soul. I knew Jesus was my closest and dearest friend. I also understood I couldn't leave until He opened the door for us to go. I let her know I would just stay lined up with God and not move out ahead of Him no matter how bad it got here. I may not know what tomorrow would bring, but I had definitely come to realize I just needed to let God take the wheel and we would be just fine.

OCTOBER 1998

Once again I was having another profound dream. The dream was so real I immediately got up and put it on the computer, wondering if this too was something from God. In the dream, the country of Honduras was flooded. I just remember being above all of it looking down at all the floating boards and debris. Nocona and I escaped by getting in the truck and driving around the Island. In the dream as we traveled I saw mountains falling and thousands of people were dying. In their desperate state people were being shot and killed. I confided my dream to only a few people, being it was so absurd.

Weeks later, Hurricane Mitch came through the Island leaving one section devastated along with the mainland of Honduras. Mountains on the mainland fell from mudslides, killing thousands of people. Over 6,500 were reported dead and eleven thousand were missing. The Island of Granaha was totally destroyed as the hurricane pounded it for days. Reports came from tourists around the world that a witch convention was scheduled to be at Granaha during that time.

Hurricane Mitch was reported to be the most powerful storm in the Atlantic, with 180 mile-an-hour winds. The schooner, "Fantone," lost its fight in an attempt to get out of the hurricane's path. Hurricane Mitch was changing its course like no other hurricane in history. Thirty-one men and women were on board the schooner "Fantone," losing their lives.

The night before the hurricane, two of our favorite missionary friends with Alternative Missions came off of St. Helene and spent the night with us. They sat at the table visiting with us, telling me their plans. They had flown to the Caymans and had to leave because Hurricane Mitch was headed that way. Now the hurricane was headed straight to Roatan. Their plans were to leave Roatan and miss the hurricane. By this time, I had picked up enough of God's ways to the point where I began to speak what I knew would come about. I listened intently as the two men went over their departure time. I knew they were Godly men, so I quietly began to explain to Matt that anytime something bad came into our lives, God always placed someone there to help us. They boldly reassured me, stating, "It won't be us! We will be leaving out in the morning." I didn't argue...I just knew it was them!

The next day the two men hurried off to the airport, only to find that all flights had been canceled! They returned to see their rooms open and waiting. I knew they would be back!

Once they got past the initial shock, they regrouped and began to work barring up windows and getting Casa Calico ready for the high winds. It was a full week of hard wind and rain. The days and nights were long with the hurricane hanging over the country of Honduras for days. We tied off my dock, but as the water rose, the wind and waves soon took it out to sea. Matt and Charles started out upstairs, but as the wind got stronger and began to sound like a freight train, they made their way down and took the spare bedroom downstairs. As the days went on, the winds were still strong and the rains continued. Out of boredom, Matt and Charles entertained Nocona by baking cookies on the outdoor gas stove and taking her for hurricane updates to Half Moon Bay Resort. The Resort was the only one around with a generator and satellite television. Half Moon Bay Resort had evacuated all their guests to a resort in French Harbour, which was on higher ground. The guests soon returned despite the risk, stating the food was much better in West End.

Casa Calico came through the hurricane, but the East End of the Island did not fare as well, and that is where Pastor David and Sister Harriett lived. Nocona and I made our way to the East End of the Island and helped the clinic at the Garifuna village. Most all of the small homes located there had been wiped out by the hurricane. Later we went to our friends in Oakridge, and helped pick up their spirits by making homemade pizza for everyone there, who were all vigorously cleaning up from the water damage.

I soon had another dream. Early in the morning, I quickly awakened to the horrible sounds of the earth crunching and grinding. I woke up to the building swaying back and forth. It was an earth tremor. Everyone was talking about it. No one heard the earth crunching and grinding, but I did.

As time went on, my whole outlook on Honduras began to change. I had struggled with understanding some of the people in this culture. Over a period of time, I suddenly began to change, realizing there was never a problem with the people—it was a problem with *me!* I was now beginning to see the change in myself. I was taking a different look at the culture, the ones that I had gotten so upset with over petty theft. I now realized, I had never been hungry nor had to live without plumbing or electricity. I began to accept and love people for who they were and not who I desired them to be. Nocona and I were now deeply attached to the people and this Island God had placed us on, called Roatan.

&

Reports back home were that River JoNey was doing well in college. She commuted to the Island as often as she could to see Nocona and I. We greatly anticipated her arrival, especially at Christmas. Her favorite thing was bringing in suitcases full of presents and watching Nocona as she would rip through them, laying claim to as many packages as possible. There were always lots of swimsuits, since everyone knew Nocona lived in them daily. Many were too small, but Nocona didn't care; she wore them all anyway. It was always fun, ending up with a lot of laughs and catching up on all the Island happenings. Nocona immediately rushed over to Naomi's to share whatever she got with all the girls.

As the day passed, River JoNey would catch up with old friends and go out for the evening. She always returned with funny stories, the latest being the lady over immigration was at the bar she went to. She immediately recognized River and they all had a good time dancing, and yes…*Still favor!*

Each year became harder and harder for us financially, especially after the hurricane. The whole Island had gone through a depression. Tourists were not coming to the Island since the news media was stating the Islands were badly damaged. The truth was within a couple of days, the airport was back up and going and so were all the resorts on the Island. The area that was actually damaged was not in an area tourists went to. With no business, it was now depressing to walk the sandy road of West End or shop the marketplaces. The hard times were showing on everyone's faces.

My mind continued to reflect on Phil, wondering what kind of person could do this to us. He never once checked on us or thought about us. My bank account continued to spiral downhill. I was not able to go to the mainland for several years. There was just no money. I was now totally dependent on the missionaries and JoNey to bring clothes for Nocona each year.

&

Nocona, Soqui, & Carly

As Nocona grew older, she became good friends with many of the American children. Carly, Docky, Ally, Soqui, and Zeke were just a few. Their parents were in various businesses on the Island or in mission work. If the girls were not in school, they were on the beach swimming, kayaking, or taking piano lessons from Kristopher Goldman, a young musician on the Island. The American children enjoyed the water as much as Nocona and were now old enough to kayak and do other water sports. As we traveled down the sandy beach road to Gregg, Angela, and Stephen's Saturday Night Celebration Church Service, the girls would frequently throw out water balloons on boys from the back of our old Chevrolet truck. When the hotel was empty, the girls stayed overnight in the big rooms upstairs.

I continued to work with Nocona and her ABeka home-schooling program each day. In the afternoon I would try to lie down and rest for a while. Nocona would come in and visit with me. One particular day, she was laying quietly beside me as I was reading. She suddenly sat straight up in the bed and said, *"Why Did I Call Trevor A Wolf?"* (meaning when she was three years old.)

Saturday Night Celebration

I was totally taken by surprise. Nocona never showed a desire to discuss her father. It was as though she had tucked the whole problem neatly away and liked it that way. I knew it was still vivid when Trevor kidnapped her at school and what he did to her teacher and friends. I explained the word *wolf* as simply as I could without having to go into details that might upset her. For some reason, I posted it on the calendar the day she made the statement.

Life on the Island was settling down and all was going well. Everyone was looking forward to the winter season for two reasons; cooler weather and hopefully more tourists.

NOVEMBER 30, 2000: HONDURAS ENTERED INTO FULL COMPLIANCE WITH THE U.S. HAGUE CONVENTION!

As I make my way through Coxen Hole shopping, I was stopped by a businessman and given more news. Honduras was now in full compliance with the Hague Convention. No one could protect us anymore! The U.S. could pick us up at any time!

A week went by, and I heard that a family was picked up by the F.B.I. in

West End, and U.S. officials were still on the Island. I could tell everyone was getting nervous for us. For some reason, I didn't dwell on it. I knew I had done the best I could and that was all I could do. I just went on from day to day running the hotel, but yet had it in the back of my mind. Months went by and still no one approached us. A year went by and still no one picked us up, nor were there reports of anyone else being picked up.

SEPTEMBER 11, 2001

I drove to the airport to check on a package that my brother Thadd had mailed to us. I casually made my way into the airport as always, speaking to all the workers. I then walked over to the T.A.C.A. Airline counter and began to question the lady on flight arrivals from the U.S. The lady looked at me with piercing eyes and said, *"Don't You Know Terrorists Have Destroyed The Twin Towers? There Are No Flights Coming In From Anywhere!"*

I rushed home, wondering what was going on in my country. Day and night, I watched the horrible nightmare on television. I was afraid of going to bed at night thinking something else might happen. I was up and down all night checking on updates. It was a horrible feeling being so far away, knowing your country is under attack. I wanted so much to be with my family. I didn't care what was going on, I just wanted to be back in the U.S.

Everyone in Honduras was equally affected and horrified by this attack on humanity. The U.S. was always a pillar of strength in Honduras's eyes, and now everyone was in a state of shock! The whole world watched in awe as the families in New York suffered and worked together in an attempt to pull their lives back together.

Over a year and a half had passed by since the news of the Hague Convention. Once again it was time for settling down and getting ready for school. Nocona was now eleven years old and starting the sixth grade in the ABeka program.

Each year I prayed God would help me with the math and language. I was definitely not a good student and I never liked math; actually I didn't like a lot of subjects. The only thing I excelled in was typing and spelling.

I was not a very motivated child, probably every teacher's nightmare. I remember my English teacher getting very aggravated with me. One day in front of the whole class, she loudly stated, "Frances, you are burdened with the inexpressible!" I froze at the statement, but knew whatever she meant had to be the truth. Most of the time I was bored in class, and when I was called on, I did not express myself well. As I think back, I am sure most of my time in class was spent daydreaming.

My time was always pretty much taken up, but the one leisure thing I continued to enjoy during the hot summer months was relaxing on the beautiful Half Moon Bay on my raft or walking the beach visiting with the islanders and resort owners. Each was so different in his or her own way and totally amusing in character. The walk wouldn't be complete without waving at Blackie on her front porch, then visiting with Welba and Sue in their restaurant. As we made our way down the road and past the Bay, Marty would always wave as he passed us picking up tourists in his van. We usually had to step to the side about that time as Larry McLaughlin rounded the curve in his truck, making his way to his favorite corner of West End. Our next stop would be Ms. Marie Woods to catch up on her wisdom and latest herb remedies. She and Sister Laura were the best! I never had to go to a physician!

It was always a good day when we ran into Donna Lynn and Aida. They were two unique young ladies, definitely with a plan and a purpose. Just being around them you could sense their deep knowledge of God. As we passed the Baptist Church, on the right were Mr. Orti and Ms. Greta. She was there with her usual big smile, big hug, and limes or a jar of jam for us to take back. As I neared the end of the beach road, we would stop in and visit with Ms. Edith, Merilina, her husband, and Vivian Foster.

On our return to Casa Calico, we would stop in and glean over the latest art and souvenirs at Waves of Art Gift Shop. Jackie, one of the employees, had a very upbeat personality and always made us feel special, taking the time to laugh and talk about the latest happenings around the Island. As we passed the Cocoanut Tree Dive Shop, our friend Gay and her children were many times out front and would wave as we passed by. As our daily walk narrowed down, sometimes we would spot Freddie and catch up on his latest building projects. Our walk would end as we made the last turn by the hammond tree where the famous West End baseball team sat as they went over their next game. Moses, Arthur, Errick, Kevin, Elmer, Piggy, Tony, and Homer were just a few. Emerson could always be seen close by, exchanging the latest baseball stories. They always had a smile and laughed as Nocona passed, with her usual antics or Petie riding on the handlebars. It was neat watching everyone's children as they grew from season to season.

SPRING OF 2002

River JoNey was attending Texas A&M. As a part of the curriculum, she was to do a project on the Mosquito coast in Honduras. Once again, A Higher Power was at work! Things just worked out with someone making it possible for Nocona and I to join her mother for the weekend. I was rather nervous about the adventure, realizing it was the most remote area of

Honduras. No electricity, no running water, just jungle! The thought went through my mind once I got there, would I find JoNey, since there were no such things as a telephone? I had learned a lot about Faith, but this was a true test! I had traveled to Palacious once with Sister Eleanor, so I wasn't afraid of landing in the jungle on the dirt runway in the tiny plane we referred to as puddle jumpers. But this, by myself, with just Nocona, was a whole new challenge. We were definitely headed to no man's land!

The plane safely landed. Nocona and I slowly made our way down the little dirt paths along the river, eventually leading to the small village. Finally we arrived, and River JoNey was nowhere to be found! It was evident everyone there knew her, but they said she was further up the river. We were hungry and it was getting late in the evening. I spotted a building out over the water that had a distinct aroma of beans, fajitas, and fresh tortillas flowing from it. It was obvious someone was cooking. My choice for the moment was panicking over River JoNey not being there, or following the scent. I chose the latter. We made our way into the large open room and sat down, hoping someone would understand our language or realize we were extremely hungry. A nice lady came over and asked if we needed something. About that time I heard a ham radio coming from the kitchen. The voice coming over it sounded like River JoNey! I listened intently, but the voice was breaking up. From a distance I heard this coarse voice holler, "It's your daughter, and she made arrangements for you to stay overnight next door. She also has a boat coming to pick you up tomorrow." A kind lady then brought us something to eat. I never really knew for sure if I was at a café or if it were just a very nice lady realizing we were totally out of our element and in need of help.

Fluent in the language, Nocona quickly made friends, visiting with all the natives as we ate the beans, tortilla, and meat. The next morning we were up and ready early for whatever came about. We were told to wait by the river. As we sat by the murky water waiting on the boat, I became absorbed watching as one of the workers crudely killed a chicken, plucked its feathers and prepared it for lunch. As the boat approached, I began to call for Nocona. As usual, she had wandered off. I became more intense with my search, then noticed she was over by a large building by the water. Nocona was entertaining herself by painting one of the masculine worker's long dreadlocks with blue water paints. The other children were looking on, but not joining in, looking fearful for Nocona's life. The dark-skinned man looked ridiculous, yet never flinched as villagers laughed at him. I quickly grabbed Nocona as the man strolled off as though nothing had happened.

The river trip was once again like a movie setting. The boat was very small. As the man paddled down the narrow river, it was as though time were standing still and totally surreal. I reflected back on all my faith walks and this was obviously another one. I could not understand anything the man said since he spoke a broken Garifuna language. At one point, I wondered,

Was he truly taking us to see JoNey or were we being kidnapped? I had previously heard stories of this sort. Regardless, I chose to relax and enjoy the moment. A couple hours went by. The boat began to go slower and slower, but all I saw was heavy jungle and then finally a small path. I sat patiently waiting, and suddenly we saw River JoNey smiling as she peered through the bush. We walked around the little area nestled in the jungle, and she pointed out her headquarters. She was quite proud of her new residence. It appeared to be a tree-house to me, but I acted impressed.

There was a physician working with her from Cuba. The whole trip was extremely hot, but memorable, with River JoNey taking us up into the mountains through the jungle on small pack horses to a Cacao farm. I was drenched in sweat. The long ride through the thick jungle was hot and tiring. Within minutes, I realized I had made a grave mistake by agreeing to this. My whole being felt at risk as intense pain and sweat ran down my body from the agony of the skinny horse and the intense heat. Totally numb and clueless to my surroundings, I began to take a deeper look into the jungle, seeing orchids and many beautiful plants and wildlife. I became more appreciative, realizing no other gringa grandmother in the world had probably experienced this.

There were guides along with us. Some walked and some rode, yet no one thought to bring water. We soon came to a fresh spring, and everyone got off and enjoyed the cool water. We finally made our way to the top and were relieved to get off the skinny horses.

The humble couple in the only home at the top of the hill quickly greeted us, showing off their cacao farm. I was in awe, not having the least idea of where chocolate came from. Somehow I just visualized it growing from a decorative box! The kind family ended the day by making us hot chocolate. I nervously drank it as the pigs and dogs casually ran through their little, open, adobe home. No running water, no electricity, but a feeling of total serenity at the top of this mountain. I was grateful for the large bundle of cacao that they gave us on our way out. I froze it immediately once I returned to the hotel, in hopes of preserving it. I enjoyed serving it to friends and telling everyone the unusual story behind it.

There was no doubt by this time, I knew no matter where God placed me tomorrow, the people of Honduras would be forever etched in my mind. I no longer had to ask, Why did God send me to Honduras? I just wondered why He waited so long! By this time not only had my whole life completely changed, but my whole thought system. The Lincoln town car was now meaningless, the big home, the travel trailer, the boat, and yes even the money and all the dive trips.

COUNTY RECORD

ORANGE, TEXAS — 1852-2002 — **CELEBRATING 150 YEARS**

VOL. 43 NO. 8

Bush pushes military action

■ BUSH TARGETS IRAQ FOR POTENTIAL MILITARY MOVE

JERRY CHILDRESS
FOR THE RECORD

President Bush emphasized to Americans Monday night that military force may be necessary to stop terrorist attempts and aggression from Iraq, an issue that Congress will vote on this week.

"I have asked Congress to authorize the use of America's military, George Bush if it proves necessary, to enforce the U.N. Security Council demands," he said in a televised speech from Cincinnati, Ohio. "Approving this resolution does not mean that military action is imminent or unavoidable. The resolution will tell the United Nations and all nations that America speaks with one voice and is determined to make the demands

BUSH Page 3A

2002 Citizen of the Year

The Greater Orange Area Chamber of Commerce is taking nominations for the 2002 Citizen of the Year. Deadline for nominations is 3 p.m. Dec. 6.

Nominations should include a detailed written resume outlining the activities of the person being nominated. The award is open to any resident of Orange County. Nominees need not be members of the chamber. The award should not be presented to paid professional leaders such as city managers, judges and others in a public office, according to a release from the chamber. However, honorable mentions may be given to those in such categories.

The award will be presented at the chamber's annual meeting and will be announced Jan. 1, 2002.

Darby Byrd, 1990 Citizen of the Year, is chairman of the Citizen of the Year Committee.

For more information, contact the chamber at 1012 Green Ave., Orange.

Anna Ocaguera returns from a detention hearing last Friday for her mother, Frances Harris.
Staff Photo By Glenda Dyer

Harris hearing postponed

Grandmother jailed for kidnapping granddaughter

GLENDA DYER
FOR THE RECORD

A former Mauriceville woman remains in a privately-owned correctional facility in Beaumont after U.S. Magistrate Earl Hines agreed to postpone a detention hearing Friday at her attorney's request.

Frances Harris, 57, is being held on a federal kidnapping charge that alleges she kidnapped her 11-year-old granddaughter, Nocona Lyon, when she and the then 3-year-old child went to Honduras about eight years ago.

Beaumont Attorney Sonny Cribbs asked that the hearing be reset until after a federal grand jury decides whether to indict Harris on the kidnapping charge.

Indictments are to be presented Oct. 17, so Hines rescheduled the hearing until 2 p.m Oct. 18 at the federal courthouse in Beaumont.

Hines had postponed the detention hearing Sept 27 to give Harris time to hire her own attorney. She has retained Cribbs, who will replace public defender Frank Henderson.

When she disappeared in 1994, Harris said she left with her then 3-year-old granddaughter to avoid abuse by the girl's father. But the child's father, 47, has maintained over the years that he never abused his child.

Frances Harris

Nocona's mother, River JoNey Burton, 30, is one of Harris' three children. Burton and never married. The families have been involved in a custody battle since Nocona was a baby.

Burton, a student at Texas A&M University in College Station, did not attend Friday's hearing but was expected to attend a custody hearing set for 10 a.m. Tuesday before visiting judge in Orange.

But about 30 of Harris' relatives and friends crowded into the courtroom

HARRIS Page 2A

**ONE NATION UNDER GOD
NEVER FORGET 9/11/02**

Proposed stamp commemorates 150-year-old Orange County

■ ORANGE CHAMBER TO UNVEIL STAMP COMMEMORATING SESQUICENTENNIAL

VICKI PARFAIT
FOR THE RECORD

Elected officials of Orange County will be honored by the Greater Orange Area Chamber of Commerce and citizens in a special luncheon banquet lasting from 11:30 a.m.-1:30 p.m. Oct. 24 at the Sunset Grove Country Club.

The ceremony is being planned with a special twist — the unveiling of a 150 Years stamp to commemorate the historic event of Orange County's sesquicentennial year.

Betty Harmon, chamber president

PROPOSED STAMP Page 2/

THE RECORD REPLAY
ORANGE COUNTY FOOTBALL PAGE 1B

DICKIE COLBURN FISHING
Head to know what's working and what's not on Orange County water. More local fishermen turn to Dickie Colburn for insights and news than any other outdoor columnist. Honest, entertaining reading everyone can enjoy.
SEE PAGE 4B

Anna, Frances Harris' daughter, at court hearing.

Prior to my arrival to Roatan I had never really known anyone that was a missionary. I remember donating to someone called Lottie Moon at the Baptist Church, but really didn't remember a thing about her. Now my life was overwhelmed in a good way with missionaries.

As the years passed, more and more ministries came in, setting up projects. I had started monthly get-togethers at Casa Calico for all the missionaries. The group was made up of both foreigners and Islanders coming from around the Island, bringing delicious food and great music. The beautiful outdoor garden with soft twinkling lights in the coconut trees once again served as a relaxing setting, making this event memorable for all who came. I had come to have great respect for missionaries. As each person shared, we came to know more and more missionaries with each get-together.

The Island was filled with gifted musicians and singers, so each gathering was quite memorable. Dolphus Stanley, Pauline Galindo, and Halcie were just a few that entertained everyone. Many times our hotel guests and tourists walking down the road would hear the music and join us. My friends, Kayte and Don, would always stay over for the night, since the Friendship Ministry was on the other end of the Island.

New events were being organized. Sister Harriett from Oakridge Chapel started monthly luncheons with women from around the Island. There was a growing response with each meeting. Harriett planned the meetings in detail, holding them at different restaurants around the Island. The next one was to be at West End.

A group of missionaries arrived from the States and stopped in on their way to St. Helene. One of them was a friend from Texas named Laura. It was great seeing her and her son Dalton. We were all greeting each other as each came in the door. As one of the young ladies stepped in the door, she looked up and said, "Frances, Is That You?"

It was the little girl from Louisiana who, with her sisters, had prayed over us when we stayed at their home prior to arriving here. Lacy definitely wasn't a little girl anymore! It was hard to picture her all grown up. She took a lot of pictures of our place and promised to show them to her sisters and family. Nocona was invited to go along with them on their mission trip for the week. I was in awe that God brought Lacy right to my front door! I thought, God is not only cool, *He is truly amazing! I had prayed to see her again, and it happened!*

Something unusual was in the air! In my spirit I was feeling of a change deep with in me. I began helping the ladies with the Church of God at

French Harbour organize a women's conference. My new friend, Brenda Anderson, was coming in from North East Texas with a group of women to be the speakers at the conference. I was also meeting with Kayte to help her with their upcoming women's conference at the Friendship Ministry.

After eight years on the Island, strange things began to surface once again deep inside me. In my spirit I was sensing ... *Now We Were Leaving!* How, I didn't know! But I felt strongly that we were going back to the States soon. From the time we arrived at the Island, I prepared Nocona each day for her return to the States. I knew God was the most important thing in our lives, so each day I taught her something new about Him. If what I was feeling was true, then it was of extreme importance I step it up. Each day as I took Nocona to school or made my way to the markets, I would have Nocona repeat with me, *"I am a child of the Most High God; Satan has no power over me. Greater is He that is in me, than he that is in the world."* I wanted Nocona to know her place with God, and who would be there for her when problems arose. I continued teaching her as much Scripture as I could.

As I was walking with Nocona down the beach one day, I began to share with her the strong feelings I was having about our return. I was surprised when Nocona said she felt the same thing—that we were leaving soon. During the week, I was visiting with Kayte. I relayed to her the thought that continued to recur in me. Surprisingly, she came back with the same; she felt as though she and Don were leaving also. I couldn't see them going anywhere. It was as though the Friendship Ministry project couldn't go on without them. The Island could certainly do without me, but not without them! They had put in so much labor there, and the project was growing in leaps and bounds.

Suddenly, Don and Kayte were returning to the States because of a sudden illness with Don. Kayte asked if I would oversee their conference at Friendship Ministry and introduce the speakers. I had been meeting with Kayte helping coordinate the conference, but this was out of my comfort zone. I felt totally inadequate, but agreed, knowing how important it was to Kayte.

The ladies in French Harbour had everything in place and were getting excited about their women's conference. Brenda Anderson, a friend I had met earlier through Sister Eleanor Cooper, and her ministry were emailing me daily, getting ready for the big event. They had previously ministered on the mainland of Honduras, but this was their first time on Roatan. They would all be staying at Casa Calico and be dependent on me to continue coordinating between Brenda and the leaders in the Church of God.

Now, Harriett was sending word for me to take her place, taking charge of the ladies' luncheon in West End. Something had come up so she couldn't attend. There was no such thing as *No's* in Sister Harriett's vocabulary! I once again agreed.

Things had turned around for the Island of Roatan. Tourists were returning, and cruise ships were pouring in with everyone falling in love with the little Island. Business was picking up for everyone. People were gathering around me as I made my daily walk down the West End beach road.

Children and adults all were asking the same question: "When were we going to start the first meetings of the Christmas On The Beach?" Each year more and more people joined in. It was easy to sense this year would be even larger than the last, and we would have to start planning early to make it happen. We had so much fun in the past with all the children, and now tourists from all over were bringing in Santa hats and goodies for the upcoming event. That was the fun part for me—just watching the way everyone joined in, including young and old, tourists, missionaries, and businessmen. It was now a huge part of the community, and everyone was excited.

People around the Island were catching the spirit. Now French Harbour was having Christmas parades and fireworks. Eldon with Eldon's Supermarket was having a fireworks display close to BoJangles by Coxen Hole. Christmas lights were always in one area of French Harbour, but now they were popping up all around the Island.

Nocona and I made our usual evening walk. It had a way of clearing my mind and relaxing me. I reflected on a particular day Nocona and I strolled down the beach. Big Mike, our West End Santa, stopped and asked if Nocona and I would join him and his wife for Christmas dinner. I thought, *It was so kind of him knowing their life was so different from ours.* They were truly unique and fit into every seam of the Island with their motorcycle and love for parties and a good time. I never saw Big Mike without a huge smile. Nocona and I did join them and had a wonderful time with him and his wife.

As I continued my stroll down West End, I wanted to get excited, but something was different this year. Deep inside me was now a Presence, stating we would no longer be on the Island for Christmas. No one said a word to me…I just knew we were leaving!

Seashell Prisoners
CHAPTER 16

I continued to meet with old friends occasionally in Coxen Hole with BoJangles being our favorite hangout. The whole Island rejoiced the day BoJangles opened. The wonderful feel of air-conditioning, clean floors, and no sand or sand fleas to contend with was a wonderful treat. My nervous system had greatly improved, and it was good getting out and feeling somewhat normal again. You could always run into old friends and meet new friends like Annie and Odessa from French Key or Dolphus and his wife. Many referred to BoJangles as my office since I frequented the small restaurant daily with armloads of emails to sort out.

More and more foreigners each day were finding their way to the little Island utopia called Roatan, building lavish homes overlooking the sea. First International Living brought groups of investors, all wanting a piece of the beautiful haven. Later additional cruise ships spotted the virgin Island, bringing in thousands of tourists weekly. West End and West Bay were two of the favorite hot spots to visit. My favorite change on the Island—there were no more sightings of men urinating along the side of the road! You could stroll along the beach to many unique curio shops, restaurants, and dive locations. Now everyone was wanting a piece of Roatan!

Jerry Hynds, a prominent businessman, had been elected mayor, and as a result, major changes were taking place on the Island, quickly bringing it up to tourism standards. Cell phones were coming into existence. The Island was definitely beginning to take on an extreme makeover with a whole new appearance. Coxen Hole had a facelift. Gift shops lined the road on each side. The city and beaches from Flowers Bay throughout West End no longer were littered with trash, but cleaned and brightly colored umbrellas began to appear along the sandy beaches. The West Bay Beach was now lined with beautiful condos and restaurants.

Foreigners from all over the world continued to settle in West End and West Bay creating irresistible, delectable dishes in their unique outdoor restaurants along the beach. Most of the tourists were flooding the West End and West Bay not only for the world's second most beautiful dive locations, but to taste the delicious recipes from Argentina, Italy, and the local Caribbean cuisine.

୨ଈ

Nocona was now eleven and an excellent swimmer. Occasionally, to relax after working with tourists all day, we would swim out to the end of the Half Moon Bay and around to the East side. The water was rough on the other side, but we always made it a goal to find the large coral with the hole in the middle. Our main priority was to free dive through the hole before returning back to the Bay.

Nocona was beginning to push me to teach her more about scuba diving. Whenever I had free time, I began to take my diving equipment out to the end of the point of the bay. The coral reefs were within a few feet. I would swim out to the coral reef and dive the beautiful reef as Nocona and her friends swam and kayaked in the bay. There were always turtles and lots of fish to watch. I would finish my dive by coming up in the bay, and swimming under the girls. Nocona would see the bubbles and dive down, swimming along, breathing off the regulator. We would then snorkel over to a little restaurant on the other side of the bay for lunch.

With each month, the sense of change got stronger and stronger with both Nocona and me. It wasn't a feeling of new beginnings or new challenges. Something deep in our spirits continued to state, "We were leaving Roatan." It was truly a bittersweet moment, knowing God couldn't seem to make changes without a tremendous amount of hoopla. I cringed each day at the thought of what He might come up with for our exit! I knew one thing from the past—it would be dramatic and full of color...*It Just Always Was!* Quiet and subtle seemed to be out of His vocabulary as far as His choices of existence in our lives. My life was always colorful, but somehow when God took complete control, it became extremely intense and unbearable at times.

SEPTEMBER 24, 2002   Nocona (Eleven Years Old)

Nocona and I had just gotten up and begun preparing for the day. It was 7 a.m. and, little did we know, nothing about this day would be normal.

Normal to us was swinging open the big double doors overlooking the garden each morning, allowing the breeze off the bay to flow through the large room. The cool morning air had a way of pushing the stifling humid heat from the night across the spacious living area and out the back door. Normal was going over our Christian journals as we had breakfast; laughing at Petie as he exited his favorite banana tree off the front porch, making his entrance, tiptoeing across the wooden floor, and quickly scurrying as Puffer chased him. Normal was Nocona's laughter as Petie crawled up my Island dress to get on the table in hopes we had fresh banana pancakes for breakfast; watching Petie and Puffer as they vied for our attention which usually went into a huge fiasco. The two of us would laugh at Petie as he raced to wipe his beak on me to clean the pancakes off. Nocona would scream and run from Petie, her laughter ringing across the room and across the Bay.

This day would be different! We never got to the door. We never had breakfast. Nothing was normal about this day!

I was brushing my teeth and partially dressed. Nocona was in the large room playing. I heard a knock on the door, and for some reason I felt uneasy in my spirit. As a rule I would have looked out of the wooden shutters that overlooked the front of the house. I felt the immediate need to go to Nocona. I heard Nocona's footsteps walking towards the door. Something told me to yell at her to wait, but fear inside kept me from reacting quick enough. As I cleared the bathroom door, the room was filled with men in uniforms carrying M-16's. As my eyes scanned the room and out the window, more men with machine guns surrounded the outside of the hotel. Five vehicles surrounded Casa Calico. I immediately had a sinking feeling, but something quickened in my spirit. I was able to keep my composure. Two of the men identified themselves—one being the Chief of Police of LeCeiba. The other was a Central American F.B.I. agent. They boldly stated they were taking us into custody and would be returning us to the States. I knew the time was close, but this was just too much to grasp. God had been preparing me, but I felt helpless. The whole scenario was overwhelming and full of drama, but I regrouped knowing somehow God was in the middle of it. It was just a matter of my getting past the moment.

    I glanced around the room to see two women with the Chief of Police, both enjoying the excitement of their assignment. I told them I needed to change clothes since I only had on shorts. The two ladies followed me into the bedroom as though I would try and escape. My wardrobe was quite limited, mostly being island dresses and shorts, but I quickly found a pair of long pants and put them on. I could only imagine what would present itself upon our arrival in Houston. As I dressed, I was searching my mind as to where I had seen the ladies before. I then remembered the two coming to Casa Calico the day before, checking on rooms to rent.

    As I exited the bedroom, I checked to see where Nocona was. When I looked up, it took all I could do to control my emotions. The impact hit hard as I watched Nocona scurrying around the room, picking up all the things she knew were important to me: my Bible, my portable CD player, and my Christian notebook that I journaled in daily.

    The Chief of Police abruptly demanded I leave with them at that moment. I looked him in the eye, making my own demands. He seemed startled as I told him, "I deserve respect…I need more time!"

    Surprisingly, there was no reply. I then joined Nocona, picking up personal items I knew were important to her.

    I struggled with keeping my focus. There were so many things I needed to do. At one moment I looked out and saw two young missionaries walking out of my drive rather casually. Josh and Erica were new on the Island. I had given them a large discount on their room to make it easier for them to live on the Island. Normally, wherever Josh went Erica joined him. For some reason this day, she stopped and looked back at the awful scene. She came back as Josh continued on. I had never mentioned our problem, but felt they probably knew from other missionaries.

I never apologized to Erica nor did she look at me with fear or anxiety. She was quite composed for her youth and lack of experience in this area. It was a total God-moment and divinely appointed. I quickly outlined Erica on the upcoming Women's Christian Conference at French Harbour, and who to contact to keep it going forward. I let her know Brenda Anderson from Texas was bringing a team of women to do the Conference, and Casa Calico was to host the group. I had been working diligently for weeks as Brenda's liaison person, making sure they had a location for the conference, food, and help. Now it would be up to God to coordinate the finish.

The F.B.I. agent insisted on my leaving, so I grabbed my plastic container with my documents and important papers. I remembered all I had was an old green duffle bag to put them in. I threw a couple shirts in the bag, took Nocona by the hand, and grabbed my sunglasses on the way out. I knew at any given time that this inner strength might leave. I was determined they would not see me cry. We rode with the Chief of Police and his female assistants.

As we drove down the road, the Chief of Police began to soften. As he talked, I then remembered his voice. He also had come up the night before looking for a room. I remember telling him my rooms were full, being I didn't feel comfortable with his appearance. I had acquired a strong gift of perception during these eight years. I knew the look of a tourist, and this man in no way fit the profile. Our first stop was the Judge's office in Coxen Hole, then on to the airport.

There was never a day on the Island that I didn't contemplate this happening. Now we were facing it head on. We boarded the plane and soon landed in Tegucigalpa, the Capital of Honduras, then on to San Pedro. There we were released to a U.S. F.B.I. agent, named Gregg Skinner, his female assistant, and John Hamilton with the Orange County Sheriff's Dept. Gregg was stationed in Beaumont, Texas, and was much more nervous and uptight about the situation.

For some strange reason, Gregg abruptly turned to me and boldly stated that I could cooperate, or he would take things into his own hands, flashing the handcuffs. I tried hard not to show facial expressions through this whole bizarre statement. My thoughts were once again, *I'm Just A Grandmother, Not A Drug Lord!* The whole thing was so uncalled for! I had not moved a muscle. I was just sitting down.

Later I was asked if I wanted to make a phone call. I looked over at Nocona, knowing she would be delighted to use a telephone. There was no doubt whom the call would go to, knowing the emotions going through her at the moment. Gregg approved, getting an interpreter to place the call. Within minutes, Nocona was relaying a message to her grandfather.

For some reason everyone's attention focused on Nocona as she picked up the phone and dialed. It was as though each person was listening intently, anticipating Nocona to pour her heart out to him or burst out in tears. Instead

Nocona, her usual self, full of drama, very boldly and in few words told him we had been picked up by the F.B.I. and they were bringing us back to the States. That was the height of the conversation, and she hung up. She had a rather amusing expression on her face as she wheeled around, looked each person in the eye, and quickly stated, *"Now it's not a secret anymore!"*

Totally confused by all the drama, I got the feeling in her mind Grandpa was next to God. Once Grandpa knew, these guys might be in a ton of trouble. It definitely had a way of breaking the powerful stronghold on the moment. John nervously asked Nocona if she wanted something to drink, and he quickly ushered her out the door.

In a strange sort of way, my mind was racing as I reflected on many things. One was on my wonderful friend, Brenda. She would be coming to Casa Calico that weekend totally unaware of this wild scenario. Yes, I was supposed to have all the arrangements lined up for a women's retreat, and she was the speaker. In a weird sort of way I found it amusing, knowing her personality. It had a way of helping me hold on to my sanity. I knew Brenda's walk with God, and she could handle anything.

It was time to board the plane to Houston. John Hamilton sat by Nocona and me. He asked if he might pray with us, and I agreed, still not sure of where he might be coming from. After we sat down, he obviously saw that I wanted to be alone with Nocona. He moved directly across from us. It was like at that moment reality became more vivid. I then began to think of all that might take place once we landed. Nocona was entertaining herself, fidgeting with all the many buttons and gadgets on the big plane. She was used to the much smaller planes we referred to as puddle-jumpers—planes in which we went back and forth to the Mainland. I was grateful, needing time to collect and organize my thoughts on what to say to Nocona that might help prepare her for what would soon be reality.

As Nocona pulled out the magazines and flipped through them, I knew there was no way she could comprehend what was soon to confront both of us. As I pondered on the soon arrival, I stared straight ahead with tears dripping out from under my dark glasses. I knew I had to say something to prepare her, but what could I say? I went over and over in my mind how it would come across to her if they placed her in the hands of the person she feared the most, Trevor! I decided to let her stay in her dream world for a while, until I could pray more.

Nocona and I were like velcro the entire eight years on the Island, and had prayed many times to return to the States. Nocona and I probably did not spend five minutes the whole eight years on the Island talking about Trevor. Her encounter of him kidnapping her from the school was still extremely vivid. It stood out in her mind with great pain. Every day on the Island was lived to the fullest, just enjoying each other and grabbing at anything that looked like an email or letter from home. Our life had been simple, but a library of books couldn't describe the love we had for each other and the impact God had on our lives. Nocona was truly a light to me and to all others she came in contact with. Not for one moment were we guilty of taking either for granted. Nocona never left the house without saying, "I Love You, Ganna!"

As the plane drew nearer to Houston, I overheard one of the men say Nocona would have Judge Herris for her judge. I lit up, knowing Judge Herris was one of the first in helping me tremendously with the CASA Program in Orange County. I admired him greatly and the reputation he had, helping abused children. I felt that was the open door to talking to Nocona. I immediately relayed what I had heard, letting her know Judge Herris was a wonderful judge and would take good care of her. I told her when we arrived that they may put her in a home, but she would be able to see her grandfather and grandmother soon.

She acted as though she understood, but within minutes asked where we would spend the night, and if I could take her to the mall the next day. Nocona was just too naïve; she was not able to conceive what would soon hit her head on.

I later regrouped, making one last attempt to instruct Nocona. I tried to subtly let her know if she was not happy where they placed her to be bold. I told her to let the Judge know where she wanted to live. If bad came to worse, make bad grades at school and they will listen to you. Right before we landed, I alerted Nocona to be careful when questioned by the legal system. In one sense Nocona was street smart, being raised on the Island, but I also knew she was totally unprepared for something of this magnitude. Orange County would be anxiously awaiting revenge and would use whatever instrument they could to bring me down, even if it meant using a small child!

The closer we got to Houston, the more nervous Nocona became. She kept pulling on me and giving me big hugs. She would follow it up with "I love you, Ganna," and then get quiet, slumping under me. I thought surely they would place Nocona with her mother or grandfather, knowing the trauma she went through with her dad kidnapping her. Nocona never wanted to leave my side after that fateful day in her life.

I thought it all rather strange that I was taken out as a high-profile criminal—probably the only female that had ever been extradited back to the States from Honduras, and I had saved a child's life!

I began to think of frivolous things like the young man handing me the game ball as West End rallied to win the championship game. I was so honored, but I would never see that ball again, maybe I may never see the Island again!

We arrived in Houston, soon to be met with even more officers and what appeared to be a female child psychologist. The lady took Nocona's hand as we entered the airport, and walked ahead of me. We all walked a long way through the terminal. Nocona never took her eyes off of me, looking back constantly with each step, making sure all was okay. At one point, I heard the lady ask Nocona who had given her the blue teddy bear she was clinging to. She quickly replied, "My mother."

We were taken to a very elegant room. Nocona sat with the child psychologist. Nocona continued to watch me, making sure I was still close.

My mind continued to race as to when I might see Nocona again, and did I say everything I needed to? I remembered all our things being in the same bag so I asked permission to separate them. I made sure Nocona's personal Christian notebook, that we worked so many hours on, would be with her when she left me. As I went through the things, I became emotional as I saw the many pictures of the Island and our friends.

The longer I sat at the airport, the more angry I became, thinking of the injustice of all of this. I had found out my eighty-four-year-old dad, whom I had not seen in eight years, was within twenty minutes of me. Dad was in critical condition in a Houston hospital, and I was being brought in as an International Kidnapper, not able to even visit him.

We sat for what seemed like hours, then it was time to board the Beaumont flight. Nocona was taken out first, and officers followed with me. F.B.I. agent Gregg Skinner sat with me, and Nocona was seated beside the psychologist down from us. Things became more intense. Nocona continued to look back at me. I gave her the high sign and a big smile, pretending I was fine. I kept my eye on her, making sure when she looked up I wouldn't miss that last glance. I thought Nocona was going to be okay, but I saw the stewardess bringing Kleenexes and handing them to her. I knew at this point reality was kicking in for her.

Before we landed, I overheard the psychiatrist state to Gregg, "Nocona is not ready to live with her father!"

My emotions were greatly mixed. I was relieved, yet extremely angry at their ignorance at the thought of ripping Nocona out of her home and country, much less placing her with Trevor! I kept thinking, *One of them would inquire concerning Nocona's health and well being.* But not one person asked if she was taking medication or had any health or emotional problems that needed to be dealt with. Ever since Trevor kidnapped Nocona from school, she had had huge fears of being away from me and being by herself. Trevor once again was taking total precedence with full support of the judicial system.

I was filled with anger not at any one person, but just the whole sick system! Nocona was once again an object in the hands of cold-hearted, self-seeking followers of our great, narrow-minded legal system! Not one thread of empathy was shed for a child, yet hundreds of thousands of dollars continued to flow, cheering on a horribly sick, abusive man and his family. There definitely was a victim, Nocona! Not one person stopped to investigate the reason I left, my character, or Trevor's.

I continued to dwell on... *how easy it was for me to find out about this abusive man!* It was also spelled out very plainly in the week-long custody suit. How difficult could that be for Orange County? If Nocona's mother got custody of Nocona through the week-long custody suit before a jury, then shouldn't they request information of the trial? Wouldn't they ask a few questions, before spending a million dollars chasing down a grandmother?

Surely there would be one person that would stop and talk to Nocona, and ask what would make her happy. Yes, yes, It would be Judge Herris! I felt sure he would take care of Nocona. He will straighten this whole bizarre scenario out! Thank God I was fed only bits and pieces of Nocona's plight.

We arrived in Beaumont. Agent Gregg Skinner told me I would have a few minutes with Nocona to tell her goodbye. I gave Nocona a big hug. I could tell she was confused. I was at a loss for words, so I just hugged her again and told her I loved her. She hugged me back, but her body felt lifeless.

They quickly led Nocona away. Gregg then instructed me not to speak to anyone. He stated the press would be there and a lot of my friends and family, but I was not to say a word. Nocona would get to visit with them, then be placed with Child Protective Services.

As we made our way down the hall, I could see family and friends from a distance. Gregg and his assistant quickly walked me past them and out the door. I glanced to the right to see who was there waiting. I felt a warm feeling as I saw familiar faces. Gregg quickly ushered me over to what was obviously his Mercedes. He, at that point, pulled out the handcuffs and leg cuffs, placing them on me. I now felt the impact of the title, International Parental Kidnapper. Yes, I was back home! I was in Texas, but it didn't feel like home. I was promptly taken to a facility in Jefferson County, where I spent my first night.

Seashell Prisoners
CHAPTER 17

It was late in the evening when we arrived at the Federal Facility. The whole experience was overwhelming as the officer escorted me to a small, grungy cell. I sat silently watching in awe as women were being brought in of all ages. The first eight hours were spent booking. It was easy to see as each new inmate entered the cell her only thoughts were, *How Can I Get Out!* Each within her own mind was desperately seeking ways to once again be free; brainstorming as though the other might be able to accomplish the feat for her. To them I wasn't even there. They had previous experience. One look obviously told them, *I was clueless!*

From our cell, we observed each new person being brought in. We each waited our turn to be taken out for fingerprinting, questioning, etc. After twelve p.m., I was taken to the physician, only to be told I would not be allowed to use the hormones that had been taken from me. My hormone was an herb. Not a prescription. I was greatly disturbed since it took me a year to get off the prescription drug, premarin, without my body reacting.

Then it was time for me to be outfitted, only to receive clothes and shoes much too large. No one seemed to care. Between twelve and one a.m., I was called out of the cell once again. Each time a different person questioned me. This time a lady asked where I would live once I was released? My mind was numb and I couldn't seem to think clearly. I wasn't sure about anything, so I just told her I didn't know, but that wasn't good enough. She seemed to be confused that I didn't know the telephone numbers of any of my family, except one. I never thought to explain I was on an Island without a phone for eight years, but at that moment, my mind was totally traumatized. I was equally confused because her main focus seemed to be to inquire about my finances, property, and bank accounts. I thought, *what a strange thing to ask! I didn't rob a bank! My case had nothing to do with money!*

During the night, I felt threatened with each hour. All the other ladies had been booked and sent to cells except me. The female officers disappeared, leaving only large, tall, dark-skinned men working up front. One led me to the back to a small room around two in the morning and explained I was to stay there the rest of the night. The room was small, approximately 5 x 8 ft., and freezing cold. On the floor was a thin plastic mattress and one sheet. The remainder of the night I walked the floor in an attempt to get warm. The eight years of tropical climate was working against me. Down the hall I could hear workers hollering at one of the inmates to get out of the shower. This went on for hours. At first I thought it strange for someone to be showering at such an hour, then realized the lady was simply staying warm the best way she could.

The following morning, my clothes were returned to me. The officer instructed me to get dressed. I once again asked for my hormones, but was refused. I became stressed, knowing my body would soon be reacting without them.

I was placed in handcuffs and my ankles in shackles, then released to F.B.I. Agent Gregg Skinner and his assistant. I soon found myself at the Jack Brooks Federal Courthouse in Beaumont, Texas. It was my first court hearing. Extremely awkward, I walked slowly, taking short steps, keeping my eyes on the chains around my ankles. My total focus had to be on my steps at all times to keep from falling. As I entered the courtroom, it was obvious no one knew I was to be there except the press.

I was slowly led into the courtroom to a large desk. The struggle to keep the chains untangled was difficult as I made my way to a chair. The unlocking of the chains was humbling. As I looked up, there was such an aura, as U.S. Magistrate Earl Hines quietly made his entrance. I glanced around to see Agent Gregg Skinner and another large man I assumed to be the prosecutor sitting directly across from me. No introductions were made.

There were two things obvious. I had no counsel, nor was I prepared, but...they were! The room suddenly appeared enormous, feeling cold with no one, but myself, present. I had one huge priority at this time, getting my hormones back! I was walking into something that I was totally ignorant of, yet I had a strange sense of peace. It was obvious someone had to be praying for me.

The Honorable Magistrate Earl Hines addressed the large man at the desk across from me. The man boldly stated I was brought in under the charge of International Parental Kidnapping. He reminded the judge that this would bring a life sentence. Even with that profound statement, I remained calm and at ease. I glanced around the room and saw what was obviously the press, taking notes.

I was then asked to approach the microphone. The judge questioned me on several things, and asked if I had an attorney or had plans of hiring one. My answer was stated quietly, but emphatically, No! Judge Hines stated the courts would appoint one and then questioned me about my finances. Once again I was surprised and stated I had given that information to someone earlier. The judge agreed stating that was sufficient.

The Judge then asked if I understood everything and if I had any other questions. I was grateful for the opportunity he was giving me to speak and used the time to request my hormones. I asked if he would please give permission for me to take the over-the-counter herb I had brought from Honduras. He appeared a little taken back by the request, yet reassured me I would have them. I was later taken to a privately owned jail in Beaumont. Once again, there was another grueling booking. It was late by the time the officer went through all the procedures.

A rather large and unusual female officer offered to take me to my cell, which included getting on an elevator. The lady obviously had great rapport with all the inmates and workers as we went from floor to floor. The elevator suddenly stopped. I thought it was the floor we were getting out on, but it wasn't. As the elevator door opened, there were male inmates everywhere laughing and making obscene comments to the guard, all of which seemed to pump her up all the more. If this was a tour, one minute was plenty for me, but she lingered as though it were her only opportunity to boost her ego. Within seconds I felt threatened, and fear raced through my mind as to the elevator door possibly not closing quick enough if they came towards us. Once again the door closed. We soon made our way to the laundry room. I was handed sheets, towels, etc., then led to a cell.

For the first time, my new life as a criminal was hitting me in the face full force. As we passed down the row of cells, I saw a group of young women in a cell. The lady stated they were from Honduras. I thought, *How strange; are these angels or real people? What would Hondurans be doing here? In all my life in the U.S., I had never been introduced to someone from Honduras.* They all watched as I passed by, each with a soft smile.

The heavy door opened to my cell. I looked around the long, cold room filled with bunk beds. A couple of the ladies began greeting me while others were more reserved. A very pretty young inmate was standing off to the side. When she looked up, she screamed, *"You're The Lady That Was On America's Most Wanted!"*

She grabbed me and gave me a huge hug! She went on to say she had been following the case for years and was so excited to meet me! I couldn't imagine where people were getting this information from, but strange as it all was, it was rather comforting to know I was being accepted into their lives. An older lady led me over to a corner in the room, showing me which bunk was mine. She immediately began helping me make up my bed and continued her caring ways throughout the stay.

Once again the room was freezing, but it wasn't just me. Every inmate walked around with blankets around them. For some strange reason, there was no cold water in the showers, just hot. You had one minute to bathe before the water was at the boiling stage! The rooms were set up shotgun with mirrored glass past the bars. Everything we did was in the open, including the commodes. We all struggled with this. At different times an inmate would put a sheet in front of the commode, only to have the guard quickly make them take it down. The constant change continued to work on my nerves, with my becoming more and more despondent. There were so many rules, and just doing little things became very stressful, like remembering what day the towels were to go in the laundry versus the uniforms.

The women were very nice, but things had a way of stressing them, with respect quickly going out the window. I was averaging two to three hours of sleep at night. Inmates laughed and hollered through the vents at male inmates throughout the night. These men were on different floors, but somehow they could hear each other. I continued each day to ask for my hormones, but never received them. My nerves were getting worse.

I was later told Anna quickly went into organizing a team of supporters in an attempt to help me. Friends, family, classmates, and prayer warriors around the world organized and sent out letters to my judge. Money came pouring in to help with defense. From $50.00 to $1,000.00 donations flooded the bank. People we had come to know from all over the world desperately wanted to help. I thought of the spunky little redhead as a child, and now she was a beautiful young lady with a desperate desire to help her mother.

Immediately, I began to have visits from several pastors. Most were local pastors from different churches, then Gregg Ruark, an American missionary from the Island. It was wonderful when I saw a familiar face!

Within a couple of days, an officer came by stating I had an attorney visit. At this time I more than welcomed a visit from anyone to get out of the cell. I jumped up and ran to the door, waiting to hear the huge iron door slide open once again. I was still new at learning the correct protocol of a criminal. I was abruptly reminded daily to walk to the right and stay by the wall, always going to the back of the elevator, and facing the wall. Today, I walked into the small room and, looking up with a huge smile was a friend of mine. I thought, *"Oh Thank You, Jesus!"* This was the only room I entered that I could touch someone, and it felt great being able to hug someone I knew.

Within hours I was called out for another visit. This time with my new court-appointed attorney, Walter Henderson. As I entered the room, his reaction was noticeably different. He turned his whole body towards the wall as though I had lice or an incurable, contagious disease. He peered across his shoulder and would ask very pointed questions, then look away from me. His demeanor was so disturbing, I quickly thanked him and let him know my daughter was seeking another attorney. Actually, I knew nothing of what Anna was doing, I just had a horrible feeling about this man. When Anna learned of the incident, she was furious. She was already upset with him. Mr. Henderson let Anna and a friend know that I had no chance, and I would definitely be going to prison for life. Anna immediately hired Mr. Sonny Cribbs, an older gentleman with unlimited experience with high-profile criminals. I knew nothing about Mr. Cribbs, but Anna had researched the situation and he seemed to be the man of the hour when it came to criminal attorneys. I thought it strange as I reflected on the daycare owner who recommended this same attorney eight years ago.

❧

Each day got harder with the constant clanging of iron doors, and people all around me. Authorities continued to refuse to bring my hormones. My mind was foggy and my nerves seemed to be falling apart. I became frantic and upset, but no one cared. I did everything, using every God-given gift, including name dropping as to the Federal Judge who stated I was to get them. The guards continued to ignore my request.

Once again I was called out of my cell for an attorney visit. It was my first visit with Mr. Cribbs. I found it odd—right off, he made a remark stating I was pretty and that could be a good thing. I didn't feel pretty and had not been told that in a while. He went on to explain that sometimes it helped in the courtroom. He appeared upset as he told me of his visit with the Orange County D.A. He asked if I had had an affair with Trevor and was jealous of Trevor and JoNey? I was totally blown away by the statement and became outraged. I knew Orange County would be tough, but I wasn't expecting lies and deceit on top of all the other betrayal. With each day, it was becoming more evident as to what I was up against.

More visitors came from pastors, attorneys and family. Some of the pastors were total strangers, yet let me know they were praying for me. One bold pastor, taking it a step further, warned me not to accept a plea bargain. He boldly stated, "Make sure you get a jury trial!" I thought, *How cool! A truly awesome man of God! He obviously knows something I don't.*

The food was similar to T.V. dinners and tolerable the first few days. I began to skip meals and eat only what little fruit appeared on the tray. I remember peering down at the canned fruit, wondering if it had even one vitamin. Only once in the three weeks did I see a piece of real meat. I am not sure what the beef was, but my stomach paid the price daily, so I deleted it from my meals. It began to play on my mind to the point where I wondered if strong cravings for fresh vegetables were similar to being a drug addict! Everything we ate was fresh on the Island. I never saw a can opener in an Islander's home!

I worried about my health, so I began to throw out hints to different workers I came in contact with. Surprisingly, it worked. I soon found a source to provide dried nuts and fruit. That's when I became a true convict. I would normally put them in my socks and bra. One particular day I failed to wear socks, so I placed them in my bra. On my return to my cell, one of the workers stopped and had me stretch to be searched. I thought, *Well, this would be different for them to find health food instead of drugs and cigarettes.* This guard had obviously been tipped off, and was angry at not finding anything. I truly knew there had to be a God. Praise God, once again! I returned to the cell doing everything I could to hide my snacks in my locker. I laid quietly on the bed, meditating over and over about what they would do if they caught me. Could I be in any worse trouble than life imprisonment? Could there be anything worse for sneaking in health food?

Within a couple of hours, one of the officers came in very upset, opened our door and just glared at us. She boldly stated she knew one of us was hiding something, and had flushed it down the commode. No one had flushed the commode, so this was confusing. With her hands on her hips, she continued to turn to each of us, staring as though she were expecting a full confession. Surprisingly, I was calm and just stared back at her. I really didn't care. I knew punishment normally was solitary confinement. I would more than welcome that. Maybe I could sleep for a change!

ða.

I soon learned how to use the phone in the dining room, and began to call family and friends. After a couple of weeks, I was told I could talk to Nocona. I knew they were monitoring the conversation, but I had no problem with that. Once again, Praise God! I was told Nocona was in the home of a wonderful Christian family, and their youngest daughter was now her best friend. The whole family surrounded Nocona in love. They poured out their heart and soul to make sure Nocona was as comfortable as they could possibly make her. The family attended a Pentecostal Church and loved the Lord. I knew Nocona could make it. When Nocona came to the phone, it was as though it took forever for her to speak. I clung to the phone trying to hear every detail of every word. The T.V. was right above the phone, so it was hard to hear. As Nocona spoke she cried. My whole body struggled, knowing the drastic change she was going through. I could tell she was totally overwhelmed. The small Island had prepared her for a lot, but obviously not something of this magnitude.

Tears flowed down my face and onto the blue uniform with each word that came out of Nocona's mouth. I could no longer pick her up and run. Nocona would have to now stand on her own and fight. She told me how much she loved me and how she was going to get me out of jail. She cried, reassuring me she could do it. The more she talked, the more I cried, as she spoke of her court-appointed attorney. The female attorney didn't listen to what Nocona wanted, and continued to state Nocona had to live with Trevor. I then asked if her court-appointed psychiatrist was helping her. Her reply was, "They all say I have to live with Trevor!"

When I learned it was Dr. Groban , I was outraged, but not surprised! I knew Orange County would be organized for our return to the States. I was concerned Nocona would have a nervous breakdown, knowing the games that were being played and the lack of empathy for her. The judicial system would definitely not be there for her, once again.

With each call, I would speak to the host family and grieve as the lady spoke of all the pressure that Nocona was under. Daily Nocona had visits with Child Protective Services workers, Trevor, and a psychiatrist doing evaluations. She was placed in a very large school in comparison to what she was familiar with. With each call, the host continued to stress her concern for Nocona, stating she wasn't doing well.

C.P.S. finished the evaluation on Nocona. I anxiously awaited the results.

Nocona scored high, being evaluated from the eighth to the eleventh grade. Praise God again! We had just started the sixth grade home-school program prior to our leaving. I didn't need any more marks against me! They also stated Nocona was unusually verbal for her age. They felt she was a little spoiled from living with her grandmother. In reality she was raised by an Island.

꿈

I soon came to know and understand the full meaning of lockdown! A hurricane was now on its way! All female prisoners were placed on another floor to make room for Jefferson County inmates. We were in a large concrete building, and Jefferson County was less protected. My tiny cell was soon crammed full with women lined up on the floor. There was no room to walk or lay down. The dining room quickly became a makeshift bedroom for many inmates.

Jefferson County inmates were used to a lot more privileges than we had. They all became outraged by not getting to smoke. Several fights erupted off and on throughout the two days. One of the ladies from my cell was passed a cigarette and lit it up in our tiny cell. We were all in a sitting position for lack of space for everyone. We didn't have room for ourselves much less for *smoke!* I had reached my limit and made the mistake of telling them to please put it out. I thought I was going to have the whole cell block on me!

OCTOBER 5, 2002

I was awakened at 6 a.m. to get ready for court. By seven I was in shackles and on my way back to the Jack Brooks Federal Courthouse in Beaumont, Texas. I waited in a 5 x 8' cold room until the afternoon. A man in a cell down from me asked if I was getting out soon. He wanted to pay me a large sum of money to help him after I was released. It definitely had a way of taking my mind off of my problem, but I let him know I wasn't up for the offer.

I was then led down the long hallway in chains by a female officer. I continued to walk extremely cautiously and nervously, knowing everyone was aware of this hearing and would be present. As the officer slowly walked me into the large courtroom, her demeanor quickly changed as she saw the huge crowd. She became more and more nervous as she led me in. As we approached my chair, she never said a word to anyone, but suddenly turned, motioned for me to turn around, and led me back out. I was moving very slowly, struggling with the shackles on my ankles. She took me back down the hall and placed me in another room. There was no explanation. I was later taken to a much larger courtroom. I then realized this one could accommodate the many friends that showed up to support me. My friends had taken up both sides of the room!

I couldn't look around since I was bound in the chains, and had to move forward with caution. I was seated next to my court-appointed attorney. I was truly feeling awkward, but desperately felt the need to attempt to keep my composure and dignity, whatever might be left. Everything about me felt exposed and cold. There was a hush across the room. Whispers could be heard stating, *"The Wrong Person Is In Chains!"* At one moment I glanced over at the crowd, but the expressions on the faces were not what I was expecting, but a look of horror! My eyes continued to scan the room, only to stop when I saw JoNey. Her face was totally void of life! It was as though everyone was watching a horror movie rather than a courtroom hearing. Yet it felt good, seeing so many friends and family present.

The courtroom was packed, but Trevor and family filled only a few seats. The Honorable U.S. Magistrate Earl Hines entered the room. You could hear a pin drop! Judge Hines' opening statement was unusual. Using my past married name, he boldly stated, *"Miss Harris, Ever Since You Arrived You Have Caused Quite A Stir. There Have Been Two Hurricanes And Two Packed Courtrooms!"* It wasn't a statement everyone expected, but it had a way of mesmerizing my friends. The judge was extremely nice, with a way of relaxing the moment.

The court-appointed attorney, Walter Henderson, quickly dismissed himself from the case, letting the judge know I had my own attorney. The judge asked if I understood everything and if I had any questions. As much as I hated bringing it up, my priority remained the same. I once again explained that the institution was refusing to give me the hormones.

Once again his whole demeanor changed, yet regrouped, letting me know that I would get them! His statement proved to be correct. It was definitely no longer a problem!

As the court adjourned, the officer was leading me out past my friends and family; one of my friends made an attempt to approach me. She was quickly cut off by security. I was then led back to the small, cold cell. At 5:00 p.m., I was placed in a van and returned to the jail. I noticed as they helped me into the van, a tall black man was seated in the back seat. He was also wearing the same attire and handcuffed. The man began to speak, referring to me as the High-Profile Case. He went on to proudly state there were two high-profile inmates in the van. I looked up at the driver as he rolled his eyes. We were the only two in the van, so I inquired as to who he was. His reply was that he was involved with the Mayor's case. The words *high-profile* began to echo more and more with each day.

With this new environment, I was determined to spend my time just being myself to the best of my ability. So did the other inmates. Despite our differences, I was determined to make the best of this. If I had to be an inmate, I wanted to be a model inmate, and do all I could to keep peace with everyone. With each morning I read my Bible, with others soon joining in. In time we found ourselves daily sharing and praying together. We would sing and march around the room in an attempt to stay warm and remain active. Once a week ladies from a local church came and ministered to us. I was always the first one to get ready. The ministry team immediately recognized me from the press. They let me know they supported me, and the whole church was praying for me. I found it hard to believe that so many strangers were aware of my circumstances and supporting me. River JoNey had mentioned to me on the Island that I had a huge support system in the States, and now from behind bars, I was seeing it firsthand.

Twice a week we were lined up in the hallway and led to the top floor. It was great seeing sunshine and fresh air. The Hondurans were allowed to be with us at this time. Most were very young, and they were always excited to see us. I marveled at how happy they were, despite their circumstances.

Prior to my next court hearing, Mr. Cribbs gave me the fatal words, words I least desired to hear: "The State (Orange County) wants you released to them!" He went on to say that the Federal courts agreed to release me if Orange County would sentence me within twenty days.

I was upset, at first telling him, "*No Way!* I would prefer being dropped into a pit of cobras! I would rather go through a trial with the Federal courts any day than to face Orange County."

Mr. Cribbs tried to explain the reasons I should not go through a Federal trial. He stated that Federal trials were much different than State, and I would be taking a big chance. I reluctantly told him that I would think about it. Later, Mr. Cribbs came back and once again reminded me I would have to face Orange County eventually. He added that the Orange County judge had agreed that, once I got there, the judge would reduce the $100,000.00 bond to $10,000.00 until my sentencing. He said I could possibly just get probation! I would be allowed to stay with Anna until my sentencing.

I talked to Anna and a friend. We all agreed I didn't have much choice. Maybe this was the feasible thing to do since I knew I would eventually have to face Orange County sooner or later.

ಶ

As soon as I returned from court, the officers had my things ready to leave. I never got to say goodbye, but I could see all the ladies through a small window. They had packed all my things and were waving me on with big smiles. It was all set—Anna and a friend would be waiting for me in Orange with the $10,000.00 for the bond. I would now have a new judge. Judge Parker would be presiding over my case in Orange County...

Seashell Prisoners
CHAPTER 18

I was now released to Orange County. An officer from the Sheriff's Department arrived to pick me up. I had no special privileges. I was definitely treated as all other criminals even though I was born and raised in Orange and had poured myself into community work for thirty years. It was made plain and simple from the arrival of the officer, that my life was now in the hands of Orange County, my worst-case scenario!

My ex-husband of twenty-two years was recently elected Commissioner and was to be sworn in within weeks, but once again, I was just another criminal, or, better yet, a high-profile criminal.

I still had to wear handcuffs and sit in the back seat with bars between the officer and myself. As we drove down Interstate-10 to Orange, it felt strange, for more reasons than one. It was my first trip back in eight years to the city I was born and raised in. The patrol car felt as though it was flying, after many years of driving thirty miles an hour on the Island. I often wondered what type of people rode in patrol cars. Now I knew! I tried to ignore individuals staring at me as the different cars passed. We were not far from the Sixteenth Street exit, when for some reason, the patrolman went off the Freeway across the grass and onto the access road. I questioned him as to whether that was legal. He laughed, stating, *"It is for me!"*

Despite the circumstances, I was anticipating seeing Orange for the first time in a long time. Everything appeared clean, and the grass looked unusually green. It was totally different from the sandy beaches we had grown accustomed to. As we approached Sixteenth Street, I crouched down, turning my head as each car passed by. I had anticipated my trip back to Orange for so long, but the last thing I desired was to be seen arriving, in handcuffs, to the very city I was born and raised in. I handled it all well up to this point. My homecoming was truly difficult.

As the officer led me through the jail, we passed cell after cell with men lying on the floor on mats. I thought, *Well, I had heard horror stories about the Orange jail*, and now I found myself struggling with the reality of it all. They quickly seated me, and gave me instructions to wait until I was booked. I looked around to see food trays going by. For the first time in three weeks, I saw fish and fresh green vegetables. One of the workers noticed my staring and asked if I had eaten dinner. I quickly answered "No," so they served me a tray.

I knew Anna was anxiously waiting with a friend to get me out, but I wasn't sure how long that would take. The fish was great and so were the vegetables.

Time was passing: an hour, then two. I began to get nervous looking for a familiar face. I could see no one. I visualized delicious boiled crawfish or something really wonderful for my long-awaited homecoming at Anna's. I knew I would be under house arrest, so there would be no restaurants for a while. At this point it really didn't matter. I just wanted to feel a warm house with family, friends, grandkids, and lots of vegetables and fruit in the kitchen.

I tried to remain calm as the officer went forward with the booking. Another hour went by and it was getting late. Too much time had passed. Something was definitely wrong! I was told Judge Parker would allow me to bond out for $10,000.00, but it wasn't happening. Anna was nowhere to be seen. The booking was going forward, and it was obvious I was not going anywhere, but to a cell.

It didn't take long to see that the Orange County Jail had zero compassion for anyone. The next voice I heard was, "Line up!"

As I stood up, the lady in charge grabbed my hair tie, telling me hair ties were not allowed here. The smell of insecticide was strong. I soon realized that it was used by inmates to wash their heads. They lined several of us up for showering before placing us in a cell. As each inmate entered the shower, someone would oversee the horrible smelling liquid as they poured it over each person's hair and body. The smell was so strong it was nauseating. My turn was coming up. As the inmate stepped out of the shower I stepped in. The person in charge was called away, and I poured the liquid down the drain, but wet my hair down quickly as though I had taken care of it. When they returned, I stepped out of the shower and began to put on the orange jumpsuit they handed me.

The lady then showed me a large plastic container full of sheets. On the side was a plastic pad for a bed. She boldly demanded I carry it to my cell. Because of its weight, I continued to drop it as I walked. At no time did she offer to help. I knew then I wouldn't be leaving this jail tonight. Something obviously had gone wrong!

I was later called to the front. It was a friend. Anna was in the car, but refused to come in since the whole deal went sour. Now it was up to Anna's friend to explain the situation. It came hard and fast.

Judge Parker was now refusing to reduce the bond. It was all a setup to get me to Orange. It was definitely revenge time for Orange County! They now had me where they wanted me, and there was nothing I could do. Once again I had been deceived, and it was hard to tell by how many. I could better understand why Trevor's abuse went unnoticed. Lack of integrity and abuse seemed to be the norm for more than one judge of Orange County.

Anna sent word in an attempt to reassure me they were still working on a way to get around it, possibly for someone that could sign the $100,000.00 bond.

• THE COUNTY RECORD AND THE PENNY RECORD • THE COMMUNITY NEWSPAPERS OF ORANGE COUNTY, TEXAS

Child's future hangs in balance

The continuing saga of Francis Harris — A grandmother's devotion lands her in jail.

DOWN LIFE'S HIGHWAY
ROY DUNN
For the Record

If I was a writer worth my salt, I tell you what I would do. I'd sit down and pen a novel about a true life story filled with international intrigue, kidnap attempt, drawn guns, imprisonment, life on a Caribbean island and a runaway grandmother. Like the perfect country song it has most of the ingredients to be the perfect novel, lacking only a killing, which in itself is surprising to some.

Over the years, I've come across a variety of intriguing suspense-filled stories. But this story is different. Well-written, my novel would surely spin off into a made-for-television movie. Real life experiences sometimes surpass the imagination. Long ago someone coined the phrase, "I gotta do what I gotta do," which brings me to the ongoing saga of Francis Harris, a 57-year-old grandmother who today is incarcerated, sometimes cuffed and shackled while being held by U.S. marshals.

The seed of this story was planted over 12 years ago. But it was eight years ago that Francis committed the actions that have landed her in jail on federal charges. She took her granddaughter Nocona Lynn and left the country.

After making stops in a couple of countries, she settled on Roatan, Honduras, to make her stand. People who know Francis well knew she was resourceful enough to make it just fine wherever she landed, and she did. But what happened in between would have to go in the novel. There's not enough space in this short column.

In 1990, Francis was a young, attractive, financially secure, divorced mother of three youngsters. She was raising her children near Mauriceville, a community that she helped through her generosity and civic endeavors. "A community leader," one lady said. Another lady added, "She didn't help push the wagon; she pulled it." I mention this so the reader will understand she wasn't a transit or lived a life of crime.

Her children owned some horses. Riding horses need shoeing. That's where enters the picture, and the story begins.

Francis hired the 34-year-old man to shoe the kid's horses. Shortly after arriving on the scene, started a sexual affair with one of the children. In January 1991, River JoNey Burton, at the age of 17, gave birth to Nocona Lynn. The custody battle started at the child's birth. A jury awarded custody to the baby's mother, JoNey. With her mother's help, they would raise the child.

Things didn't rock so smoothly with the dad. When Nocona reached the age 3 1/2, Francis made a decision that few people would have the guts to make. With dishes in the sink, plates on the table and unopened mail, Francis grabbed up Nocona, a few belongings and disappeared, leaving behind her three children, parents, siblings and friends. The custody battle had accelerated to the point that Francis feared unlimited visitation was around the corner. The reasons she stated for leaving was her belief that Nocona had been abused and would be again under 's control. These charges are unsubstantiated. She also said she feared for her own life.

I don't know what her basis was for that assumption. Maybe some of the problem from the beginning was that was considered just a donor. Anyway, Francis made the snap decision that would alter her life and that of Nocona and others. In March 1994, she and the child disappeared. In June, JoNey, joined them. Owen Burton, JoNey's dad and

Roy Dunn

granddaughter living away, they have bonded with the child. The Burtons feel the best course of action would be for them to care for the child, who is presently in a foster home. It's no doubt that his pregnant 17-year-old daughter by an adult male was a hard pill to swallow. Some men might have taken different actions than this Christian man did. The Burtons, by all accounts, are solid, good people who want only the best for their grandchild.

In a few days, a judge will decide with whom the child will be placed. In three months, Nocona will be 12 years old. Her thoughts and wishes are sure to be considered. It's not an easy call. The dad has a right to get to know his child. The best possible thing for the child's sake would be if the adults could come to an understanding and wipe the slate as clean as possible.

The scars ahead for Nocona depend in a large part on what happens to Francis, the grandmother who has cared for her since birth. In the child's eyes, she can do no wrong. So whom is she going to blame if her grandmother is serving time in prison? Will she blame herself or others? Someday she'll reach that troublesome, resentful age of 15. Stability in her life before then can lessen the blow. I know about kids this age. I raised five of them. Their imaginations run wild. What tricks will Nocona's mind play on her if the most important person in her life is in prison?

It seems obvious to me that has a lot of confidence building to do in order to build a relationship with his daughter. His future actions could determine how solid a foundation is built. He can endear himself in her eyes or become the villain. Francis made a bad choice, and more bad choices piled on top of the damage already done

was only 3 when she left the country. was at the airport the night Nocona came home but stayed out of public view, Tarver said.

"But I know he and his daughter did get to see each other that night," he said.

Meanwhile, a custody hearing is set for 10 a.m. Oct. 8 in the 163rd District Courtroom in Orange before Judge Farris.

Nocona's maternal grandfather and Harris' former husband, Owen Burton, and his wife, Nelda Burton are intervenors in the case.

Owen Burton is a Mauriceville rancher and the uncontested Democratic candidate in the Precinct 2 Orange County commissioner's race.

When they were married, Harris and Burton started the former TJA's grocery store in Mauriceville, which was later bought by Market Basket.

During her exile in Honduras, Harris has operated a small resort called Casa Calico on the western end of Roatan, which she had to leave when she was arrested.

Tarver said Harris traveled lightly on the plane from Honduras. She and Nocona sat together, and Harris was not handcuffed.

"After visiting with Mrs. Harris, it was understood that we were not going to have any trouble," Tarver said. "Plus we didn't want to create any problem for Nocona. Everything went nice and smoothly."

located them a year after they left.

Later   , his sister and others attempted to kidnap Nocona. They were successful until they got to the airport where the police surrounded them with guns drawn.

JoNey returned to the states, pleaded guilty to a charge, got probation and continued her education at Texas A&M. Meanwhile Nocona, described as a bright, stable youngster, continued her education. She speaks three languages and is fluent in Spanish.

Until a knock on the door at 7 a.m. one day last week, Francis operated a resort on the island. The extradition laws had changed, and the law had come for her and the child.

Owen Burton and wife Nelda are also victims. Despite their who is well aware of where she's 4   een and the sacrifices made on her behalf. In just five years, she will be an adult, free to make her own choices. Meanwhile, the choices of adults in her life will reflect good or bad for the remainder of her life. I know because I've been there.

In conclusion, no one knows what the future holds for Francis, who possibly faces prison for the rest of her life. No doubt that grandmother had lots of guts and love. Her journey, I'm told, has taken its toll. Nocona apparently has been well cared for and has had a happy childhood. We can only hope that the cards of life fall her way. As for me, I don't know any of the players. I met Francis Harris once, 20 years ago. I'm barely familiar with the Burtons and don't know JoNey, Nocona or   . I just know it's one heck of a story down life's highway.

Article (continued)

I was then taken to what they called the drunk tank. It made no sense, being I had come directly from a Federal jail. There were women all over the floor on thin pads. The room was very small with one commode in open view. The walls had what appeared to be fecal matter on them. There were so many women in the small space, it made it impossible to walk or move around. From what I understood, it was a place for the drugs and alcohol to wear off, of which I obviously had neither after three weeks in a Federal institution. One of the ladies recognized me from the press. I saw her running her hand up the wall, stretching, in an attempt to reach the only phone in the room. As she grabbed the phone, she called her mother, quickly telling her, *"Frances Harris is in the cell with me."*

Her mother's reply, "Try to get her autograph!"

There was a horrible stench in the cell, with one small drain in the middle of the floor. I looked around to see where the smell was coming from. There wasn't a lot of light in the cell; little was visible.

Women were coming in throughout the night. There were no pillows, so I looked around to see what everyone else did and quickly copied them, rolling up the end of the thin mattress. I was exhausted, but finally went to sleep. Strange enough—that was the first night in three weeks that I slept six hours! It had to be God, or maybe the fact there was no partying or loud noises all night. I felt so much better the next morning. The next day I was taken to the cell.

I quickly made my way to the far end of the cell in an attempt to get away from the T.V. or anything or anyone that looked noisy. The lack of privacy was playing a toll on me. There was plenty of room to walk around and a table to sit at. In a short period of time, I had made friends with all the ladies. Each was very nice and easy to talk to. I soon came to know all of them, and as the previous inmates, it bothered me as they told their stories of why they were there. I realized it was pretty much the same as the Federal Jail. No real criminals, just women with a past of different forms of abuse.

One of the ladies was there for drinking and driving. I later found out a family member was killed in the accident. The legal system's punishment could not compare with her own. It was obvious that she lived with the pain daily. Despite each individual's dilemma, we all became friends.

Praise God, these ladies slept at night—no big parties, no laughing and cutting up until three in the morning. I was on the top bunk, and once again it was not easy getting up and down, but I managed. It was obvious there was no mercy for anyone.

I observed as the female officers made their way to our cell each morning. They would holler their orders. They were so insensitive! They would open the main door, walk into this small area with bars all around it, and call out a name. Whether you were on the top or bottom bunk, you had better be there instantly or get scolded.

Early one morning they called out a young lady's name, telling her it was time for her to go to court. It was 6 a.m. We were all still asleep. The young lady jumped out of the bed and went straight to the gate. There wasn't time to wash her face, use the bathroom, brush her teeth or comb her hair. I laid there in horror, wondering if this would happen to me!

From then on, I got up at five each morning, and brushed my teeth and hair before anyone else got up. I daily observed all officers to see if just one would treat us with compassion or maybe like a human being. Six days went by before that happened! A rather plump young officer smiled as she approached us in the morning. That was the last time I saw her.

One day we heard an inmate down the hall screaming horrible screams. This went on for hours. From time to time we could hear someone trying to talk to her, but it was obvious the inmate wasn't listening. The screams continued until we heard the door open to her cell. You could hear a pin drop. Everyone was listening to see what would happen next. We never found out, but the screams stopped.

I continued to be amazed at how nice and normal the ladies were in the cell. I could just imagine what all my friends were thinking, that I was in there with all these mass murderers, etc.

੩▲

Days went by and no release. An officer approached the cell once again, this time calling my name. I was taken out to speak to Anna's attorney. David Hunt came in with Joni, stating he could not sign the bond. He had thought about it earlier, but he could not do it. Later there was another attorney visit. Sonny Cribbs came by with his fiancée and once again with devastating news. "Orange County is offering you a plea bargain of three years in prison. Frances, you need to go ahead and accept it. That is the best they will do."

Sonny apologized, claiming he did everything he could. He went on to say two of the judges had recused themselves, but Judge Parker was hanging in strong. Sarah, Trevor's mother, no longer worked in the Orange County Courthouse and was in a nursing home. Her influence was no longer required. It was just...revenge time for the Orange Judicial system!

I was innocent! I had saved a child's life, but no one was interested in that. I had built up so much anticipation of getting out and being with my family before my sentencing. If prison was my destiny, I just wanted a little time with my family. Was I supposed to smile, go straight to prison, and thank everyone in the Orange County Judicial System on my way out for being so generous? Just giving me three years in a state prison? I had already heard all the dreaded stories about state prisons, many times emphatically stating to Sonny, "I would never go to a state prison!" Inmates, after one look at me, stated I would never make it there, they were so tough.

Sonny strongly recommended the deal and let me know there was no way the judge was going to reduce the bond, nor were they giving me probation like I was told prior to coming to Orange. Outraged, I looked Mr. Cribbs in the eye and told him to go back to the courthouse and tell all of them I would just stay in jail and rot; so they could watch me, if that is what they desired. Sonny looked at me and politely let me know, *"That Is Not An Option."*

I then jumped up like I was going to leave the room! There were glass windows between me and the main office. As I looked around at the officers, I noticed piercing stares. I slowly made my way back to the chair, until Mr. Cribbs gave them the go ahead. A jury trial was never brought up.

ತ⁕

As I was battling for justice, River's father and his wife were battling for Nocona's freedom. Nocona's first hearing came up. The Orange County Sheriff stated Nocona needed to be placed with Trevor. Nocona's attorney, a psychiatrist, and a judge were all in full agreement. Nocona should live with Trevor. All were court-appointed, and all of them were united, sticking to the same story. Nocona should live with Trevor. Nocona would continue living with the same C.P.S. family until the decision on a date was made.

The judge then announced he was placing a gag order on Nocona's case. All documents were sealed and no one would be able to speak to the press about anything to do with it. It was obvious that their strategy was well mapped out prior to our arrival to the U.S. It was just a matter of forcing the pieces of the puzzle together. Laura's influence was holding strong even with her lack of presence. Nocona was eleven now, and undeniably verbal, but her voice continued to be ignored.

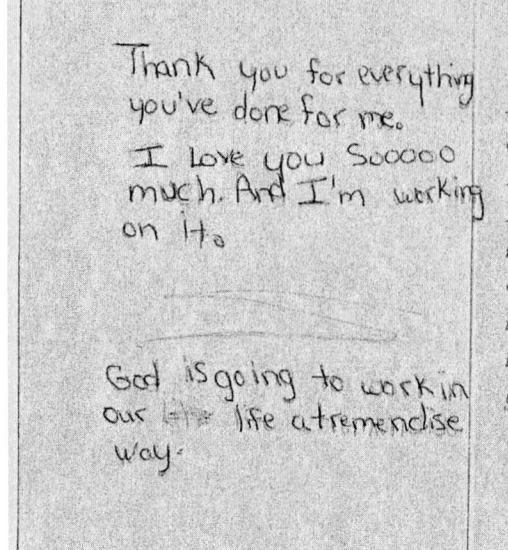

Nocona's letter to her grandmother

I requested a jury trial, but I continued to hear the same. That would not be possible! No one seemed to know why. I just would not get a trial! One morning an officer called me out as though I was going to court. They took me up to the front office and told me to sit down. This tall, very well-dressed man asked if I would speak to the press. I told him only when I got the bond reduced. The man turned and walked off and I was totally unattended. No one was watching me. The lady that had brought me out thought I was going to court, so she was nowhere in sight. I walked around a little and looked down the hall. Not one person was watching me! I saw the double doors leading outside. The thought actually entered my mind to just walk out, but I didn't.

After returning to my cell, I began to cry. Inmates, one at a time, came over and consoled me. Two of them stated they wished I would have been their grandmother and helped them when they were a child. My problems were small in comparison to theirs, but at the moment the day was overwhelming me. Mr. Sonny Cribbs was a famous criminal attorney, yet the Orange County courts continued to be in total control.

Days went by. I was now being told I could speak to Nocona. I knew they would be monitoring the call, but I didn't care. With each call, Nocona would cry, and appeared to be overwhelmed with everything. C.P.S., Nocona's court-appointed attorney, and a court-appointed psychiatrist continued to put pressure on Nocona. All of them were telling her she had no choice, but to live with Trevor. Nocona would sob and tell me she felt she had been sold out.

She told me that on one forced visit with Trevor, he was questioning her on different things, and Nocona's reply to Trevor was, *"I Plead The Fifth."* Trevor became very upset with her reply and fussed at her. I was extremely concerned for Nocona, but in another sense I found it humorous, realizing where she had picked these statements up. The term, *sold out*, was common for attorneys on the Island, but a person would think it was out of place in the U.S.

Once I was questioning Tim, a young entrepreneur on the Island, about his girlfriend. Tim smiled and said he pled the fifth. At the time I didn't realize Nocona was listening, much less would one day repeat the term.

Nocona's sobs got worse. I told Nocona to call and talk to her judge or write him letters and let him know her feelings. Previously, Judge Travis had been so compassionate with all the children in the CASA program. I knew he had to be totally misinformed on this case. He was so supportive of me and the programs I was involved in prior to my leaving. This just wasn't the Judge Travis I knew!

With each conversation with Nocona, I could tell she was wearing down and sounded exhausted. She continued to have forced visits with Trevor each week. Now they were making her go different places with him. On several occasions, Nocona asked Trevor to drop all charges against me, including the million-dollar judgment. His reply was always, "No!"

I would talk to the host family Nocona was living with, and the lady reconfirmed it was all very draining. C.P.S. and the courts weekly played on Nocona, leaving her stressed. Nocona was not doing well in school, and continued to worry about me. On one call, Nocona told me not to worry about anything—that she would get me out of jail. I thought, how sad that she feels it's her duty now to free me of my charges. She obviously felt the burden of justice was on her.

A few days later, Nocona called once again and told me she had attended a revival. The evangelist picked her out of the crowd and prophesied over her. He stated he knew she was praying for something and he saw a window opening for her and she would receive whatever she was praying for. She was excited and felt comforted by it!

≥∙

Days continued to go by. There were no changes with the courts. Nothing appeared to be happening. The whole scenario continued to play on me, sending me deeper into depression. I began to cry over little things. I would try to get up and act okay, knowing the effect my depression would have on the other ladies.

The inmates daily made attempts to encourage me. Every now and then one would look at me and say, "You're not going to have to serve any time." I wanted very much to believe that, but it didn't appear possible. I continued to pray, but it was as though my prayers hung directly over me, going nowhere.

By this time, Anna and friends would come, but they reflected nothing but fear in their faces with each visit. Anna, with the help of others, utilized the power of the Internet, with hundreds of emails being sent out to friends around the world. Letters continued to pour in. Family and friends from many years past began to get word and desired to help in any way they could.

Immediately upon our return to the States, the Island of Roatan was in a total uproar. Our support was overwhelming. Reports came back that the elite to the poorest of people were now contacting Anna, and moving forward with letters to the judge. The Mayor of the Island sent word that he would come if needed and testify on my behalf. This was all very encouraging and helped me to continue fighting for my freedom.

Missionaries on the Island were instrumental in forming an organization they called 924. To them our tragedy was as appalling and traumatizing to everyone on the Island, as 911 was to the U.S.

Gregg, Angela, Steven, and other friends were back on the Island collecting our personal things and storing them for us.

Despite the problems, everyone in West End was uniting together and working to see Christmas on the Beach go forward in my absence. On my arrival to the Island, I didn't feel I had anything to share with the people. With time, we had all learned so much from each other. It all proved to be totally life changing for me. It never entered my mind at that time from all the new friendships, I would one day gain an even larger support system!

Nocona's attorney surprised me with a visit to the Orange jail. I was shocked she and a friend came, knowing how upset I was with all of Nocona's court-appointed legal aides. I took the opportunity to unload as to how I felt Nocona was being horribly abused by the judicial system. I was surprised when her first words were, "I guess Nocona thinks we sold her out!"

My immediate thought was, *Those were the same exact words Nocona said over the phone*. The person went further, stating Nocona would be living with Trevor full–time, despite Nocona's wishes. Somehow the conversation came up about Nocona's psychiatrist. I let them know how upset I was that the courts were using him. One in the party was obviously not considering the enormity of the statement; reconfirming my thoughts on the man. The person boldly stated "Frances, Dr. Groban is a court-appointed psychiatrist, and will go with whatever the state desires for Nocona. Some refer to this as a *courtroom whore*."

I froze at the statement, since I had never heard this term or thought it possible in our courts. Within weeks, I was speaking with another attorney, who reconfirmed the statement going as far as to say that a judge had made the very same statement about Dr. Groban.

This time I had to speak up. The same psychiatrist that turned his back on Nocona in 1994 now was once again in charge of her safety? And I'm the one in jail facing a life sentence! Maybe they thought the truth would comfort me in a way, but I grew more angry with each day. I was nauseated at the thought of other children, whose lives had been affected, or even devastated like ours by this man. The word, courtroom whore, became more defined with each day.

Prior to our leaving the U.S., attorneys, physicians, and judges had let us down. Now we were back, experiencing the same. Where exactly would all this end? I knew from the time I left, one day I would have to experience this horrible nightmare, but the last thing I considered was Nocona becoming the victim of this whole bizarre tragedy!

If I could have foreseen all of this, things would have been handled a lot differently in Roatan once I found out Phil had turned us in. I would have been a lot better at hiding the second go-around with the experience I had gained.

Over a period of time, I had spoken with many attorneys, one being a very prestigious attorney. Each time I would bring up the judge that failed to listen to our case prior to my leaving, he boldly stated, "Well, Frances, I know that man, and he hates getting in the middle. He tries to please everyone."

Then later, I brought up the psychiatrist, and he went through the same scenario: "I know that man well, and he just wants to get along with everyone."

Many different professionals, that we were paying and desperately seeking to help to save Nocona from horrendous physical and sexual attacks from her father, all failed to help, because they were professional men that didn't want to get involved! Yet they took my money to defend Nocona! People were in professions that they had no business being in! They played on our every emotion, took our money, and in the end our lives were ripped to shreds! River, Nocona, and I were all mentally and emotionally raped by, not only an abusive, sick man and his family, but, most of all, a rogue judicial system! I was totally overwhelmed, as feelings boiled up within me at the mention of the word, attorney! I thought of where all these attorneys would be on Judgment Day; Jesus stated what would happen if one little hair is bothered on a child! The more I thought of it, with everything I had read in the Bible, Jesus appeared to have only contempt for attorneys!

The days continued to go by slowly in the Orange County Jail. The only good thing, other than the inmates being so nice, was the food. The cooks definitely knew what they were doing! My stomach was now at peace! No more need to smuggle in cashews, etc. I thought, *One day I am going to send them a big bouquet of flowers!* They thought of their work as a job. I thought of it as a ministry!

Once again the officer came to our cell and announced, "Attorney visit for Harris." I thought, *Great! Now what is happening?* Each day seemed to have its own new beginning.

I went into the little room, once again. There sat Anna with David. David's wife insisted he sign the bond. David's wife and Anna were High School classmates. Thank God, the young lady couldn't turn her back on Anna's tears and desperate pleas. What a glorious day! I felt like a ton of bricks had been taken off of me. I would be under total house arrest, but that was okay. Anything to get out of here!

All the inmates were hugging me! No more chains on my feet and wrists. All I could think of was, *Praise The Lord!* My feet were once again on solid ground. No more ugly orange suits! Another epitome of the whole stay—orange was definitely not my color!

⁂

I was now in the United States of America, for the first time walking on concrete roads, with cool air and crawfish within reach. Even though I was under house arrest, I could still see all these things getting closer. I would now be able to see all my family and friends! It was truly a great moment, the feeling of some sort of freedom. The very thing that we all take for granted, now felt so wonderful!

After my release, I made my way to Anna's car. I then realized I had forgotten my hormones. I told Anna as important as they were, I refused to enter the jail once again. Anna quickly jumped out, retrieving them for me.

We immediately made our way to Bridge City to Anna's home. I knew I was in trouble, when Anna swung through Sonic's drive-in window to get food. I thought,... *This is my welcome-home meal!* The welcoming dinner was now obviously on hold.

⁂

When we entered the house, there were wonderful scents that met us at the door. Candles were lit in each room, each having a wonderful fragrance. Anna's home was warm with a wonderful sense of her family. It was a beautiful home, and all the character built into it was awesome. I had not been around Anna since she was a teenager, so I totally didn't know what to expect of her as an adult. Anna's first marriage had failed, and she was now married to Louis Oceguera. The two of them had a beautiful little two-year-old son, named Julian.

We were only there a few hours when we heard a knock on the door. I was in a state of total numbness from everything, but it was wonderful seeing, to my surprise, two friends, one being from the Island. My first guests! *A Total God Moment!* These were two of my and Nocona's favorites, Jen with Alternative Missions and Laura, another truly great friend from the States.

I do not remember one word that was exchanged, but I remember the hugs and how wonderful it felt. What a miracle that her one month off the project in St. Helene, Honduras, and God had them here to encourage Nocona and me! What a God we serve! They had brought a couple of boxes full of our pictures and personal things of ours from the Island. Last but not least they also brought my cacao from the Mosquito!

After they left, I was totally exhausted, soon finding my way to the bedroom. As I entered the room, presents were sitting all around the room. Anna's oldest son, Rylan, had drawn pictures for me and placed them in my room.

I went on to bed, but for some reason I couldn't sleep. I got up and walked around the house, touching and feeling all the pictures and décor Anna had on the wall of family and friends. My mind continued to go back into time with all the memories of our home in Mauriceville. The long halls in our home were always full of family pictures. Our family trunk was packed with lots of memories and now Anna's walls reflected the same. The house was truly decorated with love.

I realized the little temperamental young lady I left had changed a lot over the years. My little girl that I had missed for so many years was now all grown up with her own family.

The next day and many days to come, friends poured in with gifts, food, and lots of hugs. It felt wonderful, but I continued to just feel numb to everything. I guess the trauma was still there despite the physical freedom. I was back in the States, yet mentally my mind continued to shut down. People were bringing gifts and food daily. Most everyone looked pretty much the same, only a few had changed. I looked on as everyone laughed and talked. The cameras were constantly flashing. I was mentally exhausted, yet I made every attempt to smile and show my appreciation.

Frances with Friends & Family

Nocona, Frances, Sister Eleanor Cooper & Brenda Anderson

Frances with Mother, Brother & Sisters

ૐ

 The day after I got out of jail, Anna took me to Beaumont to my probation officer, Jenelle McArthur. After a couple of visits, it took every ounce of energy that I could muster up to be in her presence or talk to her on the phone without becoming totally stressed. Jenelle let you know right off where you stood with her: *"You Are A Hard-Core Criminal And I Am In Control!"* There was never a moment that she varied from that visage. That was her job and she did it well.

 Jenelle lectured me on the seriousness of my house arrest, and what would happen if I did not comply with it. I was then told to go immediately and have the monitoring bracelet put on. She reminded me of the twenty-day deadline on the sentence the Federal Courts had stipulated on my release. Orange County had agreed, but Jenelle acted as though it was up to me to make sure it happened.

ૐ

Anna Oceguera and her mother, Frances Harris, pose for a family picture with Oceguera's daughter, Julia Oceguera, shortly after Harris' release from the Orange County Jail. The Record Photo By Jerry Childress

Harris free for now

■ Grandmother faces possible prison term in custody case

GLENDA DYER
FOR THE RECORD

Frances Harris is making the most of her possibly short-lived freedom after being released from the Orange County Jail last week.

Harris and her daughter, Anna Oceguera, have been hosting family and friends at Oceguera's home in Bridge City. They also planned a prayer meeting for Saturday night at the home, and Harris planned to attend church on Sunday. Plus, a missionary friend from Honduras has been visiting.

The former Mauriceville resident faces a possible prison term of two to 10 years for interference with child custody because she fled to Honduras with her then 3-year-old granddaughter, Nocona Lynn ▢ eight years ago.

Authorities arrested Harris on Sept. 24 at her home on the Honduran island of Roatan and brought her and Nocona, now 11, back to Southeast Texas that day.

Harris was released from the Orange County Jail last Wednesday but is restricted to her daughter's home because of the terms of release stemming from a federal kidnapping charge. Harris is only allowed to attend court proceedings and church, get medical care or to meet with her lawyer.

Federal Magistrate Earl Hines let Harris go from a Beaumont jail Oct. 18 and postponed a federal grand jury hearing for a month so the state interference with child custody charge can be addressed in Orange County.

The federal charge, which was brought to help extradite Harris back from Honduras, is expected to

GRANDMOTHER Page 2A

Days went by and the numbness was wearing off. I began to collect my thoughts, knowing I desperately needed money for all the attorney fees and living expenses. I decided I would make one last plea to Phil and see if he might return my money. I made the call, but Phil's wife answered. Phil was not there, she explained, but she was aware of the situation. She went on to say Phil would have to take care of it. Phil never returned the call so I called him again, and he answered the phone. He mumbled a few words and hung up the phone. I called back and he didn't answer.

The very next day I heard a faint knock on Anna's door. When I looked out, it was Phil, lurking around the house as though trying to hide from someone. It was all very strange as he came in and sat down. He was very nervous and fidgety. I found the whole scenario amusing, and asked if his wife was aware he was here. He quickly said, "No!"

He began to make excuses as to why he had not paid me back the money. I stopped him immediately and let him know that he had lied to me and that I wanted my money. He began to say he would pay me back a hundred dollars a month. Outraged by the statement, I told him that I would never live to receive it all and I expected full payment.

He then said he would sell some of his property and give it back to me. Needless to say, that never happened. He had certainly proven himself not to be the friend he portrayed to me, my family, and my friends.

Throughout the years, I had the reoccurring thought: *Phil you could have been a hero in this situation, yet you chose to be a liar and a thief!*

Oct 18

Harris resort stays busy
Jailed grandmother's Honduran resort managed

GLENDA DYER
FOR THE RECORD

A missionary taking care of Frances Harris' rooming house on the Honduran island of Roatan says the former Mauriceville woman's resort facility continues to stay busy.

"The dog, the cat, and the parrot are all well, and we've just wrapped up a wonderfully busy week of hosting a missionary group here at Casa Calico," said Erica, who asked that her last name be withheld.

The man Harris "trusted with the grounds keeping and cleaning" continues his job also, she said.

Erica has maintained administrative duties at Casa Calico since Sept. 24 when Harris, 57, was arrested on a federal kidnapping charge stemming from her leaving the country eight years ago with her then 3-year-old granddaughter.

Federal and Orange County authorities escorted Harris and her granddaughter, Nocona Lynn ____ from Roatan to Texas the day she was arrested.

When she left in 1994, Harris said she fled with her granddaughter to avoid abuse by the girl's father. But Nocona's father, ____, has main-

Frances Harris

tained over the years that he never abused his child.

Harris' Casa Calico is located in West End village on Roatan island opposite Half Moon Bay and has "the greatest tropical breeze off the bay," the facility's Web page says.

The resort has "beautiful suite size rooms overlooking the water with a garden below, 24 hour hot and cold water, air conditioning or fans and large porches with hammocks." And the lobby features

Erica said four or five vehicles pulled into the driveway of Casa Calico just before 7 a.m. the day Harris was arrested.

"Six to 10 policia (local Honduran police) armed with M-16 type rifles hopped out of the trucks and quickly surrounded the property while a few of the six or seven plain-clothed people, some carrying side arms, approached the front door," she said.

When she went inside the house, a clerk was writing out a legal document giving an account of what was happening. Also inside were a police officer with an M-16, two FBI agents, a judge, two women police officers with side arms and a woman who appeared to be a child services worker, Erica said.

"At this time the agent asked Frances and Nocona to gather a few things like a change of clothes and personal items," Erica said. "Neither of them was dressed yet that morning; the police may have woken them up."

Erica helped Nocona get her things together, and Nocona put her clothes in a backpack.

"Nocona displayed a wide range of emotions that were unusual for her from defiant to compliant, complacent to horrified," Erica said. "She cried as I hugged her."

By about 7:25 a.m., Harris was finishing gathering what she needed and explaining to Erica how to keep Casa Calico running when an FBI agent cautioned that they had to catch a 9 a.m. flight.

"They each had only a backpack, and Frances also had her purse and was grabbing important papers as they shooed her out the door," Erica said. "They did not separate Nocona from her Grandma. The two of them left the house without handcuffs and walked to the car together."

Currently Harris remains in custody in a privately-owned jail in Beaumont, and Nocona's whereabouts are under the supervision of Child Protective Services.

At a custody hearing last week in Orange, visiting Judge ____ laid out a plan to re-establish a relationship with Nocona and her father, saying it will take experts to help figure out the best way to accomplish the task.

____ said ____ wants to have a part in his daughter's life and has been denied the privilege of being with her for the past eight years.

"But you just can't uncook a cooked egg," ____ said. "You can't change the past; the future is the only thing."

Both sides of Nocona's family are unable to comment about the case because of a gag order ____ issued.

Harris is scheduled for a detention hearing Friday at federal court in Beaumont.

• THE RECORD NEWSPAPERS • THE WEEK OF OCTOBER 16, 2002 • 3A

Harris trial
From Page 1

cable television, video and "our famous lemon grass tea and fruit punch."

Erica said Harris was a respected business woman there because she operated one of the nicest hotel facilities in West End.

She also said Harris and Nocona were well known on the island.

"The entire community and beyond — everyone we come in contact with — are so sad that they're gone," she said.

Erica and her husband, Josh, first met Harris and Nocona, now 11, at the beginning of the year when the couple came to Roatan to scout out missionary opportunities.

"We were introduced to Frances by a few of the missionaries in West End," she said. "When we returned in August for a long term stay and to start a Bible study, Frances gave us a good deal on monthly rent and offered for us to use her property as a place to meet for Bible study. Sometimes Frances would invite us down for dinner."

Erica and Josh were leaving Harris' resort facility the day Harris was arrested. When Erica went back to see if she could lend support, she was asked to look after Casa Calico during Harris' absence.

An FBI agent told her Harris would be leaving and needed someone to look after the place. Otherwise a local police officer would be assigned as caretaker.

"The thought of this horrified Frances," she said. "Every other person I've spoken to has the same horrified reaction at the thought of the local police being in charge of their property."

Roatan, October 31st 2003

The Honourable Judge Thad Hartfield,
US District Court
300 Willow St.
Court Room Number One
Beaumont, Texas 77701

Re: Francis Collins contributions to the island.

Dear Judge Hartfield:

My name is Jerry Dave Hynds, I am the Mayor of the island of Roatan, Bay Islands Honduras. I would like to point out to you what Frances Collins means to our island.

Most of the foreigners that come here have their individual priorities, but with Frances things were different she made the Youth, Women & Church groups her priority. With her background in organizing youth events and programs, she has been able to bring similar activities to the island and our youth has been very benefited by her work. Being an undeveloped country, without her help and experience, we now lack such programs that were enlightening to our young ones.

Here is a list of the programs Frances has started on the island:
1. Two youth revivals for the whole island involving over 500 youth
2. Helped organize monthly Christian Women Meetings involving women from all over the island.
3. Christmas on the beach program: yearly event for the past four years involving all the youth and family of West End with Parades/Youth Drama, Dance & Drama Programs, Fireworks Display, Boat Parade with Santa as the highlight of the event, all of which Frances organizes working together with the business community of West End.
4. Pastor and Missionary Conference: had the first one at her business and later helped other Ministries with their program.
5. Has monthly dinners for welcoming new Missionaries to the island and bringing the island Ministries together.
6. Used her home and business for new Missionaries coming in
7. Worked with youth Sunday school classes in West End

CONSTRUYENDO UN MEJOR ROATAN
Islas de La Bahía, PBX: (504) 445-1299, Fax: (504) 445-1697
e-mail: roatanisland@hondusoft.com

8. Supports Ministries in Honduras with her income.
9. Started a dance team with Children from West End
10. Worked up a Youth Program for children on Halloween night
11. Helps Ministries on the island to get in contact with mission teams from the US, and works with them building web sites for their Ministries.

Honourable Judge, Frances Collins is a very important person to our island and specifically to the community of West End, her Knowledge, experience and work is needed in a place like ours, where we lack of people like her who have dedication, love and perseverance towards working with our people.

I hope that my letter will help in giving you an idea of the importance of Frances' Collins contributions to our island and we, the people of Roatan, trust that Justice will be made and we look forward to have Frances Collins here working with us where she is greatly needed by our people and most importantly, our youth.

Best Regards,

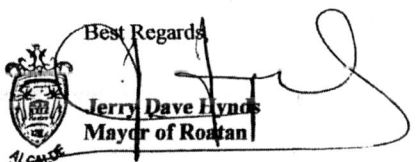

Jerry Dave Hynds
Mayor of Roatan

CONSTRUYENDO UN MEJOR ROATAN
Islas de La Bahía, PBX: (504) 445-1299, Fax: (504) 445-1697
e-mail: roatanisland@hondusoft.com

ISLAND PROPERTIES
Select Residential & Commercial Listings

October 22, 2002

RE: Character reference for Frances Collins Harris.

To Whom It May Concern,

Frances Collins Harris is known in Roatan as "Miss Frances" an island endearment normally bestowed on the honored older members of the community. This term reflects the recipient's high status of respect within the community.

I am a US citizen and have been a legal resident of Roatan, Honduras for the past 26 yrs. I have witnessed many foreigners come and go thru the years with barely a blink but I have only had the pleasure of knowing a handful of individuals that have actually made a true contribution to the island through their presence. Miss Francis was one of those very special few with her church work, charities and activities for children.

For those readers unfamiliar with Roatan or Miss Frances the recent US news coverage must seem appalling (Kidnapped to Honduras...) yet nothing could be further from the truth. It was apparent to all that spent time with the child, Nocona, or her Grandmother that Miss Francis held the child's best interest to heart. With love, guidance and tutelage from her Grandmother we watched Nocona blossom into the beautiful girl in front of you today. Miss Frances provided Nocoma with a good education, a stable home and comfortable lifestyle. Yes, it is possible to provide a child with all the necessary things even in a small third world country. I raised both of my sons from infancy to high school age on Roatan. My sons went from home schooling in Roatan to attending a Military Academy in Virginia where both excelled and held high ranking positions.

Obviously, the court has a difficult task at hand in discerning the facts and deciding the futures of Nocona Lynn & Frances Harris. Hopefully those involved in making these crucial judgments will deliberate on the father's actions. 1.) The fact that the father was approximately 34 yrs. old when he entered a relationship (which resulted in a pregnancy) with Nocona's mother who at the time was a 16 – 17 yr. old minor raises questions about this father's emotional well being. 2.) The father further engaged in criminal activity on April 23rd 1996 when he and three other foreigners illegally entered the private bilingual school Nocona was attending. With force and no regard to the safety & health of others they knocked down a pregnant school teacher; kidnapped Nocona; and raced to the airport where he had a private plane waiting. Only through the love of her teachers and fellow students was Nocona rescued. Without hesitation they chased these formidable kidnappers to our international airport and notified the airport police. It took police force to stop the abduction as it played out to the last minute on the runway with engines running. This was an extremely traumatic episode for all involved, none more than Nocoma. The school children were afraid to go back to school and had to be counseled, none more than Nocona. Again, Miss Frances through patience and diligence brought a peaceful normalcy to Nocona's life. Their relationship and bond is truly enviable. Please consider the "imposed trauma" should the court rule to separate granddaughter from grandmother. Don't prosecute Miss Francis for her selfless act of love but rather ask how can a father wanting custody perform such selfish and harmful deeds in the name of love.

Sincerely,

Mary M. Monterroso

Mary M. Monterroso

TO WHOM IT MAY CONCERN:

I am the daughter of Frances Harris, the sister to River Burton, and the aunt of Nocona Lynn. In the past two years I have lost three people that were very dear to me, at a crucial time in my life.

My mother, Frances Harris, is the most caring and loving person I know. She is also a very strong person, mentally, and spiritually. I had to have gained some of this strength, for with out it I don't know how I could have pulled through the loss of the close bond I had created with my family. I stand behind my mother completely. It had to be so difficult for her to leave at the time she did, in my life and hers. I feel it in my heart, and I'm sure in hers to, that everything happens for a reason and that God has a plan for all of us, and one day when we have to face our creator, she can be proud of the job she has done. Not many people would leave behind a nice home, close family and friends, and jeopardize such an upstanding reputation as hers to save an innocent, helpless child as she did. At the time she left, it was a few months before my graduation, and I know that it tore her up inside to have to miss her baby's senior prom and graduation. Along with that, she will now have to miss my wedding, and from the way things look, any children we might decide to have in the future.

Frances Harris is not only a mother to me, but also a role model. She made herself a successful business woman at an early age, and was able to retire in her forties. Aside from her financial accomplishments, she also found time to involve herself in outside activities and organizations. She helped create the first 4H club in Mauriceville, involved herself in the Crawfish Festival parade yearly, (and won it several times over) started the STAND (south east Texas against needless destruction)bonfire that now takes place yearly and worked hard at going to every school in the Golden Triangle to get them involved. After retirement, she decided she was going to dedicate her time to helping children that couldn't help themselves, so she took classes and became a CASA volunteer. She had began working on getting the program started in Orange, before Nocona's problems began. These are only a few things that my mother was involved in her life. She went to church regularly, and helped as many people as she could along the way.

I was surprised at how quickly people forget, and tend to jump on whatever the bandwagon might be at the time. I do want to thank anyone who has helped, believed, stood by, and prayed for my mother and our family. I do believe that justice will eventually prevail; it's just a matter of time. Thank you for your time.

Sincerely,

Anna A. Burton

Louis Oceguera

From:	"Joe Wagner WTSA" _{.com>}
To:	<roatan@yahoogroups.com>; "Hondo1Discuss List" <hondo1@peak.org>
Cc:	<loceguera@gt.rr.com>
Sent:	Monday, September 30, 2002 8:21 AM
Subject:	RE: [roatan] Frances Collins, Casa Calico

Steve/Group,

This is an atrocity. It is no longer amazing to me that our government, and the FBI in particular, will spend
the time and resources necessary to conduct this type of kidnapping during times like these, when our
country is under siege. I can speak from first hand knowledge as to depths to which the FBI and the U.S.
Embassy in Honduras will sink in order to continue to pursue this vendetta against Frances Collins.

Steve, I could write a book about what the FBI and the U.S. Embassy did to my sister when she helped
Frances and Nicona the first time this kidnapping was attempted in 1996. If there are members of this list
that are not familiar with this case, and they would like a personal opinion and more information about what
is going on, please email me off list.

Louis/Anna Oceguera, please email me off list. I think that you should have your U.S. Congressman's and Senators'
names, mailing addresses and email addresses published on this list, so that anyone familiar with this case can write
to them. Also, this is the type of international incident that news programs like 60 Minutes, Dateline, etc.
like to get involved in. Please say hello to Frances and Nicona for Mandy and me, and tell them that our prayers
are with them. Hopefully we can help.

> To unsubscribe from this group, send an email to:
> roatan-unsubscribe@yahoogroups.com
>
> Your use of Yahoo! Groups is subject to http://docs.yahoo.com/info/terms/

"Attempt Great Things For God...
Expect Great Things From God"

website address: www.alternativemissions.com

Regarding: Frances Harris

To: Whom it may concern

I am writing to share of my knowledge of and friendship with Frances Harris. I met Frances in Roatan, Honduras several years ago (6 or 7) and have been friends with her ever since. I am aware of her situation and concern for Nocona her grand daughter. It is my understanding that Frances moved to Roatan to insure a safe future for Nocona and she lovingly took care of her there. Frances showed her concern for Nocona by providing a safe, and relatively stress free environment while educating her and "giving up her life" (Frances for Nocona) for her. Frances is that type of friend to all who know her well in Roatan. To me personally; she was a kind, caring and consistent friend. She looked out for the entire community and Island. She did not "hide out". In Nocona's case, in leaving the U.S., I believe she did what she felt she had to in order to protect Nocona.

As I watch and pray for those of you that are involved in making decisions regarding Frances future I am praying that you will take into consideration factors that may or may not be obvious in court records regarding all the parties involved. Frances is by her actions and life a peace loving, caring and dedicated woman. Her family is her highest priority. They need her love and presence in their lives. In fact our country and this world need more people like Frances who are willing to lay down their lives and their futures for their families and others. I am praying for Frances to receive probation only for her sentencing and the opportunity for the parties involved to begin to build whatever relationship can be possible from here. I believe this is best for Nocona, Frances and the rest of the family.

Please contact me if there is anything I can share with you that can be of help.

God Bless;

Tom Hackett
Director

Ps: I am writing on our organizations letterhead, of which I am the president and director, to give context to how and why I know Frances and Nocona. Frances has been a friend to our entire ministry staff on the Island of Roatan. We owe a huge debt of gratitude to her for her love and friendship to us.

July 15, 2003
Dear Honorable Judge Heartfield,

I am writing to you concerning Frances Harris. I have known her for over thirty years. We worked together throughout the years our children were growing up in church and school. To say that she is a wonderful, loving, caring, human being: does not begin to tell you how she really is. Her heart has always been with the safety of the children. Not just hers, but the kids in the community as well.

I feel in a way partly responsible for what she did. We were in concert at a church in Newton one night in the spring eight years ago, and Frances and Nocono went on the tour bus with us. She shared how nocono would scream and beg her not to let the "wolf" take her. She said "I don't think my heart can stand her begging and choking me in the neck. For some reason she is terrified of that man." As we were talking about this something happened on the bus with Nocono that concerned my daughter-in-law, who was watching out for her while Frances and I talked. Lisa (my daughter-in-law) came up front, and told Frances how the child behaved with a stuffed bear. Lisa being a school teacher said a red flag went up as the child told her the "wolf" (the name she called her biological father) did these things to her.

This is a good person who would go to any length to protect the baby she was raising. She loved this child as her own. And I know that it had to be the hardest decision she ever had to make since she would not see her daughter graduate from high school, or attend her daughter's wedding; not to mention all of the birthdays, and Christmas's, and other family holidays she held so close to her heart. Her parents who were up in age, and not seeing her sisters. I can only admire her for her courage.

I know that you have the responsibility for where she spends her future, and I realize the law was broken. I can only pray that your decision will be tendered with the thought of what you would do personally if you thought your child was in danger. How far would you go to protect a little three year old baby girl who begged you not to let the stranger take her. And I would hope that you remembered this man was guilty of statuory rape. Your Honor; I will be praying for you.

Sincerely,
Pat Martin   07/15/03

Dear Honorable Judge Thad Heartfield,

My name is Denise and I would like to share some of my thoughts and feelings about Frances Harris. My brother and I were in foster care with two families. Frances and Owen Burton was the first family. We lived with them for about a year. We had to leave the Burtons because Frances, out of concern for her own family, needed to make room for her newly widowed sister and her 2 children. Then we went to live with another family in Orange County.

While in the care of Frances, we experienced what it was like to have a loving person make sure you were loved and cared for. She taught us unconditional love as well as responsibility (by helping out around the ranch and with the garden). Frances made sure our stay with them was an easy one.

I am so thankful and grateful for Frances' influence in my life when I was a child. I know I am a better person and mother just for knowing her. She has always had a big heart for children.

Since Frances took such great care of my brother and me (strangers), I understand why she has taken great care of her own family.

If you have any questions for me please feel free to call. @

Thank you,
Denise McBride
Denise McBride

TO WHOM IT MAY CONCERN

This letter is being written because I cannot believe what has happened to one of this communities' upstanding citizens. The treatment she has received at the hands of the FBI has shocked our community. Ask yourself does this respectable woman deserve to be held in chains and incarcerated for doing what any loving, caring, grandmother or mother would have done to prevent their own flesh and blood being given to an undesirable person. Her house was surrounded by machine-gun toting policeman and then she was led away. TOTALLY UNNECCASARY.

In my opinion the father of Nocona has to have some ulterior motive for wanting her. If he truly loved her, why would he be putting her through this horrendous ordeal. He is a wanted man down here on our island. He and a group of "mercenaries" entered a school, knocked over a pregnant schoolteacher and terrified a whole school of children. This is the man the authorities think should have custody of Nocona. Crazy or what!

Nocona is a happy, well balanced little girl who is dealing incredibly well with life. She had gotten over her ordeal of 7 years ago and has many friends here. Why does he want to hurt her so. If only you could see the life he wants to take her away from. I am a British citizen, I have chosen to make Roatan my home, because I believe that my two children will have a much better quality of life down here.

Ms Francis has done many good things for this community, she is solely responsible for bringing a little bit a happiness to lots of children during the Christmas festivities, when she organizes Xmas on the Beach. There's no-one here that can fill those shoes, although this year in honor of Ms Francis we are going to try to get it going. She is also responsible for organizing Christian speakers to come to the island. Ms Francis is a woman who cares…… just recently, together, we organized a clean up of the bay where we live. If it was not for Ms Francis this would not have happened. She is considered a woman who manages to get lots of good things happening here. Ms Francis if you have the opportunity to read this letter. God speed you back to us.

Yours sincerely,

Gaynor Pook
Schoolteacher and dive shop owner.

Honorable Judge Thad Heartfield
U.S District Court
300 Willow
Courtroom Number One
Beaumont, Texas 77701

Honorable Judge Heartfield:

Due to the confusion on Frances Harris's case I felt I should reroute my letter to make sure you got it. I previously sent it to Judge Clark.

First I would like to point out several outstanding contributions that Frances Harris has made to the Mauriceville community, Orange County, and the Golden Triangle.

I first met Frances when she was a student in High School. She was an outstanding student, possessing outstanding leadership ability to compliment her excellent character. After her school career, she became a 4H club leader with the Dusty Trail 4H club. The first program that she directed had six students in attendance. A year later the club had a membership of 100. Frances was instrumental in starting a series of flea markets to raise funds to promote youth activities. The first event Frances raised $5,000.00 and used the money to pour a concrete slab on grounds that are now used by the Mauriceville Crawfish Festival Association. Other money that was raised went to the Crawfish Festival and other community projects. Due to the success of Frances's efforts with the Flea Markets and the growth it went into what is now the Mauriceville Crawfish Festival.

Frances later organized a drug-awareness and prevention program which included all the schools of the golden triangle . This program was called S.T.A.N.D.. Frances was currently working on the seventh annual event when she had to leave with Nocona. These programs were held in conjunction with the Mauriceville Crawfish Festival. Attendance was great with students from schools of the Golden Triangle, averaging as many as 2000 youth the last year.. . It is unfortunate that conditions beyond her control prevent her from continuing these types of programs.

Frances deserves a star for organizing CASA and the work she did for the Chamber of Commerce in Orange to promote Orange County. Frances was in the middle of starting a Casa Program in Orange County when she left with Nocona .

As a business women in Orange County, she looked forward to the holiday seasons. Frances made an effort to make sure everyone was well fed and taken care of at Thanksgiving and Christmas. Any time during the year she could be counted on to lend a helping hand to any worthy cause.

It would be hard to find anyone, anywhere that contributed more money, time, and effort to make the people happy, promote citizenship, and improve the area where we live.

Sincerely,

Ruben Stringer

Ruben Stringer /Public School Employee (43 years)409 ... ...

Re: Francis Harris and Nocona   October 20, 2002

To whom it may concern,

    I am writing this letter to offer some insight into the life of Francis Harris and her granddaughter, Nocona on the island of Roatan – Bay Islands of Honduras.

    I have lived in Roatan for more then eight years. During this time I have know and been friendly with Miss Francis, her daughter, River, and grandaughter, Nocona. Miss Francis has always been a friendly, helpful, and contributing member of the community. She has been involved in many projects, including Christmas on the Beach (annually), beach cleanup days, as well as religious classes and events for both local and foreign members of the community. I, personally, have not been involved with their religious interests, yet still have established a good friendship with both Francis and Nocona. Francis is an open-minded, generous person and this has reflected onto Nocona. I have a son – who will be three on Dec. 25, 2003, and since he was born on the island the whole community has welcomed him into their lives, including Francis and Nocona; both stop by on a regular basis to visit us at our home – down the road approximately ¼ mile. They stay and chat about life and play with Jeter. I have had many conversations regarding educational options for my son and have talked to Nocona about her home study program; about which she is very enthusiastic. Nocona is a lively, friendly, happy, well adjusted child, whom has occasionally dropped off a present for Jeter …..just because she felt like it.

    I am a Canadian and came to Roatan while traveling through Central America. I stayed on the island – spent five years teaching home study programs to foreign children living on the island as well as working as a scuba diving instructor. I now run a successful gift shop and my husband operates a fishing charter business. I have a B.A. in Anthropology and a B.A. in Marketing from the University of British Columbia – Canada.

    After I spent my first year on the island my parents came to visit to see what it was all about. They stayed three weeks at Casa Calico I February, 1995, and enjoyed their stay. They understood the appeal of the island and loved their apartment and hostess – Francis. I was able to get to know Francis even better after the birth of my son – Dec., 1999. My parents came to visit shortly after the birth and stayed once again with Francis at Casa Calico. They once again had a great visit and since ask regularly about Francis and Nocona. Francis in turn, frequently asks after the welfare of my family. I was with my husband and son in Canada, visiting my family in Sept., 2002 when I was told about Francis and Nocona being taken away to the States. We were all very concerned about their welfare.

    In my opinion this life is a great life to offer one's children. Furthermore, I feel that by living here, children are less materialistic, very happy, and satisfied with a natural and healthy life.

    I hope that by writing this letter I can provide a better picture of the life Francis provided for Nocona in Roatan. Both are missed greatly and their welfare is of great concern to this community. We worry for Nocona and hope that the state will realize that this situation was always and still is about what is in the best interest of this beautiful young girl with an open and loving heart.

    Thank you for taking time to read this letter.

                                       Sincerely, Sara Didcott

To The Honorable Judge Thad Heartfield;

I have known Frances Collins Harris since July 1997, when our Mission Ship, "Spirit of Grace", arrived in Roatan, Honduras. Our ship arrived carrying a cargo of relief supplies along with building materials, heavy equipment, work boats, and many other items in order to establish an Industrial School and training facility to aid local residents in earning a better way of life on that island.

Frances came on board our ship along with hundreds of other visitors when we anchored in Roatan. The big difference was that most came on board in hopes of receiving something from us. Francis came offering her time and services to help us in any way she could. In time this offer resulted in immeasurable aid in many, many different ways.

Frances' small resort has been used as a gathering place for many missionary gatherings, a training location for the teaching of children in preparation for the programs presented during "Christmas On The Beach", an event started and continued annually by Francis which brings the community together in fellowship, unity, and training of children. This event has brought in many very poor children, giving them the same opportunity as the more economically affluent children on the island. Her grand daughter, Nacona has functioned almost in the capacity of an adult in helping these less fortunate children feel at home and feeling like they belong to an important group.

Since Frances' arrival on the Island, she has established and coordinated women's Christian groups from one end of the Island to the other. She has sponsored conference leaders from the USA; connecting them with local women's groups for the benefit both materially and spiritually. All churches on the Island have been included in these gatherings. It has brought ladies together in a cooperating unity unlike anything which had ever happened before. Church pastors have been ecstatic over the result, stating that the separation before had been a problem. Women are now happy, cooperating, and accomplishing good things for all people on the Island. Even though Frances must continue to do almost all of the work, because of the relaxed nature of the local residents, she was faithful to follow through and keep this function going long and strong.

She, through her caring for others and hard diligent work, has obtained the reputation of being one to get things done to the benefit of many others.

When our organization holds women's conferences, Francis, who is known and respected by everyone, is called upon by us to be the front person in gathering the women on the Island to be part of the conferences which have proven to be very beneficial to all those attending

We cannot imagine what life on the island, in the above described realm, will be without her presence and influence for the greater good for islanders, children and adults alike; ministries; and visitors to Roatan, Honduras.

We are certainly praying for true justice to be served for she and her grand daughter, Nacona, whose lives, being lived for good to others, were abruptly interrupted, along with those lives afore mentioned.

Sincerely,
Don Ashcraft
Don Ashcraft
Facility Manager, Roatan, Honduras
Friend Ships International of Honduras

Route 3 Box 132
New Boston, TX 75570
October 16, 2002

Dear Honorable Judge:

At the time of this writing, the specific judge that will be hearing Frances Harris's case has not been chosen, but I feel compelled to tell you about the Frances that I met and came to know.

I first met Frances and her granddaughter, Nacona, in Tegucigulpa, Honduras, in 1997. I have a ministry, GO Ministries, Inc., and I travel internationally as a Bible teacher. Frances attended a conference that I was teaching at. She was invited to come by a mutual friend who is the Director of Crusades of Honduras, a large mission organization in that country. Frances invited me and others there to come to Roatan Island to her home. Several of us did go to Roatan and stay at her home for a couple of days. She had a lovely 2-story home. She and Nacona lived in the downstairs and she rented the upstairs rooms out to guests.

In 2001 I returned to Honduras with a women's ministry team. We stayed at Frances' house a couple of days on that trip. I also returned to Roatan with my husband and daughter in May 2002, for a vacation time. We stayed at Frances' house for a week. During this time, Frances and I planned a Women's Conference to be held on the island this October. Frances had many friends on the island and was looked up to by the islanders. She contacted several church leaders on the island and they all worked together to have the women's conference. The conference was held Oct. 3 – 5, 2002 at French Harbour, Roatan, Honduras; however, Frances was not in attendance as the FBI had picked her and Nacona up September 21, 2002, and returned them to the USA.

The Frances that I knew and who became my friend was a good person. She loved Nacona dearly. It was very obvious that they had a close loving relationship. Nacona was a happy, fun loving little girl. She loved to show all the guests where to go for the best swimming and snorkeling. Frances came to care about the people where she lived. She helped organize community activities such as "Christmas on the Beach".

I believe that our justice system in this country is probably the best in the world, but I also know that it is not perfect. The crime that Frances Harris is most guilty of is loving too much. I believe that she truly believed that the courts were not giving protection to her granddaughter who she believed beyond a shadow of a doubt was being abused by her father. I myself have 7 beautiful grandchildren and faced with the same situation, I would probably have made the same choice.

Frances Harris is not a threat to society, unless loving and caring for the those who cannot defend themselves is a threat to our world. I would ask the Court for leniency and mercy in this case. The Court also needs to hear and give weight to what Nacona has to say; she is a very intelligent child.

Sincerely,

Brenda Anderson

November 11, 2002

Judge Pat Clark
128th. District Court
801 Division Street
Orange, TX 77630

Your Honor:

I am writing to you on behalf of my mother, Frances Collins, who will soon appear before your court. First, I will summarize her personal history in the context of our current situation in hopes that you will understand why she should be considered for the court's maximum leniency under the charges she currently faces.

As a graduate student of public administration at The George Bush School of Government and Public Service at Texas A&M University, I credit my mom for the successes I have had in life. Over the years she has ensured that we, her children, have had opportunities to develop as human beings and as professionals while helping others in the process.

Mom has continually put family first. In fact, our family's greatest memories retrace numerous holiday gatherings she assembled to bring us together. As a small business owner, her sense of family extended to her employees, as well, whom she would invite to our home for special occasions and to share summers at a beach cabin she rented each year.

Mom's virtues and talents have also benefited the residents of Mauriceville, Texas. Yearly she committed herself to developing the community in many ways. She was actively involved in 4-H, church and school activities, festivals, and anti-drug campaigns profiting local youth. To many people, including myself, she is a highly capable and dedicated public servant.

While in Honduras, mom continued serving others. She was active in local churches, assisted numerous missionary teams, started an annual Christmas program for children, and sponsored Bible studies at her home for neighborhood children. While some people cherish one-time awards for public service, mom accepts giving as a part of everyday life.

Most importantly, mom worked hardest at ensuring that Nocona, my daughter, had a quality life in Honduras. Like mom, Nocona was equally involved in community programs. Indeed, wherever Nocona went she was widely recognized and loved. This had a lot to do with mom instilling in her a genuine affection for other people, regardless of their circumstances.

From the time I spent in Honduras I know better than anyone how mom suffered from splintered ties with loved ones back home. At no time did she relish having left the country as a "law breaker." Rather, she raised us to cherish our nation's laws. Indeed, I do not ever recall her ever having broken a single one before leaving for Honduras.

In fact, we had an argument when I was much younger concerning freedom of expression. In no way did she condone the burning of an American flag. In effect, she always kept one hung outside our home in Honduras. As expected, she mourned our nation's tragic losses on Sept. 11th and cheered for Americans during World Cup soccer matches and The Olympic Games.

Like me, Mom possessed powerful reasons to believe that   was abusing Nocona and documented specific events. While some have minimized   long history of abuse to women, they can never erase the bruises and threats he regularly dealt me over the years. Normally, abuse does not end or begin with one person.

This is one of the reasons   should not gain custody of my daughter. As a much older, more experienced person he was successful in reducing me to a state of dependency and insecurity during the time I lived with him. He routinely discouraged me from visiting family and friends and told me I was incapable of attending school or getting a good job.

However, something (God, unhappiness, or both) motivated me to seek out self-improvement. When I was with ____, I felt that something was wrong with me, not with him. When I tried to better my appearance, he told me I looked "funny" wearing make-up or dresses. When I got a job, he told me I should quit since he believed it did not pay enough to cover my time or associated expenses.

Today, I realize that I was not the dysfunctional one in our relationship. Recently I had the courage to look back on the photographs of myself when we were together and was appalled by what I saw. One photo was particularly telling; I sat next to ____ with my daughter in my arms. In this photo taken in my late teens I appeared ghost-white, gaunt, and demoralized. In none of the photos did I smile, as I do in all of my photos today.

From looking at these photos I was stung with the reality that what loved ones said about me at that time was true. ____ had kept the beauty in me away from the world. Before meeting ____ I was an accomplished athlete and honors student. I had dreams of attending Texas A&M University and leading a wonderful career. During our relationship, however, I was incapable of taking care of myself much less a child.

While I am thankful for the strength of spirit and opportunity to escape this harmful relationship, ____ neglectful treatment of me has been difficult to shake. At times I feel insecure and have difficulties trusting men with whom I would like to establish a long-term personal relationship. Several friends have noted this without me having to tell them about my past. While it is still difficult for me to define love, I have definitely learned from ____ what love is *not*.

Today, without ____ I am a maturing young woman with a bright future. I am re-building family relationships he destroyed in my youth and am getting the quality education he tried so hard to prevent. Moreover, I have excellent job prospects and am a vastly more confident and capable person. I am excited about life and want to share it with my daughter.

This is what my mother envisioned for me and worked so hard to ensure. When she discovered that ____ was abusing me and worse—my daughter, she was horror-stricken. Thank God she never gave up on us. While she has forgiven ____ for what he has done, as we are instructed to do Biblically, ____ is unwilling to forgive for the sake of our daughter.

Accordingly, it seems profoundly ironic to me that mom (a life-long community servant) faces prison time, whereas ____ a long-time abuser enjoys the protection and favor of the law.

Sincerely and Respectfully,

Ms. River J. Burton

CC: Mr. Sonny Cribbs, Jr.

Honorable Judge Heartfield,

I am writing this letter in regards to the character of Francis Harris who is being tried for protecting her granddaughter, Nocona.

I met Francis when I was 19 years old and going to Lamar University to become a teacher. She owned the local grocery store, T.J.&A., and gave me a job to help me pay for college tuition. When she hired me, she was willing to work around my hours so that I could attend college and sing in a music ministry on the weekends. She was highly respected by all of her employees and assisted other students like me, as well as high school students. My family and I had visited her house on several occasions and enjoyed her family's company. She has become not only someone who employed me but a friend and a woman I consider as a role model for my daughters, students and me.

My father, as a child, abused me and I wish that someone had been there to protect me in the manner that Francis has done for Nocona. Although I am an over comer, the experience made me untrusting of those around me and forces me to make decisions differently. However, since Nocona was taken away from her situation, she won't have to struggle as much if allowed to become a normal young person with the only one who has given her protection, and the ability to become who she is supposed to be. It would be so unjust to separate Nocona from her grandmother. It has already been too long. I believe that Nocona has grown to be strong but will be devasted if our justice system fails to defend those who are defenseless, like children and if standing in harms way, at all cost, is not honored. Nocona needed protection. I experienced seeing Nocona, at three years old, stab and scream at a little stuffed bear on our bus one night when she and Francis had traveled to a concert with us. She was stabbing the bear in the groin area with great force with a pencil. When I asked her to stop, she responded, " That's what the wolf does to me!" She oftened talked about this "wolf" and referred to him as living at her dad's house.

It is my experience that we teach the kids to say no and to stand up for their beliefs, even when pressured to believe or react differently. As a 5th grade teacher, for fourteen years I have taught my students to do just that and that our government will honor and protect them. My students know that I am friends with Francis and ask me how the courts are going to handle this situation. I honestly answer, I don't really know but that the principles that we were founded on could be trusted and they should never fear doing the right thing and helping others. What kind of faith will they have then if they know that Francis was put in prison and punished for protecting an afraid, abused three year old who beats up her own toys, is angry, and hates to see her dad? Will justice be served and how will Nocona overcome all of this if Francis, a pillar in the community, businesswoman helping high school and college kids, P.T.A. activists, friend, role model, wife and mother of three and *her* grandmother put in prison? It all seems so unfair, don't you think?

    I do appreciate the opportunity to tell you how much I respect Francis Harris, in every way and pray that you will have the wisdom to consider what was happening to Nocona and how Francis felt helpless in what to do to protect her and if it were your wife, daughter, or granddaughter. What would *you* do? Please investigate her character and facts **completely** before making a decision that could allow Nocona to believe that you will continue to keep her safe and maybe even ask Nocona how she feels about her circumstances.

    If I'm not mistaken, you took your oath to protect her and I feel with certainty that you will. Therefore, I thank you for representing us with honor and respect.

    Sincerely,

Lisa Martin, 7/15/03
Lisa Martin

Seashell Prisoners
CHAPTER 19

The press was having a field day between both my and Nocona's cases. With each day the headlines became more intense. The main focus seemed to be, *What Were They Going To Do With The Texas Grandmother?* Judge Travis made the decision to cut off all calls between Nocona and me. For what reason, I was not told.

One month went by, then two. Still no sentence! My probation officer was becoming outraged, and so were the Federal Courts. Each time the State brought up the plea bargain, I refused and requested a trial. If that was so strong in my spirit and the pastor reconfirmed it, then it must be the way to go. I certainly had nothing else to go on other than human instincts. My lack of legal knowledge was evident from day one, and I knew Orange County would take full advantage of it. Finally, Orange conceded—I would get a trial! We were all in shock, but happy with the decision.

Sentencing dates were set up in Orange, Texas, then suddenly the sentencing dates were canceled. Each week, I would meet with my attorney, but there were no explanations other than *"Frances, They Don't Know What To Do With You! Frances, You Are Every Judge's Nightmare!"*

I began to feel my only chance for truth to come out was the press. I was ready! It was time to make an attempt to get my story out! Everything was on hold, so I definitely had nothing to lose. The courts were obviously stalled. Who knows, maybe something miraculous could come, once the public saw the truth from this. Or was it the public that kept this case from going to court?

From then on, it was nothing for Anna to return from work except to see her driveway filled with television and newspaper reporters! Nocona's case was picking up momentum more and more with each day. It was getting more intense with each problem arising. It was obvious Orange County was prepared for whatever came up. Closed door meetings had brought about one common goal among C.P.S., the D.A, the Orange County Sheriff, Judge Travis, the court-appointed attorney, and the court-appointed psychiatrist; they continued to come on strong with one common goal—Nocona would live with Trevor! The abusive father had been deprived of his child. I was becoming more livid with each day! They stood strong in not allowing me to see or talk to Nocona.

I received a telephone call from Nocona's attorney, Lisa Hurst, stating Nocona's judge made a strong suggestion that I stop speaking to the press. He would allow me to speak to Nocona on the phone again if I would agree. I quickly weighed out what may help Nocona the most and stated, "I will stop when Nocona's court-appointed legal defense, court-appointed psychologist, and court-appointed judge will listen to Nocona." Nocona needed someone looking out for her best interests and not Trevor's.

Shortly after that statement, I received another call from Lisa stating the judge said I would never speak to nor see Nocona again. Later I met with another attorney with them backing up the statement, stating the same: I would never see nor hear from Nocona again, ever! I heard the harsh statement, but I knew a Higher power, and His statement was not aligned with theirs! I chose not to accept man's report, therefore I never gave the threat another thought.

&

The monitor continued to be an endless problem with relentless phone calls from the monitoring company, stating I had left the house during the early morning hours for fifteen minutes. Sometimes it went off during the day for no reason. Despite it, I would hear the same echo: continued threats from my probation officer...."The monitor never makes mistakes! We have never had problems with anyone else on the monitor."

Upset by the remarks, I would contact different attorneys all saying the same thing: "Frances, everyone has problems with the monitors! Don't worry about it!"

With each new day I found that truth takes on a whole new definition with whomever states it. A lie can be the truth or the truth can be a lie. It's all a matter of who states it as to how it takes precedence. Now I would just have to bear the glares and hateful statements from my probation officer on each return.

&

Most of the time, I felt handpicked by God. I felt like Moses when he led the people out of Egypt. I knew that I knew that I was totally God-centered in every way, yet now depression was coming down hard on me. Satan reminded me daily that I had lost everything. I now had no home, no car, nothing.

My Sunday services were not a day of uplifting, but a matter of life and death! I was attending church with Anna and her family. The first church they took me to I refused to go back to. The church was going through a split, and the only thing you felt during the service was tension. Everything changed when they took me to Community Church. The warm presence of God met us at the door. Pastor Berkheimer and his wife Melba were having their own personal battle with her health. Despite that, his sermons grew stronger and stronger with each Sunday service. I found comfort and reassurance, seeing their strength and perseverance with their own problem.

Every day, I was doing what I could to stay focused. Each Wednesday I attended my care group, with Pat, Miriam, and Valda keeping me covered in prayer. Valda had an anointing such that the worst of demons vanished as she embraced and prayed over me. Miriam and Pat had a gift of words of knowledge that often had unusual humor. They were always right on and I left the meetings feeling as though heavy weights had been taken off of me. Others in the church continued to send me encouraging words.

There was never an hour of peace. If there weren't distressing reports on Nocona's case, there were depressing reports coming from Sonny Cribbs. Just the continued thought of the ten-million-dollar lawsuit hanging over all of us wreaked its own havoc. Friends made statements in regard to Nocona struggling with the many demands being made on her life. It was obvious Nocona had her own battlefields: Keeping up with school, pleasing the court-appointed attorney, C.P.S., the Judge, and the court-appointed psychiatrist, and having forced visits with her father—all was overwhelming daily making things worse. The weekends with Trevor were always stressful for her.

Reports were Nocona was going downhill emotionally, and now academically. Finally, the judge stated Nocona could live with her grandfather, instead of the appointed family with C.P.S. She would still be forced to go to Trevor's every other weekend until Nocona made the adjustment living with Trevor.

It wasn't surprising when I heard there were many problems coming from weekends with Trevor. Nocona always referred to him as Trevor and he would become outraged by it. Trevor cursed and smoked. Nocona was not used to either. Nocona's pleading with Trevor to drop all charges on me continued to keep him agitated.

Prior to Nocona's arrival to the States she was a very happy child, but now I saw a totally different picture. Nocona was losing ground under the pressure. As pictures were brought to me of her, I cried as I saw the changes. The bubbly little girl wasn't there anymore. She had taken on another appearance, one of seriousness and a quiet demeanor. Nocona would write to me and through the words I could see huge changes in her personality. With each letter I became more and more outraged, not with Trevor as much as the Orange County Courts for putting her through this. She had nothing to do with any of this, yet she continued to pay the price. It all appeared to be a battle with Goliath, in a no-win situation!

Reports continued to come back to me that Owen and his wife Nelda were diligently working with their attorney on the custody suit. They were building a case to go forward to gain full custody of Nocona, hopefully, in the future, relieving Nocona of all problems. How awesome that would be for Nocona, but this too was moving way too slow! It all appeared impossible with the Orange County judicial system being so organized.

Owen and Nelda chose Karl Perry—once again, the very attorney that failed us before! I knew he was the best in Orange County, but deep down I deeply resented the choice. I still had contempt for Karl when he represented JoNey in the custody case. A friend reminded me that there really wasn't much to choose from in Orange County, and Karl wouldn't take advantage of a Commissioner; also Sarah's influence was no longer there. He went on to remind me that attorneys also treated men differently than they would treat a woman.

Reports were coming back to us that Judge Travis was now totally outdone with Trevor's flagrant and brazen quotes in front of the press. Trevor continued to make threats and remarks of suing people and was obviously not abiding by Judge Travis's demands. Travis was now seeing a whole new side to Trevor.

છે.

Two and a half months went by and still no sentence! The news media continued to make it front page coverage with everyone anticipating the grand finale. I spent every moment preparing and pushing for a jury trial. Orange County saw I was not backing down and finally agreed on another date and it appeared they would go forward with it. The date was set and weeks went by. I was up night and day on the computer. I would now have my opportunity to get all the facts out, and everyone would know the truth about Trevor and his dysfunctional family.

I then got a call from Mr. Cribbs. Orange County had canceled the court date! They were giving me one last option. Now I was to accept the plea bargain or my case would be kicked back to the Federal Courts.

My reply came easy. *"Send Me Back To The Feds!"* The information was quickly passed on to the Federal Courts. I began to receive calls from attorneys stating the Federal Courts were furious with Orange County! Orange County's mess was now thrown back on the Federal Courts to resolve, and they were not happy about it. Mr. Cribbs then stated the Federal Judge would release me on a monitor until sentencing. No date had been set up for sentencing. Everything went back to the roundtable. No one seemed to know what to do with Frances Harris!

છે.

Freedom, Freedom, the wonderful feel of Freedom! I had been at Anna's now three months. I do not know who was the happiest the day the judge gave me the okay to relocate!

After another trip to the probation officer, with the same intensity Jenelle went over and over with me the fact that the judge was going out on a limb to allow me this privilege of freedom, and told me not to jeopardize it. I would stay on the monitor, but I would now be able to circulate during the day between the hours of 6 a.m. and 10 p.m., but be unable to go out of the State.

By this time everyone was growing weary of the three-month vigil. Anna and Louis's faces lit up, with each jumping through themselves, helping me pack and get my things in their vehicle. My staying up at night on the computer had definitely become annoying to them. I am sure that was only one of many irritating things about my three-month vigil in their home.

Being at Arlene's, my sisters, would put me closer to Mother and Dad's. My sisters were happy to get more help, with both my parents in need of full-time assistance. Both parents were still at home. Dad had throat and lung cancer and Mother had dementia. Both parents were in need of full time help.

Somehow in the middle of all the confusion, I was not only relocating, but the two boys, Rylan and Julian, were going with me for the night. Anna, with her special gift of organization and manipulation, within seconds quickly planned a night out to celebrate what began to look like…Granna's departure!

It was an unusually cold night. Normally, Anna, being the overly protective Mom, met the boys' every whim and emotional need. Tonight was different! Both kids were tossed in the back seat with neither socks nor shoes. Everything was packed in their little backpacks. Rylan, and his one-year-old brother, Julian, were rather wide-eyed at it all. I quickly regrouped and threw a blanket over Julian, and off we went singing songs all the way to Mauriceville. Actually, we were delighted, but no one considered it was my first time to drive in the States. I was totally freaked at the traffic! Cars were constantly blowing their horns and passing me. I was moving very slowly!

The boys did great! Anna and her husband appeared more relaxed when they arrived to pick them up the next day. In the course of conversation, they told me they ran into Jenelle, my probation officer, at the club on Crockett Street in Beaumont. Now I could better understand why Jenelle could call me at two in the morning to check on me during my transition.

More friends and family continued to call and come by. My ministry friends, Sister Eleanor from Honduras and Brenda Anderson from North Texas, came and spent the day with me. We all found it humorous at Brenda's surprise when she arrived to Roatan with her ministry team, and Nocona and I were nowhere to be found. Don and Kayte Ashcraft with

Friendship Ministry also dropped in the following week, all encouraging me and praying for a miracle. Friends from all over continued to pray and lift me up, knowing what was fast approaching.

⁂

Now I was, for the first time, faced with something totally different. Strange things began to circulate through my mind. Like, *how is everyone going to treat me now that I am in the public and back in the community of Mauriceville?* Now, I can actually get out and move around. *Am I going to be looked at as a joke, a total fool, or the bad guy with my unusual homecoming back to the States?*

My Dad generously loaned me his old '96 pickup truck. It was a long way from the Lincoln town car or the Cherokee jeep I was last seen in, but I was grateful. A few trips to the local stores, and it was apparent that even all my old employees were driving new cars and owned homes. I now had neither. I dreaded facing people when I went to the grocery store or local churches. I just wanted to lock the door and pull the curtains at the house rather than go through the pain of watching people's reactions towards me. *Would I be attacked by angry men that had lost their children in custody suits or be laughed at for losing everything I owned?* Despite my thoughts, I had no desire to answer any questions. I just wanted to sleep and be left alone. I continued to be numb to everything. The trauma hung on with each day.

Arlene graciously gave me her largest bedroom. It was quiet and the room was very private. I badly needed that. I tried hard to take each day one hour at a time and not become overwhelmed. I was still struggling within my mind and emotions with everything that was happening in my life. Now that I was back in Mauriceville, my thoughts kept going back to my home on FM 1130. I wanted so much to be there and just lock myself off from the whole world. I wanted my children back young again, running in and out of the house with their boots and jeans. I wanted to see all the pictures on the walls and grandpa's trunk in the large family room heaving with all the family pictures. I longed to see Todd cooking at our crawfish boils, and dancing at the New Year's Eve parties. I was missing my home and the past so much!

Arlene encouraged me to attend church with her, but I struggled with facing all the people in the community that had known me as a successful business woman.... *Not a criminal!* I finally conjured up the boldness to join her. I called Johnny Ruth, an old friend, to make sure she was going to be there, but it was cold and rainy. I had a strong suspicion she would never make it out from under her electric blanket. I knew if she would just show up she would say something off the wall that would make me laugh, and laughter I badly needed.

On our arrival to the First Baptist Church in Mauriceville, I noticed right off the church hadn't changed much. Arlene opened the door to the Sunday School classroom, and Johnny was nowhere to be found. I glanced around the room, and there were soft smiles from familiar faces. As my eyes quickly surveyed the room, I saw someone staring at me very profoundly with tears flowing down her face. It was Beth, an old friend of mine. I knew then someone present could relate with my pain. That felt good.

My stronger desires to go into a real grocery store, see Wal-Mart, and sit in an air-conditioned restaurant quickly overrode all thoughts of people's reactions. On my first day of release, my niece Cynthia called, asking me to go with her to Wal-Mart. There was little to no pause. Off I went! I bit my lip and laughed as we drove down the road, thinking of the reactions of people when they heard I chose Wal-Mart on my first day of freedom! Only if you sit on a little virgin Island for eight years, in jail for three months, and under house arrest for three months, could you comprehend this decision!

Wow, that long awaited moment! There it was—the entrance of Wal-Mart. I hesitated as I slowly approached the door thinking, Jenelle or the F.B.I. were going to apprehend me the moment I stepped in the front entrance! The legal system's presence and control over me was deeply etched in my soul.

I became immediately overwhelmed by the size of the store and the many people. Total strangers began to approach me, stating they were praying for us and they were so proud of me! I was previously told I had the public's sympathy, but it was a welcome treat seeing it firsthand. I continued to stroll around the store, but hastily made my way to the produce aisle in awe at the abundance of vegetables and fruit. For the first six years on the Island, I never saw firm tomatoes or cauliflower without a layer of mold. The tomatoes on the Island would be what most grocers would dump in the U.S. It was only the last two years that fresh vegetables began to appear on Roatan, all of which were shipped from the U.S. As I filled my basket at Wal-Mart, I thought the people in the U.S. were so blessed!

The whole time I was on the Island I considered their prices to be outrageous. I always thought how wonderful it would be to shop in the U.S. and pile my basket up with groceries. Well, I did just that, surprising myself with a bill of over two hundred dollars—twice the price I had remembered!

Once I became established at Arlene's, I began to work on my health and nervous system once again. Many times I felt my mind was leaving me completely, and I did all I could to keep it intact. It was like doing such simple things had become difficult. I wondered at this point if I would ever get my health back together. Once again I began my study of herbs on the Internet and get the help of friends like Sissy, a daughter of one of my good friends.

It didn't take long to see that most Americans lived their lives too fast in comparison to the Island. They purchased many gadgets yet they never had time to use them, much less repair them. Cynthia, my niece, had a house beaming with them. My addiction to gadgets soon was fulfilled by this wonderful niece and other family members. Arlene's kitchen previously was void of life, but now was running over with my new earthly addiction, "gadgets." In less than a few weeks I owned a gazelle exercise bike, electric skillet, three George Forman grills, a bread machine, etc., etc. Once friends and family found out, I had appliances coming in from all directions!

Within weeks I received a call from Faye, a lady that had not only been a wonderful employee, but a true friend. Faye informed me the pastor's wife of the Assemblies of God Church had asked if I would speak at their Women's Luncheon.

This caught me so off guard! I am sure the pause was confusing. Number one, here I am a high-profile criminal and on the news daily. Number two, among my few talents was never, ever public speaking! What if my mind gave way right in the middle of the talk? My spirit kept saying, "Remember it's a testimony. It's not about you. *It's All About Him.*" At this point, with my knowledge of God, the thought of what might happen if I didn't, quickly outweighed the possibility of making a fool of myself. Things like this continued to reconfirm the platform that I knew God was laying out for the testimony that He so vividly told me would go out from all of this.

The more I thought of the invitation the more content I became, feeling the sense of support from so many. Christians saw me for who I really was and not what any entity accused me of.

୨ଲ

I soon received a call from Bill Childers, my old dive instructor. He called letting me know he was taking a group to Roatan and asked if I needed him to do anything. My mind was searching desperately, knowing there were so many things I had left behind. My mind kept going blank, but there was one thing that took precedence, Puffer! I knew it was illegal to bring Petie to the U.S., but I said, "Bill, is there any way you might bring our little dog, Puffer, back?"

There was a long pause, which wasn't unusual for Bill with his huge Texas drawl.

A month later, Bill was on his way back with Puffer, family pictures, and Nocona's keyboard. Meeting me at the door with Puffer was a dream come true! A million dollars couldn't touch that moment! What a day! I do not know who was the happiest—me or Puffer. It was as though I had a total blood transfusion!

❧

Family members continued to relay Nocona's dilemma. Nocona was struggling more and more with each return to Trevor's. I was still unable to speak to Nocona. Nocona continued to stay with Trevor on the weekends and Wednesday nights. Problems came up with each visit. Nocona would repeatedly write her judge with her concerns. One day it all came to a head with Trevor and his wife reprimanding Nocona for her actions. Nocona broke down under the pressure and cried. No matter what angle Nocona approached to get help, she would be shut down. I continued to send word through friends to encourage Nocona to write her judge until he responded. "Tell your judge everything that is happening until he gets sick of it and responds!"

After months, a break came. Judge Travis no longer relayed the messages to Trevor's attorney. The feedback from different ones stated Trevor had totally lost ground with Judge Travis. There seemed to be a different feel in the air, but Nocona continued to return to Trevor's.

Nocona's grandfather went forward with Karl Perry to go to trial against Trevor and gain full custody of Nocona. Nocona regrouped, realizing a lot would be dependent on her. It took a while, but the whole scenario was sinking in and now coming together. There was a certain amount that would be up to Nocona to help Nocona! She couldn't depend on the court-appointed help.

❧

Trevor made his usual trip to Nocona's school to pick her up for his weekend visitation. This day was different. Nocona refused to go with him! The school counselor and principal backed up Nocona, calling security and the Sheriff's Department to assist in the situation at the Little Cypress Mauriceville School. Trevor and Nocona battled back and forth in a closed-door meeting. Nocona stood strong as to what she planned to do. Nocona was adamant despite Trevor's demands.

She stated once again, *"I am not going home with you anymore."* This time Nocona won, returning to her grandfather's house!

Nocona's decision was now back on the news and growing with intensity. Many thought I would be completely released at this time, but that didn't happen.

I was now seeing the powerful Caleb prophecy of the End Time Hand Maidens taking effect. Nocona definitely conquered an area that no one else dared enter. Nocona was an unusual child from day one, so it didn't surprise me when she stood her ground with Trevor and the Orange County Legal System. I knew she was set apart for a big task. Little did I know as an eleven-year-old she would be coming against giants in the form of F.B.I. agents, judges, the C.P.S., court-appointed attorneys, and a court-appointed psychiatrist! As one person put it—Orange County's dream team!

I never raised Nocona to be dependent on me for more reasons than one. Actually, I never raised my own three children to be dependent on me. I think the main thing with Nocona was just not knowing from one day to the next when we might be separated and she would have to be on her own.

The word was out, with everyone anxiously waiting to see what was going to happen next. Would the law by force rip her once again from Owen, taking her back to Trevor's? I thought for sure my case would be dropped now! Many theories were circulating. People were getting the word back to us, from Louisiana through Texas, all letting us know, "We are behind you and praying for you." It was truly comforting and helped us all to go forward.

Trevor began calling Owen (Nocona's grandfather) as though nothing happened. Trevor would make excuses as to why he was not picking Nocona up. He never asked how Nocona was or if she needed anything.

More news began to surface. Trevor's wife was filing for divorce. Things were beginning to unravel for him now.

❧

Daily I surrounded myself with strong Christians and clinging to prayer warriors. Friends called, emailed, and came by. Letters from all over the world continued to flood the courts as the press went forward headlining the new Burton/Harris dilemma. Total strangers approached me at church, stating they were proud I was attending their church. Each continued to pick me up after each discouraging visit with my attorney. With each return appointment with Mr. Cribbs, the news was never: "Frances Harris, it looks like they are going to drop your case or let you go free!" It was always devastating words like: *"Get Ready For Prison!"*

❧

I attended the Community Church on a weekly basis with Anna and family. Pastor Berkheimer had an unusual anointing, and the followers of his church were strong prayer warriors and encouragers. You could expect anything to happen during their service. Prayer warriors would approach me at different times to pray over me during their services. On one Sunday during Praise and Worship, a man came up to me, spoke my name and requested to pray with me. At the time I was not aware of who he was or the fact that he was a judge. He prayed as any normal Christian did, then suddenly his prayer became more intense. He very humbly stated, *"One day people will bow down at the feet of Jesus because of what has happened in your lives."*

After the service a friend took me to one of the prophets in the church. The first words that came out of the lady's mouth as I approached her were that I was writing a book. I was taken back at the statement. I thought, *That would truly be a miracle of God!* My English teachers would vouch for that. I knew there would be a book, but River JoNey had an unusual talent in writing...I didn't!

Still later, another member said he saw huge angels surrounding me as I walked into the church. The message and the testimony all continued to reconfirm once again the Holy Spirit's words to me prior to leaving with Nocona. The end result would be a testimony that would help people come to know God.

I soon ventured out more and more into the restaurants, and all the places that had been deleted from my new life as an International Child Abductor. Strangers constantly approached me, requesting to shake my hand or just hug me and thank me for being so bold in helping Nocona. One even paid my bill at a restaurant! Instead of mocking and sneers that I had feared, I was treated like a hero! It was a nice feeling. It was truly humbling as time went on, at the numbers of people that approached me. It all just reconfirmed why Orange would not allow a jury trial.

Confirmation after confirmation continued to feed my spirit that God was setting up a platform. I continued to pray daily more for what I saw God possibly bringing about rather than the life sentence I was facing. My biggest fear became my inadequacy or inability to fulfill whatever purpose this was all for. I knew there was reason, but it all felt too big for me.

Seashell Prisoners
CHAPTER 20

My meetings with Mr. Cribbs became more frequent and extremely tense. I was now at the mercy of the Federal Courts. I was desperately making an attempt to comprehend all the legal jargon coming at me. My background was as a mom, a retired grocery store owner, a hotel manager, and now a high-profile criminal. I was definitely not prepared! Most of it continued to go right over my head, but the words Life Sentence rang out loud and clear. No matter how much explaining Mr. Cribbs did, I continued to think, *One day, yes, one day someone in the judicial system will want the truth, and not just put the lady in prison and get on to the next case!* Surely someone is interested in the fact that I saved a child's life! What other reason would I leave my family and home? I didn't just wake up one morning and decide to run off with a child! Everyone else seemed to understand it. *What Was Their Problem?*

With each attorney visit there was always more news. I was not only to go to prison but pay Trevor, the victim, $24,000.00. Just where does all this sickness end? I try to help a child, the Feds spend hundreds of thousands chasing and monitoring me, and now the abusive psychopath destroys a family, walks free, and is handed a bonus of $24,000.00, as a small stipend?

Anna's time was maxed between her husband, her older son Rylan, Julian who was two years old, a full time job at a chemical plant, and now her mother facing a life sentence. I tried not to call her any more than I had to. My friends were wonderful and great prayer warriors, but equal to me as far as understanding criminal law.

Sonny was throwing tough questions out on each visit. The day was now approaching that I had to make a huge decision as to which route I would go with the Federal courts. Mr. Cribbs had made it clear what his thoughts were—*Plead guilty!* He kept telling me the Federal Court worked much different than State. Things could go wrong, and I could easily be sent up for life. I would try to listen to Mr. Cribbs, but the intensity and unfairness of decisions being made were overwhelming. In the end, I would be the person at the end of the rope!

The thought kept flowing through my head: *How Can I Plead Guilty When I Am Innocent?* Too much was coming at me too quickly, but I had to make a decision. I had no other option than to trust in my attorney. Once again I made the decision to follow my attorney's advice and plead "guilty."

A pre-sentence study would be done. Mr. Cribbs explained he felt my sentence would bring at the most six months prison or probation. I wanted my day in court, but it wasn't going to be. All I wanted was one day just to lay out all my proof of this abusive man. I wanted so much to clear myself and see justice! But the decision had been made, and it was now only a matter of going forward with it.

This was one of those times when I could not feel one ounce of God. I felt total darkness, and I was just hoping to catch on to something that would eventually pull me out of this. I had prayed so many times, but all I could feel was an inner voice saying, *"Just keep going forward."*

I continued to stress over my ignorance of the legal system. I hated the fact that I had to plead guilty. For weeks, I could not cry, but now I was beginning to have spells of uncontrollable crying. I thought at times I was truly cracking up. I wasn't fearful of going to prison, but fearful of my decisions. I would sit down at my computer and journal. Now all I could write were the words, *"This too shall pass!"* I sat and gazed at the sentence and continued to read it over and over, gaining solace in knowing my spirit was telling me the truth. It would pass, but when?

My reputation was considered spotless in comparison to Trevor's. I was a model citizen of Orange County. Trevor's reputation was of total abuse. Surely the Federal judge would still see this with a pre-sentence study and the whole case would be dropped after they did the comparison. I thought this was what the pre-sentence study was about, right! They would glean over the case for truths, and now at last the truth would be out.

FEBRUARY 2003

I met with Mr. Cribbs at the Jack Brooks Federal Courthouse. We went before Judge Crawford. My nerves were fractured. I knew I couldn't handle any more hoopla, so I told no one, keeping it as quiet as possible, hoping I would be the only one present. If I felt so confused about my plea of guilty, how would my friends and family react as they heard it in court? Everyone had been so good to me, and the last thing I wanted them to think was that I was giving up. Totally unstable about the decision, but right or wrong, I had made it and was determined to ride the wave out despite the storm. I just prayed Mr. Cribbs was right and my character would truly come into play at some point.

I immediately entered an even larger Federal Courtroom, once again in total awe of the room. It was obvious they were expecting the usual large crowd. The courtroom was huge and beautiful. I was so distracted, with my thoughts continuing to stray to the intensity of the judge, how he handled himself, and to the awesome room we were in. I worked hard in an attempt to keep my mind focused on his words. Both Federal judges were dignified with an unusual calming presence about them. Sensitivity I was not expecting, yet it was present in each courtroom. I had never felt this before with Judge Davis or other state judges. The only "presence" we felt in Judge Davis's courts was totally demonic and cold.

At one point as the Judge was explaining my plea of guilty, reality kicked in! He was going over my decision, yet it was like words were being added that were confusing. I began to feel I was placing my own neck into a noose. I felt uninformed in such areas. I am sure my face expressed that as the judge spoke. At one moment I noticed he paused as though he knew I was unsure of myself. Then a strange peace came over me. *"Yes, you are out of control, but I am still in control. Just Trust Me,"* the voice kept saying! So I rested in that thought. Not what I felt in the physical, but what I knew in the spiritual realm would be God's plan.

As soon as the judge recessed, a very strong-willed young lady came over and introduced herself as Ms. Willis. She then presented me with a stack of papers to be filled out in a short length of time. I quickly looked it over thinking it would have something to do with my case, and possibly my chance to prove my innocence. As I looked the paperwork over, it looked more like an intense income tax audit, not what a pre-sentence study or what I thought a pre-sentence study would be.

After a few short weeks I was informed this very lady would determine my fate. A lady that had no law degree would carry more weight than my judge in the decision to send me to prison or free me? The more I learned that her decision would take precedence over the judge, the more upset I became.

Later, I let Mr. Cribbs know I would never have agreed to this guilty plea if I had known this. All I ever wanted was to go before a jury. Mr. Cribbs reassured me he felt this was my only alternative, and he felt everything would go well for me.

I continued my visits with Jenelle, my probation officer. Jenelle was obviously reading my face as she saw how disappointed I was at how the case was going. Jenelle sat back in her chair and began to reassure me, Mr. Cribbs was very respected amongst the courts. I knew she was in earnest with her statement and helped me in a weird way to stay focused.

Deep down I felt Mr. Cribbs' indebtedness to the judicial system outweighed his interest in me! Who was I? Just one of thousands that would cross his path. I knew the courts just wanted me out of their lives. He said himself this case was obviously every judge's nightmare. Orange County had made this mess and now the Federal Courts just wanted it behind them.

Rumors were flying around the courthouse. Steve Carter, my attorney prior to leaving the U.S., was now passing the word around that he hoped I got the maximum in prison. I wasn't surprised. It only reconfirmed my thoughts of him when I left with Nocona.

I soon became attached to a new friend named Trudy. I had met Trudy at Community Church. She worked for an attorney, so I latched on to her warm personality, strong belief in God, and obvious knowledge of legal terms. She volunteered to go with me when I met with Sonny Cribbs.

My life continued to be a struggle. River JoNey's graduation from the Bush School of Government and Public Service and Texas A&M was approaching. George Bush Sr. would be the speaker! I took a huge leap of faith with the help of friends and family and chartered a bus for this great occasion. I pictured myself being at the ceremony even though I was clueless as to whether they would allow me to go. I was still limited in the area I could travel. I, along with my family, just wanted it to be so special for River JoNey and, most of all, I wanted to be there. What an awesome triumph for River JoNey, after going through so much in her life! Many times she had started college only to be knocked out by this abusive man.

I was so fearful of asking my probation officer, that I decided I would bypass her and ask the judge personally, being it was so important to me. I just knew from past experiences Jenelle would say *NO!*

Sonny had promised to ask the judge for me, but weeks kept going by, and he always forgot. As the date drew nearer I decided I would bypass Mr. Sonny Cribbs and just stop by and speak to the judge myself. That was the only time I saw the judge as a normal human being. As I made my way into his office, I knew immediately I had made a huge error. The normal wisdom and professional appearance left him at that moment. The judge immediately let me know I was completely out of order, but he would hear my request! After I explained my situation, I quietly exited, but I was far from giving up!

I quickly regrouped, and contacted all my prayer warriors, and went at it at a totally different angle. I knew I had to face Jenelle. Something came up in my spirit so huge—the voice was saying take Jenelle an invitation to the graduation! The whole time I thought, *The last person I would desire to see at the graduation would be Jenelle!* It was so off the wall, I just hoped it was a God thing, so I did it!

As I walked down the long hall to her office, I went over and over in my mind as to how she would react. Would she be angry, thinking I was playing up to her? To my surprise, she didn't react! For some reason all the bad vibes I felt in the past were not present. As she read over the invitation, it was as though the stronghold somehow was broken between us. Remarkably, she approved my attendance to the graduation.

Jenelle was very nice from there on out. For the first time, I felt I actually became human in her eyes. I am not sure if it had something to do with the invitation or stating George Bush Sr. would be the speaker. As I glanced around her office, I saw pictures of Jenelle standing by George W. Bush, Sr. I assumed I had finally found common ground.

River JoNey, Frances, & Anna at Graduation

The grand day finally came. River JoNey's big graduation day was here. Many friends and family loaded up on the beautiful chartered bus. Posters and decorations were all over inside and out congratulating River. Laughter filled the day as we continued to decorate the bus and eat homemade cookies as we traveled down the road, making our way to College Station. We may not have been the most prestigious group, or maybe we were! But we definitely got the most attention with our decorated bus and large group.

It was a fun-filled day with River graduating with honors from both schools, Texas A&M and The Bush School Of Government and Public Service. It was really neat seeing George Bush, Sr. in person.

River JoNey with Friends & Family at Graduation

The way home was filled with laughter as each reminisced on the day. We all found it amusing that we were the only ones recognized outside the graduates in President Bush's speech. He was quite amused with our large group and all the spirit. Little did he know the depth behind it all.

Reality soon kicked back in the following Monday as I met once again with my attorney. Mr. Cribbs reassured me everything would go well and arranged a meeting with Miss Willis. Prior to the meeting, I questioned Mr. Cribbs more about Miss Willis, only to hear the same thing—no law degree, not sure if there was any degree whatsoever. Totally confused by it all, the pre-sentence study began. I tried to think positive as I pondered on the thought that this lady might just be on my side once she saw all the evidence I had. Justice would soon come about.

She asked very few questions, one being would I do the same thing over if it presented itself? I explained the reason I left and my strong feelings that, if it came to life or death of a child, I would have to do the same. I could tell it wasn't the answer she wanted. I quickly filled out the papers Miss Willis had given me in court and turned them in.

Once again, there was another huge letdown. The meetings I had with Miss Willis went totally the opposite of what I was expecting. There were two things plain and clear. It wasn't about my character at all or truths that may lie behind this whole case. Miss Willis' main focus was the financial statement I handed in. No matter what information I gave her, she was not interested in anything but my finances, and she became more and more irate with me. I originally felt Miss Willis was prejudiced against me, but now I felt total betrayal. I knew I had taken the wrong course of action. I didn't have to wait on her decision. It was obvious this lady's one desire from day one was to bury me!

Mr. Cribbs knew my position on attorneys. I made that clear the first day. I had been sold out by three prior to him and truly did not trust them. Once again I entered his office upset, but as always, Mr. Cribbs had his own way of settling me down. He always quickly agreed with me and began telling many unusual stories from his past. Being an older experienced gentleman, he had obviously learned the quickest way to resolve an upset female. Many days I would like to have said more, but refrained, knowing my lack of ability to go forward without him. From time to time, Sonny would remind me, boldly stating, "Frances, you have to keep in mind—You are every judge's nightmare!" It never helped matters, but he made sure he kept that up-front in my mind at all times!

I continued to totally depend on the fact that God was still God, and I would come out okay. I knew despite Miss Willis, the judge, or any attorneys' decision, God was in control of the whole situation, and they were just tools He would use to bring about His will, *Whatever It Might Be!*

Over a period of time, I grew to relax with Mr. Cribbs and discern where he was coming from. I caught myself calling him by his first name Sonny and other times it was Mr. Cribbs. It seemed to be according to the mood at the time.

From the beginning, I was not treated as other clients, as several noticed, nor did I feel ordinary. We had our differences, but I knew he was the best criminal attorney in Beaumont. I would just have to do everything I could to keep my demands up front. I felt more like a distant relative than a total stranger, so I always went straight to his lounge instead of waiting in the main entrance room. I would fall back on his comfortable sofa and pray until it was my time to meet with him. I knew I came second to the court system, but I was just hoping second would keep me out of prison!

Despite my lack of confidence in the pre-sentence study, I poured my whole body and soul out to the young lady, realizing this was it! She was my last chance! I offered her documents, cassette tapes, etc., hoping she would take the time to study them, praying something would make its way to the judge. Because of her intense frustration with the information on my assets, I ended up having one of my attorneys redo the paperwork in hopes of satisfying her.

Mr. Cribbs called me in once again. The pre-sentence study finally came back and, as I felt in my soul, it was not in my favor! As I read it over, most everything in it was either incorrect or distorted. I was outraged by the wording in the report that I felt was totally deceptive. I brought documents to Mr. Cribbs, disproving the accusations.

Devastated by the report, I quickly called the F.B.I. agent that made one of the statements against me and asked him as to why he made the statement listed on the report. His answer was, "I never said it."

Why all truths continued to stay concealed was far from clear. I knew at this time the truth would never come about with my case! My sentence was obviously set in stone the day the U.S. Marshalls brought me back to the States.

Mr. Cribbs made his objections to the pre-sentence report, but little change came from it. I was still looking at possibly twenty-three months in prison and one year in a halfway-house. I felt like Daniel approaching the lion's den!

With each visit, Mr. Cribbs talked of downward departures being my only chance. All these words continued to confuse me. Just as I would learn the meaning of one term, another one would be thrown at me. Friends and family immediately began to check the Internet to study *downward departures*. From everything I read, I had a bunch of them, yet Mr. Cribbs was never interested in our suggestions. I felt a decision had already been made, but I was going to fight it to the end.

Court dates continued to be set and canceled. I was beginning to see that, with each delay, it was as though God was positioning me for something.

There was a positive side. At least no one was stating *Life In Prison* anymore, nor would I be going to a State Prison! That was a blessing and a miracle.

Once again the sentencing date was set. The Honorable Judge Thad Heartfield would preside over my case. I felt uneasy about everything going on. At one point, I actually broke down in tears when I was in Jenelle's office. Something I swore I would never allow her to see was my weak side. I told Jenelle I was confused as to the pre-sentence study and the result. I thought my and Trevor's character would come into play, yet it obviously hadn't. Jenelle told me once again to have confidence in my attorney. She emphasized again how respected he was amongst the courts.

With each letdown, more and more letters continued to pour in to Judge Heartfield from Mayors, Congressmen, businessmen, and friends around the world on my behalf. Anna, River JoNey, and Nocona all wrote heart-wrenching pleas. Nothing appeared to be helping. The judge would make remarks that made it appear that he was for me, but there always appeared to be pressure from a higher level.

JUNE 2003

The press continued in full force, but this time with something totally different! Judge Davis was now making headlines in the newspapers and television. The Judge that should have helped Nocona in 1994. Praise God! *Darkness comes to light* was my first thought. Judge Davis was being sued and investigated for allowing children to go back into an extremely abusive home. C.N.N. and FOX T.V. were having a field day! Bill O'Reilly was outraged with Judge Davis, making the scandal the topic of his program.

This was the same judge that failed to listen to us, causing me to flee with Nocona. With each event, my supporters jumped back on the Internet in an attempt to gain outside support. By the time everyone found out, it was too late. O'Reilly had spent several days and was going into a different topic.

FOXNews.com

Talking Points

We Are Not Protecting the Kids

Thursday, June 12, 2003
By Bill O'Reilly

NEWS

To watch "The Talking Points Memo" in the Screening Room click here.

Hi, I'm Bill O'Reilly. Thanks for watching us tonight.

We are not protecting the kids. That is the subject of this evening's *Talking Points Memo*. Last night we played you a harrowing 911 call from a 12-year-old named Tyler Kay, who was pleading with Houston operators to save him from his parents. Katherine and Kendall Kay went to prison for savagely beating Tyler and his six siblings went to foster homes.

Now, Mrs. Kay is out of jail, and incredibly Judge _____ has returned the children to her custody; excepting Tyler, who's living with his grandparents.

Since the kids were all found to be neglected and sexual abuse was suspected in the case, what Judge _____ was doing was what, atrocious, right? The answer is he was clearing the case; at least that's what's on the record, because the cowardly _____ will not talk.

And what about the court-appointed attorney for the kids, Michelle Merendino? Well, she's all for the kids going back to the abusive mother. Makes her life easier as well.

In just a few moments, we'll tell you about this alleged monster in California who authorities say kidnapped and raped a 9-year-old girl. He was arraigned today.

But all Americans should be getting the picture here. We as a society are not nearly as vengeful as we should be against those who abuse children. Adults who brutalize kids should never again be allowed that opportunity. One strike and you're out. Society must put down the gauntlet.

Instead the ACLU is fighting for the rights of the North America Man-Boy Love

http://www.foxnews.com/story/0,2933,89219,00.html 6/13/2003

On my free days I helped with Mom and Dad. Dad continued to go downhill with his health and needed a lot of attention. Mother's dementia was at its worse. She was unable to comprehend anything and had to be supervised at all times. One day I went with Dad for his doctor's appointment. As I was leaving, I saw someone that looked familiar in the hall. As we drew nearer, I smiled as an old friend recognized me. I am not sure who was the happiest to see the other. It was like he had seen a ghost. We had been on dive trips together.

The first thing that came out of his mouth was, "How can I help you, Frances?"

I quickly responded with, "A letter to the judge!"

Within minutes, he had made an appointment for me with the secretary of Congressman Jack Brooks. Within a few days, my judge received a letter on my behalf from Mr. Brooks.

Each time I went to the Jack Brooks Federal Court House, I always stopped and looked at Congressman Brook's pictures. Little did I know, God would soon have this great figure of a man sending a letter on my behalf!

As the court dates approached, the press repeatedly splashed across the airways not my best, but my worst, pictures. I cringed with each viewing.

The court date was now August 15, 2003. I truly felt this was it, and immediately emailed everyone that we would have a victory party the night before. I felt a total peace about it, and knew no one could imprison my mind anymore. They may place me in a physical prison, but they could not imprison my mind.

No more prayer meetings—only victory parties! Anna continued to forward each change to all our friends and family. Many from the Island continued to call and email, hoping to make a difference. Jerry Hynds, a prominent businessman from the Island, was now a congressman in Honduras. Jerry called and encouraged me, letting me know how upset he was with the way Nocona and I were being treated in the U.S. He went on to say he would fly down to testify on my behalf if needed. I only knew the people for eight years, but daily I was getting letters and support from many businessmen and friends from Roatan. It was all so encouraging.

JULY 30, 2003

Every day, I tried to focus on nothing but positive things. On this particular day, I was to pick up River JoNey at the Bush Airport in Houston. She was coming in from Haiti where she had been working as a teacher. Prior to leaving, I picked up a couple of cassette tapes I found in a drawer.

As I traveled, I quietly listened to Todd Bentley tapes. He mentioned that when God started turning things around, to ask Him to rain it in. I did not know who Todd Bentley was, but I was desperate and would try anything. I began to do just that. I began praying for lots of rain, God's rain, blessings and more blessings to pour in. "Lord just flood me, I need help!"

Within minutes, my cell phone was ringing. It was a call from Owen's wife, Nelda, stating, "Wonderful News! Trevor just relinquished all his rights to Nocona!" The news was totally unanticipated and absolutely a God thing!

I wanted to pull over and shout and dance around the car, but I was running late to the airport. I missed the turn to the airport as my mind reflected on the rain—*Yes, God's Awesome Rain! It Was Beyond My Comprehension! Nocona Would Be Free Of This Man The Rest Of Her Life. What A Miracle!* Surely my case would be dropped now! I was late picking River JoNey up and had to pull out Dad's handicapped card to find a close parking spot.

I knew Owen and Nelda were preparing for a trial to get full custody of Nocona that week. Everyone said Trevor would be a fool to show up in court with all the evidence and individuals prepared to go up against him. Fourteen years of living a nightmare and, at the stroke of a pen, it's all over for a child. Trevor knew he would not win and obviously did not want to pay child support.

The next day they were ready to go before the judge and make it legal, finished, etc. I knew I couldn't go to this great event, so I joined a friend and her daughter at the lake. I got a call from Nocona. "Ganna, I Have My Freedom; come celebrate with us at Tuffy's Restaurant in Mauriceville. Let's celebrate!" JoNey got on the phone stating the judge dropped the gag order. She went on to say that when the press began to corner Nocona, she was a little shocked by it, yet boldly spoke out when asked questions concerning her grandmother going to prison. Nocona went on to tell the press she was so excited that she could turn cartwheels! Blessings were definitely beginning to rain!

Nocona was soon over to spend the night. What a long awaited moment! We stayed up for hours looking over pictures and laughing about different happenings on the Island. Normally, Nocona never slept with me on the Island, since she moved around so much in bed. Tonight was different, she could do anything she wanted! Before she returned to her grandparents' home, I made her do a couple of cartwheels just to see if she could still do them.

KFDM-TV Channel Six News

- Home
- News
- Weather
- Sports

-Quick Links-
6 News This Morning<<
Live at Five<<
Fish/Game Forecast<<
6 On Health<<
Community Calendar <<
HDTV Questions <<
Download WeatherBug<<
Job Opportunities<<
Contact Us<<

Nocona Burton Custody Battle Finally Ends After 10 Years

Reported by Courtney Zubowski
July 30, 2003 - 8:36PM

The custody battle over a girl from Orange County has made national headlines.
Tonight, the fight for Nocona   , who now goes by the name Nocona Burton, has ended.
Courtney Zubowski was at the Orange County Courthouse Wednesday where the decision was made.

Nocona's biological father,   , voluntarily gave up his rights to Nocona after a 10-year-long custody battle.
It started in 19-94 when Nocona's grandmother, Francis Harris, fled with Nocona to Honduras because she said   was abusing Nocona.
         has denied those charges.
Wednesday   officially denied himself custody of his daughter.
Nocona Burton:
"He gave up his rights to me and so I'm really happy right now."
After 10 years, Nocona Burton has a permanent place to call home.
Nocona Burton
"I'm just going to jump up and down and do cartwheels."
Something you'd expect of a 12-year-old.
But she's not your average pre-teen.
Nocona Burton:
"It's been really different, pretty scary."
When Nocona was three years old, her grandmother, Francis Harris, fled with Nocona to Honduras.
She spent the next eight years on the island of Roatan knowing at any moment, the FBI could arrest her grandmother and bring them back to the U.S.
That happened last September.
Nocona hasn't seen her grandmother, Francis Harris, since then.
Nocona Burton:
"I'd say, 'I love you and I miss you.'"
Nocona will be living with her maternal grandfather Owen Burton and his wife Nelda.
Nelda Burton/Nocona's Grandmother:
"She told me I was home now, so it's quite emotional for us."

http://www.kfdm1.com/engine.pl?station=kfdm&id=2238&template=breakoutlocal.html   7/31/2003

THE BEAUMONT ENTERPRISE ♦ Thursday, July 31, 2003

Father walks away from fight for custody

FIGHT: Daughter 'relieved'

By KEVIN J. DWYER
THE ENTERPRISE

The long-running, international custody battle for a 12-year-old Orange County girl came to a sudden end Wednesday when her father voluntarily gave up parental rights to his daughter.

In a surprise decision following 10 years of court battles, _____ officially severed his parental rights to 12-year-old Nocona Burton.

"It was a good conclusion," said _____ ; Nocona's attorney, in a phone interview. "Any time you can resolve a case without putting the family through a trial, and

FIGHT, page 15A

Continued from page 13A

doing what the child wants, it ends the uncertainty of the litigation."

After severing parental rights, Judge _____ awarded permanent custody of Nocona to Owen and Nelda Burton. Owen Burton is Nocona's maternal grandfather.

"Her dad gave up his fight for her today and she is in my custody," Owen Burton said, adding that he and Nocona feel "great" about the outcome of the case.

_____ also granted River JoNey Burton, Nocona's mother, parental rights.

Nocona was also able to change her surname from _____ to Burton during the hearing.

"This has put an end to it," _____ said. "(Nocona's) relieved and she's happy. She got to change her surname to 'Burton.' Nocona's really relieved that she can lay her head down in a bed and know she won't be uprooted again."

Nocona's case made national headlines in March 1994 when her grandmother, Frances Harris of Mauriceville, abducted the then 3-year-old girl and fled to Honduras. Harris has said that she fled the country with Nocona because the girl's father abused her, a claim _____ says is untrue.

Federal and Orange County authorities arrested Harris in Honduras after eight years as a fugitive and brought her back to Southeast Texas on Sept. 24. Harris ran a small island resort there on the island of Roatan.

Harris pleaded guilty in federal court to international kidnapping Feb. 3 and is scheduled to be sentenced Aug. 15. She could be sentenced to as many as three years in prison on the charge.

Reach this reporter at:
(409) 833-3311, ext. 413
kdwyer@beaumontenterprise.com

Nocona's fate was sealed, but mine was still on the burner. I was anxiously waiting to meet with Mr. Cribbs. I thought, *Well, I would assume he now had the downward departure he needed.* Trevor obviously didn't care to fight for his child. I thought, *Surely my case would be dropped now!* My next meeting was with my probation officer, and she asked if my attorney had mentioned anything on my case possibly being dropped. It certainly sounded logical to me.

Once again Trevor's decision to relinquish his rights to Nocona was all over the television and front pages of the newspapers. It was the talk of everyone on the streets, obviously reassuring anyone that didn't know me who the real villain was in this case.

Once again I was to meet with Mr. Cribbs. When I entered his office, everything about him was different, with him abruptly stating not to concern myself with the August 15, 2003, court hearing. I anxiously awaited for him to say those golden words, that my case had been dropped. That didn't happen, but once again my sentencing date had definitely been canceled, and he didn't know when it would be rescheduled. He went on to state that the judge wanted him to get together with the D.A. and work on the case some more.

I had already heard this several times and now, once again, "No Sentencing Date!" At one point, Mr. Cribbs relaxed and chuckled when he told me the judge had already received seventy-five handwritten letters as of that date, all in support of Frances Collins Harris. His law clerks were making sure they were brought to his attention. I didn't say anything, but I knew at least a hundred or more were on the way.

I brought to Mr. Cribbs' attention that Trevor had relinquished his rights to Nocona. "Wouldn't that cause my case to be dropped?"

He replied, "Frances, there seems to be people higher up than the judge making decisions on your case. Washington seems to have interest in your case." As I left, I was totally confused with our legal system. What more did they need to know if the man wouldn't even fight for his child?

I regrouped. As bad as I wanted it over, questions continued to surface. What else could happen?

As I continued to meet with Mr. Cribbs, he refused to allow me to think all this would help. Pressure appeared to be on different ones, obviously one being my judge. As of right now, I would still be going to prison!

I found myself choosing not to believe what came out of the mouth of man. I stayed focused on who I knew I was as a person and what I deserved!

I began to reflect on the Congressman and Senators that were fighting for Trevor while we were in Honduras. More and more we began to feel that my sentencing would have nothing to do with the Beaumont Federal Courts, but whoever had political strength in Washington. The political strength was obviously not in favor of Frances Harris!

Seashell Prisoners
CHAPTER 21

Each new day brought a change in headlines. Roy Dunn with *County Record* continued to go out on a limb in an endeavor to help our imminent attempt for justice. Friends said he remembered me from my past community work in Orange. Roy was obviously a man of much integrity from the reflection of his newspaper and comments made by many. He occasionally threw out timely remarks stating I was a classy lady and beautiful, all of which had a way of picking my spirits up.

Letters from friends and family from different parts of the world continued to pour in to Judge Heartfield's court. With each passing week, the more intense things became. More letters and calls came from Roatan. Everyone was appalled at our U.S. judicial system.

Old classmates continued calling and sending letters and dinner invitations, somehow working me into activities including a class reunion out of town. Several escorted me home from Houston, making sure I was in by my ten o'clock curfew. Each supported and sympathized, but Linda, one high school classmate who frequently found humor, stated "I was their claim to fame."

Pam Guidry, a close cousin, called and told me her son Benji had just come in from serving in Iraq. On his return, Benji brought in the Iraqi local newspaper, *Stars and Stripes*, headlining news from Texas—the grandmother and her struggle to fight a life sentence for kidnapping! It never ceased to amaze me as to the unusual places our story would pop up.

This week all eyes were on the news. Every attorney in the Golden Triangle was watching to see the judge's decision on the trial of the mayor of Beaumont. Would the mayor receive a downward departure on his charge of bribery, money laundering, mail fraud, and conspiracy? I along with many others were glued to the television, anxiously watching and awaiting the judge's decision in hopes it might influence my case in some way.

Weeks went by, then Mr. Cribbs announced the inevitable—another court date had been set up for October 23, 2003! Still no change with the judge—I would go to prison! They had reduced the court fees to $3,000.00. I had become numb to all the ups and downs, yet continued to stand fast as I refused to listen to anything negative. Despite my determination, I felt my nervous system slipping in and out. There were just too many changes, but I was determined I would not allow it to bring me down. I knew God was in control. It was just a matter of me staying in control. Daily

I burned the midnight oil on the computer, pouring every thought into it, somehow thinking it might solve the whole matter. I journaled for hours, then repeated over and over, *"This Too Shall Pass."* It had to pass, it was just too overwhelming!

Mr. Cribbs continued to prepare me for what was appearing to be my fate: Prison! It was evident the Honorable Judge Thad Heartfield was going to sentence me to prison, despite the letters, the calls, and the press support. As the court date approached, Trevor appeared on T.V. stating he would be at the sentencing and that I should get a life sentence.

Sonny explained the hearing would be simple and short. I would get a split sentence—seven and seven, and there would be no possible changes: seven months in prison and seven months of house arrest. Something in my spirit continued to stir, telling me I needed to tell my story despite the preconceived report. No one ever gave me the opportunity to defend myself nor would I get the chance in the future. I sat at the computer at night, off and on, going over what I would say if the opportunity arose. I finally got up the nerve to tell Mr. Cribbs I wanted to make a statement. He discouraged me, saying it could possibly cause problems. He said "Frances, It is your right, but it won't do you any good."

I called him two days before the hearing, letting him know I would be making a statement. He replied, "Fine," but continued to discourage me. He then asked how long it would be? I reluctantly told him a couple pages. I knew he would be irate with the five I had on my computer.

The closer the court date came, the more intense family conversation became. Each had their own fears. I began to go by Nocona's school so I could be close and reassure her. I sat at a distance as I watched her many friends clamor around her.

OCTOBER 23, 2003

The big day arrived. Over a year of court dates had been set and canceled. What originally was to be twenty days had ended up being over a year! My family and I were exhausted, but we were ready. Prior to the sentencing, I had a quiet evening. I went to bed early. I felt very good, but wondered exactly what God had in store the next day. I was clueless, but felt a sense of peace. I woke up early the next morning laughing at what was so strong on my mind. I had this Reggae song deep in my spirit like I was ready to dance!

The phone rang. Pat Martin, a good friend, called to reconfirm my thoughts. She told me she dreamed I was in a mini-skirt dancing on the table. Pat could always find humor even in the most bizarre situations! I truly did feel good, but not like dancing on the table. My spirit was free and that was a good sign! I knew that regardless of what happened, I was going to be okay.

I went to my computer and printed out my statement. It may have been crude since I'd stopped and started so much, but I would take it just in case I still had the nerve to read it. Traci (an old school friend), JoNey, and Anna were on schedule to pick me up. River JoNey and I pulled out our usual humor tactics, trying to pick each other up as Traci drove. JoNey could always find something funny in everything that came up in our lives.

I had all my probation visits at the Federal court, so I knew the security protocol. Today was different. Everything had changed and Sonny was eagerly awaiting us at the door. My attention suddenly changed. It was odd seeing him dressed up and not in his usual casual attire. He truly took on the appearance of a high-profile attorney. I was impressed as he approached us wearing a black, tailored suit.

Security stood to the side as Sonny, in his quiet, distinguished manner, quickly ushered me past security and walked us down the long hallway to the elevator. Sonny's demeanor had changed. I could tell he was deeply concerned as to what I might say in court. As we made our way closer to the elevator, I glanced around to see many friends and family along the long hall. All had somber expressions as though a public hanging was in the making. As we approached the elevator, Sonny leaned over and once again discouraged me from making a statement. "Frances it will not help and possibly do harm."

Deep down I knew I had to go with my gut instincts, hoping a big voice from heaven would give me the go-ahead. After getting off the elevator, Sonny took me over to the side before entering the courtroom, again stating he was afraid I would slam everyone involved. He once again explained the judge and everyone had done all they could do. Traci spoke up, reassuring him I had no plans of attacking anyone.

In reality we never discussed any of it, but Traci knew me and knew I would do whatever I could to keep from seeing my family hurt again. She also knew leaving my family and going to prison would definitely be another huge slam and let-down for all of us. Furthermore, I would only be speaking truths, and if the truth offended, then so be it! My thoughts were, *If the legal system had an uncomfortable moment, so what, the legal system was the reason I had to leave to begin with. They were the reason my granddaughter, my daughter, and my whole family had been put through hell for so many years! They certainly deserved an uncomfortable moment!*

At least fifty friends gathered around as we neared the entrance to the courtroom, all anxiously waiting to pray prior to going in. Bold prayers went forth by everyone with Pat, Miriam, and LaDonna leading off. Pastor Berkheimer and Bro. Robert came in shortly after them. As we were entering the huge courtroom, we could feel the tension.

I overheard someone whisper, "Judge Heartfield received a call from another judge's wife, asking him to please not send the grandmother to prison." As I entered the courtroom, everyone filed in with Nocona, her mother, River JoNey, and Anna sitting on the front row. Many had to sit on Trevor's side since there wasn't enough room. Once again there was the usual aura in the huge courtroom.

For a brief moment I remember thinking, Praise God! My nerves are still intact. I quickly scoped out the crowd, but Trevor was nowhere to be seen. This huge battle continued to stir in my spirit: *Read the story. No don't read the story; read the story; no forget it! If you read it, it's just going to make things worse. What if it caused you to get a life sentence! Nocona would definitely be hurt by bringing up the past.* She will be hearing things for the first time, things I never told her about the past. A true battle of spirits was definitely in full force. Then this voice rose up saying, *Just Be Still.* So I obeyed!

I intensely watched Mr. Cribbs, relying on him for the tiniest details. We all stood until he motioned for me to sit down next to him. Everything got quiet. The Honorable Judge Thad Heartfield entered the courtroom. In very few, very simple words, and way too fast, he gave the verdict. I was listening, intensely concerned I wouldn't understand his intellectual legal grammar, but it came plain, simple, and quick.

It was not good! *Seven Months Confinement in a Federal Correctional Institution and Seven Months Home Detention.* I was numb as I thought surely I am not understanding this man correctly. He politely went on to explain that I had the right to speak if I wanted. I fidgeted momentarily, wondering if it really would upset the judge, with him announcing a recourse. Could he back up and give me more time if I told my story? Was I going to make a total fool of myself? My mind swept to Nocona. Sonny sat quietly in his usual dignified manner, saying his own prayers.

All of a sudden I stood up and commenced to go forward with my five pages in my hand. I paused as I approached the microphone. I began to silently pray that God would just help me speak without crying, or without the honorable judge abruptly stopping me, only to have me chained and marched off to prison.

I quietly began to read my statement. I was pouring my heart out as to the many years this sick man and his family had destroyed our lives. It was all coming straight from the heart and soul. I was so nervous that I felt my legs were going to collapse. As I spoke, I began to hear a noise behind me. It was weeping! Then the weeping turned into sobs. It was hard to tell who it was. Everyone directly behind me was immediate family. It was obvious this was not just my story, but our whole family's story. The distraction helped, but as I continued to speak my voice began to get shaky once again. Then something rose up in me strengthening me to go forward, speaking about our fourteen-year vigil with a psychopathic, abusive man and his family. The words came out hard and fast, not leaving anything for guesswork. My daughter and granddaughter had been brutally abused by this man and our whole lives were devastated from it.

At this point I didn't care if the whole world knew my weaknesses or most embarrassing moments. I would have laid face down on the floor, if I thought it would have made a difference with Judge Heartfield's verdict. I knew this was my last chance to be heard—my last chance for justice. I would do everything I possibly could on my part to see justice from this noble man. I had been forced to be humble about this far too long, accepting every form of punishment from this scapegoat position. My whole family had hurt long enough! Every legal professional, male and female, had let all of us down. If he did go forward with the sentence, I wanted to know at least I did everything I possibly could. It really was time for all this to halt.

I continued to read on with no doubt now that I was supposed to be doing this. Even though I was reading, I felt the emotion of the courtroom. I began to glance up and look around for response or lack of response. I couldn't look at the judge, but I glanced over at the District Attorney's face. His head was down with a look of remorse, or maybe just wishing he could have been anywhere but here. I glanced over at the court reporter and he looked extremely sad and expressionless. There was a quiet hush throughout the courtroom. I didn't really know who was or was not affected, but I desperately hoped the judge heard every word.

Halfway through my talk, Judge Heartfield interrupted me. I thought, *This is it! This noble man is going to tell me to sit down or have me taken out.* As I looked up, I was totally shocked at his response. He looked me in the eye and very professionally, yet politely, asked me to slow down. He went on to say I was reading too fast for the court reporter. I breathed a sigh of relief, caught my breath, and finished. His timing was perfect, I felt faint from holding my breath, reading so fast. When I made my finishing remarks, I made my way back to my chair and sat down. I expected to feel the presence of total wrath from Mr. Cribbs with harsh glares, etc. He continued to look forward, keeping his very notable composure as he sat quietly waiting to see the judge's response from this unexpected speech. I knew Mr. Cribb's experience with many previous bizarre psychopathic clients. It had obviously prepared him for this day!

Judge Heartfield never changed his distinguished demeanor as he made his finishing remarks. He brought up the fact that over one hundred and fifty people sent letters of support. He recognized the pastors, Congressman Jack Brooks, Congressman Jerry Hynds, and Honduras citizens' responses. It was evident Judge Heartfield had made up his mind and there would be no change. Frances Collins Harris would go to prison!

I fought back tears struggling with his sentence, but I tried not to show it. I was so in hopes of seeing justice done. He emphasized the time already served would be taken off of the sentence. As a last-minute gesture, he delayed my departure until January 5, 2004. The victim payment had also been dropped. It was pretty obvious, *We Were The Victims!*

Lauren and Nocona were next to me as I exited the courtroom. Anna and Traci were directly behind. I looked back to see River JoNey distraught, struggling to walk. Reality obviously kicked in full force as she listened intensely to our story. As we exited the courtroom, Traci wanted to bypass the press. As much as I desired to take her up on it, I felt so deeply this was God's platform, not mine, and I was not to turn away from it. Deep down I felt I was the judicial system's scapegoat or even a sacrificial lamb, but I had to go forward and somehow God would be in the middle of this, too. With each step I thought of what must be going through the minds of my children, family and friends. As we drew closer to the press, I turned and wiped back the tears. I decided that despite the sentence, we were not losers, and winners smile! Smiling is what I chose to do even though my heart was breaking. It was going to be so hard leaving my family once again. As we walked outside and down the sidewalk, the press was waiting. I pulled it off, by telling them I was okay. The truth was I was totally in shock once again at the decision by the only system we had to protect the innocent. Maybe it was the world's best or the Federal Courts' best, but it definitely wasn't justice!

Nocona was deeply disturbed with the verdict, totally shocking me with her statement as the press turned to her with questions. Her only reply was, "I am the reason my grandmother is having to go to prison!"

I was concerned about her statement, but I continued to walk forward, smiling as though the statement was never made. I looked around to see all my friends standing over to one side. I walked over to give them all a hug. I was so grateful to have them by my side.

Someone spoke up and suggested going to dinner. I knew they would try to make the best of this awful day. Totally traumatized, I did what I had become good at—faking my feelings. I joined everyone at Papadeaux's Restaurant.

> **Grandmother sentenced**
>
> **TX** BEAUMONT — A grandmother was sentenced Tuesday to 14 months in prison for kidnapping her 3-year-old granddaughter in 1994 and taking the child to Central America, where the pair lived for nearly nine years.
>
> Francis Harris, 58, was also fined $3,000 by U.S. District Judge Thad Heartfield.
>
> Nocona Lynn , now 12, was located in Honduras with her grandmother last year and has since been returned home to southeast Texas where she is now living with her maternal grandfather in Mauriceville, according to the U.S. Attorney's Office in Beaumont.
>
> Harris pleaded guilty to a charge of international kidnapping in federal court in February.
>
> *Stories and photos from wire services*

*Mid-East-Stars & Stripes
International Press Release*

As everyone sat around the table, I quietly listened and occasionally made an attempt to add to the conversation. LaDonna casually mentioned my going to prison in a limousine. We all laughed, but soon grabbed hold of the thought. It certainly had a nice ring to it, and was definitely appropriate for the occasion.

Vol. 8, No. 30   October 2-8, 2003

THE EXAMINER

The Independent Voice of Southeast Texas

Nocona   's
plea to judge

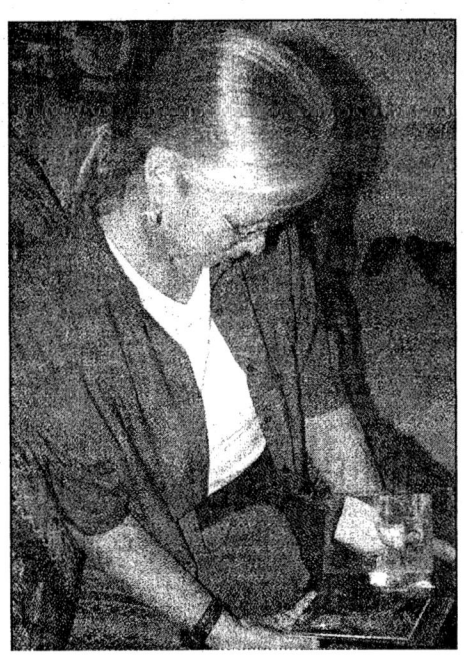

'Please, please don't send my granna to jail'

Page 7

Sunday morning I attended church as though all were fine. I was there in spirit only. I felt total numbness as though not one organ in my body was functioning. Pastor Berkheimer's sermon was once again exactly what I needed. Somehow he gracefully brought my sentencing into his sermon. By the time he finished, the congregation was standing, applauding my plight. It was definitely confirmation that my five-page letter, pouring my heart and soul out to the judge, obviously wasn't stupid, but was looked upon as being what it truly was—a last attempt for justice. I really did have a lot to be grateful for. I was frequently reminded that I was facing a life sentence.

As I began to make my way out into the public once again, people embraced me wherever I went with hugs, handshakes, and even meals paid for. Prophecies continued to come forth on the book, ministry in prison, and prosperity coming forth. The world poured out great compassion, but the Judicial System continued to be steadfast, even with the knowledge that they were sending the wrong person to prison. Someone had to pay and obviously it was going to be Frances Harris and family. Letters appeared in the newspapers from total strangers, stating I should get a medal and a key to the city—not prison! Thousands were appalled by my fate, and so were we!

I later regrouped and decided to give praise as the Bible states and embrace the moment—yes, even for prison! I had fought the fight and God obviously had something else in mind. I began to take advantage of every opportunity to be with family and friends. The holidays were coming up. With my daughters, nieces, and friends' strong gifting of organization, November and December were quickly packed full of dates. At times it seemed strange. Nine years ago, I was in total control of all the party planning in the family, and now with all the nieces, all I had to do was sit back and show up! It took some adjusting, but truly felt wonderful!

I continued to help with Mother and Dad. Mother's dementia condition continued to get worse. She did not know any of us and was now unable to walk or communicate. Between my sisters and I, we were taking Dad to Beaumont for treatments every day for seven weeks. It was neat getting to see the big smile on his last day of treatment when they presented a large certificate showing completion of his treatment. He was eighty-six years old, but he embraced it as a small child. We celebrated at the Black-Eyed Pea Restaurant. I knew his thoughts, it was as though possibly he would regain some control of his life again.

Within just a few weeks we received a call from his physician, requesting the family to come in. We knew it wasn't good if they were calling in the family. The physician announced Dad had throat and lung cancer and it had spread. Once again our hearts fell. Everyone had jobs to get back to, so Dad and I made our way to his favorite restaurant, the Cracker Barrel. I put on my happy face in an attempt to ignore the horrible report. This time I could not pull it off. With each attempt to make conversation, I couldn't talk for tears rolling down my face. It was like his whole world had been ripped from him, and we should have been able to fix it. Why did this have to happen?

How could I go to prison when it looked as though Dad might not have long to live, and he needed so much help with Mother. Depression set in with the thought that I was of no help to anyone. I kept wondering whether they would even be alive when I got out!

DECEMBER 2003

Things began to pick up with the Christmas season. Each day was filled with Christmas shopping, parties, birthdays, class reunions, and trips with the grandkids to see the Nutcracker. I was allowed to go to LaGrange to celebrate Sam and Todd's birthday. Everyone made sure there wasn't one moment to dwell on anything.

I did get to organize one thing, a Christmas-light tour on a chartered bus with all my grandkids and friends. What fun we had! I felt in some way I still had it. Whatever it was! As with everything I organized, it had its funny moments. Homeowners in the neighborhoods stopped and asked who we were. I am not sure who they thought we were—terrorists or some famous persons in the big bus? Actually, we could claim the latter.

Things were picking up for Nocona with her school grades and personality reflecting her success. She was enrolled at Mauriceville Jr. High and competed for Miss Mistletoe and won. I laughed as I thought of her Caleb personality as she also jumped out and ran for President of the Student Council, even though she had never held office in anything. She lost by only a few votes. The school was proud to have her. The counselors and teachers let me know what an unusually good child she was. I continued to go by the school, reassuring her I was okay. Many kids clamored around as she walked down the halls. It was neat seeing them laugh and talk.

I was no longer being monitored. The freedom was nice, but I was still helping with the family. Both Mother's and Dad's health were quickly deteriorating. As usual I went overboard decorating their home for Christmas. I prepared the turkey and dressing using Mother's recipe. Family members brought additional dishes. Two days in advance, I set the table with all of Mother's favorite Christmas plates and glasses. Mother might not know they were out, but the rest of the family did.

The big day arrived with many tough moments. At times, we didn't think we were going to pull it off with Dad exiting to the bedroom with spells of heart problems. One o'clock came and Dad slowly made his way to the head of the table. Yes, it was definitely one of my proudest moments! We had worked so hard and once again we were all sitting at the table for Christmas dinner. What an awesome meal with Dad at the head of the table, and Mother sitting beside him! No one cared if vile words came out of Dad's mouth or if he grumbled when we said the blessing. We were just happy to be together.

ᛞ

The Christmas holidays were over and now it was the countdown. New Year's Eve was, as most things in my life, spent differently. Nieces were still in town from the holidays visiting, so we all loaded up and went to two movies. This was something I occasionally did in the past with an old friend whenever life got boring. The neat thing today was Nocona got to join us.

The first movie was *The Return Of The King*, from *The Lord Of The Rings*, and then we made our way to *Cold Mountain*. My sisters were with us. With everyone exhausted from the holidays, little thought went into checking the rating. After a couple of surprising scenes, we all wanted to sliver out of the theater! Nocona thought at one point she was under attack, as hands rushed towards her, so she closed her eyes at a couple scenes. Afterwards we made our way to I-HOP. We had breakfast as we watched the fireworks in the distance going off on Crockett Street, bringing in the New Year, 2004.

JANUARY 2004

The holidays went good and everyone was working hard to keep my morale up. The idea came up of having a going-away party for me. It was cold and raining. I was so tired from the holidays and stress from the sentencing. My deepest desire was to take the first boat to a desolate island, bury myself in the sand for a month, and then bake quietly in the sun.

I thought, *There is no way anyone will show up, considering everyone is worn out from court hearings, the holidays and this whole depressing ordeal.* Just the opposite happened! Not only did friends and family show up, but the press made their way there. We made it a combination birthday

---

From his experience, reader says Harris treated unjustly

I have not written a letter to the editor in several years now because nothing I have read has really "ticked me off." I even agreed with you on all the state constitutional amendments, which is kind of rare in itself. However, this Frances Harris case has made me want to put pen to paper once again.

The subject of grandparents taking care of their grandchildren is something I do have some firsthand knowledge about. Because of something I did really stupid in 1978, my mother undertook the enormous responsibility of raising all five of my daughters, from pre-teen through high school graduation and then until they married and moved away from home.

I have watched the Harris case through the media since 1994. It is my opinion that not only should this case not have been brought to trial, but I believe Harris should have been given a medal and maybe even a key to the city for having the courage to stick her own neck out to protect her granddaughter.

DOYLE F. McKEOWN JR.
Silsbee

party for Nocona plus a going-away party.

The party was wonderful, with Sam and Sissy being most gracious in opening up their beautiful home—designed, constructed and decorated by the two of them. Pat and Lisa sang a beautiful song. As the conversation slowed, Sissy entertained the ladies with all of the latest herbal remedies.

Carlos and Ginger, out of boredom, turned on their favorite Cajun music. Yes, it was a victory party and a time to dance! We all joined in and finished the evening dancing. I refused to make my worst moments in life dark. There truly was a huge victory. I wasn't going to prison for life—Just for six months! The night was typical as with all my friends, full of personality and life!

Seashell Prisoners
CHAPTER 22

With each letter I received and service I attended, prophets continued to lay the same word on me…*I had a mission…It was for one person!* A prophet from Community Church stated angels could be seen surrounding me and preparing me for my new journey. I truly felt the same, but was totally confused as to why. *Why me? Haven't I been through enough? Haven't I learned enough about God? Wasn't this book thick enough?*

The night before I left, my last words to my sister Arlene were, "There's one thing I have learned about God. When He's leading you off in a different direction you just lay everything to the side and go into it 100%. Arlene, I'm entering that prison totally focused on what God's desire is of me, to accomplish whatever it is He wants…and get out!"

I had learned that, in order to get through your planned destiny with as much ease as possible, you just…take a deep breath and totally submit!

JANUARY 3, 2004

It was time to depart for Carswell Prison at Fort Worth. Travel by limousine seemed to be somehow God's plan, yet it wasn't large enough for the many desiring to go. I quickly checked out the possibility of a chartered bus, but it was totally out of the budget. Details became too stressful, so whoever had $100.00 left over from the holidays went to Fort Worth in what was obviously the predestined limousine!

The thought of an extra day in Fort Worth was soothing to my mind, giving me time to regroup before I entered the prison. Everything within me was exhausted from my sentencing, holiday activities, going-away parties and the press. The only positive thing about my predestined trip was that I didn't have to concern myself with packing for a six-month stay!

The limousine was all I'd dreamed and more. My friend Trudy and her husband Charles, with their gift of organizing, planned and escorted the long ride to Fort Worth. The day was everything and more, with some of my best friends and family beside me—Nocona, Judy, Vonnie, Pam, Sissy, Anna, River, Arlene and Charlene, Trudy and Charles. Earnie, the driver, was also hand-picked and full of humor, quickly joining in with us with everything, including praying.

We quickly scoped out the limousine, finding a full bar with beautiful glasses, ice, and cold drinks. A large bottle of champagne was iced down, and snacks began appearing from everywhere. Laughter and funny stories filled the small space with Sissy later picking up momentum, entertaining us with one of our favorite conversations—herbs. It was an awesome trip!

Frances with Friends & Family on Limo Ride to Fort Worth

Just having a man for the day taking care of every detail, yet not complaining about the frequent bathroom stops, was well worth the $800.00. The P.A. kept us in touch with Earnie to communicate with him at all times. Thank God he had a good sense of humor! The stops were numerous! For so many years, my life was filled with color and drama. Why not go out with the same!

As Sissy took the floor, others chimed in, leaving me to relax and go over last-minute details, making sure I had covered everything prior to leaving. Yes, I had paid all my bills, sent off my donations to Sister Eleanor and Harriett, and gotten the letters off to all my prayer warriors, care group leaders and the Pastor of Community Church.

I desperately needed all the prayers I could get. Somehow I knew, even with God by my side, from past experiences with Him, prison would probably be full of surprises, color, and drama!

My exhaustion continued to cloud my mind, but with Trudy and Charles, the mind wasn't needed. Trudy was totally focused, ensuring all details were covered as far as getting me to the prison on time, making sure we had a comfortable hotel to stay in, and getting River to the airport on time. Not one stone was left unturned. They were definitely divinely appointed for this season.

The press called, wanting to meet us in Fort Worth. I discouraged them, convincing them there were no parties, no celebrations. Not one thing newsworthy would be happening!

Friends and family extended themselves throughout all the fourteen-year ordeal to the point where it was embarrassing for me, and had to be tiring for them. The few supporters that didn't know me as well probably thought I was thoroughly enjoying the limelight with all the press and hoopla that seemed to go with it all—but it was a total drain! I prayed hard each time the press arrived, hoping everything I said would meet God's approval and not show my hurt angry side.

There were weeks I didn't think I could handle one more moment of being the focus of anything. I longed for the one thing I enjoyed the most—yet lost with this whole ordeal—my privacy! Six months of being a total recluse would be heaven to me if they would just lock me up by myself and leave me alone!

As we drew closer to Fort Worth, we pulled over for the farewell dinner. By this time I was feeling the effects of the long trip. We had a quiet dinner, each not knowing exactly what to say. We knew it was time to say our farewells, yet how would we say them?

As with all situations, we quickly found humor with everyone gathering around the beautiful limousine, taking pictures pushing the limousine! The day ended in a prayer circle with Earnie joining in. Not only was Earnie handsome and humorous, but also quite a gentleman.

After many hugs and kisses, family and friends departed for the long trip back home, with Trudy, Charles, River and I staying behind. It was extremely hard hugging Anna. Eight long years were spent without her, and once again, another separation! We both had so much that we wanted to say, but hugged, wiped the tears, and made our farewell.

Earnie frequently called, letting us know they were all fine and had each safely arrived home.

Friends & Family Traveling to Fort Worth

River and I soon found ourselves tucked away in a hotel to regroup and have some quiet time. As I lay in bed reading, River entertained herself going through all the brochures of the city.

On the following day, Trudy, the organizer, was insistent on making a trial run to ensure we could find the prison and make River's flight. I suggested taking River to the airport beforehand, but there was no way. River was determined to see me to the finish!

Everything was now beginning to catch up with me. I was feeling totally exhausted as though I was coming down with something. This was the night before I was to experience my first day in prison, and it wasn't looking good. My health was giving way. Right before I went to bed, I called Todd to let him know I was doing just fine. In all truth I was feeling horrible.

I lay down and finally went to sleep, only to be awakened in the middle of the night by what felt like strep throat. I had mentioned my throat did not feel right to Sissy before she left, with her recommendation being tea tree oil. I did exactly as she said, and woke up feeling great!

We were up early and, praise God, I was spiritually strong and physically much better. It was like a miracle! I may have reeked with tea tree oil, but I felt ready!

River JoNey & Frances Traveling to Fort Worth

Seashell Prisoners
CHAPTER 23

JANUARY 5, 2004, CARSWELL PRISON—FORT WORTH, TEXAS

Trudy and Charles were prompt in picking us up. I was, for the final time, Queen for the Day! For lunch I was taken out to an elegant restaurant and the food was wonderful. After we ate we slowly made our way to the prison. With each mile, silence dominated the air space. No one seemed to have words for the moment. A few more miles and we would be inside the main entrance and entering a small metal building.

As we made our way into the building, I immediately looked around the room. Everything was totally different from what I had imagined. As I looked to the side there were young ladies crying as they prepared to leave their children and husbands. I looked up to see River JoNey totally focused on one of the young girls watching her as though it were her. I patiently waited my turn to speak to the officer in charge. I grimaced as the officer immediately requested my social security card and driver's license. One of my huge accomplishments after arriving back to the States was acquiring these cards, and now I was once again relinquishing them.

The officer's questions were simple and to the point. It was now my turn to walk away from family and freedom. My farewell to River, Trudy, and Charles was short. I knew I had to take it from here. I hugged everybody one last time. As I turned to walk off, I glanced back at River once again. She was totally distracted as her eyes stayed focused on one of the young girls as she handed her baby to her mother and husband, and then made her exit to the prison entrance. It was intense and extremely sad.

&

My warm fuzzy surroundings full of friends and family quickly diminished as we made the walk towards the main prison entrance. It was cold and wet with an added chill as we were ushered past a fifteen-foot chain-link fence with barbed wire topping it off. We were quickly led into a long hallway with rooms leading off each side. Everyone was quiet as we waited to hear the next order. Within minutes we were called into another room. One at a time we were told to strip, and one at a time we were searched. I was watching intensely as the officer handed each of us uniforms, with one of the girls being handed a green uniform. It was evident green uniforms would not be going to the same place we were. Someone noticed my concern and whispered, "That lady is going to the camp."

The rest of us were given khaki slacks with brown T-shirts. Right off they were rushing us from one room to another, not allowing anyone to ask questions. I had no choice but to go forward with everyone else. I was in deep thought the whole time, wondering why I was not separated out and on my way to the camp. Why didn't I get the green uniform?

We were dressed, shackled, and led to a small, dingy, holding room with no bathroom facilities. There was no place to sit down so we all leaned up against a table. The lady in the green uniform was nowhere to be seen. I looked down at my shackles as we waited for the officer to return. The moment was tough for all of us. Each of us continued looking at each other, not knowing what to expect next. An overwhelming sensation came over me, once again reminding me of my arrival to the States and the jails. Tears began to flow as I became unnerved, not knowing what was to take place.

Reality slowly began to kick in full force. I now had no control! It was only a small taste of what I would soon realize prison was all about, zero control of your life and zero control of your mind! It was as though they dismember your brain from your head at the entrance, leaving only room to comprehend their daily commands and the mental and emotional pain from the new existence. My life and my mind were totally in their hands and now considered of no value. No one cared that I was an outstanding citizen, good mother, and grandmother. Nothing meant anything to them except they were in control, and I wasn't.

Within a short length of time, we were each placed separately into maximum-security cells, normally used for the discipline of inmates. There were two bunk beds on each side of each tiny, dark cell, with three feet in between the beds. The commode was sitting in the open at the end of the bed. These cells were referred to as the SHU, with every inmate dreading to hear that word.

Two ladies lay on the bunks, giving me their prison welcome. One looking up boldly asked, "Weren't there any black girls?"

From listening to their conversation, they had gotten into fights on the main compound over their girlfriends and were now being disciplined. I was a quick learner. If you wanted food, you would have to quickly make your way to the large iron door as the officers shoved food in between the bars. It was real simple—if you didn't show up, you didn't get food. If anyone had to leave the cell, everyone was handcuffed before they would open the door. Our entire day was spent in this tiny space with nothing to look at, but each other.

My mind was racing as to what went wrong. I knew I was sentenced to the most minimum security, which was the camp. I thought somehow they had made a mistake. I saw an officer pass the tiny window. I asked if he would please check my sentencing paperwork in an attempt to explain that my judge had sentenced me to the camp. The large man hollered, "Ma'am, your judge is a liar."

I asked him if I might call my attorney, but there was no response other than the sound of his footsteps as he continued walking down the hallway.

I immediately made my way to the top bunk in hopes of dropping off to sleep and waking up back home! The three other cellmates continued with their conversation, having no problems expressing their lifestyle.

There was no pillow. The harder I tried to go to sleep, the more difficult it became. I was needing to use the commode, but holding off as long as I could. The younger lady acknowledged me, but the thick heaviness surrounding both of them shouted their strong personalities and different lifestyles. Every inch of strength that I may have had, spiritual or otherwise, was no longer present. I couldn't feel anything, nor could I seem to pray. I was shutting down. I knew deep down God still had His eye on me despite the huge void and emptiness I was feeling.

The next day the cell door opened. My name was called out. Yes! Yes! I was excited, knowing they had realized their error and I would be taken to the camp. I quickly turned as they began handcuffing all of us. I was definitely ready to leave this horrible place! I was excited as they escorted me two cells down, only for the bars to open once again. Within seconds, I was back in the same type of cell, only with different women. I looked down to see a large mattress on the floor and an even larger lady named Ellis standing to the right of it. Few words came from either women in the room, but it was evident if I wanted the mattress on the bed; I would have to move it myself. I saw the same disappointing look from them. I was definitely not the right color nor type they anticipated. One thing was for sure, it was evident I was not going to get special treatment from them.

I climbed up to the top bunk. As I made my bed, I glanced over to the bed across from me and noticed a young lady. She was unusually quiet and appeared to be despondent and depressed. I sensed she was happy to see me. As I glanced up the second time, I saw a slight smile, so I asked her name. Her name was Gayle.

Ellis carried a countenance that maybe she had total control of wherever she might be, and this small cell was definitely her turf. She was in the SHU for getting into a fight with her girlfriend, Alloni. Alloni was small in stature and a black belt. Ellis was to be in the SHU until they transferred her to another prison. She had been in and out of the SHU many times, so Carswell obviously had all they could handle with Ellis.

I finally fell asleep from exhaustion. Late in the night I was awakened by Ellis quietly talking with her friend about her family. Something deep inside began nudging me to get down and join in. I thought, *This is crazy*, but within minutes I made my way down to the bottom bunk.

Ellis was in an unusual mood. At first I sat and listened, then I began to share my life experiences and testimony with them. It was all kind of strange and just came out, obviously having nothing to do with my strength. They were intrigued and listened intently. I guess I just didn't look the type for the unusual story I was telling.

I explained some of the things that had happened to our family and how God had brought us through this whole thing. As I finished my testimony I asked if anyone wanted to join hands and pray. It took them a little off guard, but Ellis was the first to join hands. Within seconds, Gayle made her way off the top bunk and joined the three of us.

Ellis sat back down on her bed, but the Holy Spirit was obviously not through. My last words to Arlene continued to surface; stay focused, do exactly what God wants so He will get me out of here hopefully in one piece! Now an even stronger urging prompted me to ask Ellis if I could pray with her again. The two of us sat quietly by her bed praying together about her personal walk with God. The Lord was giving me words for this lady and I poured them on her with boldness. I felt a high calling on Ellis's life and I was not to leave her until I told her. I knew this had to be the Holy Spirit because my mind and body was void of all life, with total fear of this whole new environment and especially this tough lady I was now facing. Just as I got up from her bedside, an officer passed by. Praise God! I was told I could have been in even more trouble for sitting on Ellis's bed.

On the fifth day, Ellis began to get concerned about me. I was not handling the tiny enclosed environment well. I saw a guard go by and inquired once again when I would go to the compound. The burly officer stated there was another busload of women coming in from Oklahoma, and they would go before me. I began to cry. My mental state was once again crumbling with the small surroundings and just the lack of not knowing what lay ahead. I had always disliked a closed-in feeling, and this was now my fifth day.

All of a sudden, I heard Ellis boldly holler at the officer, "The lady needs a room!" I was in total shock!

Ellis had obviously been a problem in the main compound, but she had gained respect in the SHU, earning the title of custodian. Thanks to Ellis, once again my name was called out. This time it was to go to the main compound. Nothing could have made me happier! I jumped up as though it was an invitation to dinner! Strangely enough, the ladies gave me a hug as I left. I let them know I would be praying for them.

ॐ

Once I was released from the SHU, I was given an ID card. I remember looking at it intensely as I walked the long hall down to the compound. The picture was horrendous looking! I looked at it thinking, *That Is Me?* Despite my numbness to everything, vanity continued to hang on.

I was soon placed in one cell, and by the time I made the bed and put my things up, I was assigned to go to another cell. As I was making my bed for the second time, I looked around for my ID. I couldn't find it! The ID is like losing your passport in a third-world country. The officer had cautioned me when she handed it to me.

I thought all hell was going to break loose when the female officer from Two North found out. That seemed to be the highlight of her day, making sure I knew how low and ignorant I was for losing it. Along with her scolding, she added a long list of other rules that seemed to fly right over my head. I slowly made my way off to the side and sat down in a chair by the door. I was totally overwhelmed with tears flowing once again. I thought there is no way I am going to make it here. Where are all those people that said God was sending me here?

I looked up to see this large African-American inmate looking down on me, smiling. She patted me on the arm and said, "It's okay." She told me her name was Miss Gail. It soon became evident she was well known throughout the prison. Miss Gail was a wonderful person, but she could also be your best friend or your worst enemy. It was all according to how you treated her. It didn't take long to see she had everyone's respect.

Miss Gail pointed out that my caseworker was down the hall and stated that he was nicer than the others. I was now being escorted down the hall to my caseworker, Mr. Derrick. Drying my tears, I quickly explained to him my problem. Mr. Derrick momentarily let down his rigid demeanor and instructed me as to how to remedy my problem.

As I walked out, tears began to flow again at the thought that someone here actually acted like a human being. I knew I would only see him for less than a few minutes a month. Leaving him was like leaving Mom on the first day of school!

On the following day I noticed a sign on a door stating *Counselor*. I thought, *Praise God! Wow, they actually have people here to help with our concerns!* As I drew close to the door, the tall masculine lady sitting at the desk glared at me as though she would attack if I took one step closer towards her office. I slowly backed away from the door. I soon learned this officer was the last person to seek help from. The name *Counselor* was strictly a name plate. Her salary was obviously drawn for her ability to do paperwork or possibly her inept ability to stare people down.

I was now in what was called the high rise on the second floor of Carswell Prison adjacent to the hospital. Two North as it was referred to was an immaculately clean compound housing 200 women on the upper floor and 200 on the bottom. The cells were the same size as the SHU, holding four women to each cell. There were no doors on the cells and no exposed commode in the cell. At least you could see out in the other part of the compound and the bottom floor. There were at least fifteen hundred women in this prison with the hospital next door to the high rise.

I met a few Christian women in my compound. Ninety percent of the inmates were in a gay lifestyle. Many problems arose from it. The same heaviness I came to know lurked throughout every building. Some inmates entered in already in a gay lifestyle, but most within weeks out of loneliness and depression quickly made the transition.

The majority of the population was Spanish with the rest being African-American, white and Indian, etc. The prison remained maxed my entire stay. Most were between the ages of thirty to thirty-five.

As I looked out the small window, I saw that it overlooked the high-security facility with hardened criminals. They had a very small outdoor area where you seldom saw anyone present. I definitely wasn't in the camp, but it was a huge step up from the SHU.

&

I soon found my biggest problem lay with my title, International Parental Kidnapper. It was like a red flag drawing attention to the Bureau of Prisons (B.O.P.). I would have to adjust to what the B.O.P. considered equal punishment, despite my judge's orders.

As I met with them, I became disturbed at their comments concerning my sentencing. I sat respectfully as they spoke. No one told me the prison system could overrule a Federal Judge's decision and place me anywhere they wished. As they harshly judged me, I began to explain the background knowledge of the case versus the B.O.P's lack of knowledge. With each day, they stuck to their decision. I would stay in the compound and not go to the camp next door.

On the next visit with the B.O.P. I listened intently as they once again went over my case for the final time. I saw they were not going to release me to the camp. I then felt the need to tell them there was talk when I left a Federal Judge from our area stepped down from his position because of the very disrespect they were getting. Surprisingly, they quietly listened and didn't appear to take offense.

&

I soon learned there were many hardships being in prison. The worst was the officers' lack of patience and coldness that seemingly ran through all their veins. The place was run very military style. As all prisons, there were enormous problems with so many human beings caged up in small areas. I'm not sure if the officers were trained to act the way they did, or if it was more man's natural instinct and deep desire to be in control. Regardless, it wasn't good.

There was no space to call your own in the compound, no place to relax and just be to yourself or read and collect your thoughts. Every inch of you was monitored and under the constant watchful eye of uniformed officers or cameras, whether you were sleeping or eating.

Intense tutoring preceded my trip to prison by compassionate friends and my attorney on all the do's and don't's in prison. The one that puzzled me the most was, "Be a fly on the wall and draw as little attention as possible." This definitely was not my personality, but I knew their intensity in making the statement, so it must have great depth. It didn't take weeks nor a degree to soon figure this one out. Almost daily someone was going to the SHU. The officers were loud and so were some of the inmates. The less the officers knew about you, the less apt you were to be called by name and get into trouble.

Ninety percent of the inmates seemed to be limited in verbal skills. All their sentences started and ended with what kids call the F-word. I lay in bed night after night, wondering why God would drop me off in this Sodom and Gomorrah. Each morning as I awoke, I remembered how devastating it was when my eyes opened and I realized I was still in prison.

꽃

Back home, conversations were never about prejudice, but here it was of major importance to many of the inmates and officers. When Black History month approached, I didn't think it would ever end. There were plays, pictures on the walls, and all television and all programs were on the violence of the past. Everyone referred to it as being important in keeping up with their cultural history. Regardless, it had an intense way of adding to the heavy depression and darkness that surrounded each day.

I was now receiving an education in more ways than one. I knew only from history books that prejudice against blacks ran rampant at one time, but now it was in my face daily. Mauriceville didn't have that many African Americans, but the ones we had worked hard and were greatly respected. They were welcome in my home at any time and were always at the crawfish boils or New Year's Eve parties we gave. They were like family and, at times, helped me with making sure the girls got to their rodeos and horse shows.

I continued to wonder when would we just all come together and work towards the same goal! When would people realize that we are all going through attacks from someone or something. White people are attacked daily by white people. Blacks and Mexicans are daily attacked by their own culture. Whether you're Jew or Gentile, greed, prejudice, bullying, rape, crime and injustice don't really have a color or a culture. I continued to think, *If we could all just get the "love conquers all" scripture down, and drop the bitterness, hatred, and abuse from the past!*

As I observed the interaction of different cultures, I noticed how each culture is very protective of individual races. The black and Spanish cultures had very strong protective bonds for each other.

During my stay, there were three officers whose parents had obviously not transferred that bitterness on to them. This group treated us all the same. It was such a blessing being in their presence. I didn't get to see them much, because they taught classes. I just passed them in the hall occasionally at meal time. I always tried to make eye contact with them in hopes of gaining possibly a smile, a nod, or a moment of normalcy with them. Each and every day was surrounded with a feeling of hostility, so I daily searched for people that were at peace with themselves, the world, and God.

Over the fifteen years of hell with my own personal nightmare, my brain cells seemed to continue to deteriorate. I was determined to get past this. I had worked hard at being a wife, mother, and a role-model citizen. Likewise, I was determined to embrace and in like manner get through my prison stay and keep my mental state up and going. I was determined to keep my nerves intact despite my surroundings.

With each new day I knew I would be leaving this prison with many things that would be deeply engrained forever. I observed inmates as they went about their daily tasks. I couldn't comprehend the long prison terms they would be serving. Daily I searched buildings for inmates or officers that had normalcy about them. I found it harder and harder to comprehend how prisoners could be locked up for rehabilitation, yet all the officers treated us like hardened criminals—no love, no compassion, and no empathy would be found here. The few officers that would be considered role models were not around the inmates on a daily basis.

From listening to all the inmates that had frequented prisons all over the U.S., Carswell was listed at the top and definitely had the best food. Their reason seemed to be because the Medical Center was here.

Prior to my coming, the decision was passed back and forth on which prison I would go to. I knew God had divinely intervened when I walked into the dining area of Carswell and saw their huge salad bar with lots of oranges and apples. I knew I could survive! The many starchy foods were rough at times, but I was grateful daily for the abundance of salads.

Inmates were not allowed to take food back to their cells. We were all checked periodically as we exited the dining room. I never understood it, knowing all the leftover food was thrown away. Despite the rule, the inmates were unusually talented in finding hiding places getting food back to their cells. Occasionally, one would be caught, then all hell would break loose as the one went off to the SHU.

I counted my blessings daily as I reflected on the inmates in Honduras jails and prisons. How excited they would be just to have the leftovers thrown away at Carswell! The only food Honduran inmates saw was whatever their family could bring them. The rule in the kitchen was they could not reheat anything, so lots of food was thrown out at the end of each meal.

The more I came to know the ladies, the more overwhelmed I was at the fractured lives of inmates from drugs and bad choices. Probably 70–80% were drug-related. From overhearing conversations, there was a lot of built-up anger over the lengthy sentences where the men involved in the cases either got less or no time at all. Many of the women's children would be grown by the time they got out. Many were in for life! Some took the rap for their husbands or boyfriends, later finding out their mates were with other women, never sending them money. Watching women have their babies and giving them up for adoption was shocking. My mind kept searching over and over for an answer for this, but there didn't seem to be an answer.

My cell was located in Two North, making it exhausting for me to climb the stairways each day going to cafeteria, courtyard, or church services. Once I returned to the compound, then the pressure was more intense in the large compound. I was once again with an officer in my face daily. It was a twenty-four-hour, military-style presence, never relaxing for a minute. Officers were at hand at all times. With each move we made, passes had to be obtained. All had to be returned within a couple of hours.

Count times went on day and night. Two were stand-up counts with a third to ensure you were in your cell. Every inmate had to be in their own cells or they were sent to the dreaded SHU! No one ever walked inside another inmate's cell unless they were assigned to live there.

Lockdowns were frequent; most of the time we never knew what the reason was; they were always counting, making sure everyone was there. One morning there was a heavy fog, so, not being able to see the fence to guard, they instituted a lockdown. One week Federal Judges were visiting the prison so once again there was another lockdown. Officials were putting their best foot forward by locking us all up. It was obvious the fewer inmates out, the better impression it was for the judges.

❧

So many hours coupled up together made the ladies restless. All three of my roommates were strippers prior to their stay in prison. They obviously did whatever it took to get the drugs in their previous life. I was amused as they entertained themselves, acting out old barroom routines during lengthy count times. Once inmates directly across the large compound noticed them, they would join in, making sure the officers did not see their antics.

Privacy continued to be a thing of the past. There was no place to pray or relax and regroup. I was forever face to face with another inmate or officer. Learning to cope with all the personalities around me was a prison in itself, much less meeting the demands of the loud officers. In order to watch TV you had to put up with the arrogance of young, controlling women. Their lives were shattered and everyone around them would pay the price. They always had the controls to the television.

I continued to be a misfit as a whole, and that was okay. I moved out daily, knowing I was there for a short stay and I was there with a mission. Despite their arrogance or the way I was treated, I felt deep compassion for each of them. The chances of these ladies getting help were slim to none. All I saw were women falling into more complex problems as the environment continued to swallow them up in depression, with the hardness of the surroundings and loss of families and friends. The system describes it as *rehabilitation*. I often thought, *How could I shed light on this horrific situation?* Would humanity help or did they already know and choose to ignore it?

It was also obvious that many inmates didn't have support systems once they got out, or if they did, it probably wasn't the help they needed. The daily topic of conversation between inmates was trying to keep in contact with family members in different prison institutions.

༄

Each week we were given two different times to wash clothes. We had one hour and were assigned one machine. If you missed it, you were just out of luck! There was always mass confusion and arguments going on in the laundry room. One of my roommates was short on money, so I readily let her take that stressful responsibility and in exchange purchased commissary items for her. My nervous system continued to fail me, and the wash room only added to my problems. I was slow at getting all the rules and regulations—when to go and where to go, but quick to pick up when a window opened for help.

Day in and day out, the fear of catching someone else's disease also kept the arrogant inmates even more arrogant. If you accidentally touched another inmate, there could be serious repercussions from it and, once again, fights, and everyone involved went directly to the SHU.

I never saw physical abuse from an officer, but neither did I see role models in our compounds or love and compassion shown. Our officers continued to curse loud and often. The long-term inmates found it amusing to join in with them. Some officers made demeaning remarks about Christians. There were definitely favorites, but the majority of the inmates were treated as the worst criminals.

It appeared to be easier to punish all of us rather than to punish the same ones over and over. One day the vending machine was broken by an inmate. Even though they knew who it was, we were all punished by their not repairing it. If someone talked at mail call, then the officer didn't give out the mail. If a fight started in your cell, then everyone in the cell had to go to the SHU.

Mr. Cribbs with all his unusual cases and years of experience once pointed out to me that psychiatrists state that human beings can possibly get over physical abuse, but mental abuse they never get over.

I cringed as I thought of the masses of human beings in prisons around the world. I knew they daily faced mental abuse just from lack of empathy, much less other forms. I often wondered what we were creating in our prisons. Mankind is so strange. They spend countless hours on animal awareness, yet what is being done about human-being awareness in the prisons? The long sentences for simple drug charges. Would mankind even do anything if they knew? Or, as with Nocona's case, just cover it up with lengthy legal jargon, and eventually it will pass, leaving no empathy or concern for the victims being oppressed by the system! I knew there had to be a way of disciplining many of these people without taking them out of their homes, away from their families, and their jobs. I often thought of the tremendous expense for the taxpayer to now provide for housing when the inmate and their families were left without income providers. Most of these people had never physically hurt anyone.

Two North and Two South had reputations that definitely reflected the inmates. You never knew what to expect next. Daily someone was falling out with a seizure or getting into a fight. One day I was in the shower when a fight broke out on my floor. The young ladies were very loud. I froze, hoping it didn't make its way to the bathroom. Normally, it was short lived as the officers came out of the woodwork taking charge. That day, it took longer. It was on the second floor, making it more difficult for the officers to get there.

Depression ran rampant, with women attempting suicide often. Suicide watch was one of the many jobs available at the prison. The antidote for depression seemed to be strong medication which was given out to many.

Each morning I silently prayed and only spoke to other inmates as the Holy Spirit led me. My normal personality would have been extremely dangerous within this angry, hurting environment.

TV rooms were available, but the inmates were so loud and arrogant I rarely joined them. You always had to watch what the toughest person desired for the evening. One day, out of total boredom, I joined the ladies, but no one offered me a chair even though they had their feet propped up on them. I stood around for a minute, then asked very politely for a chair. No one got up. This day my patience was wearing down and I was having a problem with their disrespect. I commenced to ask one more time, very patiently. One of the nicer ladies quickly jumped up and gave me her chair as though my life was in serious danger if I would have pursued the matter.

One day I was eating in the lunch room when a lady fell out on the floor with a seizure. Within minutes another inmate ran out screaming. Officers quickly appeared, chased after her, apprehended her, and placed her in lockdown. The lockdown seemed to be the cure for everything!

Each new inmate cringed as officers assigned them difficult jobs, most being in food service, plumbing, or as an orderly. Somehow God blessed me with the easiest job there. I was only there for six months, so I was told I was already being processed out. I worked thirty minutes every evening, changing out five trash cans and putting clean liners in them. At 7 p.m., I was to join other inmates in taking the trash over to the large dumpster. I always had volunteers since inmates were looking for excuses to see their girlfriends in the SHU. The SHU was above the dumpster! Even though it was several floors up, just a small glimpse of their girlfriends seemed to give them a moment of contentment.

ð·

Many hours were spent in the small cell, with my main responsibility being to make sure we passed inspection. Everything in the cell had to be kept immaculate since officers were in and out, inspecting daily. My other roommates worked hard jobs and didn't need the extra duty and penalties bad inspections brought on us. The inspection officer was tough and delighted in finding any personal items out of place. These items were confiscated and thrown into a huge sack. The officer always laughed as she walked away, writing up bad reports. She made sure at all times our minds and lives were stressed and void of existence. So I worked hard, making sure she never found anything out of place in our cell. I detested her lack of empathy for humanity! Every day at the prison felt like a month!

Each morning, once I cleaned the tiny cell, I would face the small window overlooking maximum security. I prayed daily for all the inmates, but especially the ones in maximum security below us. My life was miserable, but I could only imagine theirs being totally shut down, with a small dog run as their only escape from their cells. Seldom did I see any of them outside. If we did see the presence of these ladies in our buildings, they were shackled down, and everyone was forced to leave the area until they were out.

From time to time they would bring someone from maximum security into our compound to live. We were not sure if they were out of room or what the reason was. We would notice a new face down below, and everyone would inquire as to who, what, and why they were there. Normally, there would be a busload entering, so we always knew she was from high security if just one appeared.

I will never forget this one small-framed lady. I noticed her on the second floor in her cell. When I asked what she was in for, they replied: "She was on a plane with a dead baby that was stuffed with drugs. The stewardess noticed there was never any movement with the baby." My mind continued to wonder, *What kind of mind would do something like that?*

These inmates normally stayed in their cells all day. One day I saw this lady in a small sitting area downstairs. I walked in and realized that she was the lady everyone was talking about. I started to leave, but then decided not to. I sat down and began to read my magazine. I observed as she was so intently coloring a picture with crayolas. I walked over and looked at it and was surprised that her actions were so childlike. As I sat and watched her, she drew and colored pictures of simple things like rainbows and the sun shining over a small house.

One morning I began to notice a horrible odor that appeared to be in our cell and surrounding me. I would wake up at night overwhelmed with the odor. I noticed it was not only around me, but on my pillow. I began to bathe several times a day trying to get the smell to leave. One day I asked Celena, one of my cellmates, if she was noticing the same thing, but she said no. I thought of Pat Martin when she and her family did ministry at the prisons. She said the presence of demons had a smell of sulfur, and that is obviously what I was smelling.

From week to week you never knew what was going to happen. After a month I was awakened by a male officer at two in the morning, loudly stating my name and number. He insisted I follow him immediately. I was still in my night clothes, yet he led me out ordering me to follow him. I was then ordered to sit down and wait outside his office. I watched him close his door and get on the phone. Totally confused, all I could think of was the horror stories you see on television. I had been told that one of the physicians was under investigation for having sex with several of the ladies prior to my coming, and one of the officers had raped an inmate. I tried to stay focused.

I was then instructed to go down the flight of stairs and outside by myself. It was dark outside with just the security lights on. As I walked down the sidewalk, another inmate joined me. We were met by another officer that instructed us that we were there to be drug tested. I actually felt a huge relief and thought, *No problem with that, unless it was in the food.* What normally came easy was now next to impossible, because the officer stood inches away, facing me, as I strived to urinate into a container.

The following day the news circulated the prison, since many were tested during the night and greatly concerned about the results. Inmates were pacing the floor. Throughout the next two days, we watched as high officials went from dorm to dorm pulling everything out of lockers. One by one, inmates were quietly taken to the SHU until further punishment was decided. Rumors were that drugs came in from friends during visitation hour. There were also rumors that officers had traded drugs for sexual favors. We never knew the truth.

During the same week at the camp across the street, inmates got busted for having a cell phone, and liquor was confiscated. The SHU once again was maxed with inmates receiving longer sentences. I compared my life here to life in a communist country, living every moment not knowing when or what time an officer would approach you, call your name, and take you off.

ða

A new face entered Two North Compound. The young lady had just gotten out of the SHU. I watched her as she walked proudly through the compound. Something deep inside was telling me it was Alloni, Ellis's girlfriend. You could hear inmates whispering as she passed, *Hey gang, she finally got out of the SHU; she's a Black Belt!* You could tell they were impressed with Alloni.

Once again, something inside of me was giving me a bold statement to relay to this girl. I thought, *Not In My Lifetime!* Alloni was a young, tough, very pretty African-American black belt! *Lord, I am staying in my comfort zone!* Up until now, I had done an excellent job being invisible, but now this same message just got stronger and stronger inside me.

I began praying daily that if God wanted me to tell Alloni anything, then He would have to bring Alloni right up to me in the cell and make me say it. I was grateful the rules were that no one was allowed to be in my cell other than the inmates assigned to it. The chances of my getting an opportunity of speaking or even passing Alloni were little to none. She was not in a cell on my floor or anywhere around us, and I would be the last person she would approach.

Alloni may have been small in stature, but she walked with an air that got my respect and everyone else's. Her head was always held high, and she dared anyone to come against her. Everyone knew her long term in the SHU would definitely put her in a bad mood.

ða

Changes were made in cellmates often. I had grown to respect the young spunky ladies, Barbara and Celina. We had shared a lot of stories. It was now time for Barbara to leave. Celina became extremely nervous at the thought of her best friend leaving. A young, dark-skinned, Haitian girl named Asmath replaced Barbara in the empty bunk. Asmath was totally to herself, extremely spoiled, and arrogant. I hung in there, comparing myself to Paul as I tried daily to find common ground with young girls. I soon found it! As the girls searched newspapers daily for guys to become pen pals, I approached them with my background in promotions. Life had become so totally boring, that I soon found myself putting together a resume that made this young Haitian sound like every man's deepest desire. We laughed as she envisioned him sending her money and living happily ever after once she departed Carswell. I was now considered cool! My approach to her problem worked, and she was receiving letters from several young men.

All the girls found many ways to cope, spending endless hours on their hairstyles, and dreaming of someone to save them from their desperation. Asmath softened, joining in with Celina and myself from time to time as we talked about God. Once she dropped the arrogance, she had a beautiful side to her, spending many hours laughing about the weird things that happened every day.

I continued to pray daily and read my Bible. From time to time Celina would join with me. It was neat. Asmath quietly listened. One day we were all laying quietly reading in our beds when Alloni walked up to the entrance of the cell. I momentarily froze, not realizing she and Asmath were friends. Alloni was standing inside the cell at the door. They began to laugh and talk. I was lying in my bunk wishing I were a million miles away. This was totally against the rules, going into another inmate's cell. No one had ever come into our cell except the inspection officer, and this could get us all in the SHU.

Then I was reminded, *Oh No, Is This God Again?* I lay in my bed as the two girls whispered over the different happenings of the day. My immediate thought was, *It sure looks like God is setting something up, and I am supposed to know what to say to this girl.* Fear was racing over me as I lay on my bed, contemplating what to do. As my mind continued to focus on fear, Alloni turned and left. I was so relieved!

The next day Alloni popped into our tiny cell once again to laugh and go over the latest wild prison stories of the day. This time she was bolder as she came on into the room. I was lying in my bed as she sat down on the tiny stool in between the beds. This put this black belt inches from my head as I lay reading. My mind raced as I wondered what God was going to do next. I thought this better be God or I am in major trouble. Within minutes Asmath exited the room.

Momentarily, it was just me and Alloni. I couldn't believe it, but I knew this had to be God. Once again, it just came out! Never ever having said a word to this young lady before, I quickly blurted out, *"God Gave Me Words For You."* I was so scared that I lay quietly, expecting her to attack me! She stared straight ahead as though she was shocked I even spoke to her. There was no major reaction, but just a quiet serious demeanor as I went forward speaking the very words God had given me for this young black lady.

I didn't have to think for one second, the words just came out. I told her, *"God said it's time for you to quit running from Him. Alloni you have been running for a long time, and it's time to stop and go forward with your walk and your purpose in life."*

She silently stared down at the floor as I spoke and didn't say a word. She had a very serious look on her face as she suddenly got up and left out of the room without a word!

I thought, *Praise God!* I felt a huge relief. I said it and I didn't even get hit or anything! I knew it had to be a God-thing, despite her lack of response. I was now excited—mostly because I was still alive, and then again wondering if she was possibly waiting for a better time to retaliate!

A couple of days went by, and once again Alloni entered the room. I froze and acted as though I didn't know she was present. I lay on my bunk reading and continued to read on. Asmath and Alloni began to talk. Alloni paused, then turned and looked over at me. I felt her eyes glaring down at me, so I looked up. She then softly stated, "Thank you for telling me. What you said is exactly what I have been doing. I have been running from God. I had a long talk with God last night, and I rededicated my life to Him once again." *It was a powerful moment! Hopefully, this was the person the prophet at Community Church spoke of prior to my arrival here. Hopefully, I would get out of this place now!*

⁂

Once you went outside the compound and outdoors, the grounds had a beautiful layout with plenty of chairs outside and a large track. Despite the large area, there was never a place to sit and read or pray, without confusion. Ladies arguing or just foul language filled the airspace wherever you went. I had met a few women that were very nice, but most of the time I sat by myself.

Miss Gail and I continued to be friends along with a few other women. We had many conversations about family and God. From time to time we prayed together. Miss Gail had been there a long time and would always fill me in when special ministries were present. She and I would also attend services together on occasion.

Miss Gail was continually surrounded with friends wherever she went and loved pointing me out, boldly stating as she passed, "This lady may appear to be alone, but honey, she is far from alone!" Then she would walk off with a big smile!

God had connected me with not only Miss Gail, but with other young Christians struggling for survival. I began to encourage them to come together once a week to have cell meetings. It had to be done discreetly since organized meetings were not allowed outside the chapel.

Prior to my coming I had heard prophecies that God would use the prison to raise up His end-time army. I could see it coming about with some of the ladies. Once they got the vision of Jesus, it turned their lives around, causing them to go forward in a positive and peaceful manner.

In one of our services we had seen a video of Joyce Meyers ministering in the Angola Prison in Louisiana. The Warden told Joyce Meyers the only change he ever saw in inmates was when they found Jesus!

I had soon gained an even deeper appreciation for television evangelists, as I attended evening services by representatives of T.D. Jakes and Kenneth Copeland Ministries once a week. I swore I would never listen to anyone that put television evangelists down again! The libraries here were full of Joyce Meyer, Chuck Swindoll, Bennie Hinn, and Tommy Tenney books along with all the other great ministries. Beautiful Feet Ministry blessed the ladies once a month as they not only ministered, but loved on the women. Touching was not allowed day to day, so each inmate had a tendency to withdraw and feel guilt as the ministry reached out to hug us. There were always lots of tears at their meetings.

Some of the ladies were getting free Bible studies and books from Joyce Meyers, Salvation Army, and the Copeland Ministry. These were truly lifesavers for the ladies that were doing them. Christian speakers, videos, and their books were like fresh oxygen pumped into the prison. It soon became evident that the only inmates that would leave the prison and not return would be the ones that had found the inner peace that came with knowing Jesus. Sad to say, the numbers were easy to count since most inmates never entered the Chapel.

Each day at a designated time, everyone would go to the bottom floor for mail time. We would all sit in a big circle and wait for our names to be called out. I was receiving a lot of cards and letters, so my name was becoming well known as each week went by. It was always sad watching so many in the circle, yet so few letters were presented.

I had made several attempts to call my attorney. It was hard using the phone, since you could only do it at certain times, and there was always a line. I finally get word to my attorney to check with the Judge and see if he could get me into the camp. I let him know I was upset and explained the camp was next door, as though they didn't know. I emphasized over and over how hard it was for me in this part of the prison.

I tried prayer. I tried everything to keep from going into depression. It continued to be overwhelming just being around so many women in such desperate states. I'd often tried to visualize hell—I thought, *This must be it!* Being next to the hospital, we saw many elderly women in wheelchairs with debilitating diseases, with no legs, or paralyzed. It all continued to play on my mind. I wondered...*Shouldn't empathy come into play somewhere with all of this at some point?* I finally scraped my nervous system together and wrote my attorney a letter, leaving nothing out to guesswork. I was now extremely upset and needed an explanation! *What happened to the camp?*

I always looked forward to Sunday when we came together in the Chapel. It was a time when we were around everyone that was seeking some form of peace whether it be from God or just time out from all the problems that went on during the week. It appeared to be a form of expression as many were in the choir and would march down the aisle on Sunday morning, singing their way to the choir loft. I always looked for Miss Gail. She could always be seen with much enthusiasm leading them off. They weren't exactly the Mormon Tabernacle Choir, but they were quite colorful and sang with a lot of soul.

I loved the young minister that taught each week. Chaplain Lee's sermons were lacking in enthusiasm, but he taught straight from the Bible and had a very humble heart. One of the last services I attended will be forever etched in my mind. The moment we all entered the Chapel, we felt an unusual presence in the air. This Sunday everyone seemed to enter in one accord. We had a tough week with many problems amongst the inmates. The Chaplain Lee was sitting in his usual front pew. For some reason, I was glancing over at him watching his expression. As the choir began to sing, I focused on Miss Gail since she was always so full of drama and amusement at times. They sang their upbeat songs as usual, then went into slower worship songs.

Suddenly, their voices were overtaken by new voices much louder and much softer. There was a hush throughout the building. It had to be angels! It was in such perfect harmony and so much more beautiful than I had ever heard at any service anywhere.

I looked back over at Chaplain Lee, and his face was frozen, yet glowing. There was an unusual hush throughout the building. Everyone there knew... *We Had An Awesome Visit By Jesus!*

It was the very thing we all needed to get by another week. As the minister made his way to the front to speak, his face continued to glow. Miss Gail and I talked about it for days! Everyone had witnessed the same thing...*Jesus Showed Up At Carswell Prison!*

MARCH 2004

I desperately waited for mail from Mr. Cribbs. I never got a reply, but within weeks I was awakened at six a.m. one morning, and told to pack out. They never said where I was going—It was just, *Pack out!*

At this point, I didn't care. I thought, anything would have to be an improvement. Tears began to fall as my fellow inmates hugged me as I made my way out of the big compound. By this time, many of the arrogant ones had softened towards me and nodded their heads and gave me the high sign, as they saw me leave the room. I soon found myself exiting the fifteen-foot chain-link fence and was on my way to the camp.

As I walked past the high fence something very strange happened. I felt this huge presence come off of me. It was like weights were taken off my shoulders as I felt this presence of demonic spirits leaving me. From that day on, I never experienced the harsh sulfur smell that I had sensed before.

❧

The camp was beautiful, a totally different environment, but the threat of lockdown continued to exist. No loud cursing, no hollering officers, no high fences. Inmates sat quietly on the outdoor benches. The camp was built next to a large, quiet lake with beautiful, large oak trees and a presence of life everywhere. Squirrels danced under the trees and ducks walked around.

The Carswell Navy Air Base was adjacent to the prison camp. Daily we could see the men and women on the track jogging adjacent to the prison. I always stopped and watched each time I heard the fighter planes taking off. I was in awe of the huge Falcon jets as they raced down the track and made their entrance into the blue clouds. That was totally exciting!

We were the first to know when our country was under high alert. Intensity at the base picked up. No one was on the track jogging. All planes were in the air.

The other prison had strict rules. If we saw an animal, we could be sure of one thing…it would be killed! The camp had its own track for jogging. There were places to sit around it. Huge oak trees surrounded it, with squirrels and rabbits racing across the lawn approaching you for food. I now had a place to escape. What an awesome blessing! I could finally get by myself and pray, write letters, and listen to Christian music on my small radio, one of the few luxuries allowed here. I spent many hours under the beautiful oak trees trying to forget the horrible memories of my new-found prison existence.

I now had a place to cry. There continued to be depressing news. Today, it was over the recent news of a young lady that had hung herself the day before I left the other facility. She had been in prison a long time and was to get out within a few days. The sick environment to some becomes a crutch over a period of time to those with long terms and no support systems on departure....

❧

Many letters continued to go out daily as I responded to the many prayer warriors around the world that never forgot me: Old dive buddies, missionaries, family, current friends and high school friends wrote. One in particular had a keen ability for humor, bringing up funny things in our childhood as we lived in Brownwood. His encouraging words were such a glimmer of life and hope in a seemingly hopeless situation. I held on to all my letters, and read them over and over.

Friends and family wanted desperately to visit, but I found myself repeating over and over—even the President of the U.S. would have problems getting past these gates! There was so much red tape I felt I would be out before anyone got approved. Despite my warnings a few went forward in an attempt to get in. The first that sent their paperwork in were accepted. Two up for visitation were Dennis and Linda Vaughn. Dennis was my Sunday school teacher in Mauriceville prior to my leaving for Honduras.

What an awesome couple and a wonderful day! The big bear hugs, prayers, and smiling faces were greatly appreciated with each visit, but obviously hard to believe by the officer. I was strip-searched after Dennis left from a later visit. With each visit, I would explain to security that Dennis was my Sunday school teacher, but his big burly hugs seemed to give a different message to the officer, who assumed we had to be up to more than just hugs!

I received a letter from my old friends, Ron and Judy, from the Island. They let me know they had driven a long way to see me and were turned down at the gate. It brought a huge smile to my face, knowing Ron's rough Island appearance, with a bandana and beard that he was famous for. Ron helped me with all my plumbing at Casa Calico, and Judy worked as a teacher in a private home school program in West End. They were both huge supporters in the Christmas on the Beach program each year, and were well known throughout the Island. Weeks later they wrote a letter to me stating that they saw the lake and wondered if the institution knew I could easily swim it! It was people like this that kept me going each day!

Anna Trudy
Frances
Rylan Brac Julian Kai Nocona

Anna, Nocona, Rylan, and Julian finally got their approval from Carswell to come for a visit. Trudy and her grandsons, Brack and Kai, joined them. I was so happy to see all of them. It was a great occasion, but I was sad when they left. Anna and Trudy looked around in awe. They couldn't believe all the inmates' appearances were just like the person you sit next to in church! I told them, "That's right. They just made a bad decision and are having to pay a heavy price."

As they left, I wondered if the kids actually knew they were inside a prison.

☙

I was grateful for the move to the camp, but anxiety kicked in, realizing I would now be reassigned another job. I prayed hard, knowing most everyone had hard jobs. I was soon placed in what was called the dish room. My heart fell as I visualized tons of huge, dirty pots and pans, and soapy water. It soon gave way to praise as it turned out I was loading the dishes onto a twenty-foot, stainless-steel dishwasher—it became a delightful escape!

Anna quickly reminded me of my love for gadgets, and we had a good laugh. Only then did I realize I had never worked for anyone! I soon found it a challenge, learning to interact and work together with others rather than be the boss!

The officers here were much better. Many enjoyed their positions being in control, but as a whole everything went a lot smoother with a strict, but more relaxing atmosphere. Every now and then the officer over the kitchen would let down his guard and join us in a humorous situation. On special occasions he would let us eat anything we wanted after we got through with our work. That was a fun day since the freezers were full of ice cream treats and unusual things we normally didn't see on the serving tables. They would also let us prepare new recipes, so I fixed the chimichurri I had learned to make on the Island. Everyone loved it and requested it often.

After a week of working in the kitchen, I desperately wanted to reorganize the kitchen operation. I struggled daily with this deep desire to simplify our work day, despite the resistance from officials in charge. We all had our struggles, but all the workers soon became some of my best friends.

☙

It was during the time I worked in the kitchen when I met Debbie. Debbie was very intelligent, independent, and quiet-mannered. She had a tough reputation and no one crossed her during my stay. She had an office job in the lunch room area and was obviously respected. I am not sure why Debbie invited me to her table. I certainly wasn't tough, and definitely no one was afraid of me. I always enjoyed visiting with all of her friends.

I had met another young lady in the lunch room that was a scuba diver. We would get off by ourselves and laugh about the big lake they had on the side of the compound, knowing our ability to swim it.

God continued to connect me with many women, praying, encouraging, and uplifting them as God gave me words. My Bible quickly filled with names and numbers of women to pray for in hopes of eventually getting back with them after I left, for instance, Loretta, Vickie, Sheila, Elsa, Rosa, Music, Lina, Shelia, and Kathy. There were many.

All the Christians were young in their search for God. Not one was a mature Christian! What I needed desperately was a good prayer warrior to pray over me like Ms. Ruth or Ma Gibbons.

I soon found one of the ladies I worked with was in Tapachula, Mexico, the same time we were. I marveled at her as she walked ten miles a day on the track in an attempt to lose weight and keep her mind off her extended sentence. Once she realized my stay was short-term, she came over and thanked me, stating that with each lap around the track she felt a strong presence of God as she passed me. She said, "I knew you must be praying or reading your Bible."

❧

Many inmates were on strong anti-depressant drugs which were reacting with many mood changes. I often felt the prison was giving them out in an attempt to keep everyone calm. I was having my own problems with nerves, but I didn't dare complain. I didn't want the after-effects I was seeing with many inmates.

One lady in particular, named Kathy, struggled with her nervous system as she grieved over the absence of her small children and older daughter. Kathy's daughter was having her first baby, and it was tough not being there. Kathy and I spent time together and sometimes prayed together. As I would pray we could both feel this strong presence coming off of her. I made sure she understood what it was, and she felt instant peace as a result. I encouraged her to continue studying God's Word and seeking Him.

Kathy was a wonderful young lady, but her life had been full of drugs and personal failure prior to her arrival. I was determined to keep them focused on the only Person that would be there with them always, and that was Jesus—not me! I knew He would be there when no one else was there, and He was the only one with power.

❧

Lockdown was once again announced. On that day, it was bad weather. No one said anything. The officers told us to go to certain floors. They were expecting a tornado. The winds picked up and, sure enough, limbs and branches were flying past the windows. It was the first tornado I had ever experienced, but almost everything was okay afterwards.

The prison continued to stay maxed out, despite a few leaving each month. It was great seeing women going home, but the glad moment was quickly replaced with sadness as another big bus rolled in from Oklahoma each week to fill the empty rooms. Carswell was always maxed out.

⁂

The rooms in the camp were like small hotel rooms. Most had five women, all in bunk beds. We had a private bath to each room. We had more space than the other facility. But every room was struggling with all the different personalities. The blacks hated the cold air-conditioning, and the whites were hot-natured. Most of the time, the one that arrived in the room first ruled the room, and no one usually crossed her.

There were two African-Americans and one white lady in my room. Myisha, the youngest girl, let us know right off she was in control of the room. Kisha, another African-American that shared our room, didn't see color, but Myisha daily showed disrespect, doing her best to intimidate myself and Margie, the lady on the top bunk above me.

Kisha quickly became one of my closest friends in the prison system. She had high morals, a gift of humor, and a lot of integrity despite her bad decision. We shared a lot with each other since we were both deeply involved in family, friends, and God. Kisha had held a high position in her job prior to her life here and was very business-minded. We talked about God and both seemed to be on the same level. One would never suspect her to be in a prison. Actually, most of the women there you would not relate with prisons. Kisha often reminded me how grateful she was that we had been roommates.

Myisha was very pretty and smart, but clung to her prejudice daily and was extremely haughty.

Margie's disposition was different, taking a lot of flak from Myisha, but I continued to hold my ground. I did my best to ignore Myisha's arrogance and controlling nature, and avoided her as much as possible. After several months it grew old, with Myisha pushing her authority more and more. Myisha and I had words on several occasions. We had been told by the officers to keep the rooms cold to hold down bacteria. Myisha insisted the rooms be hot. The A/C was by my bed so I would turn the temperature down each night. The closer it came to Kisha's departure, the more arrogant Myisha became. One could tell she was deeply concerned as to who might replace Kisha, since she could possibly lose power once Kisha was gone. Kisha was the only one in the room that Myisha tried to have a relationship with. I was now learning the word prejudice first hand, but not as the textbooks taught.

One evening I was tired and not ready for Myisha's arrogance. I finally told Myisha face to face she had best not touch the A/C dial, nor was she to speak to me in a derogatory manner. I reminded Myisha that I was raised to have respect for people, and she should respect me not only because I was another human being, but because I was much older than she. Kisha and Margie looked on, waiting for Myisha's reaction. You could cut the tension with a knife, but Myisha turned over and went to sleep.

❧

The camp was definitely its own Venus flytrap, having its own problems. The officers were more relaxed at the camp, but still lacking in compassion as a whole. They had their own set of rules and everyone as a whole worked hard meeting their daily demands.

The administrator of the camp, Miss Kranton, was tough and was outfitted daily with men's attire, even to her hat. All but a few of the officers met her every whim, one going as far as making up things against the inmates to impress her. One attempt was made against me prior to my leaving. I confronted the male officer about it in a nice manner just to let him know, *We may be inmates, but we were not animals nor were we ignorant.*

Once a year they had a family day. Every inmate looked forward to it, inviting their families. It was a full day together. I observed the inmates' children and families as they arrived from different states. Never did I see the officers approach the families with an introduction or a kind word. I witnessed the lack of organization of visitation and family days by the officers. Many families were turned away after long hours of travel, preparation, and anticipation to get there. The officers didn't process everyone in quick enough for them to get in, so they had to return home, with some driving a long distance.

The problems of the prison system were vast, yet few would ever know about them. All were being neatly tucked behind the walls of the prison!

❧

My departure date was now set up with Miss Kranton for my release. As the administrator questioned me, she was totally confused at the number of people that were making arrangements to pick me up. She kindly informed me of the normal procedure of one person or two at the most. She later stated she didn't look for it to be a problem.

I wanted to blurt out, *It would be a whole busload if I thought it wouldn't slow me down getting out of this awful place!* I desperately wanted all my friends and family to share this special day with me. I didn't dare make the phone call to ignite this response, since I knew it could delay or cancel my departure with the strict procedures of entry. The prison system was clueless as to this being such a grand event in our lives. I always said with all humility,

"Whatever affects you affects everyone around you." I definitely wanted everyone to enjoy the fruit of years of prayer and individual efforts.

July 2nd couldn't come quick enough for me! Kisha packed out two weeks before I was to leave. She laughed as I jumped up and commenced to do the same. I just had to do something, I was so excited. I would be next! I was past ready to get out of the coldness and lack of life in the prison system. As much as I strived to be the wall flower, it just wasn't working.

One of the officers had failed to post my payment on fines. They were taking the money out of my commissary account, sent in by friends and family: A total of $335.00. I had given them several months, but the money never appeared in my account. Inmates kept telling me that if I didn't push them I wouldn't get it back. Realizing I would be leaving soon, I approached a higher authority, which didn't set well with the camp administration. From there on, the vibes were not good, with subtle remarks and glares being thrown at me during the week, then later at my last team meeting. I knew by the uncalled-for remarks by my caseworker that I was leaving just in time.

I prayed and prayed before my last meeting, sensing it was going to be rough. For some reason I was always called last. As I entered the room once again, it was as though my very presence was stressing the officers in charge. As I sat down at the table I felt a heaviness in the room. I knew the importance of being humble as I looked at each person sitting around the table. No one made eye contact with me as though I wasn't there or didn't exist. I stayed in total control, taking all their remarks without becoming upset, not wanting to do anything that might delay my departure.

My caseworker at one point quickly flipped her head towards me, asking if I had a problem being in the room with them. Shocked at the remark, I quickly looked around the room at each person present to see why they were stating that. I replied, "I don't have a problem with anyone. I'm just ready to get out and get on with my life."

I knew whatever she said had to be an attack over my attempt to recover my money, or about one of the officers lying about me. I remained calm and focused, answering all their questions as though I were not offended.

It was definitely time for me to get out of Carswell! I struggled with many things, one being the institution going out of their way to please all religions. I knew it had to be a law, but shouldn't there be a limit when they were spending taxpayers' money to build a place for demon worshippers? These people were divisive and had no plans of contributing anything morally good to anyone other than their cult.

Our laws need to define religion, and religion should not be an organization that would in any form or fashion be a threat to other citizens or our country.

Kisha was now gone and the days got longer. Each day seemed like a month as I patiently counted the hours until I would get the report to go to R&D: A notice on the callout sheet every inmate desired to see. This meant, *You Were Leaving!* I quickly put numbers on a lot of papers and had a drawing amongst the inmates. I gave everything away out of my locker down to my watch. It was like a game, and everyone loved it!

Prior to my job ending, Rosie, Vicky, and Elsa gave me the traditional last-day farewell in the dish room. Catching me totally off guard, I was soaked from head to toe with all the sprayers as I tried to make my way out at the end of the shift. The night before I left, the ladies I worked with gave me a private going-away party. I was always in awe at their creativeness with so little, but they did an awesome job with things from the kitchen somehow appearing in the refreshments they served everyone.

After my going-away party, I slipped over to spend the last hour with a couple of my other friends, Kathy and Loretta. By this time it was evident why God had sent me to this place. We joined hands in a prayer circle, and then I reminded Kathy of the medication. She looked me in the eye with a big smile, stating, "I'm already off the strongest drugs. The physician said I didn't need them anymore."

I approached each person God had connected me with, making sure they knew how honored I was to have met them. Throughout my stay I was daily graced with beautiful remarks from inmates for encouraging and uplifting them. I desperately wanted them to know how they had blessed my life with their friendship.

The day before I was to leave, news was out that someone was in the SHU. It was all very strange since this was that inmate's day to leave the prison. The lady was in a unit down from me and had been waiting for years to get out. She had gone through every step in her release and was packed out. She made her way to the main office as her family waited on her paperwork to be completed, only to get the horrible news she would not be released! The family had to turn around and go back home. The inmate collapsed and was placed in the SHU. The news spread throughout the camp, making everyone nervous as to who would be the next to be turned down on their departure.

JULY 2, 2004

The big day finally arrived! All my prison friends were excited and trying to make arrangements to be close by to see me off. It was a tradition to walk your friends down the sidewalk to a certain point. Loretta was the first at my door to help me collect all my things and help me take them over to R&D. I had previously hugged friends and given all my farewells, but some came by, hugging me as they made their way to their jobs. Some were anxiously waiting to walk me as far as they could across the grounds. My clothes arrived that Arlene had sent for me to wear home. I didn't take into consideration I had gained a few pounds. I quickly resolved the dilemma since I may have looked like a hussy leaving out in my tight jeans, but at this point I really didn't care! As I made my official walk, other friends were passing, bidding me farewell as they went to their jobs.

Kathy then heard the infamous announcement...*Compound Closed!* Loretta and Kathy's faces fell, realizing they wouldn't be able to finish the traditional last-day walk with me. I breathed a sigh of relief, as it seemed to be the door to escape the long, sad goodbyes. I gave Loretta, Kathy, and Emma one more hug, then watched them go to their rooms.

Bonnie, another inmate, was leaving for the halfway house on the same day. As I was walking off, I looked back towards the lunchroom and all my co-workers were waving me good-bye. My brain was kicking in—I was truly leaving! My feelings were mixed with so much joy yet so much sorrow, leaving all these women behind.

Loretta hollered, "We will all be looking out the window, so give us the high sign as you drive off."

As Bonnie and I made our walk across the long sidewalk together, she told me about her background as a stripper. She said she'd found God while in prison. She noticed my red lipstick and requested to use it. I told her she could have it. As she painted her lips, she began to step a little taller in her tight black pants and T-shirt, revealing her stomach. The guard told her to cover her stomach until she cleared the fence, and laughed, knowing her background.

Once we got to the main office, Bonnie realized they were not going to pay her last wages, leaving her without enough money to go to the halfway house! Bonnie began to panic, and her officer became stressed, so I turned and slipped Bonnie some money. The officer rolled her eyes and turned her head, but had a look of gratefulness that the problem was solved so quickly.

Anna & Frances
Carswell Prison Release

The release only took a few minutes as they handed me my personal items. I looked around to see Anna, Nocona and friends with huge smiles. We all embraced. I hugged Anna. As I looked up, huge tears were flowing down her face. I was still numb and anxious to get beyond the gates. I knew my release was not complete until I passed those huge iron gates. I would not relax until I cleared the Carswell Prison and Forth Worth!

There were no words to express my emotions at that moment! As we stepped into a big dually and drove off, we all rolled down the windows and gave the high sign as we passed the prison camp. I saw the ladies waving. I felt so blessed in so many ways. It was awesome leaving, but it was humbling to first-hand witness that awful state of life, or rather lack of it. No one in a thousand years could have portrayed such a life to me without my being a part of it, first-hand!

※

I had totally exhausted myself from anticipation of clearing the prison walls and being back to normalcy. Family, friends, animals, anything that had a feeling of life, a future, or a positive nature had been put on hold for six months. By the time we arrived home, I was ready to collapse!

I couldn't help but laugh as I saw fireworks going off as we drove up to my sister's house. How creative of my sister! It was great seeing everyone. Freedom felt wonderful, but quickly became overwhelming!

I made my greetings, eventually slipping off into my bedroom to lie in my bed. The next morning, my first thoughts were to check the refrigerator for fruits, nuts, vegetables, and anything with life! As soon as everything was clear with my probation officer, I raced to the grocery store, loading up my basket with everything that looked green!

Once again another party was quickly put together; I assumed it was my prison homecoming party. Fifty friends gathered at Sartin's Restaurant in Beaumont, Texas, and celebrated the long-awaited end to our dilemma. As everything else in my life, it had its own story with another new beginning!

With each victory over the years, I had purchased a little present for myself. With Nocona's assistance, I soon purchased a little, black, spunky puppy, a porch swing, and a new Scion—all of which I felt, each in its own way, would be a small beginning, once again, in pulling my life back together.

Treasures of wickedness profit nothing,
But righteousness delivers from death. Proverbs 10:2

Seashell Prisoners
Conclusion

I think Anne Graham Lotz best captured my feelings on life after death… not a physical death, but death to the old…Frances Collins, and now life once again…as I now look at it. Not through my rose-colored *me, myself, and I* glasses, but through the way God originally intended for it to be.

Through my deep search for life's meaning, I've read many awesome books by very anointed men and women of God. As I began to settle in at my sister's house once I was released from prison, I picked up a book a dear school friend gave me by Anne Graham Lotz. It was the first book I had read of hers, but I think it best explains my new view of life and the world in terms of the God that our American forefathers fought and died for.

In Anne Graham's book, *Just Give Me Jesus*, she quotes:
"If you are questioning the sufficiency of God's power to resolve your problems and pressures, your suffering and stress, (or) your crisis and change, His answer is the same. The infinite power of the Living Logos of God is adequate for any need you or I will ever have."

We may intellectually grasp the truth that God's power is adequate, but we can never know that by experience if we stay in our comfort zone. If all you ever attempt is what you know you can do yourself, if all your needs seem to be met through someone or something other than God, if you never have any difficulties that are greater than you can bear… how will you know the awesome greatness and personal availability of His infinite power? It's when the Red Sea is before you, the mountains are on one side of you, the desert is on the other side, and you feel the Egyptian army closing in from behind that you experience His power to open up an escape route. Power to do the supernatural, the unthinkable, the impossible!

The three very things I vowed I would never do:

1. I would never raise my grandkids.
2. I would never live in Honduras.
3. I would never have a resort.

All three are the very things God used to turn me around so I might truly know Him. In Matt.16:15, when Jesus asked Peter, "Who do you say that I am," I too can now answer that question correctly. I probably would never have known the answer without going through this experience. I would never have come to know Jesus personally without this experience. I am so grateful I kept my eyes on Him and not the situation engulfing our lives.

Every day, God is doing such neat things as He is pulling my life back together—this time, with Him at the helm. My life, now totally different, is richer with purpose and anticipation for each day.

Yes, this life of mine and my family was shattered from this now fifteen-year struggle. We have physical, mental, emotional and financial scars as a result. All of these will take many years to heal. Maybe some will never heal, but the one thing I know for certain that I know—we each have a plan, a purpose, and a planned destiny. The God we serve can do all things, so as God's children, "We can do all things through Christ that strengthens us" (Phil. 4:13).

Nocona asked me a question recently: "What were the two things that happened in your life that made the biggest change in you?"

I didn't have to even think about it. My answer was: "Living in Honduras eight years, and going to prison." As difficult as each was, I wouldn't take anything for the lessons learned and the growth that came about through the whole experience. Along with my previous fifty years, it made me who I am today...a much better person!

I feel through great pain and suffering, I was taken on an extraordinary and amazing treasure hunt, and at the end I found the treasure...JESUS!

In 1994, the Orange County Sheriff made a statement to the press that if I did not return with Nocona,...they would have me back in their custody within a week. Nocona remained in the country of Honduras for eight years until September 24, 2002, the year God prepared her to stand on her own two feet.

In 1995, an F.B.I. agent stated to me via telephone conversation that if I did not turn myself in, they would apprehend me immediately. Six years later, Nocona and I were still in Honduras!

Also in 1995, the same F.B.I. agent stated I was facing a life sentence for International Parental Kidnapping.

In 2002, upon my arrival to the U.S., the same statement was made in the Federal Court and later by a public defender—that I was facing a Life Sentence for International Parental Kidnapping.

In 2003, a judge and two attorneys stated that I would never see or talk to Nocona again! By August of 2004, Nocona was once again living with me.

In October of 2003, I was sentenced to a total of seven months in prison and seven months of home confinement.

※

River JoNey Burton, Nocona's mother, repeatedly had custody taken away from her when we left the U.S. in 1994, yet in May of 2005 it was returned to her, and Nocona's father relinquished all his rights to Nocona.

※

Satan made three different attempts to kill Nocona and one attempt to steal her from God's hands. Nocona is now twenty years old, and remains a vibrant, happy young lady enjoying living in the U.S.

Nocona has interpreted for churches on mission trips and served as a Levite counselor at Camp His Way. She enjoys playing golf and loves Jesus!

Nocona is in her second year of college, but returns to Honduras each year to enjoy the place she considers her home, and the many relationships she acquired during her eight years of living on the Island of Roatan.

Nocona now returns to Roatan and volunteers her time wherever needed. In the year 2010, she helped out at Peggy's Clinic, children's Christmas parties in various villages, and First Baptist Church of West End.

Nocona's mother, River JoNey Burton, went on to graduate with honors from Lamar State College, Texas A&M, and the Bush School of Government and Public Service.

※

Would I ever go to this length again? In a heartbeat, but only with God's leading! There's man's laws and God's laws, both of which I deeply respect and am fearful of ignoring. When you know you're following God's leading, you never go wrong, and awesome things come about as a result. I truly know for certain that I know, that as I stumbled through sixteen years of pain, agony, heartache, and tears, keeping my focus on Jesus, awesome things came about in the spiritual world. I can truly say I witnessed the power of Almighty God.

I allowed myself to be used by God and now have a better understanding of destiny; one of which many never venture to receive. I witnessed the supernatural. I learned God cannot be self-contained or, as some say, put in a box. He is Almighty God and there are no limitations on what He can do.

Because He is God, He can do what He wants when He wants. As a result of my submission to Him, I walk with my head held high. People approach me with a different kind of respect than the old Frances Collins Harris. I am now on a new platform and seeking more each day. Only the Most High God, Jesus Christ, could have turned this around!

Since I made the decision in 1994 to step out of my comfort zone and keep my focus on Jesus, I came to know a new man in my life (Jesus), a new country (Honduras), and new people that greatly extended my family.

Nocona and I now return with great enthusiasm to Roatan, Honduras, each year, enjoying friends around the Island that we came to know and love in our eight years of living there. I also return each year to see with great anticipation what God is doing. I always return home blessed!

&

Just as I placed my life and my family's lives in God's hands, the same I do with this book. I wait with great anticipation to see come forth what the Holy Spirit repeatedly spoke in me seventeen years ago. This book—this story—is a message to people around the world. I only repeated that to a few people in 1994 because it appeared so out of context and impossible at the time. Now it appears quite clear and simple. I now have a testimony and I use it as frequently as possible.

I continue to seek God daily and realize there's so much more available to anyone that desires it. I now realize I can hear from Him daily and feel His presence. It's just a matter of taking the time and listening.

I know that every part of me belongs to Him. I not only focus on feeding my spirit the right food daily (Bible), but also practice feeding my physical body the right food, so I can continue to tap into the destiny God planned for me thousands of years ago.

&

As far as the many paid professionals that should have stepped up to the plate and who had the opportunity to help an innocent child and her mother, I pray for you and the many others around the world. I only hope you one day reconsider and realize the consequences of your daily actions and the impact on the lives you represent. From many years of suffering, I can tell you first-hand the price the innocent pay is beyond human comprehension.

The ones that had the opportunity to come to know and love Nocona, yet chose selfish gratification—you are the real losers. Nocona is one of the most unique individuals I have ever come to know. She is definitely set apart and has a way of bringing light into dark places. I daily anticipate seeing what God has in store for her life.

All of my children and grandchildren are special and set apart. I see in each a special gifting that I do not have, and know God has great plans for all of them, just as He did in someone that was as ill-structured, burdened with the inexpressible, and unfocused as myself!

My deepest desire for this book is that each person that reads *Seashell Prisoners* might relate with some part of it. That each person might have a better understanding of human nature whether it be professionals or your best friend. Most of all that you might have a better understanding of God.

I was told by several to use real names of everyone in the book to make the book more credible. I only used the names of our friends, since I fully believe that God did not want me to use this story as a weapon to condemn, put down, or attack anyone. My hope is that each reader will take a second look at their lives, reevaluate, and grow and improve themselves as an individual....*Just As I Did.*

> *"Therefore do not fear them, for there is nothing covered that will not be revealed, and hidden that will not be known."*
> *"Whatever I tell you in the dark, speak in the light; and what you hear in the ear, preach on the house tops."*
> *"And do not fear those who kill the body but cannot kill the soul. But rather fear Him who is able to destroy both soul and body in hell."*
> *Matthew 10: 26, 27, 28*

We Appreciate Each And Every Reader And Look Forward To Your Comments.

Contact us on Seashell Prisoner Facebook

West End Ministry
Roatan, Bay Islands, Honduras
Website: www.westendministry.org

Re: Frances Harris

To whom it may concern,

When reviewing the case of Frances Harris, please consider the following: My family and I live and work on Roatan as Christian missionaries whose focus is the resident foreigner community. We have known Frances for approximately two and a half years. We met her the very first night we visited Roatan and in the course of our acquaintance Frances made no effort to hide her situation regarding Nocona Lynn. It is our opinion that Frances made a brave and sacrificial decision for the ultimate good of her granddaughter Nocona.

As the West End Ministry's focus is the resident foreigner community, Frances and Nocona were included in our target people group. However, Frances' strong Christian character and community example actually provided a starting platform and ongoing support *for* the West End Ministry.

And, regarding Nocona Lynn, I would like to point out that she is a child whose life clearly indicates that she is a very loved and well-cared-for young lady. Nocona has been a regular attendee of the West End Ministry's Children's Bible Study and proven repeatedly to be a healthy example to the other children in the group. Her only fears seemed to come from vague memories of her biological father and having to return to that situation.

I believe Frances is a hero in Nocona's life and certainly not deserving of incarceration for any length of time.

Thank you for taking this information into consideration. Please contact me for any further information or details.

Sincerely,

Greg Ruark
Director

On staff with:
  Alternative Missions   Outreach Christian Fellowship

Phone: (Honduras)
Email:

Dear Judge Clark,

I know that everyone has an opinion on the subject of Frances Harris and Nocona ⸺. I would like to add my opinion:

I want everyone to know that they are one of the nicest families I have ever known. Nocona was always number 1 in all their lives. Her happiness and safety were their top priority. It truly saddens me to think that all the goodness they have put into her life was all in vain!!!

I have 2 wonderful, beautiful grandchildren ⸺ and I have thought numerous times what I would have done in Frances's situation and I always come back to the same answer: I would have done the same thing!!

I do not know ⸺ I have never met him personally, but from total strangers I have never heard anything good regarding him.

During one of the hearings before Frances left, my husband attended and he came home shaking his head saying "I can honestly see that Frances does not have a chance with the Orange County Court System." He said that you could tell it was one sided and definitely not on her side, no matter what the testimony was. They were listening with deaf ears when it came to Frances.

It seems to us that the court system today wants it to be a Father vs. Grandmother issue and it seems like no one is listening to Nocona. Children are smarter that some people give them credit, Nocona knows right from wrong and it seems to me, no one is listening to her or the family that is taking care of her at this time.

How heartbreaking it is to me that anyone would even consider Frances a criminal. Why???? For doing what she thought at the time was the best thing for her grandchild? Step out of your shoes and walk in hers a while and then tell me what you would have done if you thought your voice could not be heard, you were constantly going up against a brick wall and your grandchild was being hurt!!!!!! No one would listen then and no one is listening now, I can't figure this problem out!!

My heart is very heavy right now and has been since Nocona and Frances were returned to the states. I worry about them constantly because it seems there is no fairness here in Orange, the town I have lived in all my life.

Please consider everything, and dig deep into the problems that have been presented. Listen to Nocona!!! She deserves to be heard!!!!!!

Respectfully,

Alison Fore

Mrs. Angelina Gruner
#16 Sundancer
Sandy Bay, Roatan
Honduras, Central America

November 3, 2002

Honorable Sir or Madame,

    I have known Frances Collins since my family and I moved to Roatan, Honduras, in August of 2001 to do mission work for the people of the island. Miss Frances graciously introduced us to the many people she knows here, both directly and indirectly by inviting us to many potluck dinners she hosted at her home. She was instrumental in helping us to adjust to our new surroundings and feel more at home here. She has done the same for numerous other people as she has tried to create a sense of community in a place where many people of quite diverse cultures live.

    One major way that she has attempted to develop a sense of community on the island is by creating the annual "Christmas on the Beach" and organizing the business people of West End to sponsor and participate in this event. "Christmas on the Beach" is an evening of celebration consisting of a children's parade, a talent show geared toward children and families on the island, and a culmination of a visit from Santa and fireworks. This special evening, which takes months of planning by Miss Frances, has become an annual tradition to which the children look forward each year.

    Perhaps the best way I can communicate the character and parenting skills of Miss Frances is in my observations of her granddaughter, Nocona, with whom I have had at least weekly contact for over a year now. I help to lead a Bible study for the children of West End each Tuesday, and have found Nocona to be respectful of authority and attentive during the lesson times. Her answers during discussions show that she has been taught the difference between right and wrong, proper ethics, and strong morals. She is well-liked by the other children because she is pleasant and friendly, but she also is not afraid to speak out for a friend who has been wronged.

    On a more personal level, my daughter considered Nocona a friend. Like normal American pre-teens, they enjoyed having "sleep-overs", during which they would swim, play games, eat pizza, paint nails, watch movies, talk, and giggle. Nocona, again, was always well-behaved and displayed good manners. She always answered "yes, ma'am" or "no, ma'am" in response to questions, a southern tradition to which I am not accustomed, being from Illinois, but which I recognize as good training on the part of Miss Frances.

    Miss Frances has made sure that Nocona has received an excellent education while living on Roatan. Being a teacher myself, I extensively researched the different possibilities for educating my children here. I concluded that home schooling my children with the well-respected A Beka curriculum from a private school in Pensacola, Florida, was the best option. This is the same curriculum Miss Frances has been using with Nocona. After teaching my children from this curriculum for over a year, I am confident that my children, and Nocona, are getting an education as good as, or even better than, they would be getting in the States. A Beka is an expensive curriculum, but Miss Frances looked at the benefits for Nocona, not the cost.

While one criticism of home schooling is that students do not get the socialization which they would get in an American public school, Nocona is very social - - out-going and at ease with any culture. I have seen her interacting with Americans, native Caribbean islanders, and Spanish Honduran nationals, in each of their native tongues. In fact, Nocona certainly has a broader world perspective and a deeper understanding of peoples of different cultures than most American children her age.

Miss Frances has also made sure Nocona has had socialization opportunities by organizing field trips and inviting other children, including mine, to come along. In addition, she arranged for Nocona to join other children in a home school group for special activities each Friday morning. Considering these activities, plus the "sleep-overs", potlucks, and individual guests at their home in addition to attending church and Bible study each week, I would not consider Nocona to be lacking in socialization.

Thank you for taking the time to consider my observations. I hope I have given you some insight into the Frances Collins I know: the gracious hostess, the community leader, and the devoted, responsible parent.

                                                        Respectfully yours,

                                                        Angelina Gruner

From:	"Jerry Kerin"
To:	"Louis Oceguera (Francis)"
Sent:	Wednesday, November 06, 2002 12:00 AM
Subject:	Support Letter for Francis

November 6, 2002

RE: Frances and Nocona

To whom it may concern:

My name is Shelley Kerin and I have known Frances and Nocona for 2 years. I have visited the island of Roatan for the past 2 years as a missionary and have worked with Frances in ministry outreach. I have not only worked along side her, but also stayed in her home.

I know Frances to be extremely generous and hardworking. I know her to be honest and take deep concern and involvement in other people's hurt and pain. I also know that her first priority in life has been Nocona. She has been an excellent example of self sacrifice to Nocona; putting others first before herself.

This past August 2002, I spent a couple of nights in their home. I watched and observed as Nocona would walk us down to the island cafe for breakfast in the morning. The people there knew Nocona and loved her. That whole part of the island in which they lived knew her and respected her and Frances. The whole community was like a family to each other.

Many conversations Frances and I had were about Nocona and what she studied in homeschool. I homeschooled my children for a year and have a deep appreciation for the dedication, sweat and tears, it takes to undertake such a task. We talked about how smart Nocona is and how well she was doing in school. Nocona decided she wanted to learn a Spanish dance we brought to the island and several of us had just recorded it so she and her friends could learn it and perform it for the community there. I've been amazed at how blessed she has been to be exposed to so much in her education.

I know Nocona to be well rounded and educated because of the exposure to knowledge Frances gave her. I know her to be quiet and confident in whom she was created to be. She had good friends and a structured, steady home life on the island. Nocona would be described as a responsible, smart, and creative young lady with a bright future ahead of her.

Frances would talk often about how obedient and respectful a young lady Nocona is becoming. Being a parent of 2 teenagers myself, that speaks loudly of the parenting Frances has done.

I know both Frances and Nocona have been deeply involved with church and ministry on the island. They truly have lived a life of serving others at no gain to themselves other than the gift of the privilege to give to others.

Frances has done a great job at raising Nocona, as evident of the character and strength portrayed in that young lady. She has a bright future ahead of her. I pray that the courts would see the stability she once had and return her to the love and care she has known all her life in Frances.

Respectfully,

Shelley Kerin

--- Jerry Kerin

--- EarthLink: The #1 provider of the Real Internet.

2626 Honeysuckle Walk
Spring, TX 77388
October 29, 2002

In support of Frances Harris

Anna Oceguera
198 Live Oak
Bridge City, TX 77611

To Whom It May Concern:

I became acquainted with Frances Harris many years ago through The Wet Set Scuba Diving Club, a Non-Profit SCUBA Club promoting the safety and enjoyment of scuba diving to the Golden Triangle community. Frances was an outstanding member of the club as well as a good friend. She was a prominent member of her community and, to my knowledge, was always held with high regard by all who knew her.

Recently, in the summer of 2000, I visited Roatan Honduras on a dive trip and visited with Frances and her granddaughter Nocona. Frances has done so much for the impoverished people of her island community by creating Christian-based gatherings at her house and initiating functions for the island children. Nocona was a marvelous child and just a delight to be around. I believe Frances should be proud of how well rounded and adjusted Nocona is.

It takes a lot of courage and love to leave your whole life behind to protect someone you love. There are not many people that could make such a commitment. I do not believe anyone could interpret her actions as ill intended.
She is one of the nicest and sincerest people I have met and I am proud to be her friend.

Best regards,

Keith Walker

45 West Hill Avenue
Epsom
Surrey
KT19 8JX
England
25th November 2002

Your Honour Judge
755 Goodhue
Beaumont,
Texas
77706
USA

Your Honour

I am a Forensic Psychologist working for Her Majesty's Prison Service who has carried out an extensive review of the adoption of traumatised children. I wish to write to let you know how deeply I feel about what may become a miscarriage of justice in the placement of Nocona Lynn Burton.

In the literature, the title of traumatised children refers to children who have been abused, whether physically, sexually or emotionally or suffered from neglect. It is quite clear that being able to form attachment bonds again after such a trauma is a gradual and very important process. If attachment bonds are repeatedly broken, then research shows there is limited recovery and the results can be psychologically and in some cases physically devastating for the individual. To be forced into contact again with the perpetrator of the abuse must be unimaginably traumatic and I am convinced will have grave consequences.

I have been a friend of Mrs. Frances Collins Harris and Nocona Lynn Burton since I stayed with them in Roatan, Honduras. During this time I was able to see the happy and well-adjusted life Nocona was leading, with her home-schooling hours and with her social circle of friends that were living nearby. I was able to spend time snorkeling and swimming with Nocona in the beautiful waters right next to their home and it was wonderful to see her so free and happy, despite the dreadful physical and sexual abuse that she suffered as a child.

I ask you to reconsider the decision to stop contact between Nocona and her grandmother Mrs. Frances Collins Harris, who has become her Primary Caregiver.

I further suggest that you obtain details of the offences of sexual and physical abuse committed against Nocona Lynn Burton by Mr.

I implore you to consider Nocona's voice in your verdict.

Yours sincerely,

Elizabeth Webster-Gardiner

2/4/96

To whom it may concern.
As Pastor of the first conservative Baptist Church in the comunity of West End, Roatan Bay Island of Honduras in Central America. I hereby declare, after keen observation of the Collins family. My wife and I both have come to respect and appreciate them very much, as we find nothing reproachable in their conduct.

They attend our Church regularly. Mrs. Frances teaches our youth class. Nocona is a very healthy and happy little girl, who attends a class of begginners, and is very Brilliant and active in whatever takes place at our church. So if there is any way you can assist in keeping her that way please do so.

While we remain forever gratefull.
  Yours in Christ love
Pastor & Mrs. Eddy Bush

PINEHURST
PENTECOSTAL CHURCH

A Haven of Grace on the Westside

Rev. Bill Smith
Pastor

RECEIVED
AUG 0 7 2003

U. S. District Court
300 Willow
Beaumont, Texas 77701

Judge Heartfield;

I am sending this letter on behalf of Frances Harris. I understand that she will be sentenced in this court and I am appealing to you that you show her as much mercy as the law allows.

I believe that Frances is a very good and loving person, and certainly does not deserve to be put behind bars.

I believe that when she fled the country, she really felt that her grandchild was in danger and felt that was the only way that she could protect her.

Thank you for your attention to this matter.

Sincerely,

Rev. William W. Smith

Rev. William W. Smith
Pastor
Pinehurst Pentecostal Church
Orange, Texas

cc: Attorney C. Haden (Sonny) Cribbs, Jr.

Weekly Celebrations

Sunday School
10:00 am
Sunday Evening Experience
6:30 pm

Wednesday
Word and Worship
7:30 pm

2111 N. 40th St.
Orange, TX 77630
(409) 886-2408

July 24, 2003

The Honorable Judge Thad Heartfield
U.S. District Court No. 1
300 Willow
Beaumont, TX 77701

Re: Frances Collins Harris

Dear Judge Heartfield:

Thank you for taking a moment to read this unsolicited letter.

When Frances Harris first started attending Community Church I was cautious as to her true motives since she was under indictment. However, since then I have changed my mind and believe she is truly a sincere and upright woman.

She has in no way attempted to get my attention. She attends a small group (We call them care groups.) and has asked for prayer and counsel from some of our elders. She has never claimed to be in the right only to have done what she thought was best.

It is my opinion that she will never repeat her crime and that she has suffered enough economic and emotional losses already.

Thank you for hearing me.

Sincerely,

David Berkheimer
Senior Pastor

HONERABLE JUDGE THAD HEARTFIELD:

MY NAME IS RANDY BECKER. I WORK FOR THE MARKET BASKET IN MAURICEVILLE, TEXAS. I AM THE STORE MANAGER AT THIS LOCATION.
ON JANUARY 2, 1990, MARKET BASKET BOUGHT THE STORE FROM FRANCES HARRIS. THE PREVIOUS NAME WAS T.J.&A. GROCERIES AND FRANCES WAS MANAGER, OWNER. SHE AIDED US IN A SMOOTH TRANSITION OF OWNERSHIP, BY STAYING ON AND INTRODUCING US TO MANY OF OUR CUSTOMERS.
DURING THIS TIME, I GOT TO KNOW FRANCES, AND LEARNED TO LIKE AND RESPECT HER. SHE WAS ALWAYS INVOLVED IN COMMUNITY ACTIVITIES, SUCH AS DRUG AWARENESS FOR KIDS, MAURICEVILLE BONFIRE, AND CRAWFISH FESTIVAL. SHE DONATED A LOT OF HER TIME, AND MONEY TO HELP THE KIDS, AND THE COMMUNITY, AND ASKED FOR NO REWARDS.
FRANCES SEEMS TO BE A GOOD AND TRUSTWORTHY CITIZEN, AND DISPLAYS GOOD NATURE WHEN VISITING MY STORE LOCATION.
I FEEL THAT IT IS A PRIVALIDGE AND HONOR TO HAVE KNOWN FRANCES HARRIS, AND HER FAMILY.

THANK YOU.

RANDY BECKER
MARKET BASKET #42
11916 HWY. 62
MAURICEVILLE, TEXAS 77626

First Baptist Church
P O Box 56 11540 Hwy 12
Mauriceville, Texas 77626
Ph. (409) 745-3013 Fax (409) 745-3989

August 15, 2003

The Honorable Judge Thad Heartfield
U. S. District Court 300 Willow
Courtroom Number One
Beaumont, Texas 77701

Dear Judge Heartfield,

As a friend of the court please allow me to submit a letter of support for Ms. Francis Collins Harris. Having served the Mauriceville community as pastor of the First Baptist Church for the last three years the story of Francis Harris was one of the first things I heard about. Members of her family attend the First Baptist Church of Mauriceville and many others know and support her. Ms. Harris had been respectable businesswoman in our community before she fled the country with her granddaughter Nacona   Burton. She had made a positive impact in our community and in the lives of others.

Since her return I have had many opportunities both to talk and pray with Ms. Harris. I have discovered she has a spirit of humility and a heart of compassion. Her faith in God is strong, as is her determination to do what is right. Upon her arrival back to the States, Ms. Harris has followed the demands of the law and has resigned to obey the decisions of the court.

Your Honor, I know you are faced with many difficult decisions each day. I respect the work you do for the people of this country. I will pray for you and all involved as you make the very difficult decisions related to Ms. Francis Harris. I believe, given the chance, Ms. Harris can and will make a model citizen of the State of Texas and the United States of America. On her behalf I plead for leniency from the court. May God grant you His wisdom.

Respectfully Yours,

Dr. Robert Netterville, Jr.
Robert Netterville, Jr., D. Min.
Senior Pastor

Judge Dunn

I am a native of the Island of Roatan Honduras. I have served the people here in many capacities. I serve as Pastor of the First Baptist Church of Roatan and Honorary Ambassador of the city of New Orleans.. Since I serve in the capacity of overseer of all the Baptist Churches and meet weekly with pastors of many denominations I feel confident I can speak not only for myself but for the many other pastors and residents around the Island. We have a deep concern and have been in prayer for three U.S. citizens: River JonNey Burton, Nocona Lynn████, and Frances Ann Burton Collins. Many of us have observed them from the time they have arrived on this Island and have become very concerned about their safety and well being. I spoke with Frances recently and she was expressing her concern about the case with Nocona her granddaughter.

I'm writing this letter at this time to express our feelings and observation of these U. S. citizens and hope in some way it will help resolve their problem. River and Frances have worked very hard from the time they arrived on this Island not only in an attempt to make a home for themselves and Nocona and they have also involved themselves with many projects in helping their neighbors. River has started youth projects such as cleaning the public beaches in her neighborhood. She organized a women's softball league on the Island. River is presently managing a restaurant for a retired couple as they are unable to manage it themselves due to medical problems.

Frances has been working with Christian youth and women's groups throughout Roatan. Through these efforts a Women's Prayer Group has been formed with over a hundred and twenty women meeting once a month.. Frances was instrumental in organizing one of the largest Youth Revivals that was held here

Nocona has been a big part of all these activities. She has attended school from the time she arrived. She is a regular in church each Sunday. She is a joy to be around and is dearly loved by all her neighbors.

The people of Roatan embrace River, Nocona, and Frances as fellow residents. We have gained three wonderful people to our small island. We are saddened by the events that took place last April in regard to Nocona's father attempt to kidnap her.

Hopefully there will be some resolution to this unfortunate situation as they are unable to be with family and friends in the US. In the meantime we will remain in prayer and support of River, Nocona and Frances.

Sincerely

Reverend Glenn Solomon
Pastor, First Baptist Church of Roatan